D1593453

England's Long Reformation
1500–1800

The Neale Colloquium in British History

Charity, self-interest and welfare in the English past
Martin Daunton (editor)

England's Long Reformation, 1500–1800
Nicholas Tyacke (editor)

England's Long Reformation
1500–1800

Edited by
Nicholas Tyacke
University College London

UCL
PRESS

© Nicholas Tyacke and contributors, 1998

First published in 1998 by UCL Press

UCL Press Limited
1 Gunpowder Square
London EC4A 3DE

and

1900 Frost Road, Suite 101
Bristol
Pennsylvania 19007–1598
USA

The name of University College London (UCL) is a registered
trade mark used by UCL Press with the consent of the owner.

British Library Cataloguing in Publication Data
A CIP Catalogue Record for this book is available from the
British Library.

ISBN: 1-85728-756-8

Typeset in Bembo by Acorn Bookwork, Salisbury, UK.
Printed by Arrowhead Books Limited, Reading, UK.

Contents

v

Preface

This is the second volume in the Neale Colloquium series, which honours the memory of Sir John Neale – the Astor Professor of English History at University College London from 1927 to 1956. It largely comprises the papers discussed at the Colloquium in January 1996. The Neale lecturer on this occasion was Dr Eamon Duffy of Magdalene College, Cambridge, and author of the justly acclaimed *The stripping of the altars: traditional religion in England 1400–1580* (1992). Having chosen the 'Long' English Reformation as our theme, we were both amused and encouraged to discover that several other historians claimed independently to have invented the concept. Some 140 participants attended the Colloquium, and most seemed to find consideration of the Reformation over three centuries a stimulating challenge. We are grateful to Jonathan Cape for its continued support of the Neale lecture, and to the British Academy, the Graduate School of University College London and the Royal Historical Society for financial assistance.

Nicholas Tyacke
University College London
February 1997

Notes on contributors

Jonathan Barry is Senior Lecturer in History at the University of Exeter. His recent publications include two co-edited volumes on *Reformation and revival in eighteenth-century Bristol* (1994), with Kenneth Morgan, and *Witchcraft in early-modern Europe* (1996), with Marianne Hester and Gareth Roberts. He is currently completing two books on the religious and cultural history of Bristol.

Patrick Collinson is Regius Professor of Modern History Emeritus in the University of Cambridge. He is the author of numerous studies of English Puritanism, and of *The birthpangs of Protestant England: religious and cultural change in the sixteenth and seventeenth centuries* (1988). He is now preparing a collection of essays on the Long English Reformation, to be called *From Tyndale to Sancroft*.

Eamon Duffy is Reader in Church History in the University of Cambridge, and author of *The stripping of the altars: traditional religion in England 1400–1580* (1992). He is currently working on a study of the impact of the Reformation in rural Devon.

Jeremy Gregory is Principal Lecturer and head of the History division at the University of Northumbria. He contributed to *A history of Canterbury Cathedral*, edited by P. Collinson et al. (1995), and is writing a book on the English Reformation and its effects on society from the sixteenth to the nineteenth centuries.

David Hickman recently completed his doctoral thesis at University College London on the religion of London's ruling elite during the sixteenth century. He is currently visiting tutor at Goldsmiths College, and research assistant on the Boyle Project at Birkbeck College.

Ann Hughes is Professor of Early-Modern History at the University of Keele, author of *The causes of the English civil war* (1991) and co-editor with Richard Cust of *The English civil war. A reader* (1997). Her present research interests include Thomas Edwards' *Gangraena*, and other aspects of the English political culture of the mid-seventeenth century.

Peter Lake is Professor of History at Princeton University and author of a number of studies on politics and religion under Elizabeth and the early Stuarts, including *Anglicans and puritans? Presbyterianism and English conformist thought from Whitgift to Hooker* (1988). He is now working on English conformist thought from Hooker to Laud, and the rise of the funeral sermon and godly life.

Christopher Marsh is Lecturer in History at The Queen's University of Belfast. He is the author of *The family of love in English society, 1550–1630* (1994), and is currently completing a book on popular religion in sixteenth-century England.

Muriel C. McClendon is Assistant Professor of History at the University of California. She has recently completed writing a book on the Reformation in Norwich. Her research interests concern the changing relationship between religion and society in Tudor England.

Michael Questier is Research Fellow at the Chichester Centre for Ecclesiastical Studies and the author of *Conversion, politics and religion in England, 1580–1625* (1996). He is editing a volume of early seventeenth-century newsletters, and (with Peter Lake) a collection of essays on conformity and orthodoxy in the Church of England between 1560 and 1642.

Joy Rowe has written a number of articles in *Recusant History*, jointly with Patrick McGrath. Her particular interest is in religious dissent, both Catholic and Protestant, in Norwich diocese, and on which she has also published recently.

Nicholas Tyacke is Reader in History at University College London. Most recently he has completed editing *Seventeenth-Century Oxford* (1997), in *The History of the University of Oxford* series. His next major project is a joint book, with Kenneth Fincham, on the Caroline remodelling of English religious worship.

W. R. Ward is Emeritus Professor of Modern History in the University of Durham, author of *The protestant evangelical awakening* (1992) and editor (with R. P. Heitzenrater) of *The journals and diaries of John Wesley* (1988–95). His research encompasses eighteenth-century religion in Britain, Europe and North America.

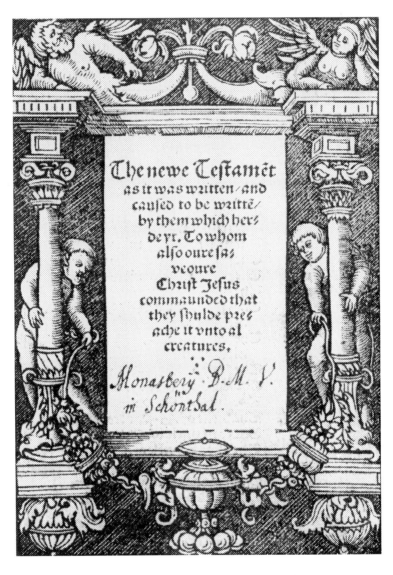

The newe Testamēt
as it was written / and
caused to be writtē /
by them which herde
yt. To whom
also oure saveoure
Christ Jesus
commaunded that
they shulde preache it vnto al
creatures.

Monastery: D. M. V.
in Schöntal.

The recently discovered title-page of William Tyndale's 1526 translation of the New Testament (reproduced by the kind permission of
the Württembergische Landesbibliothek).

xii

1

Introduction: re-thinking the "English Reformation"[1]

Nicholas Tyacke

Historians of continental Europe are accustomed to taking a long-term view of the Reformation. Thus the modern discussion of its "success and failure" ranges across both the sixteenth and seventeenth centuries, while Jean Delumeau's seminal treatment of the Counter-Reformation employs an even wider time frame.[2] The case as regards England, however, is somewhat different, where the Reformation remains largely corralled in the mid-sixteenth century and the recent "revisionist" accounts seek only to edge forward a few decades. Part of the explanation for this historiographical contrast lies in the still dominant English tradition of political interpretation, which treats the subject as first and foremost a succession of legislative enactments – culminating under Elizabeth I and followed by a fairly rapid collapse of Catholicism.[3] Continental historians, on the other hand, have been more willing to see the Reformation as a religious movement, and one furthermore that continued to be strongly contested.

Apart from this difference of approach, the English model requires glossing over a number of problems. Catholicism may have withered away, but how did a religion of the word (Protestantism) fare in a predominantly illiterate society? At least according to one account, itself a notable exception to the historiographic rule, magical beliefs came partly to fill the gap.[4] Related to this question are the deep divisions among Protestants, which resulted during the seventeenth century in the temporary destruction of the Elizabethan "settlement of religion", with the Puritans and their Dissenter successors claiming to be the true heirs of the Reformation – a conflict of interpretation

1

which the 1689 Toleration Act only served to institutionalize. There are indeed analogies to be drawn here between this internecine Protestant strife and the struggle on the continent between reformers and counter-reformers. Moreover, the subsequent Enlightenment critique of all such bands of competing Christians, mounted during the eighteenth century, also owed a debt to English thinkers.

Nevertheless, considerations of this kind are far removed from those of most historians of the Reformation in England, where since the 1970s much energy has been consumed in a prolonged bout of revisionist enthusiasm.[5] According to this new account, the Reformation was imposed from above upon an unwilling people, by a process both officially inspired and markedly piecemeal; religious change came about only gradually and largely because of the manoeuvrings of a section of the political elite; such was the enduring strength of Catholicism that Protestantism remained for long a sickly plant, its survival far from assured. These views are associated especially with the historians Christopher Haigh and J. J. Scarisbrick, although they have received powerful reinforcement from Eamon Duffy whose book concentrates more on the fifteenth century. While the centre of gravity of Scarisbrick's *The Reformation and the English people* is the earlier sixteenth century and the focus of Haigh's various writings is rather later, they are two parts of a related argument about Tudor religious developments. The thesis appears firmly grounded on the evidence of bountiful Catholic religious giving as recorded in the wills of the period, the building and adornment of churches right up to the Reformation, items of expenditure in churchwardens' accounts during the first half of the sixteenth century, flourishing lay confraternities almost until the moment of their statutory abolition, and the high clerical standards revealed by pre-Reformation episcopal visitations. All in all, the English Church emerges from these documents as being in excellent shape at the accession of Henry VIII. Hence revisionists reject what they see as an essentially Protestant and triumphalist story of events thereafter, portraying them instead as an accidental by-product of Tudor politics.[6]

Closer inspection, however, reveals this "new" interpretation to be an old one resurrected. Specifically, it is a Catholic version propagated at the beginning of the twentieth century by Cardinal Aidan Gasquet and his protégé H. N. Birt. Gasquet's book *The eve of the*

Reformation, published back in 1900, now seems remarkably prescient, drawing as it did on wills, churchwardens' accounts, records of lay confraternities, and visitation materials, among other sources, to illustrate the healthy state of the pre-Reformation English Church. Gasquet also suggested that the importance of anti-clericalism had been much exaggerated, and this argument too has recently been revived. But his main contention was that "up to the very eve of the [Reformation] changes the old religion had not lost its hold upon the minds and affections of the people at large".[7] On the other hand, the concern of Birt, in his 1907 publication *The Elizabethan religious settlement*, was with the fate of Catholicism under Queen Elizabeth. His conclusion was that

> as in the case of the clergy, so in that of the laity, while some without doubt heartily embraced the change of religion, the majority of them were not favourable to it, but acquiesced outwardly for the sake of peace, not fully understanding the details of the differences between Protestantism and Catholicism.

At the same time, so Birt claimed, large numbers of Marian priests refused to submit to the Elizabethan regime, ministering instead to the Catholic laity, whom he characterized as numerically "not only considerable, but formidable, far into the reign". Readers will be struck here by the distinct anticipations of Haigh's arguments especially about the "continuity of Catholicism" across the Reformation, and the merging of the old Marian priests with the younger generation of seminarians trained abroad, as well as the alleged religious conservatism of many nominal Protestants.[8]

There is, of course, nothing shameful about following in the footsteps of previous historians, even if it does rather detract from revisionist claims to novelty. Nor is a Catholic version of events inherently any worse than a supposedly Protestant one, although it may be no better. Yet doubts arise, particularly concerning the *relevance* of the type of evidence used by Gasquet and his modern equivalents to understanding the Reformation process. Revisionist historians usually distinguish the Reformation in England from that elsewhere, but similar signs of Catholic health can be found in many parts of continental Europe which were to turn Protestant.[9] Here indeed the original Gasquet version was distinctly superior, allowing as it did for a "Lutheran invasion" concurrent with the Henrician break from Rome, whereas Luther does not rate a single mention in Scarisbrick's index – a telling, if extreme, example.[10]

Haigh offers us a stark choice between conceiving of the English Reformation as either "from above" or "from below". Despite a further subdivision into "fast" and "slow", these are the basic options.[11] Reformation from below is linked pre-eminently, in this scenario, with the name of A. G. Dickens, who attempted the praise-worthy task of trying to provide a popular dimension to more tradi-tional political accounts, along with emphasizing "the development and spread of Protestantism".[12] But this Haighian "choice" is largely illusory. Thus the concept of a Reformation from below, which we are asked to reject, is something of a revisionist straw man. In comparative continental terms it implies a broad popular movement only really conceivable if some kind of peasant revolt,[13] as in Germany, had interacted with the early stages of the English Refor-mation, yet even then the attitude of the magistrate would still have been decisive in the long run. Conversely Haigh's Reformation from above is defined extremely narrowly, in the high political terms of court faction. As a consequence a whole range of other possibilities are ruled out.

What, for example, of the intelligentsia and the role of ideas more generally? As on the continent, we need to take into account the very important part played by a clerical vanguard. Increasing signs of alarm were also registered by the English authorities over the influx of printed heretical literature. Thus May 1521 saw the formal burning of Luther's works at St Paul's Cross in London, with an accompany-ing sermon from Bishop Fisher of Rochester which sought, among other things, to refute the doctrine of justification by faith alone. There were similar book-burnings in Oxford and Cambridge at this time, as part of a nationwide campaign.[14] Yet by the mid-1520s a heretical network had developed, which embraced London and both universities. The upper echelons included at least two heads of Cambridge colleges, Thomas Forman of Queens' and William Sowode of Corpus Christi. Forman masterminded a trade in forbidden books from his London parish of All Hallows, Honey

Lane. Arrested in 1528, he died the same year – his "Lutheran" views on justification recorded for posterity in the hostile pages of Thomas More. Nevertheless the successors of Forman at Queens', Simon Heynes (1528) and William May (1537), turned out to be of a similar religious persuasion to him, as was Matthew Parker who followed Sowode at Corpus Christi in 1544. By this last date St John's (John Taylor: 1538) and Pembroke (Nicholas Ridley: 1540) had joined the roster of colleges with reformist heads. We should probably add to the list Peterhouse, where the master John Edmunds died a secretly married man in 1544, and Christ's whose master Henry Lockwood sponsored the performance that year of a Lutheran play. In addition, between 1528 and 1538 King's had a reformist provost in the person of Edward Fox.[15] Fellows of like mind can be found across the university as a whole and heretical works regularly show up in the inventories of individual Cambridge scholars from the 1530s onwards. During the same decade William Turner of Pembroke College was translating, for English publication, continental propaganda in favour of the "new" religion. Oxford undoubtedly lagged behind, only acquiring a clearly reformist head with Richard Cox, already in trouble for his religious views in the late 1520s, as dean of Christ Church in 1546, and continental reformed theology seems to have been much less widely available there.[16] Even one English university, however, was springboard enough.

By the beginning of the 1530s the authorities had condemned over twenty heretical works in English and many more in Latin.[17] Whereas a few years earlier it had been thought sufficient to catalogue the errors of Luther, now this treatment was extended to his fellow reformers as well as to a new breed of English language authors. From the mid-1520s some of the most intrepid English evangelists had journeyed to Luther's Wittenberg itself, while a favoured port of call by the later 1530s was Bullinger's Zurich, this last with the personal blessing of Archbishop Thomas Cranmer. Also during the 1530s works by Bullinger and Luther became available in English, along with others by Bucer, Lambert and Osiander; Melanchthon and Zwingli were added to the list in the early 1540s.[18] Here, however, revisionists are able to counter that the bulk of the population was illiterate. Yet the spoken word is not constrained by such barriers and, as on the continent so in England, preaching proved central to the spread of what retrospectively was called Protestantism. The amount of preaching is unquantifiable, but we can cite as indirect evidence an instruction on this subject issued by Archbishop Cranmer in 1534. It appears to have been triggered by the reformist sermons of Hugh Latimer at Bristol but clearly had a much wider reference, other foci for example being the similar preaching of John Bale at Doncaster and that of Thomas Rose at Hadleigh in Suffolk. Cranmer stipulated that no one for a year should preach either for or against "purgatory, honouring of saints, that priests may have wives, that faith only justifieth", the making of "pilgrimages" and the working of "miracles", since these "things have caused dissension amongst the subjects of this realm already".[19] But that the orthodox Catholic view should now be a matter of doubt shows just how rapidly ideas were changing, courtesy in part of the pulpit.

Revisionists usually couch their accounts of the English Reformation in terms of the history of parliamentary legislation, yet this produces a very distorted picture. At the official level indeed it remains vital to distinguish between the Henrician and Edwardian Reformations, because only after 1547 was Protestantism established. Nevertheless there is an underlying trajectory of evangelical activity from the 1520s and through into the 1550s. At this unofficial level the allegedly piecemeal nature of the Henrician Reformation makes much less sense. Granted considerable wells of indifference or plain muddle, plenty of evidence also exists of growing polarization between the advocates of the "new learning" as opposed to the "old learning", by which is meant religion. (The contemporary state papers are littered with such references.) Compared with this, the leading parliamentary issues of the 1530s, such as the royal supremacy and the dissolution of the monasteries, were relatively uncontentious matters. Therefore the argument that the Reformation crept up unnoticed on the educated classes presupposes an extraordinary insensitivity on their part to what was happening under their noses.[20] Take, for instance, the electrifying sermons preached to the Convocation of Canterbury, in June 1536, by Latimer. Having previously been accused of "erroneous preaching" on purgatory and the veneration of images, he now daringly threw the charges back in the faces of the assembled clergy. Even more boldly he bracketed his own case with that of William Tracy, a Gloucestershire gentleman who was posthumously burned in 1531 for having made an heretical will. Speaking of "purgatory pick-purse" and "deceitful and juggling images", Latimer invoked instead "Christ's faithful and lively images" – the poor – lying "wrapped in all wretchedness". Originally preached in Latin, the sermons were published in English translation the following year.[21]

It is true that royal proclamations against the publication and sale of heretical books continued to be issued until the end of Henry VIII's reign. In practice, however, during the 1530s it became much easier to publish such works in England. For example *The parable of the wicked mammon* by William Tyndale, originally printed at Antwerp in 1528, came out openly in a London edition of 1536 and moreover under his own name. Teaching "justification by faith only" in combination with a powerful statement concerning the necessity of charitable "deeds" by the righteous, this book had previously been condemned by royal proclamation.[22] Similarly London editions of works by Luther himself now appeared, albeit not identifying the author. One key figure here was the printer James Nicholson of Southwark. There was also a range of quasi-official publications, which propagated the thinking of continental reformers. A treatise by Martin Bucer, arguing against the placing of images in churches, was printed at London in 1535, the translator William Marshall being a publicist regularly employed by the royal minister Thomas Cromwell. The latter was also the dedicatee next year of an English translation of the Augsburg Confession – the Lutheran formulary of faith.[23]

Most striking of all, however, is the so-called "Matthew Bible" published in 1537 under royal licence. Largely the work of Tyndale, this not only included his notorious prologue to the Epistle to the Romans, and other heretical marginalia but was further supplemented with a "table" of "principal matters" lifted wholesale from the first French Protestant Bible of 1535. This table, by the unacknowledged "Matthieu Gramelin", provided a conspectus of reformed teaching which was quite uncompromising in its message. The "mass", for example, is condemned as not to be found in the Bible, the reader being cross-referenced to "supper of our Lord" which is defined as "an holy memory and giving of thanks for the death of Christ". "Free will" is rejected as equally unscriptural, religious "images" are described as "abominations", and there is a ringing declaration that "we are all priests to God". Dismissed too are auricular confession, ceremonies, holy days, merit, purgatory and traditions. Justification by faith alone is affirmed, and a predestinarian strand runs throughout the whole. This was the Bible, published by Richard Grafton and Edward Whitchurch, about which Cranmer wrote to Cromwell that the news of its licensing was more welcome than the gift of a thousand pounds. Drawing on both French and German sources, the work is truly international in character. As for "Matthieu Gramelin", he was in reality Thomas Malingre, pastor of Neuchâtel, which perhaps best explains why the English compiler John Rogers chose the pseudonym Thomas Matthew.[24]

Between 1534 and 1538 annual numbers of English reformist publications, printed both at home and abroad but omitting Bibles and prayer books, rose from about four to ten, at which point they heavily outnumbered equivalent works of Catholic orthodoxy. Moreover by 1536 Tyndale's New Testament had gone through at least seventeen editions, published abroad and smuggled into England; with its notes and prologues partly derived from Luther, this was one of the most important sources of reformed teaching available. (As early as November 1526 Archbishop Warham had complained of the "great number" of Tyndale New Testaments circulating in the province of Canterbury.)[25] The widening opportunities in the 1530s for English reformers, whether in press, pulpit or academe, undoubtedly owed a great deal to the benevolent patronage of Queen Anne Boleyn, Cromwell and to a lesser extent Cranmer.[26] Conversely the "reaction" which set in from 1539 is graphically illustrated by the history of religious publication. Reformed output collapsed that year, with only some three possible candidates and remained at around this level until 1543 when numbers briefly surpassed the previous peak of 1538. For the rest of Henry VIII's reign the figure averaged about six books, although they were now generally published abroad. It was also during these last years, however, that Parker at Cambridge and Cox at Oxford were moving into strategic university positions, as vice-chancellor (1544–5) and dean of Christ Church respectively. Cox was to become chancellor of Oxford in 1547, when Parker was again elected vice-chancellor of Cambridge.

A fascinating glimpse of the febrile religious situation at late

Henrician Cambridge comes from a letter which has been ascribed to early 1545, written by Roger Ascham of St John's College to Cranmer. Ascham reported that "the doctrines of original sin and predestination" were being debated between supporters of the modern Catholic theologian Albertus Pighius on the one hand and the followers of St Augustine on the other – among whom he numbered himself. But what he did not spell out was that the two principal targets of Pighius's book were Luther and Calvin.[27] At about the same time Christ's College had staged a performance of a play by Thomas Kirchmeyer, entitled *Pammachius*. A full-blooded attack on Catholic teaching from the Lutheran standpoint, this had been published at Wittenberg in 1538 with dedications to both Cranmer and Luther. Despite certain cuts having been made in the original, Stephen Gardiner, the university chancellor and a leading religious conservative, was still furious. Nevertheless Parker, as vice-chancellor, stood his ground, claiming that "none . . . were offended with any thing that now they remember was then spoken".[28]

Historians are understandably hesitant about using the word "Protestant" in the early phase of the Reformation, because of the fluidity of the situation. They prefer instead the term "evangelical". But the problem still remains how far the first generation of English evangelicals developed out of orthodox Catholicism or were recruited instead from a still-living heretical tradition. Thus the significance of Lollardy has been much debated. The work of Dickens, among others, has clearly demonstrated the continued existence of Lollards, often wrongly categorized as Lutherans by the ecclesiastical authorities. There are also recorded instances of Lollards making contact with the new continental reforming current, and literally discarding their old Wycliffite Bibles for Tyndale's New Testament. In addition, they played some part in the distribution of illegal printed literature.[29] Yet it would appear, on the face of it, that the intellectually deracinated nature of Lollardy made for a fairly limited role by the time of the Reformation. Academic Lollardy had been effectively wiped out during the first half of the fifteenth century, and it is striking that the majority of Lollard writings which survive do so in manuscripts dating from the same early period. Nevertheless there exists at least one reference to an apparently Lollard scriptorium, or writing shop, in Henrician London. More tantalizing still is the possibility of Lollard involvement in the production of Tyndale's New Testament.[30] Lollards may also have participated in the growing popular iconoclasm, which is detectable from the late 1520s. This involved both the destruction of wayside crosses and the burning of roods, although these outbreaks seem to have been stimulated by radical preachers such as Thomas Bilney and Thomas Rose. Some of the heat was subsequently taken out of the situation, when the Henrician government itself embarked on a policy of limited iconoclasm in the 1530s.[31]

Anticlericalism is an especial *bête noire* of the revisionists. They are quite correct that most parishioners seem to have been satisfied with their local clergy. There is also the obvious point that clerics spearheaded the Reformation. Yet in seeking to reduce anticlericalism to the grievances of common lawyers, hungry for the business of church courts, revisionists are in danger of scoring an own goal. For it is precisely the legal fraternity that one would expect to produce a challenge to the near-monopoly of learning exercised by the upper ranks of the late medieval clergy. Not for nothing have the London Inns of Court been called the "third university" of England, and only in the course of the fifteenth century was the previous clerical dominance of the central government bureaucracy undermined by members of the laity.[32] Some of the earliest and most committed lay support for the Reformation was in fact to come from lawyers. Here a particularly interesting group comprised James Baynham, Simon Fish and Richard Tracy. Tracy's father William was, as we have already remarked, posthumously burnt as a heretic in 1531. Tyndale, who knew the family, later remarked that Tracy senior "was better seen in the works of St. Austin [Augustine] twenty years before he died than ever I knew doctor in England". The son followed in his father's religious footsteps, while Baynham who was William Tracy's nephew, and like Richard a member of the Inner Temple, was burnt to death as a heretic in 1532. Baynham had also married the widow of Simon Fish of Gray's Inn – author of the notorious *Supplicacyon for the beggers* (1529), which attacked the doctrine of purgatory, monasticism and the clerical estate in general.[33] Fish was in addition involved in importing the earliest editions of Tyndale's New Testament from abroad and in their sale in England. Not surprisingly merchants too were crucial in this clandestine enterprise, and one very important early figure was Richard Harman of Antwerp, London and Cranbrook in Kent, operative from about 1526.[34]

Revisionists are prone to belittle the power of ideas in bringing about the Reformation, emphasizing what they see as almost the irrelevance of theology. Yet this is seriously to neglect the subversive potential particularly of the doctrine of justification by faith alone, undermining as it did the whole panoply of medieval Catholic teaching and practice built on the notion of spiritual good works. Reformation teaching had the effect of making largely irrelevant the great round of masses, prayers, penances, pilgrimages and related observances. It also radically reduced the role of both priests and ecclesiastical institutions. At the same time material grievances against the clergy certainly existed, and in the early 1530s cases as far apart as Devon and Lancashire can be found of literally murderous assaults on priests seeking to levy mortuary or burial fees. Resistance on this issue, however, appears to have been greatest in London.[35] There too the question of church tithes provided a long-running dispute, particularly from the late 1520s to the mid-1540s, and one initially linking up with attacks on Cardinal Wolsey. Religious reformers were not slow to capitalize on such material grievances, some of which spilled over into the parliament which met in 1529.[36]

For much of the 1530s the evangelicals appeared to be riding high, their aims increasingly coinciding with official government policy. Yet it was always something of a marriage of convenience, influenced by the exigencies of the international situation, and Henry VIII was never truly won over. But although the reformers failed in the event to capture the Henrician regime, they were not dislodged from their English strongholds. Susan Brigden, for example, has drawn attention to "the activities of a band of more than fifty reforming clergy in London in Henry's last years". Like the London printers of reformist works, most lived to fight another day and indeed attracted new recruits to their ranks.[37] Moreover even in 1542 an almost despairing note crept into a draft proclamation against heretical books in English which have "increased to an infinite number and unknown diversities of titles and names". Meanwhile at Norwich, the second city of the kingdom, in February 1539 the conservative Bishop Rugge had been publicly refuted by the evangelical Robert Watson in a classic continental-style debate on the freedom of the will, as a result of which

Watson apparently won over the mayor and corporation to his views.[38] With the change of monarch, both cities witnessed religious reform at the parish level running ahead of government orders. In London images began to come down almost immediately on Edward VI's accession in 1547, and by September iconoclasm was far advanced. Similarly, on 17 September 1547, the Norwich Mayor's Court debated

> a great matter . . . concerning diverse curates and other idle persons within the city, which hath unlawfully and without authority and commandment enterprised to rifle churches, pulling down images and bearing them away.[39]

The same month, in what threatened to become a major scandal, the pyx over the altar at St John's College, Cambridge was desecrated. That October the parishioners of Great St Mary's, the Cambridge University church, voted to sell their silver-gilt crucifix.[40]

Also unauthorized was the subsequent attack on the mass, London preachers and printers weighing in along with "irreverent talkers" and "revilers" more generally. A rash of books and ballads appeared on this subject in 1548, some of them extremely scabrous. While the government moved forward rather gingerly, Londoners especially were making a much faster pace – emboldened by the knowledge that Protector Somerset and his circle favoured change.[41] At Cambridge too the evangelicals can be found straining at the leash. Thus in late 1547 a group of reformist fellows at St John's College held a disputation on whether the "mass" and the "supper of the Lord" were the same thing. Proceedings were then transferred to the divinity schools, until halted by anxious university authorities. In these circumstances Ascham put pen to paper, excoriating the "Romish abuses" of the eucharist and proclaiming "behold the mass of the Pope which takes away the supper of the Lord".[42] Not until mid-1549 was the mass formally condemned by the universities, the year when altars began to be demolished in Norwich – again in advance of official instructions.[43]

Yet between 1547 and 1549 a Protestant Church was established in England. During the summer of 1547 a Book of Homilies was issued, the central reformist message of which was that works played no part in justification. Chantries were abolished that December, the parliamentary statute including an explicit attack on the doctrine of purgatory. This was followed by an Order of Communion, introduced in April 1548 and subsequently expanded into the Prayer Book of 1549. As regards the latter, Eamon Duffy has commented that it represents a "radical discontinuity with traditional religion", eliminating "almost everything that had till then been central to lay eucharistic piety". These and other changes were enforced by accompanying visitations, commissions and injunctions. In February 1548 the Privy Council ordered all images to be removed from churches and, on the evidence of surviving churchwardens' accounts, the process of iconoclasm would appear to have been "virtually complete" by the end of the year. The same source indicates that windows were reglazed and walls whitewashed, as part of the purge. Although parishes were slow to acquire the Book of Homilies, purchase of the Prayer Book, published by Grafton and Whitchurch, was enforced effectively – the old Catholic service books being either destroyed or sold. More generally, Ronald Hutton concludes that at this time there "crashed a whole world of popular religion."[44] In addition, from 1549 priests were allowed to be married. At Oxford and Cambridge Peter Martyr and Martin Bucer were installed respectively as regius professors of divinity – thus bringing continental reformed theology more directly to bear on the English universities. Meanwhile reformist literature poured off the London printing presses. Along with the greatly expanded numbers of works by English and continental writers now being published, Matthew Bibles and Tyndale New Testaments became much more widely available in various sizes, and on a sliding scale of prices.[45]

In the course of 1549, however, England was wracked by social disturbances, some of which escalated into full-scale rebellions. That in the west country took the religious form of Catholic opposition to the liturgical changes introduced by the Edwardian regime. But, as Diarmaid MacCulloch has noted, the "further east one goes, the more positive enthusiasm for the new religion one finds" among the protesters. This is especially the case as regards Essex, Norfolk and Suffolk. We know from the reply of the Privy Council that the Essex rebels buttressed their grievances with biblical texts, and claimed to "greatly hunger" for "the Gospel". Other letters to the Norfolk and

Suffolk rebels speak of them "professing Christ's doctrine in words", while showing "the contrary fruit" by their deeds.[46] Given the combined influence of Cambridge, Norwich and London, the distinctive religious tone of social protest in this part of England is perhaps not surprising. The sole surviving list of articles from these three counties is that drawn up by the group of Norfolk rebels led by Robert Kett, and camped on Mousehold Heath outside Norwich. It was A. F. Pollard, today a deeply unfashionable historian, who suggested a possible link between the Kett list of requests and the Twelve Articles of Memmingen produced in 1525 during the German Peasants' War. Comparison of the two documents tends to bear Pollard out, especially if allowance is made for the different socio-economic context and the more polished nature of the Memmingen articles.[47]

Both the Kett list of requests and Memmingen articles combine calls for change in religion and society, each asking for clergy to be *chosen* by their parishioners and able to preach the "word of God" (Kett no. 8) or "holy gospel" (Memmingen no. 1). The Kett list of requests elaborates further on the imperative for a resident minister, to give religious instruction (nos. 15 and 20). The two lists also share a desire to limit tithe payments (Kett no. 22 and Memmingen no. 2). As regards secular grievances, there is a mutual concern with the need to reduce rents (Kett nos. 5, 6 and 14 and Memmingen no. 8), the restoration of rights to common land (Kett nos. 3, 11 and 13 and Memmingen no. 10), freedom of river fishing (Kett no. 17 and Memmingen no. 4), and the abolition of serfdom – albeit there was only a remnant left in England (Kett no. 16 and Memmingen no. 3). At the same time the Kett list of requests exhibits many specific differences from that of Memmingen, not least because the former itemized more than twice as many grievances. Moreover unlike the Memmingen articles, which speak of "Christian justice", those produced by the Norfolk rebels do not enunciate any underlying philosophy.[48]

Contemporary rumours existed concerning "Anabaptist" involvement in East Anglia, yet the rebels seem to have taken their cue from more mainstream reformers. Interestingly Cranmer, in a sermon preached at the height of the disturbances in 1549, spoke not of Anabaptists but rather of a report "that there be many among these unlawful assemblies that pretend knowledge of the gospel and will needs be called gospellers". On the other hand it is important to remind ourselves that barely a decade previously the government had nipped in the bud a Norfolk conspiracy which involved similar social grievances, although combined on this earlier occasion with Catholic opposition to religious change. Among those then executed were a number of priests.[49] During 1549 a servant of the Catholic Princess Mary was said to be active in Suffolk and a Catholic priest, John Chandler, seems to have played a leading role in the rebel camp outside King's Lynn in Norfolk.[50] The rebels, however, under Kett's captaincy were ministered to religiously by reformers such as John Barret, Thomas Conyers, Matthew Parker and Robert Watson. After the event these clergy were keen to explain their role exclusively in terms of attempting to persuade the rebels to rely on the goodwill of central government and go home quietly. But some of them may have had a hand in formulating, and possibly toning down, the list of grievances.[51]

The rebellions of 1549 took place against a background of galloping price inflation, fuelled by the government's own policy of debasing the coinage, and in the context of what many contemporary commentators perceived as a loss of social cohesion due to the rise of unfettered economic individualism, which they characterized in the traditional terms of "avarice", "covetousness", and "greed". Moreover by the eve of the rebellions a printed literature on the subject was already in existence, among the best known examples being *An informacion and peticion agaynst the oppressours of the pore commons of this realme*, written by Robert Crowley and published probably as early as 1547. Crowley was at this date a layman and reformist London printer, subsequently being ordained in 1551. Ostensibly addressing parliament, Crowley put the case for social reform in terms of Christian stewardship. "Take me not here that I should go about to persuade men to make all things common", but "if the possessioners would consider themselves to be but stewards, and not lords over their possessions, this oppression would soon be redressed". Such, says Crowley, is the teaching of the Bible, and he compares himself to a prophet sent by God, quoting Isaiah 5.8: "Woe be unto you therefore that do join house unto house, and couple one field to another, so long as there is any ground to be had". Landlords were lashed by Crowley as "murderers" of the "impotent", who died "for lack of necessaries", and "causers" of "stealing, robbing and revenge", by withholding the earth from the "sturdy" who "should dig and plough their living". He was equally unsparing of the "hireling" clergy. Particularly arresting, however, is the following passage from his conclusion

> Wishing unto you (most worthy councillors) the same spirit that in the primitive church gave unto the multitude of believers one heart, one mind, and to esteem nothing of this world as their own, *ministering unto every one according to his necessities.*

Crowley and his like trod a narrow path here between permitted criticism and social subversion, as his disclaimer of communism makes plain.[52]

The genealogy of the ideas expressed in Crowley's *An informacion and peticion* can be traced back to the earliest writings of the English reformers and via them to the very beginnings of the continental Reformation. Such social teaching was indeed much older, but had been recast by the reformers in the light of their attack on Catholic views concerning good works. Not only does faith alone justify, but the works which are its necessary fruit differ. Essentially one should give to the poor and not to the Church. The reformers aimed to transfer the urgency with which Catholics strove for a place in heaven to the living of a truly Christian life on earth. This twin-track agenda is evident, for example, in Tyndale's *Parable of the wicked mammon* (1528). "Deeds are the fruits of love, and love is the fruit of faith". These deeds "testify" to faith and relate above all to the manner in which Christians treat their neighbours. "Among Christian men, love maketh all things common; every man is other's debtor, and every man is bound to minister to his neighbours, and to supply his neighbour's lack of that wherewith God hath endowed him". Furthermore, "Christ is Lord over all; and every Christian is heir annexed with Christ, and therefore Lord of all; and every one Lord of whatsoever another hath". This line of argument can also be found in *The summe of the holye scrypture*, a translation of about 1529 by Simon Fish from a Dutch original of 1523. Moreover the social teaching of both works was explicitly condemned by the English Catholic authorities in 1530. By 1548 the *Parable* and the *Summe* were in their fifth and seventh editions respectively.[53]

Similar views had now penetrated the government itself, most famously in the case of John Hales, Clerk of the Hanaper, who was appointed to a commission set up in 1548 to enforce the existing legislation against enclosures. Hales and five others were made responsible for the counties of Bedfordshire, Berkshire, Buckinghamshire, Leicestershire, Oxfordshire, Northamptonshire and Warwickshire. The actual commission, dated 1 June 1548, talks of "the corruption and infection of private lucre grown universally among our subjects". On 24 July and near the end of the first tour of these seven counties, Hales can be found writing to Protector Somerset that "the people . . . have a great hope that the iron world is now at an end, and the golden is returning again". He also made clear the intimate connection in his own mind between the social and religious programmes of the government.

> If there be any way or policy of man to make the people receive, embrace and love God's word, it is only this − when they shall see that it bringeth forth so goodly fruit, that men seek not their own wealth, nor their private commodity, but, as good members, the universal wealth of the whole body. Surely God's word is that precious balm that must increase comfort, and cherish that godly charity between man and man, which is the sinews that tie and hold together the members of every Christian commonwealth, and maketh one of us to be glad of another.

The ideal held up is that all "shall live in a due temperament and harmony, without one having too much, and a great many nothing at all, as at this present it appeareth plainly they have".[54]

Only a few weeks later, on 12 August, Hales had to defend himself, in a letter to the Earl of Warwick, from the accusation that he "should by hortations set the commons against the nobility and the gentlemen". While rebutting the charge, Hales none the less adjured Warwick to "remember the poor, have mercy and compassion on them, go not about to hinder them". Reading his later account of the proceedings of this commission, written up in the summer of 1549, one can understand why the arguments used by Hales generated alarm among members of the propertied classes. As he explained, in his meetings with "the people" Hales had provided an exposition of the commission and accompanying instructions from the government. His local audiences were in effect treated to sermons on the social ills of the day. He spoke of "the great dropsy and the insatiable desire of riches of some men . . . this most hurtful disease of the commonwealth, private profit", while making plain his credentials as a religious reformer. Masses and prayers for the dead will not save the uncharitable rich from damnation. Hales also glossed the oath taken by the juries of presentment as being "not by all saints, but as you trust to be saved by the merits of Christ's passion". Now, in this time of the Gospel, men must be doers as well as "talkers of God's word". Hales hammered away remorselessly at his central theme, "to remove the self love that is in many men" and to restore a charitable "mean", backed up by threats of divine judgement. Like Crowley, he too quoted Isaiah, concluding "let it not appear that we have received the grace of God, and the knowledge of his word, in vain". Only at the very end of his harangue did Hales warn the aggrieved not to take matters into their own hands, and "go about . . . to cut up men's hedges and to put down their enclosures". In retrospect he denied any responsibility for the ensuing collapse of law and order, laying the blame on "papists" and "Anabaptists", along with the failure of the local rulers to implement government orders.[55] But the sermonizing of Hales and others is likely to have produced both a general heightening of expectations, and an enhanced sense of mismatch between ideal and reality in a county such as Norfolk, where no enclosure commission appears to have been at work.

Enclosure became a great symbol during the 1549 rebellions, although in much of East Anglia overstocking of the commons by landlords was the leading agrarian issue. Certainly this is true of the list of grievances drawn up by the rebels under Kett. It was the principal concern too at Landbeach, in Cambridgeshire, which has been described as Kett's rebellion "in miniature", with the crucial difference, however, that here matters were resolved peacefully, whereas in Norfolk the situation developed into a pitched battle. In this village an archetypal grasping landlord, Richard Kirby, had come into conflict with the tenants of Corpus Christi College, Cambridge. The master of the college, the reformist Matthew Parker, was also rector of the parish. Having failed to pacify the rebels on Mousehold Heath, Parker secured agreement at Landbeach.[56] Anti-enclosure riots actually broke out in the immediate vicinity of Cambridge at this time, but order was restored by the mayor and vice-chancellor with little use of force. A set of verses relating to this episode survives, which takes the side of the rioters and expresses sentiments not unlike Crowley and Hales. This is especially true of some lines spoken by Harry Clowte:

> Good conscience should them move
> Their neighbours quietly to love,
> And thus not for to wrinch,
> The commons still for to pinch,
> To take into their hands
> That be other men's lands.[57]

The events of 1549 in East Anglia would seem to have involved an upsurge of popular religious fervour not so far removed after all from Haigh's concept of a Reformation "from below". It is all the more remarkable that this occurred in one of the heartlands of late medieval Catholic piety. Nor did social criticism, by religious reformers, die away in the aftermath of the rebellions. Crowley, for example, continued to hold forth as loudly as ever on the subject of oppression, while John Hooper's treatise on the Ten Commandments expounded "Thou shalt not steal" partly with reference to "avarice". Likewise some of the fiercest denunciations of greed by Latimer postdate the rebellions, when he also denied that preaching against "covetousness" had been the cause of the troubles. Moreover such teachings also informed the official Edwardian primer of 1553, especially as regards the prayer for landlords,

> We heartily pray thee . . . that they, remembering themselves to be thy tenants, may not rack and stretch out the rents of their houses and lands, nor yet take unreasonable fines and incomes after the manner of covetous worldlings, . . . and not

join house to house, nor couple land to land, to the impover-
ishment of other.

Again one hears the echo of Isaiah. The accompanying prayer for the
clergy includes the request "Take away from us, O Lord, all such
wicked ministers as deface thy glory, corrupt thy blessed word,
despise they flock, and feed themselves, and not thy sheep".[58]

MacCulloch has plausibly argued that the "evangelical establishment grouping knew from the start in 1547 exactly what Reformation it wanted" and, as a consequence, "there was an essential
continuity of purpose in a graduated series of religious changes over
seven years". Hence the second Edwardian Prayer Book of 1552,
primer, catechism and Articles of Religion of 1553 represent the
elaboration of an original intention rather than a radical redirection of
religious effort. During 1550 all stone altars were ordered to be
demolished, and Cranmer published his *Defence of the true and catholike
doctrine of the sacrament* which developed the view that "only the
faithful consume the body of Christ" and, as he put it, "with the
heart, not with the teeth". This teaching informed the communion
service in the new Prayer Book. The catechism and Articles are also
notable for including fairly uncompromising statements of uncondi-
tional predestination. But, possibly as a balance to the anti-land-
lordism of the primer, one of the Articles was devoted to condemning
"Anabaptist" teaching on "the riches and goods of Christians". These
are "not common . . . notwithstanding every man ought, of such
things as he possesseth, liberally to give alms to the poor, *according to
his ability*".[59] At the parish level altars were generally removed and
the Prayer Book again bought.[60] Time, however, was running out for
the regime, as Edward VI became increasingly ill and the Catholic
Princess Mary waited in the wings. Moreover the evangelical
preachers began to turn the edge of their social criticism against the
government itself – now led by Northumberland (the former
Warwick), after the fall of Somerset. The context was the continuing
plunder of what remained of ecclesiastical wealth, for private profit.
Northumberland was, in addition, still remembered as the butcher of
the Norfolk rebels in 1549, and this may partly explain why Mary
was able to win crucial support in East Anglia, during 1553, when
successfully resisting diversion of the royal succession to Queen Jane.[61]

Under Mary, between 1553 and 1558, Roman Catholicism was restored. Revisionist historians have rightly taught us that there existed no intrinsic reason why this reversal should not have endured, save only that Mary was in turn succeeded by her Protestant half-sister Elizabeth. The grass-roots evidence of Catholic restoration, as detailed by Duffy and Hutton, is especially impressive.[62] Yet it remains worth pondering that when, at the end of October 1553, the Marian regime introduced a composite parliamentary bill repealing the Edwardian religious legislation a quarter of MPs present in the Commons voted against it, and the debates were drawn out for a week. These eighty or so dissenters appear to represent the kind of significant minority commitment that the history of the Reformation elsewhere would lead one to expect. They may also link ideologically, if not in direct terms of personnel, with Sir Thomas Wyatt's rebellion of the following year in Kent. An insurrection, predominantly of the gentry, aimed at deposing Mary, the inner ring of conspirators does seem to have consisted mainly of evangelicals.[63]

In the counties the commissions of the peace had already been purged of politically unreliable and, by implication, evangelically inclined gentry. As early as 13 and 16 August 1553 respectively all clergy in the City of London and Norwich diocese were inhibited, by the Privy Council, from preaching without special royal licence. At Cambridge, in marked contrast to Oxford, nearly all the heads of colleges were removed, either by deprivation or resignation, and there was also a loss of college fellows – including over twenty from St John's. Some went into exile abroad, but others stayed in England unreconciled to the official changes. (Northumberland had been chancellor of Cambridge University, and was in fact arrested there in 1553, along with the vice-chancellor Edwin Sandys.)[64] In London, by Easter 1554 approximately a third of all benefices "had been emptied by the deprivation, resignation, or imprisonment of their Edwardian reformist incumbents". Although some Londoners fled, the city continued to be religiously divided, the bravest evangelicals going underground and forming a secret church.[65] During 1554, the "poor men" and "lovers of Christ's true religion in Norfolk and Suffolk" went so far as to petition the Marian commissioners not to restore the mass. Meanwhile at Norwich itself the irrepressible reformer Robert Watson was for a time imprisoned, but the civic authorities seem as far as possible to have turned a blind eye to the undoubted religious diversity in their midst. More generally there was probably widespread resort in England to "Nicodemism", that is to say, dissembling of one's true beliefs.[66] Of course, the situation to the north and west differed, where reformers were thin on the ground – notoriously so in counties such as Lancashire or Devon and Cornwall. But this constituted no mere aborted English Reformation "from above". Furthermore in the war of printed propaganda, the reformers maintained their lead even during Mary's reign.[67]

The undoubted strength of Marian Catholicism, however, proved inadequate defence against the lottery of hereditary royal succession. During the years 1558 to 1563 the Edwardian Church of the reformers was in effect restored, courtesy of Queen Elizabeth. Catholics were thenceforward faced with the choice of either compromising with the new religious establishment, and ultimately being absorbed by it, or retreating into the ecclesiastical wilderness. Despite their far greater numbers, in the longer term they were in no better position than the "Protestants" under the Marian dispensation. Yet we are still here only at the start of the Reformation process, with probably a large majority of the population remaining to be won. Moreover it was not a question of a once-for-all conversion, let alone of simply waiting for those who had known a fully functioning Catholic Church to die off. Each new generation required to be nurtured afresh, as Jeremy Gregory reminds us in the concluding chapter of the present volume, lest they be lost in some irreligious void. The ensuing split, from the later sixteenth century onwards, between the Puritans and their conformist opponents was more a dispute over means than ends, the working of saving faith within the individual as opposed to the collective immersion of the parish in reformed religious beliefs and practices. This latter and less confrontational approach was arguably the more successful; such at least appears to be the message of the following chapters by Muriel McClendon, David Hickman and Christopher Marsh.

McClendon sees the Reformation in Norwich as being mediated by a magistracy mindful of the need to live with the reality of religious diversity, and hence her epithet "quiet" to describe it. So far as possible, the Norwich civic authorities avoided active persecution. A not dissimilar picture for Elizabethan London is provided by

Hickman, where parochial life, as mirrored in the wills of the ruling elite, seems to have been successfully adapted to the official requirements of religious change without sacrificing a sense of community. Moreover the earlier concern with social reform translated into increasingly elaborate schemes for dealing with the problem of poverty and its assumed causes, both in London and Norwich. Although associated particularly with the "godly", these efforts attracted a much broader body of support.[68] Marsh's study of the Family of Love indicates, in turn, the variety of establishment responses to this esoteric sect. Andrew Perne emerges as a somewhat unexpected hero in his dealings with the Familists of Balsham near Cambridge. Gentle persuasion by this most moderate of Protestants worked better, so Marsh argues, than the coercion favoured by more zealous colleagues, such as John Knewstub. Taken together these three chapters imply the need for a more sympathetic approach than has been customary to the "Laudianism" which emerged in the reign of Charles I, as catering at least in part to the needs of a lay piety in revolt from "Calvinism" in its various guises.[69]

Conversely the Catholics of Elizabethan and early Stuart England come across in the joint chapter by Peter Lake and Michael Questier as more like the Puritans – especially in their rival attempts to missionize the prison population. At the same time Lake & Questier challenge the notion that such activity lacked widespread appeal. Ironically the imprisoned Catholic priests were sometimes more effective than when at liberty. (There is in fact an analogue here with the Marian period, when reformers can also be found propagating their gospel from prison).[70] Conversion on the gallows was a prize particularly coveted by these competing evangelists and this often provided the subject matter of cheap pamphlet literature. Furthermore as public spectacle it "was a form of popular evangelism with a vengeance". For a more low-key but none the less important account of the history of Catholicism at the parish level, in this case Suffolk, the reader needs to turn to the chapter by Joy Rowe. What particularly impresses is the survival of the same geographical enclaves of Catholics down at least to the end of the eighteenth century, often only intermittently serviced by priests who were themselves not necessarily based on gentry households. Meanwhile Eamon Duffy, versatile "revisionist" that he is, agrees in his Neale lecture with Lake

& Questier that Puritanism, by the mid-seventeenth century, was effectively reaching out to the population at large. Indeed his contribution to the present volume goes much further, talking in terms of the Reformation's "runaway success" in "late Elizabethan and Jacobean England", and he clearly sees illiteracy as no insuperable bar. But this is very much Protestantism defined as "conversion", in the sense of spiritual "awakening", and an approach to Christianization associated with Richard Baxter in the 1650s and the Dissenters generally after 1662. Duffy concedes, however, that a work such as Richard Allestree's *The whole duty of man* (1658) had a comparable role to play in the propagation of religion by the establishment. Baxter, he notes, even recommended it, although the Calvinist George Whitefield, one should add, later condemned the book.[71] Ann Hughes also makes a case for the popularity of Puritanism, in this case as represented by the Presbyterians Thomas Edwards and Thomas Hall. Edwards' polemical engagement with the religious radicals, notably in *Gangraena*, is complemented by an account of Hall's ministry at Kings Norton near Birmingham.

Duffy sees increasing religious fragmentation from the Restoration period onwards, and a growing tension between godliness and formalism. Another way of putting this, however, would be to say that Laudianism had re-emerged in a more strongly rooted form than before. We need also to recall that this represents a fault line in English Protestantism running from the sixteenth century, and not itself irreconcilable with the continued existence of a national church. Peter Heylyn, the first biographer of Laud and apologist for the movement associated with him, is only one among many spokesmen for a tradition which requires accommodation in any comprehensive history of England's Long Reformation.[72] Moreover, unlike Duffy, a number of other historians of the eighteenth century do not regard the 1689 Toleration Act as the final parting of the ways. They include Jonathan Barry and Jeremy Gregory. Using a broader definition of Protestantism than Duffy, Barry's chapter locates Bristol in this later period as a "Reformation city", and demonstrates the existence of a richly diverse parish religion. The concern with the "reformation of manners" at this time represents, as Barry recognizes, a variation on an old theme. He also makes the point that the sacred and the secular remained intimately connected, while the existence of religious pluralism was regarded by most as, at best, a "necessary evil". Among Barry's exemplars is the history of Methodism, which in turn provides the subject of the penultimate chapter by W. R. Ward.

"Early Methodism", Ward reminds us, "was a movement which never became a denomination". It grew out of the religious reform societies to which both Duffy and Barry draw attention in their respective chapters, and derived its support from a very wide religious spectrum within the establishment. Contingency, rather than strategy, is what comes across in Ward's account of the subsequent development of Methodism, something most glaringly illustrated by the activities of Wesley in Scotland and Ireland. On the other hand, itinerant preaching emerged as a central Wesleyan plank, an element which Duffy and Collinson see as generally missing in the Protestantism of the sixteenth and seventeenth centuries. Membership remained fluid, however, and at least as regards English Methodism there survived a hankering after "a Catholic church order, which affected even those resolved to do without it". Features such as these, still present in a movement which represented the main religious alternative to the Church of England during the eighteenth century, allow Jeremy Gregory, in the final chapter, to see this period as part of a continuing Reformation process which involved both Protestantization and Christianization. Moreover he suggests that the Long Reformation model still has relevance for the Victorian era. But we have chosen to end our volume at *circa* 1800, in the belief that the ideas spawned by the Enlightenment had now come to pose an unprecedented challenge to the previous religious consensus.

Notes

1. This introduction seeks, among other things, to open up debate on the early stages of the English Reformation. It also aims to redress what some felt was a chronological imbalance in the original Colloquium proceedings, from which the present volume derives. I am most grateful to Diarmaid MacCulloch for his comments on earlier draft versions, and to Philip Broadhead and Christopher Coleman for advice concerning particular points.
2. G. Strauss, "Success and failure in the German Reformation", *Past and Present* **67**, 1975, pp. 30–63; G. Parker, "Success and failure during the first

century of the Reformation", *Past and Present* **136**, 1992, pp. 43–82; J. Delumeau, *Catholicism from Luther to Voltaire* (London, 1977).

3. C. Haigh, *English Reformations: religion, politics and society under the Tudors* (Oxford, 1993). This is the most recent general statement of the revisionist position, and is rather more nuanced than C. Haigh (ed.), *The English Reformation revised* (Cambridge, 1987).

4. K. Thomas, *Religion and the decline of magic: studies in popular beliefs in sixteenth- and seventeenth-century England* (London, 1971); cf. R. Hutton, "The English Reformation and the evidence of folklore", *Past and Present* **148**, 1995, pp. 89–116.

5. In retrospect, Haigh's book *Reformation and resistance in Tudor Lancashire* (Cambridge, 1975) can be seen to have adumbrated the agenda of subsequent revisionist accounts of the English Reformation.

6. Haigh, *English Reformations* and Haigh (ed.), *The English Reformation revised*; J. J. Scarisbrick, *The Reformation and the English people* (Oxford, 1984); E. Duffy, *The stripping of the altars: traditional religion in England c.1400–1580* (New Haven & London, 1992). Of these three historians, Haigh has proved by far the most combative and my remarks about revisionism relate primarily to his work.

7. F.A. Gasquet, *The eve of the Reformation: studies in the religious life and thought of the English people in the period preceding the rejection of the Roman jurisdiction by Henry VIII* (London, 1900), pp. 13, 43, 119, 323–415. For the famous controversy concerning Gasquet's scholarship, see M. D. Knowles, *Cardinal Gasquet as an historian* (Creighton Lecture, London, 1957); cf. Haigh (ed.), *The English Reformation revised*, pp. 56–74.

8. H.N. Birt, *The Elizabethan religious settlement: a study of contemporary documents* (London, 1907), pp. xi, 191, 537; cf. Haigh (ed.), *The English Reformation revised*, pp. 176–208 and C. Haigh, "From monopoly to minority: Catholicism in early modern England", *Transactions of the Royal Historical Society*, 5th series **31**, 1981, pp. 129–47. Birt was in part responding to H. Gee, *The Elizabethan clergy and the settlement of religion 1558–1564* (Oxford, 1898). Whereas Gee put the figure for deprived priests in the early years of Elizabeth at about 200 (p. 247), Birt upped this to approximately 2,000 – defined as those "who abandoned their livings from conscientious inability to conform" (p. 203). Ironically, the larger the number the more profound the religious break with Catholicism produced by the Elizabethan settlement.

9. B. Moeller, "Piety in Germany around 1500", in *The Reformation in medieval perspective*, S. E. Ozment (ed.) (Chicago, 1971), pp. 50–75; cf. Haigh, *English Reformations*, pp. 12–13.

10. Gasquet, *The eve of the Reformation*, pp. 208–35; Scarisbrick, *The Reformation and the English people*, pp. 197–203. Another absentee is Tyndale.

11. Haigh (ed.), *The English Reformation revised*, pp. 19–33.

12. A. G. Dickens, *The English Reformation* (London, 1964), p. v. In the second edition of this book (London, 1989), Dickens defends his argument.

13. For analogies, however, between Kett's rebellion of 1549 and the German Peasants' War of 1525, see pp. 13-19 above.

14. R. Rex, *The theology of John Fisher* (Cambridge, 1991), p. 80 and R. Rex, "The English campaign against Luther in the 1520s", *Transactions of the Royal Historical Society*, 5th series **39**, 1989, p. 86.

15. J. Fines, *A biographical register of early English Protestants and others opposed to the Roman Catholic church*, pt. 2, unpublished typescript (West Sussex Institute of Education, 1985), F 10, G 3–4, G 12, S 25, H 18–19, M 12, P 4–5, T 2–3, R 7–8, F 13. I have used the copy at the Institute of Historical Research, University of London; C. H. & T. Cooper, *Athenae Cantabrigienses*, vol. I (Cambridge, 1858), p. 86; for the Lutheran play performed at Christ's College in 1544, see pp. 8–9 above; T. D. Hardy (ed.), *Fasti ecclesiae Anglicanae*, vol. 3 (Oxford, 1854), pp. 685, 681, 692, 674, 668, 690, 683.

16. E. S. Leedham-Green (ed.), *Books in Cambridge inventories*, vol. 1 (Cambridge, 1986), pp. xxi, 1–3, 9–11, 16–18, 20, 22, 29–30, 32, 39–42, 51, 57, 62–6, 71, 82–6; W. R. D. Jones, *William Turner, Tudor naturalist, physician and divine* (London & New York, 1988), pp. 10–11; J. Fines, *A biographical register of early English Protestants and others opposed to the Roman Catholic church 1525–1558*, pt. 1 (Abingdon, 1981), "Cox, Richard". Professor Fines very kindly supplied me with a copy of this part. A revised edition of both parts is to be published by Headstart Press; R. J. Fehrenbach & E. S. Leedham-Green (eds.), *Private libraries in renaissance England*, vol. 2 (Marlborough, 1993), pp. 265–75.

17. J. Foxe, *The acts and monuments*, S. R. Cattley & G. Townsend (eds) (London, 1837), vol. 4, pp. 666–70, 679.

18. C. E. Foerstemann (ed.), *Album academiae Vitenbergensis* (1502–1560), vol. 1 (Leipzig, 1841), pp. 125b, 149b, 186a; D. MacCulloch, *Thomas Cranmer: a life* (New Haven & London, 1996), pp. 176–7; *RSTC* (*Revised Short Title Catalogue*, by W. A. Jackson, F. S. Ferguson & K. F. Pantzer, London, 1976–91), nos. 4054, 16962, 16979.7, 16999, 24238, 15179, 18878, 17793, 17798, 26138.

19. J.E. Cox (ed.), *Miscellaneous writings and letters of Thomas Cranmer* (Parker Society, Cambridge, 1846), pp. 460–1; M. C. Skeeters, *Community and clergy: Bristol and the reformation c.1530–1570* (Oxford, 1993), pp. 38–47, 229; A. G. Dickens, *Lollards and Protestants in the diocese of York 1509–1558* (Oxford, 1959), pp. 140–3; MacCulloch, *Thomas Cranmer*, p. 110.

20. R. Rex, "The new learning", *Journal of Ecclesiastical History* **44**, 1993, pp. 26–44; J. Gairdner (ed.), *Letters and papers, foreign and domestic, of the reign of Henry VIII*, vol. 12, pt. 2 (London, 1891), pp. 593, 643; cf. Haigh (ed.), *The English Reformation revised*, pp. 6–7, 10–11, 15–17.

21. G. E. Corrie (ed.), *Sermons and remains of Hugh Latimer* (Parker Society, Cambridge, 1845), pp. 218–20; G. E. Corrie (ed.), *Sermons by Hugh Latimer* (Parker Society, Cambridge, 1844), pp. 36–7, 46, 50, 55; *RSTC*, nos. 15285, 15286.

22. P. L. Hughes & J. F. Larkin (eds), *Tudor royal proclamations*, vol. 1 (New Haven & London, 1964), nos 122, 129 (*Parable of the Wicked Mammon*), 186, 272; *RSTC*, nos. 24454, 24455.

23. *RSTC*, nos. 16962, 16999, 17000, 24238, 908. M. Aston, *England's iconoclasts* (Oxford, 1988), pp. 203–10; J. K. McConica, *English humanists and reformation politics under Henry VIII and Edward VI* (Oxford, 1956), p. 170.

24. *RSTC*, no. 2066, *La bible qui est toute la saincte escripture* (Neuchâtel, 1535), fos. 95–105v at end; MacCulloch, *Thomas Cranmer*, pp. 196–7; A. L. Herminjard (ed.), *Correspondance des reformateurs dans les pays de langue française*, vol. 3 (Geneva, 1870), pp. 257n. 289n. 290n. Gramelin is an anagram for Malingre, although Matthieu works less well for Thomas (Mathos). This French Bible was the work of Pierre Robert (Olivétan) and includes prefatory material by John Calvin. To the best of my knowledge, I am the first to offer this explanation of the name Thomas Matthew.

25. It should be emphasized that the publication figures given in this paragraph are only my rough calculations, based on *RSTC*; D. Wilkins (ed.), *Concilia Magnae Britanniae et Hiberniae*, vol. 3 (London, 1737), p. 706.

26. M. Dowling, "Anne Boleyn and reform", *Journal of Ecclesiastical History* **35**, 1984, pp. 30–46; E. W. Ives, "Anne Boleyn and the early reformation in England: the contemporary evidence", *Historical Journal* **37**, 1994, pp. 389–499; S. Brigden, "Thomas Cromwell and the brethren", in *Law and government under the Tudors*, C. Cross, D. Loades & J. J. Scarisbrick (eds) (Cambridge, 1988), pp. 31–49; MacCulloch, *Thomas Cranmer*, pp. 173–236, cf. G. Bernard, "Anne Boleyn's religion", *Historical Journal* **36**, 1993, pp. 1–20.

27. L.V. Ryan, *Roger Ascham* (Stanford, 1963), pp. 45–6; J. A. Giles (ed.), *The whole works of Roger Ascham*, vol. 1 (London, 1865), p. 68; A. Pighius, *De libero hominis arbitrio et divina gratia* (Cologne, 1542).

28. T. Naogeorgus [Kirchmeyer], *Pammachius* (Wittenberg, 1538); T. T. Perowne (ed.), *Correspondence of Matthew Parker* (Parker Society, Cambridge, 1853), pp. 20–9.

29. Dickens, *Lollards and Protestants*; Dickens, *The English Reformation* (2nd edn. London, 1989), pp. 52, 56–7.

30. A. Hudson, *The premature Reformation: Wycliffite texts and Lollard history* (Oxford, 1988), pp. 17–18. Hudson, however, draws attention to "a number of early sixteenth-century copies" of Lollard works (p. 17); S. Brigden, *London and the Reformation* (Oxford, 1989), pp. 106–9.

31. Aston, *England's iconoclasts*, pp. 210–19.

32. Haigh (ed.), *The English reformation revised*, pp. 56–74, and Haigh, *English Reformations*, pp. 72–87; R. L. Storey, "Gentlemen bureaucrats", in *Profession, vocation and culture in later medieval England*, C. H. Clough (ed.) (Liverpool, 1982), pp. 90–129.

33. J. Craig & C. Litzenberger, "Wills as religious propaganda: the testament of William Tracy", *Journal of Ecclesiastical History* **44**, 1993, pp. 421–5; H. Walter (ed.), *An answer to Sir Thomas More's dialogue, . . . and Wm. Tracy's*

testament expounded, by William Tyndale (Parker Society, Cambridge, 1850), p. 279; *RSTC*, no. 10883; radical lawyers in turn overlapped with gentry of the same ilk, Baynham being visited in prison by the brothers William and Ralph Morice, along with William's brother-in-law Edward Isaac: Corrie (ed.), *Sermons and remains of Hugh Latimer*, pp. 221–2.

34. Fines, *A biographical register*, pt. 2, F 6, H 10; E. F. Rogers, *The letters of Sir John Hackett 1526–1534* (Morgantown, 1971), pp. 156, 161, 173–4.

35. R. Whiting, *The blind devotion of the people: popular religion and the English Reformation* (Cambridge, 1989), pp. 225; Haigh, *Reformation and resistance in Tudor Lancashire*, pp. 35–6; S. E. Lehmberg, *The Reformation parliament 1529–1536* (Cambridge, 1970), pp. 6–7, 81–2.

36. S. Brigden, "Tithe controversy in Reformation London", *Journal of Ecclesiastical History* **32**, 1981, pp. 285–301; Brigden, *London and the Reformation*, pp. 49–52; Lehmberg, *The Reformation parliament*, pp. 76–104.

37. Brigden, *London and the Reformation*, pp. 399–404, 345–6.

38. J. Gairdner & R. H. Brodie, *Letters and papers, foreign and domestic, of the reign of Henry VIII*, vol. 17 (London, 1900), p. 79; G. R. Elton, *Policy and police: the enforcement of the Reformation in the age of Thomas Cromwell* (Cambridge, 1972), pp. 138–9.

39. Brigden, *London and the Reformation*, pp. 424, 430; M. C. McClendon, *The quiet Reformation: Norwich magistrates and the coming of Protestantism, 1520–1575* (PhD thesis, Stanford University, 1990), p. 125.

40. Ryan, *Roger Ascham*, p. 92; J. E. Foster (ed.), *Churchwardens' accounts of St Mary the great Cambridge from 1504 to 1635* (Cambridge Antiquarian Society, Cambridge, 1905), pp. 114, 117.

41. Brigden, *London and the Reformation*, pp. 433–9.

42. Ryan, *Roger Ascham*, pp. 92–6.

43. C. H. Cooper, *Annals of Cambridge*, vol. 2 (Cambridge, 1843), p. 31; J.K. McConica (ed.), *The collegiate university*, vol. 3 of *The history of the university of Oxford* (Oxford, 1986), pp. 369–72; McClendon, *The quiet Reformation*, pp. 58–9 and M. C. McClendon, "Discipline and punish? Magistrates and clergy in early Reformation Norwich", in *Religion and the English people 1500–1620: new voices/new perspectives*, E. J. Carlson (ed.), in press.

44. MacCulloch, *Thomas Cranmer*, pp. 369–75, 384–6, 410–12; Duffy, *The stripping of the altars*, pp. 454, 464; R. Hutton, "The local impact of the Tudor reformations", in *The English Reformation revised*, Haigh (ed.), pp. 120–5.

45. *Statutes of the realm*, vol. 4 (London, 1819), p. 67; McConica (ed.), *The collegiate university*, pp. 134–5, 318–19, 368–74; C. Hopf, *Martin Bucer and the English reformation* (Oxford, 1946), pp. 12–29, P. M. Took, *Government and the printing trade, 1540–60* (PhD thesis, London University, 1979), pp. 134–223, 343–5.

46. MacCulloch, *Thomas Cranmer*, pp. 432–3; British Library, Add. MS 48018, fos. 388, 389v, 391.

47. A. F. Pollard, *The history of England from the accession of Edward VI to the death of Elizabeth (1547–1603)* (London, 1919), pp. 33–4. Pollard was sensitized to this issue having written a chapter on "Social revolution and Catholic reaction in Germany", for *The Cambridge modern history*, vol. 2 (Cambridge, 1907), pp. 174–205. It remains unclear whether a copy of the Memmingen articles was actually available to the leaders of Kett's rebellion, or whether the link was more indirect. There would appear, however, to have been a common ideological context.

48. A. Fletcher, *Tudor rebellions* (3rd edn, London, 1983), pp. 120–3; P. Blickle, *The revolution of 1525: the German Peasants' War from a new perspective* (Baltimore, 1988), pp. 195–201.

49. Cox (ed.), *Miscellaneous writings and letters of Thomas Cranmer*, p. 195; Elton, *Policy and police*, pp, 144–51.

50. D. MacCulloch, "Kett's rebellion in context", *Past and Present* **84**, 1979, pp. 49, 58. This article is the essential modern starting point for discussion of Kett's rebellion; Norfolk Record Office, NCC will (John Chandler) 1553, 22 Wilkins (MF 49). This will, hitherto unnoticed and dated 1550/1, establishes Chandler's Catholicism; B. L. Beer, *Rebellion and riot: popular disorder in England during the reign of Edward VI* (Kent, Ohio, 1982), pp. 141–2.

51. MacCulloch, *Thomas Cranmer*, pp. 433–4; J. Cornwall, *Revolt of the peasantry 1549* (London, 1977), pp. 149–50; McClendon, *The quiet Reformation*, p. 125.

52. C. E. Challis, "The debasement of the coinage", *Economic History Review*, 2nd series 20, 1967, pp. 441–66; J. M. Cowper (ed.), *The select works of Robert Crowley* (Early English Text Society, London, 1872), pp. 154, 156–7, 161, 164, 175. My italics. Crowley refers to the Act of Six Articles as still unrepealed, which dates his writing to before December 1547 (p. 170).

53. H. Walter (ed.), *Doctrinal treatises and introductions to different portions of the holy scriptures by William Tyndale* (Parker Society, Cambridge, 1848), pp. 57, 59, 95, 97; *RSTC*, no. 3036; Wilkins, *Concilia Magnae Britanniae et Hibernia*, vol. 3, pp. 728, 731–2; for the related teaching of Zwingli, see L. P. Wandel *Always among us: images of the poor in Zwingli's Zurich* (Cambridge, 1990), pp. 36–76; cf also S. Brigden, "Popular disturbance and the fall of Thomas Cromwell and the reformers, 1539–1540", *Historical Journal* **24**, 1981, pp. 270–2.

54. J. Strype, *Ecclesiastical memorials relating chiefly to religion . . . under King Henry VIII, King Edward VI and Queen Mary I*, vol. 2, pt. 2 (Oxford, 1822), p. 349; P.F. Tytler, *England under the reigns of Edward VI and Mary* (London, 1839), pp.114–16.

55. British Library, Lansdowne MS 238, fos. 322r–v; Stype, *Ecclesiastical memorials relating chiefly to religion . . .*, vol. 2, pt. 2, pp. 352–8, 364; E. Lamond (ed.), *A discourse of the common weal of this realm of England* (Cambridge, 1954), pp. lvi–lix.

56. MacCulloch, "Kett's rebellion in context", pp. 50–3; J. R. Ravensdale, "Landbeach in 1549: Kett's rebellion in miniature", in *East Anglian Studies*, L. M. Munby (ed.) (Cambridge, 1968), pp. 94–116.

INTRODUCTION

57. Beer, *Rebellion and riot*, pp. 143–4; Cooper, *Annals of Cambridge*, vol. 2, p. 36–44. Pyrse Plowman says (p. 41):
    I wonder at this covetous nation
    That scrat and get all out of fashion.

58. Cowper (ed.), *The select works of Robert Crowley*, pp. 131–50; S. Carr (ed.), *Early writings of John Hooper* . . . (Parker Society, Cambridge, 1843), pp. 387–404; Corrie (ed.), *Sermons by Hugh Latimer*, pp. 246–50 J. Ketley (ed.), *The two liturgies . . . with other documents set forth by authority in the reign of King Edward VI* (Parker Society, Cambridge, 1844), pp. 457–8. Cf. also the prayer "for rich men" (p. 460). These prayers are in fact taken from T. Becon, *The flower of godly prayers* (London, c.1550).

59. MacCulloch, *Thomas Cranmer*, pp. 365–6, 458, 463–4, 504–12; Ketley (ed.), *The two liturgies*, pp. 511–13; E. Cardwell, *Synodalia*, vol. 1 (Oxford, 1842), pp. 96–7, 105. My italics.

60. Hutton, "The local impact of the Tudor reformations", pp. 125–6.

61. MacCulloch, *Thomas Cranmer*, pp. 531–3; D. MacCulloch, "Debate: Kett's rebellion in context", *Past and Present* **93**, 1981, pp. 172–3.

62. Duffy, *The stripping of the altars*, pp. 524–63; Hutton, "The local impact of the Tudor reformations", pp. 128–31.

63. J. Loach, *Parliament and the crown in the reign of Mary Tudor* (Oxford, 1986), pp. 77–8; M. R. Thorp, "Religion and the Wyatt rebellion of 1554", *Church History* **47**, 1978, pp. 363–80; P. Clark, *English provincial society from the Reformation to the revolution: religion, politics and society in Kent, 1500–1640* (Hassocks, 1977), pp. 87–98.

64. D. MacCulloch, *Suffolk and the Tudors: politics and religion in an English county 1500–1600* (Oxford, 1986), pp. 232–3, 416; J. R. Dasent *et al.* (eds), *Acts of the privy council of England*, (London, 1890–1907), *1552–1554*, pp. 317, 321; Cooper, *Annals of Cambridge*, vol. 2, pp. 83–4; Hardy (ed.), *Fasti ecclesiae Anglicanae*, vol. 3, pp. 668, 671, 674, 679, 681, 683, 685, 687, 688, 690, 692, 699; H.C. Porter, *Reformation and reaction in Tudor Cambridge* (Cambridge, 1958), pp. 75–6.

65. Brigden, *London and the Reformation*, pp. 575–6.

66. Foxe, *The acts and monuments*, Cattley & Townsend (eds) (London, 1839), vol. 8, pp. 121–30. The petitioners emphasized their loyalty to Mary in 1553. My dating of this document disagrees with Foxe; McClendon, *The quiet reformation*, pp. 176–8; A. Pettegree, *Marian Protestantism: six studies* (Aldershot, 1996), pp. 86–117.

67. Haigh, *Reformation and resistance in Tudor Lancashire*; Whiting, *The blind devotion of the people*; E. J. Baskerville, *A chronological bibliography of propaganda and polemic, published in English between 1553 and 1558, from the death of Edward VI to the death of Mary I* (Philadelphia, 1979), pp. 5–10.

68. McClendon, *The quiet Reformation*, pp. 227–72; I. W. Archer, *The pursuit of stability: social relations in Elizabethan London* (Cambridge, 1991), pp. 149–203.

69. This will be one of the themes of a joint study currently being undertaken by Kenneth Fincham and myself.

70. Foxe, *The acts and monuments*, Cattley & Townsend (eds) (London, 1838), vol. 7, p. 145.

71. *A modest and serious defence of the author of "The whole duty of man" from the false charges and gross misrepresentations of Mr. Whitefield* (London, 1740).

72. P. Heylyn, *Historia quinqu-articularis* (London, 1660), *Ecclesia restaurata* (London, 1661), and *Cyprianus Anglicus: or the history of the life and death of . . . William [Laud]* (London, 1668).

2

The Long Reformation: Catholicism, Protestantism and the multitude[1]

Eamon Duffy

It is now twenty-five years since the first appearance of Jean Delumeau's *Catholicism between Luther and Voltaire*, in which he argued that despite their apparent mutual contradictions, "the two Reformations – Luther's and Rome's – constituted . . . two complementary aspects of one and the same process of Christianization".[2] The Christian Middle Ages, according to Delumeau, was a legend, at least "as far as the (essentially rural) masses are concerned". Christianity, he thought, had penetrated medieval society only superficially, and the whole of Europe in the sixteenth and seventeenth centuries was, therefore, *"pays de mission"*, just as surely as the newly discovered pagan Indies, East and West.

Some scepticism is in order about Delumeau's central contention, and was in fact expressed by John Bossy in his introduction to the English translation. Something profound, and profoundly new, did indeed happen to European Christianity in the early modern period, but it seems maddeningly wrong-headed to describe that something as the achievement, after an apparently ineffective millenium of Christian activity in Europe, of "Christianization". Elsewhere, indeed, Bossy has suggested that it may not always be very satisfactory even to describe the transformation by the term "reformation", for to do so is to go along too easily with the notion that "a bad form of Christianity was being replaced by a good one".[3]

However that may be, in this chapter I want to focus on an insular aspect of the broader renewal or recasting of Christianity in the early modern period which Delumeau made much of, and which lent powerful support to his thesis. I want to consider the English dimension of the move all over Europe to devise new evangelistic methods, missionary strategies to reach populations widely thought of by zealous clergy as not merely unchurched, but actually unchristened. While such an assumption fitted particularly well with the Protestant conviction that the Reformation had rediscovered a gospel suppressed by centuries of popish error, it was not in any sense peculiar to Protestants, and indeed in many ways Counter-Reformation Catholicism embraced it with far greater energy and inventiveness than did the Protestant reformers. Catholic missionary strategists talked of the populations of rural Europe and of the great cities as pagans, and equated non-Christian "heathenism" and the superstitious beliefs and practices of the European peasantry and urban poor. When the seventeenth-century missionary St Francesco de Geronimo asked his Jesuit superiors to send him to Japan and martyrdom, he was told instead to become "the Apostle of the Indies of this city and kingdom of Naples".[4]

Catholic Europe was of course no stranger to the idea of large-scale conversion or mission. The century before the Reformation had been marked by the activities of hugely popular urban evangelists such as Vincent Ferrar or Bernardino of Sienna.[5] But this was hit-and-run work by travelling friars: Vincent Ferrer averaged an annual three hundred lengthy sermons in the restless travelling of his last twenty years, sermons often devoted to apocalyptic warnings about the imminent end of the world. Sixteenth- and seventeenth-century Europe came to feel that something with a longer-term perspective and a more gradualist and consistent pastoral strategy behind it was required, a pastoral strategy moreover which reached not merely the urban audiences which had gathered to hear St Bernardino or St Vincent, but which would touch and transform the much larger body of the rural poor, served as they often were by clergy as saturated in ignorance, cow dung and domestic cares as the people themselves. Trent took it as axiomatic that the solution to this pastoral dilemma lay in the rejuvenation of the parochial system, yet the engine eventually devised to breach the darkness of the parishes was not routine parochial ministry, but the revivalist machinery of the parish mission.

A sixteenth-century invention in which Spanish Jesuits played a key role, the parish missions of the Counter-Reformation came into their own in the seventeenth and eighteenth centuries, and received their decisive shape in the activities of Vincent de Paul's Lazarists or Priests of the Mission, and Alphonsus de Ligouri's Redemptorists.[6] Preached by organized teams of specially-trained religious, the missions were carefully adapted to the rhythms of peasant life. In its classical, and simplest, form, devised by St Vincent, it consisted of sermons preached at dawn for the benefit of those who had to be early in the fields, and which were designed to be awakening in more senses than one, catechizing of children and young people in the afternoons, and the "great catechism", systematic but also awakening instruction of all the parish, each evening. Mission preaching was concerned with practical reform, as well as the salvation of the soul, and targeted the objectionable features of popular culture – dancing, drinking, gambling, bad language, profanation of Sunday and holidays: there were ritual burnings of novels and ballads, smutty drawings and prints. Most missionary theorists – and the period saw a blossoming of missionary textbooks from John Eudes' *Catechism of mission* to Alphonsus de Ligouri's *Exercises of the missions* – emphasized the desirability of saturation bombing of a region. Missionaries stayed for anything up to eight weeks in an area, congregations were systematically bussed or rather processed in from the surrounding villages and the wider region, to ensure that the mission target area did not become a vulnerable island of the godly in a sea of sin and infidelity. Eyewitness accounts of the missions of St John Eudes record crowds of 12,000 or 15,000 covering the hillsides to hear him preach in the open air, and of confessors besieged by troops of penitents who had queued for a week or more to confess their sins. For the object of all missions was to bring the people to a state of penitence and to get them to make a general confession, intended to be the beginning of a much more regular penitential regime.[7] Ideally missions were arranged in four-, six- or eight-year cycles, with the aim of creating what was in effect a revivalist culture, periodic awakening consolidated by an intensified sacramental and devotional life between revivals. The lost souls of the country people of Europe were to be saved by conversion, confession and catechism.

Since Tridentine Catholicism was committed above all to the renewal of Christian life through the agency of the parish, there is a deep irony in the fact that the most effective and most characteristic Counter-Reformation machinery for that renewal should have been in essence non-parochial, the itinerant preaching of revival by specialist bands of vowed religious. Yet it was a brilliant and enduringly successful improvization, which retained the integrity of the pastoral unit of the parish, while providing a disciplined machinery for injecting into the parishes the element of revivalist fervour and personal appropriation of religion which was central to Counter-Reformation spirituality.

But for Protestant Europe such a solution was not an option. The abolition of the religious life in effect reduced all ministry, at least in theory, to parochial ministry, and although within reformed church polity there was a recognition of diversity of function within the ministry, the essential localization of such ministry within the parish everywhere in Protestant Europe set the agenda for all attempts at reform. Reform of the Christian life meant reform of the parish ministry, its conversion into a preaching ministry, and the Christian ordering of the lives of the people by parochial discipline. It has become something close to an historical orthodoxy that in this endeavour English Protestantism by and large failed, that the Reformation, unpopular to start with, never won the allegiance of the majority of the nation, and that the godly were at last forced to accept "the incorrigible profanity of the multitude".[8] Even Patrick Collinson, the subtlest and most sympathetic of modern historians of Puritanism, has reluctantly conceded that "the pastoral ministry in post-Reformation England was a long-term failure, the religious plurality and secularity of modern Britain its ultimate consequence and legacy".[9]

I would be the last one to contest the unpopularity of the early Reformation in England, or to minimize the difficulties of its first promoters in establishing it as a working religious system, but it does seem to me that Protestantism in late Elizabethan and Jacobean England must be judged, by any rational standards, a runaway success. I am struck by the extent to which, within two generations, England's Catholic past was obliterated, and how deeply impregnated seventeenth- and eighteenth-century English culture was by Protestant values. The criteria for success in the Reformation set by some historians seem to me as unreal as those set by Delumeau for the success of medieval Christianity. Certainly clerical activists in eight-eenth-century England were complaining of the heathenism and ignorance of the people in much the same terms as sixteenth-century reformers, and the leaders of the Evangelical Revival spoke of the state of religion in England in terms uncannily similar to those used by the first reformers about medieval Catholicism.[10] But much the same complaints had been voiced by clerical activists in the tenth, thirteenth and fifteenth centuries, part of the perennial rhetoric of reform, and we should not try to deduce too much from them about what was happening on the ground. The achievement of a Christian society is, or was, an ongoing project which those charged with its attainment have never believed to be complete. The rhetoric of reform is not so much a measure of the failure of that project, but of the vitality of their commitment to it. My concern in this chapter, however, is not to attempt to adjudicate the successs or failure of the Protestant project in England, the long Reformation,[11] but to trace the history of just one of the preoccupations and problems it shared with the Counter-Reformation, the role of the parish ministry in the conversion of England.

In the first stages of Protestant evangelism in England the problem was acute. However much it might be feared, as Thomas Bilney told Cuthbert Tunstal, that "Christ hath not been purely preached now a long time", short of a wholesale replacement of the existing non-preaching and popish ministry there was little that could be done.[12] Itinerant Protestant preaching was a vital factor in establishing islands of Protestant conviction, but without a base in the parishes could hardly sustain the communities thereby brought into being.[13] And itineracy itself had no guarantee of a hearing. Hugh Latimer, a leading episcopal patron of itinerant preaching, told in a sermon before Edward VI how he himself on the eve of a holy day which fell during one of his episcopal journeys had sent word ahead to the next town that he would preach in the morning, for "methought it was a holiday's work", only to find when he arrived the church locked and the congregation absent. At last one of the parish came to him and said "Sir, this is a busy day with us, we cannot hear you; it is Robin Hood's day. The parish are gone abroad to gather for Robin Hood: I pray you let them not".[14]

Latimer's courtly hearers dissolved in laughter that his "rochet . . .

was fain to give way to Robin Hood's men", but for him it was no laughing matter. A rampant semi-pagan popular culture which set the word of God at naught was the result of an unpreaching prelacy, the missionary failure of a Church which was content to have the people "continue in their ignorance still". The attempt to construct a Protestant missionary ministry in just such circumstances can be seen in the remarkable career of Bernard Gilpin, Elizabethan rector of Houghton le Spring in the diocese of Durham. Gilpin, an Erasmian humanist somewhat to the left of, but very much in the mould of, his great-uncle and patron Cuthbert Tunstal, whom he served somewhat gingerly as archdeacon in Mary's reign, was an almost equally uneasy conformist in 1559, but then, as pastor with responsibility for some of the wildest border country in Northumberland, threw himself increasingly enthusiastically into a pioneering protestant ministry until his death in 1584.[15]

Gilpin was much troubled by the "desolation of the Church, and the ignorance of the common sort" which sprang from the abuse of lay impropriations. The parishes of the north-east were full of "poor base priests", only able to read the services, so that in many places "the word of God was never heard of to be preached among them" and many congregations "even dispersed and destitute of pastors".[16] Gilpin therefore undertook an annual tour of itinerant evangelistic preaching in the most isolated and "uncivil" parts of the region, Tynedale and Redesdale. He chose the Christmas season for this work, to take advantage of the great concourse of people in the churches then, thereby encountering head-on and even harnessing, the festal culture which had defeated Latimer's attempt at itineracy, and which was to feature so consistently as the great enemy of godliness in every account of protestant ministry before George Herbert.[17]

In a region so sparely served with Protestant clergy, itineracy was an obvious expedient, and in the late 1570s Bishop Barnes drew up a circuit for every licensed preacher in the diocese, although few were willing to venture into the wilds as Gilpin did.[18] Yet Gilpin knew that these were stopgap solutions, and he tackled the need for settled preachers of God's word in two ways, coaxing able young clergy into the poorly endowed livings of the region, and co-operating with a godly London merchant who had purchased the dissolved estates of a local hospital to found and endow Kepier Grammar School at Houghton. It was a foundation marked out by a distinctive emphasis on the godly formation of the pupils, explicitly intended to produce a stream of preachers for the region, "the maintenance of Christ's holy gospel". He also maintained a series of scholars at university, for the same purpose.[19]

Stopgap or not, however, Gilpin's missionary preaching had numerous parallels in the Elizabethan and Jacobean Church. The Elizabethan authorities appointed itinerating preachers not only for the Borders, Wales and Lancashire, but for other "dark corners of the land".[20] Collinson has shown that the preaching of occasionally itin-erating ministers, often accompanied in their journeyings by clusters of godly groupies, "gadding people", remained a feature of English Protestant life up to the Civil War. Such preaching was a central element in the forming of a devout Protestant culture — it was too widespread and in many places too dominant to be called a sub-culture — which took in weekday lectures in other parishes, fast days, exercises and combination lectures, all extra-parochial dimensions of a ministry which nevertheless saw itself essentially in parochial terms. By such means the unity of the godly was fostered "as if they had all been of one household".[21]

In our context it is worth emphasizing, however, that it was also a missionary device, part of the project to convert England, and such ministry, easily categorized as a process of consolidating and servicing a Puritan consensus, was rarely described or conceived by those who practised it in isolation from the language of awakening, conversion.[22] Samuel Clarke's ministry in the Wirral in the 1620s, although based in Shotwick, was in effect an itinerant circuit, funded "by a voluntary contribution" of "divers godly and understanding Christians" scat-tered up and down the peninsula. The region was *pays de mission* with a vengeance, "scarce a constant preacher besides my self" and remi-niscent to that extent of Gilpin's Northumberland. The pattern of Clarke's ministry there, the "public ordinances" of regular preaching and monthly sacraments, supplemented by "days of conference" in the wealthier houses of the region, marked by searching catechizing of young Christians, was well adapted to a region where the godly were few, and surrounded by the "ethnical pastimes and sinful assemblies" of the ungodly: it was a ministry of the godly to the godly.[23]

Yet it was not addressed simply to the godly. Clarke commented that "In this place I found the first seal of my ministry, by being an instrument of the conversion of many souls to God" and it was by the conversion of many, particularly among the young, that he reckoned the success of his subsequent ministry.[24] Conversions were indeed the distinctive "seal" of a reformed ministry. The Cheshire preacher, William Hinde, complaining that the majority of the people round about him were "Popish and prophane", "strangers from the commonwealth of Israel", with the "mists of Samaria . . . yet in their eyes, and the calves of Bethel . . . yet in their hearts", nevertheless thanked God that "he hath given me a seale of my ministry in the parish amongst them, and in the country round about them", by the converts he had "gathered together into the fold and flocke of Christ Jesus".[25] Hinde was a veteran of the wars between Popery and Protestantism which were endemic in the north west, and Collinson has rightly emphasized the particular resonance and appropriateness of the language of conversion in a region in which a committed Protestant career might well begin with an act of renunciation of Catholicism.[26] Nevertheless, the language of conversion and new birth was by no means confined to the north west, and in the seventeenth century in particular is a ubiquitous feature of Protestant discourse.

For the rhetoric of conversion and of mission did not lapse as England became a more securely reformed nation. Even in the Popish fastnesses of the north west by 1625 a zealous Protestant such as John Bruen could contrast the mid-Elizabethan period, when he had first begun "to professe religion", being almost the only man in the shire "acquainted with the power and practice of it . . . like a pelicane in the wilderness", with the happy present, in which "the borders of the Church are much enlarged, the numbers of beleevers wonderfully increased, and blessed be God, every quarter, and corner of the countrey is now filled with the sweet savour of the Gospel".[27] This was a conventional perception: late Elizabethan and Jacobean Protestants, however zealous in outreach to the perishing mass of the people, believed themselves to live in "happy days . . . in this our peaceable land".[28] Yet for all the growing company of preachers, they believed that the work of the Gospel remained still to do, and even in this peaceable land, tens of thousands were on the way to perdition. "If we come to reason", Arthur Dent wrote in a well-known passage,

> we may wonder that any shall be saved, than so few shall be saved. . . . First let there be taken away from amongst us all Papists, atheists, and heretics. Secondly let there be shoaled out all vicious and notorious evil livers: as swearers, drunkards, whoremongers, worldlings, deceivers, coseners, proud men, rioters, gamesters, and all the prophane multitude. Thirdly let there be refused and sorted out all hypocrites, carnal Protestants, vain professors, back-sliders, decliners and cold Christians. Let all these I say be separated and then tell me how many sound, sincere, faithful and zealous worshippers of God will be found amongst us? I suppose we should not need the art of arithmetic to number them: for I thinke they would be very few in every village, town and city. I doubt they would walk very thinly in the streets, so as a man might easily tell them as they go.[29]

There were two contrary energies operating in such a vision of society. One lived by and imaginatively fed on the notion of the necessary smallness of the number of the elect, and there was in such a theological vision an undertow towards separatism. Another, quite different energy saw in the heedlessness of the multitudes not a sign of God's unsearchable decrees and their own condemnation, but a summons to vigorous activity, the task of awakening the people who "be like the smith's dog, who can lie under the hammer's noise, and the sparks flying, and yet fast asleep".[30] For men of this mind, the Protestant conformity that Christopher Haigh has christened "parish Anglicanism" simply would not do: they were determined to sort out and transform the tepid religion of carnal Protestants and cold Christians into something more fiery and consuming.

> Hath God nothing to do with his mercy (think you) and Christ's blood, but to cast it away on those that can scarce think they need it, or will scarce thank him for it? No, God's mercies goe not a begging yet . . . Now we his ministers, his almoners to distribute his comforts . . . dare not lavish them

out, and promise them to such lazy indifferents as these: but if wee see any ready to faint for want, saying, give me drink or else I die, then we reach the cup of consolation to him, and bid him drink of it; neither dare we give it to any other.[31]

Conversion, therefore, meant not merely bringing the heathen to knowledge of the gospel, but bringing the tepid to the boil by awakening preaching, creating a godly people out of a nation of conformists. Converts were often the already decently conforming members of godly households, stirred to a personal appropriation of a religion which until then had been in some sense second-hand. Richard Baxter, the son of a Puritan father, recalled how even as a child hearing sermons and reading good books had made him "love and honour godliness in the general" but that, until he was fifteen, he had "never felt any other change by them on my heart". A tattered and bowdlerized copy of a Counter-Reformation awakening treatise by the Jesuit Robert Parsons changed all that, for by it "it pleased God to awaken my soul, and show me the folly of sinning, and the misery of the wicked, and the unexpressible weight of things eternal, and the necessity of resolving on a holy life". What he had known in theory before "came now in another manner, with light, and sense and seriousness to my heart".[32] The reproduction of that movement on a universal scale, to bring the commonplaces of Christian catechesis "with light and sense and seriousness" to the hearts of the people at large, was one of the fundamental drives of English Protestant ministry, and in England, as in the practice of Counter-Reformation missions, it led to the linking of catechism and conversion. Hinde's remarks about converts as the "seal" of ministry come not from a book of sermons, as one might expect, but from the preface to a catechism prepared originally for use with the people of his own parish, and the linkage of catechesis and conversion is entirely conventional.

Ian Green has alerted us to the centrality of catechesis in Protestant ministry before the Civil War. The sheer volume of works produced to help in this ministry is mind-boggling – Dr Green has identified literally thousands of different catechetical works published in the century after the first appearance of the Prayer Book Catechism in 1549, many of which ran to 30, 40 or 50 editions. Speculating as to why so many catechisms should have been produced in addition to the short form in the Prayer Book and the longer official work by Alexander Nowell, Dr Green rules out in all except a handful of cases theological disquiet about the content of the Prayer Book Catechism. He suggests rather that practical considerations were decisive: what was wanted was a medium length text, fuller than the Prayer Book form but not so long as Nowell, and one which would ensure that learners would interpret Christian fundamentals "in a fully Protestant way".[33]

This is perfectly right, but only so long as we don't confine "in a fully Protestant way" to a matter of doctrinal understanding. The missing concept here is conversion. As a summary of the essentials of the faith as they had been defined at least since the Fourth Lateran Council – Creed, Commandments, Lord's Prayer – the Prayer Book Catechism was admirable: as an instrument of conversion, however, it was virtually useless. This was not a matter of its silence about such arcane matters as double predestination. The problem was that the Prayer Book form might have been written at any time since 1215, and it said nothing whatever about the distinctive Protestant *ordo salutis*, nothing about the Fall or Original Sin, it never discussed the nature of salvation, except in terms of duties towards God and neighbour, and it never once used the word faith. For a catechesis designed not merely to instruct in basics, but to arouse to faith, such a form simply would not do. So, William Hinde's catechism follows roughly the same layout as the Prayer Book form, but replaces the opening section of the Prayer Book version, which deals with the child's acceptance of the promises made by its godparents, with a section entitled "Man's misery by Adam. His recovery by Christ", emphasizing our need of a new birth, a share in the covenant of God, and the grace "so to profess and maintain the Christian faith, that (we) may feel the power, and show forth the fruit of it".[34] In the same way, William Perkins warned the ignorant people to whom his catechism was addressed not merely that they must rightly understand the Creed, Lord's Prayer and Commandments, as opposed to merely parroting them, but that they must also "apply them inwardly to your hearts and consciences, and outwardly to your lives and conversation. This is the very point in which we fail".[35]

The recognition of the role of catechesis in conversion modified Protestant emphasis on the uniqueness and centrality of the sermon. Whereas in sermons, declared George Herbert, "there is a kind of state, in catechising there is an humbleness very suitable to Christian regeneration".[36] This was no High Church eccentricity. That ardent Protestant, William Crashaw, declared in 1618 that "I find that catechising is the life of preaching, and such a meanes of knowledge as without it all preaching is to little purpose".[37] There might be very much more to catechism than mere instruction. Catechizing might lay bare the heart: as Herbert remarked, "at sermons and prayers men may sleep or wander; but when one is asked a question, he must discover what he is".[38]

When in the late 1620s Samuel Fairclough launched what was to become a model Protestant ministry in that cathedral of West Suffolk Protestantism, Kedington, he found a people emphatically in need of conversion, and the whole town, in words which by now will have a familiar ring to them, "very ignorant and prophane, being generally aliens and strangers from the commonwealth of Israel". Fairclough set himself to "pull and snatch . . . sinners, as brands out of the fire, by any ways or means he could think of". Conversion dominated his thinking and pastoral strategy, and "he left in his diary the names of some hundreds recorded there, who had all expressly owned him to be their spiritual father, and the proper means of their first conversion". In this work preaching, which he did four times a week, played a central part, as anyone will know who has seen the great pulpit erected for Fairclough by his friend and patron, Sir Nathaniel Barnardiston, looming still in a church nowadays adorned with the Stations of the Cross and other Romish abominations. But preaching was only one element in his campaign to "awaken the consciences of obstinate sinners; and then to make known to them the way of salvation". His great aim, Samuel Clarke tells us "was to instruct the ignorant, which he found a very hard work to do". He was assisted by Barnardiston, who persuaded the substantial men of the town to join him in ensuring the attendance of their whole households and dependents at catechizing, "both young and old, both governors and governed, one and other", and themselves participating in the questions and answers, *pour encourager les autres*. As the second prong of this process, catechizing was linked to admission to the Lord's

Supper, Barnardiston and all the rest of the communicants agreeing that they would "first publicly own . . . [their] baptismal covenant for once . . . and that afterwards, they should submit unto admonition, in case of the visible and apparent breach of that covenant". Barnardiston therefore made a public declaration of "his faith in God through our Lord Jesus, and did undertake (through the assistance of the Holy Spirit) to perform whatever his sureties had promised in baptism upon his account".[39]

Fairclough's activities at Kedington, at least as presented by Clarke, were a spectacularly successful example of a not uncommon type of godly ministry, a characteristically Reformed or Calvinist style in which a form of parochial discipline centred on rigorous catechizing became the principal instrument not merely of instruction but of awakening, conversion and Christian formation and reformation. Sixteenth-century Protestant writing about the nature of ministry focused almost exclusively on the role of the preacher, but in practice, in England as elsewhere in the reformed world, and in contrast to Lutheran Europe, a more complex, nuanced and resourceful understanding of ministry prevailed.[40]

The activities of Fairclough in Laudian Kedington testify to the centrality of evangelistic concerns in the pre-Civil War Church of England, but they became acute in the Cromwellian period. A heightened sense of expectation as the collapse of Laudianism and the establishment of Presbyterianism seemed to place within grasp the achievement of a godly and converted nation submitting to discipline, gave way to growing dismay at the non-arrival of a new godly order, and at the disorganization and vulnerability of the Cromwellian Church to its enemies in the sects, and to its own internal disagreements. Yet these were years in which many yearned, worked for and expected the conversion of England. Almost any page at random of Samuel Clarke's hagiographic collections will yield examples, but the career of John Machin, a Staffordshire minister active in the 1650s, will serve. Himself converted from a youth of "vanity and sin" at Cambridge in the 1640s, Machin became a dedicated evangelist, beginning with his own family, and then embracing a converting ministry based at Astbury. A tireless preacher in his own place, he set himself "to promote and drive on the work of conversion whereever he came", his letters and prayers punctuated by fervent exclamations of longing, "*O that all Staffordshire and Cheshire might be saved!*" His spare days "he laid out to the utmost example of the Gospel, by forecasting for heavenly work in the moorlands and other dark corners in Staffordshire, where the Gospel in the power of it had scarce ever come before". He endowed a monthly lecture to be preached in towns "of great concourse" in the region – Newcastle, Leek, Uttoxeter, Lichfield, Tamworth, Walsall, Wolverhampton, Pentbridge, Stafford, Eccleshall, Stone and Mikleston. To reach the rural population, he organized groups of fellow ministers "to meet him in those parts, and to preach at several places near to each other, sometimes three or four days together", an activity which had ample precedent in Puritan pastoral practice, but which also carries resonances of the contemporary activities of Eudist and Lazarist Counter-Reformation rural missions.[41]

Machin was a relatively obscure figure. Joseph Alleine of Taunton was altogether more notable, and in the Restoration period was to publish one of the most best known and most influential missionary tracts of the century, his *Alarm to the unconverted*. His ministry in Cromwellian Somerset, like Machin's in Staffordshire, demonstrates an overriding concern with conversion. It was also characterized by one of the most distinctive features of mid-century pastoral and evangelistic strategy, namely household instruction and scrutiny. Settling at Taunton, he established a model ministry there, preaching not only to his own large congregation, but going frequently "into other parishes about the country, amongst poor ignorant people that lived in dark corners, having none to take care of their souls". He organized many of the local clergy to do likewise, and with them established combination lectures in several places. He shared in the almost universal missionary preoccupation with the propagation of the Gospel in Wales.[42] Alleine laid enormous emphasis on the practice of catechizing, and in particular on the characteristic reformed pastoral practice of house-to-house visitation, in which he spent five afternoons every week, to scrutinize the knowledge and the morals of every parishioner. Far more was involved in such visitation than the testing of knowledge of Christian fundamentals, for Alleine used it as an explicitly evangelistic device, "labouring to make them sensible of the evil and danger of sin, of the corruption and depravation of our natures, the misery of an unconverted state, provoking them to look after the true remedy proposed in the gospel, to turn from all their sins unto God, to close with Christ upon his own terms, to follow after holiness, to watch over their hearts and lives, to mortify their lusts, to redeem their time, and to prepare for eternity".[43]

Closely similar ministries, manifesting the same pastoral techniques and the same preoccupation with conversion, are a characteristic of the clergy who, after the great ejection of 1662, would form the Presbyterian party. Joseph Woodward of Dursley, a schoolmaster as well as a minister, brought his educational concerns to bear in an attack on illiteracy among the poor of his parish: his assistant, Henry Stubbs, was said to have spent a tenth of his income on teaching the poor to read and providing them with books. Woodward, "in desire of reformation", christened his eldest son Josiah, although "when he saw little hopes of it" he christened the next child Hezekiah.[44] Fairclough at Kedington had organized schooling for poor children, and he regularly distributed Bibles, catechisms and good books, including Bibles "of a larger print" for the aged poor with decayed eyesight, and for the same purpose, gave away "an incredible number of spectacles".[45] Thomas Gouge, minister of the "great and populous" parish of St Sepulchre's in London from 1638, devoted himself to a mission to the poor, pioneering work-relief schemes for the able-bodied, and catechizing every morning throughout the year, to classes "especially of the poorer sort", whose presence at classes he encouraged by random distributions of doles on a different day each week.[46]

Thomas Wadsworth, incumbent of the slum parish of Newington Butts, set himself to evangelize the tenements and alleys there. Once a week he would "bespeak a house in the street at the end of an alley, and thither would he send for the poor people out of the alleys, and spend much time in instructing them, and praying with them". These meetings were followed up by lay assistants, who gathered the poor families in subsequent weeks to answer catechism questions, to hear sermons repeated, or to have awakening tracts read to them. Wadsworth, whose pastoral strategy was deliberately modelled on that of Richard Baxter at Kidderminster, favoured Baxter's *Call to the unconverted* and his *Making light of Christ* for the latter purpose. Wadsworth also hired a young graduate to come three days a week to teach the poor of the parish to read, and distributed tracts, catechisms and free copies of the New Testament.[47]

The pastoral and missionary ideals of these men and others like them were given decisive expression in the 1650s by Richard Baxter, whose own Kidderminster ministry became a model for others, and whose key role in the Association Movement helped shape the most important single pastoral and ecclesial development of the mid-century. The Association Movement was at one level a response to crisis and breakdown, an attempt to provide a basis for unity within a voluntary structure for the parishes of the Cromwellian Church of England, by federating single ministers who agreed on the implementation of parochial discipline, along loosely "Presbyterian" lines. It was consciously a ministerial response to a sense that the godly magistrate could no longer be relied on to protect and promote true religion. But it can also plausibly be thought of as the culmination of a century of Puritan pastoral practice.

The movement aimed to give spiritual reality to the geographical entity of the parish in ways which would not have struck Greenham or Bolton, Hinde or Fairclough as unfamiliar, by persuading the laity to accept catechizing, scrutiny and discipline, and to associate themselves formally with the parish and the ministry of their pastor in an adult church covenant, based on acceptance of the Apostle's Creed and a commitment to the pursuit of holiness.[48] Out of Baxter's experience came a classic textbook of Puritan pastoral practice, *Gildas Salvianus, or the reformed pastor*, a landmark in English Protestant reflection on the nature of mission, conversion, reformation. In it he specifically and deliberately subordinated preaching to the practice of personal supervision, instruction and scrutiny of the flock. It was, he declared "but the least part of a minister's work, which is done in the pulpit", and like his contemporaries in Counter-Reformation France and Italy, he placed the main emphasis in conversion on catechizing. He had found by experience, he claimed, "that an ignorant sot that hath been an unprofitable hearer so long, hath got more knowledge and remorse of conscience in half an hours close discourse, than ... from 10 years publike preaching".[49]

So much many a minister had said before him, but for Baxter the perception that the conversion of the nation must come less from preaching than from a systematic development of household instruction and scrutiny, a pastoral revolution, changed the familiar landmarks by which Protestant expectations were orientated. Ministers and private men had too long been prone to

> talk and write, and pray, and sigh, and long for reformation, and would little have believed that man that should have presumed to tell them that for all this their very hearts were against reformation, and that they that were praying for it, and fasting for it, and wading through blood for it, would never accept it, but would themselves be rejecters and destroyers of it. Yet so it is . . . they thought of a reformation to be given by God, but not of a reformation to be wrought on and by themselves. They considered the blessing, but never thought of the means of accomplishing it. As if . . . the Holy Ghost should again descend miraculously; or every sermon should convert its thousands; or that the law of a parliament, and the sword of a magistrate would have converted or constrained all, and have done the deed. Little did they think of a reformation that must be wrought by their own diligence and unwearied labours, by earnest preaching, catechising, personal instructions, and taking heed to all the flock[50]

For Baxter and his circle, the parish was indeed mission territory, containing many who "really know not what a Christian is", men that "know not almost any more than the veriest heathen in America". Their conversion was a task to be tackled systematically, and through the later 1650s he issued a series of works designed to further different dimensions of that work. These included not only the *Reformed pastor* and its 1658 pendant, *Confirmation and restauration the necessary means of reformation*, with its fascinating account of Baxter's own parish of Kidderminster but also a series of awakening works directly aimed at conversion.[51] The famous *Call to the unconverted* (1658), which he was later to claim sold over 20,000 copies in a single year, was aimed at impenitent sinners "not yet so much as purposing to turn". His *Directions and persuasions to a sound conversion*, published in the same year, by contrast was aimed at those that are already "about the work", that they "miscarry not in the birth".[52]

In this perspective, conversion was a "work", the new life a matter of what one of Baxter's associates called "laborious holiness", and "active and busy religiousness".[53] It was also a social vision of conversion, in which the renewal of the individual meant the cleansing of society, reformation of manners. Henry Oasland, curate of Bewdley in Worcestershire, and an ardent evangelist who "went up and down preaching from place to place", yet considered preaching "the least part" of his work. He groaned for the conversion of his unregenerate flock and neighbours

> the sight of their faces, terrifies my conscience . . . I cannot go along the street without grief to see and meet the ignorant and unreformed. Oh the wound, the words and time of sinners spoken and spent in alehouses have given me every time I go by the door! How many times have I stept in amongst them, to reason the case with them, though I might loose my life or limbs![54]

So the conversion of England was for them a process which might, and must, make use of every available means, from the laborious fostering of devotion by good books or the encouragement of private meetings for edification of the godly, especially the godly young, to the enforcement by the magistrates of laws against vice and drunkeness, profanity, scorn of godliness and sabbath-breaking.[55] What these men were after was not merely the conversion of individuals, but the transformation of a community, and accounts of their work are peppered with idealized pictures of such transformations. Fairclough at Kedington made

> a very effectual reformation in that town. Former prophaneness was forced now to hide its head; drunkenness, swearing, cursing, bastardy, and the like, as they were not practiced, so they were scarce known; divers persons having lived many years in that parish . . . never heard an oath sworn, or ever saw one person drunk, as they have professed

Even in godly Suffolk,

> it was expected . . . that every inhabitant of Kedington should be distinguished from others, not only by the more savouriness

of their discourse, but also by the universal strictness and piety
of their lives and conversations.[56]

Alcester, where Samuel Clarke laboured "which before was called
Drunken Alcester, was now exemplary, and eminent for religion, all
over the country".[57] At his coming to Dursley, Joseph Woodward's
son recalled, it was

> a place at the time very dissolute insomuch that it had the
> name of drunken Dursley, but if he found it so it was very
> much altered by his labours . . . and became one of the most
> wealthy and best trading towns in the neighbourhood. Some
> of them having told me that they cleared a thousand pounds
> a year by the trade of clothing, in the time of his residence
> there. His presence in the streets . . . made the sober to
> rejoice, and the guilty to hide themselves in corners . . . and
> every one's zeal seemed inflamed by the flame he beheld in
> his neighbour; so that I have heard that there was the most
> composed and affected congregation that could anywhere be
> seen.[58]

When Baxter came to Kidderminster first, he recalled,

> there was about one family in a street that worshipped God and
> called on his name, and when I came away there were some
> streets where there was not past one family in the side of a
> street that did not so. . . . And those families that were the
> worst, being inns and alehouses, usually some persons in each
> house did seem to be religious.[59]

Baxter believed that the Commonwealth years had brought the
dream of the conversion of England closer than it had ever been. He
marvelled that he himself should have achieved so much, "when the
reverend instructors of my youth did labour fifty years together in
one place, and could scarcely say that they had converted one or two
of their parishes!" The godly had always had an uneasy relationship
with the parish community, passionately committed to the notion of
a preaching minister in every parish, yet gathering the godly from

outside it, gadding abroad to sermons, forging loyalties at exercises, fasts and combination sermons, which transcended it, and always haunted by a theology which refused to equate the elect with membership of the visible church. The activities of Baxter and his associates in the 1650s represented the reformed tradition's best shot in England at coming to terms with the parish, of establishing a stable relationship and a substantial overlap between the visible and the invisible churches. We need not, indeed we should not, take them at their own estimation. Baxter's success in persuading the majority of households in his parish to accept discipline and submit to his pastoral regime was as unusual in mid-Stuart England as the five galleries he had to construct to hold the hearers who flocked to his sermons, and probably led him to exaggerate the effectiveness of the pastoral revolution which he saw around him in the 1650s. The problems of operating a voluntary discipline of this sort within the parochial system, involving as it did the exclusion of substantial numbers of the parish from communion, were more evident elsewhere than they were at Kidderminster, where most of those excluded "yet took it patiently, and did not revile us as doing them wrong".[60] Nevertheless, Baxter came to believe that the pastoral experiments and successes which culminated in the 1650s established beyond all doubt the centrality of the parish in the work of conversion, and that "it is a better work to reform the parishes, than to gather churches out of them".[61]

But any such success was destined to be short-lived. With the exodus of almost 2,000 ministers in 1662, many of them the most committed practitioners of the Baxterian parochial model, the Restoration put an end to short-term hopes for the conversion of England through the parishes. It did not however eclipse the ideal, even within the Church of England. Many moderates who shared Baxter's hopes and methods conformed in 1662, and the children of many who could not do so carried their fathers' ideals into the establishment. Joseph Woodward rejected the Restoration settlement, but his sons Josiah and Hezekiah, named for reformation, conformed and pursued clerical careers, and, as we shall see, the cause of reform, within the national church.[62] But in the 1660s and 1670s the missionary impulse we have been discussing was more evident within the ranks of Nonconformity, as Alleine, Wadsworth, Baxter himself and a host of others pursued evangelistic careers outside the law. In some cases at least, their methods could be as histrionic as any of their their Counter-Reformation opposite numbers, and not such as were likely to win approval in a church increasingly suspicious of the enthusiasm that had overthrown church and state. Henry Oasland would press on his Nonconformist congregation the need to accept Christ, and then demand that anyone present who made light of the offer and "refused Christ" should leave the building: he would then sit down and a long wait ensued, which ended only when Oasland "perceiving that they all stayed . . . rose up as one in an extasy of joy, and said 'Now I hope every one of you is espoused to Jesus Christ'".[63] Exclusion from parochial ministry forced on them other expedients, some of them, such as the gathering of congregations, profoundly distasteful to them, others hallowed by long practice among the godly, such as wide-scale itineracy.[64] They also developed further existing Protestant sensitivity to the role of print.[65] Baxter and his associates poured out a stream of material designed to convert, from Baxter's own tract *Now or never* in 1662, to Alleine's *Alarm to unconverted sinners* in 1672, and a life of Alleine, by his wife and others, in the same year. Baxter did much to maintain this stream of publications, providing prefaces to a number of them, such as the *Alarm* and Alleine's biography, and later to a posthumous edition of awakening sermons of Thomas Wadsworth, and to Samuel Clarke's *Lives of sundry eminent persons* of 1683. Clarke's collection gathered together a set of biographies of figures like Machin, Alleine, Wadsworth, and of older, prototype figures such as Fairclough, and it can be read as a manifesto for the evangelistic enterprise choked off by the Restoration settlement, a gallery of portraits illustrating and designed to illustrate the pastoral tragedy of 1662.[66]

For English Protestantism, then, 1662 marked a parting of the ways as momentous as any event since the break with Rome. Not unnaturally, there has been a tendency for historians to be mesmerized by it into editing the "godly" dimension out of Restoration church life, to see the ideals and practice of the pre-Restoration Puritan tradition as having been decisively excluded from the national church in 1662, and having thereafter flowed into separating Nonconformity. This is particularly true in the area of soteriology: we are accustomed to think of the Restoration as the period of "the rise of moralism", the replacement of an earlier evangelical emphasis on faith and grace by a laborious and somewhat gloomy works religion, represented in devotional classics such as Allestree's *The whole duty of man*. It is a picture which leading Restoration churchmen themselves encouraged. Simon Patrick denounced the rhetoric of Puritan conversion as a cloak for antinomianism:

> It is called a casting of ourselves upon Christ, a relying on his merits, a shrouding our selves under the robes of his righteousness; and though sometimes it is called a going to him for salvation, yet there is this mystery in the business, that you may go, and yet not go. you may go, and yet stand still . . . or if you take one little step, and be at pains to come to him, the work is done, and you need not follow him.

He urged the devout reader to "put your hands to pull down that idol of faith, which hath been set up with so much devotion, and religiously worshipped so long among us: that dead image of faith which so many have adored, trusted in, and perished (by)".[67] John Eachard spelt this out:

> I do most heartily wish that such as have spent their time in reading of books and sermons about experiences, getting of Christ, and the like, would change them all away for *The whole duty of man*, that abounds with very pious and intelligible rules of godly living, and useful knowledge tending to salvation.[68]

As will be plain from what has been said about the Puritan ideal of a "laborious holiness", however, and from Baxter's denunciation of those who "thought of a reformation to be given by God, but not of a reformation to be wrought on and by themselves", there was an element of shadow-boxing about all this. Insofar as these insinuations of an antinomian emphasis on faith were aimed at the mainstream of Nonconformity, they were wide of the mark. *The whole duty of man* was promoted by Restoration bishops, and distributed by the basketful to Restoration parishioners, but it was also one of the "helps" specifically recommended to the godly by Baxter and other Puritan activists.[69] A shared godly culture persisted into the Restoration, with no impermeable walls between conforming and noncon-forming participants in it. In the margin of page 108 of the Trinity College Cambridge copy of Baxter's *Treatise of self-denyall,* published in 1660 and containing a resounding puritan attack on play-books and romances, sabbath-breaking, sports and profanity, someone has written, "July 6th 1662 Francis Limly was convinced of his sins by the hearing of this place read at Christ Church on a sabbath day morning".[70] The awakening literature which poured from the presses of Restoration England, in the production of which ejected ministers played a major role, sustained a culture within which conversion and missionary concerns remained central.[71] In the process, some of the missionary forms associated with the end of the century, and generally interpreted as a response to the new problems created for the Church of England by the calamities of the late Stuart period, emerged from the roots we have been discussing. In the early 1670s Thomas Gouge, ejected minister of St Sepulchre's in London, read the life of Joseph Alleine, and was fired with zeal by the account of Alleine's involvement in the propagation of the Gospel in Wales. Gouge devoted the remaining years of his life to an extraordinary peripatetic mission to Wales, which focused on the provision of schools for the poor, and the translation of good books into Welsh for them to read. Gouge established a trust to print Welsh Bibles, and he distributed Puritan favourites such as Lewis Bailey's *The practice of piety.* But he also distributed Welsh editions of the Book of Common Prayer, the Church Catechism and commentaries on it, and *The whole duty of man.* His work, which was carried out in co-operation with Nonconformist activists, nevertheless also had the somewhat uneasy blessing of the Welsh episcopate, and forms a striking link between the evangelistic ferment of the 1650s and the later work of the SPCK.[72]

But if there was still a shared culture of the godly, it was one which had been profoundly fractured by the exclusions of 1662, above all along the uneasy and fragile junction between that culture's parochial and its charismatic elements. The Restoration Church of England continued to seek fervour and conversion from its members, but its profound distrust of the traditional godly language by which that fervour had been elicited and expressed left it prone to a duty-bound formalism: Restoration piety can seem stifling, scrupulous, churchy.

The godly Anglican now was encouraged to express a deeper dedication and a changed heart by a closer attention to the duties of a churchman, more frequent attendance at the sacraments, a devouter celebration of the Church's year. Such a calendrical piety, however deeply felt, was bound to alienate those of the godly who had suffered exclusion because of their objections to Prayer Book observance. Penitential, joyless and duty-bound, it could seem not much better calculated to attract the multitudes of "parish Anglicans", for whom the Prayer Book and its feasts were valued, not so much as the framework for a profound and scrupulous conversion of life as the scaffolding for social decency, and markers in the natural cycle of rites of passage and the hallowing of time. Conversion of life and parish conformity, successfully joined in Counter-Reformation Europe, were decisively divorced in England in 1662.

It is in the light of this growing rift in the godly tradition that we need to consider the extraordinary flurry of pious and evangelistic activity in the last decades of the seventeenth and the early decades of the eighteenth century, of which the SPCK was to become the epitome. Modern discussion of the religious societies, the societies for the reformation of manners, of the SPCK, and the charity school movement has usually placed these various movements for reform against the polarizing of church politics in the era of the Glorious Revolution. The religious societies have been seen as self-consciously and exclusively Anglican devotional groups dedicated to consolidating a Church-based piety, while the societies for the reformation of manners, in which many Dissenters were involved, have been seen, by contrast, as a mark of Low Church abandonment of distinctive claims of Anglican hegemony in society. Where High Churchmen sought a cure for society's moral corruption in the revival of the discipline of the Church and its courts, Low Churchmen settled for the enforcement of public morality by the secular arm.[73]

The religious societies, with their scrupulous and self-consciously exclusive Anglicanism, seem on the face of it the least likely candidates for inclusion in a pedigree which stretches back through Richard Baxter to the English Puritan tradition. Origins have been sought for them in the *collegia pietatis* of German Pietism, or in the sodalities and confraternities of the French Counter-Reformation, as mediated through the life of De Renty, a favourite book with many

Protestants in Restoration England.[74] Yet our best and earliest contemporary account of their origins, by Josiah Woodward, leaves little doubt that it is primarily in the tradition we have been discussing that they should be placed. Woodward describes how the awakening sermons of two London preachers in the late 1670s, William Smythies, curate of St Giles Cripplegate, and Anthony Horneck, preacher at the Savoy Chapel, had converted groups of young men. Josiah Woodward interviewed one of them,

> who with floods of tears lamented that he had not till then had any affecting apprehensions of the glorious majesty and perfections of Almighty God, nor of his infinite love to men in his son Jesus Christ. And that he had not before felt any just convictions of the immense evil of every offence against God. . . . But now he saw, and groan'd under all this, in very sharp and pungent convictions. And withal, perceiving the universal corruption of human nature, and the deplorable crookedness and deceit of man's heart, and with what a world of temptations we are encompass'd. . . . when he considered all this, his soul was even poured out within him, and he was in danger of being overwhelmed with excessive sorrow.[75]

The gathering of young men of this mentality to take advice from their spiritual guides, to pray and to perform works of charity was in conformity with the well-established practice of the godly, for such weekday meetings "about soul affairs" were a normal part of Puritan pastoral practice. The activities of these Anglican societies also conformed to well-tried formulae, like the society in the parish of St Martin-in-the-Fields in 1681 which met for prayer, bible-reading and sermon repetition, or the society begun by the minister at Old Romney in Kent about 1690, to revive "the divine ordinance of singing psalms", to increase "spiritual fervency" among the young, and to encourage attendance on the "public ordinances of God".[76]

But there were significant differences, and a decisive narrowing of appeal about the societies. In the fraught climate of Charles II's reign it was inevitable that the piety of the societies should be self-consciously loyal to the Church. Meetings about soul affairs in the godly tradition had always been vulnerable to charges of conventicling, and it was inevitable that the societies should self-consciously distance themselves from any association with separatism. Moreover, the revival of sacramental piety which is a feature of Restoration devotion meant that the meetings of the societies were initially largely concerned with preparation for reception of communion. Fervour at the sacrament was a characteristic of the Puritan tradition too, and such preparation meetings had been a feature of Puritan devotion, but in Restoration England reception of the sacrament was a political as well as a devotional act, a barrier between the godly rather than the bond of their fellowship. The societies might have a devotional root in the Puritan tradition, but the circumstances of the time made them a stumbling stone to the principal heirs of that tradition, excluded as they were (or as others thought they should be) from the sacramental sealing of the unity of the godly.

The movement for the reformation of manners was closely connected to a providentialist reading of the Revolution of 1688. The God who had shown his special favour to the nation by delivering them from the tyranny of popery, would now demand a corresponding response, the cleansing of the nation from sins which cried out to heaven for judgement. As Josiah Woodward declared,

> A public sinner does not only sin against his own soul, but against the community of which he is a member. . . . Our overlooking of any gross sin is a taking the guilt of it into our own bosom; yea, 'tis a spreading and diffusing of the curses due unto it upon the face of the whole city and nation in which we dwell.[77]

To invoke the magistrate against public vice, therefore, was not a secular but a religious act, the search for a godly nation through the conversion or at any rate the containment and punishing of the vicious, in the time-honoured alliance between minister and magistrate. As Woodward declared,

> thou shalt appeal to the minister, and to the magistrate; not against the man, but against the sin. Thou shalt tell it to the Church, and thou shalt inform the bench (the seat of justice) of it, that all fit spiritual censures and temporal chastisements may

be applied to him in time, that his soul perish not to all eternity.[78]

Josiah Woodward, as already remarked, had been "named for reformation" by his Puritan father, and it is hardly surprising to find him deploying the familiar rhetoric of godly reformation. His own career was devoted to a strenuous campaign of education and catechesis in his own parish of Maidstone, and also, through pamphleteering and preaching, against sabbath-breaking, profanity and vice in every form, in works with titles such as *A kind caution to profane swearers*. In him the godly agenda of the 1650s and before can be seen still alive and active. But he was by no means alone. Another key figure in the movement for reformation of manners was the remarkable and eccentric Gloucestershire lawyer Edward Stephens, who founded the first Reformation Society and was a tireless publicist for the movement.[79] His later liturgical preoccupations, his advocacy of the 1549 Prayer Book and foundation of a Protestant convent, and his desire for reunion with the churches of Greece and Rome, make Stephens seem an unlikely heir of the Puritans. Yet he too had direct links backward to the Baxter circle, for he was the son-in-law of Sir Matthew Hale, and there is no mistaking the provenance of the reforming rhetoric he pressed into service in the aftermath of the Glorious Revolution. In a series of pamphlets in aid of religious and moral reform beginning in 1689 Stephens advanced a providentialist reading of the history of England under the Stuart monarchy which would not have disgraced the fast sermons of the long Parliament. He denounced the moves by which the godly had been squeezed out of the national church – the discouraging and oppression of true piety "by reproachful names of Puritans and precisions", particularly by "that impious and abominable project of the Book of Sports", and "the cursed dividing of the church and nation, by that mischievous Act of Uniformity", by which "many good and useful men" were excluded from service in the Church.[80] For Stephens, enforcement of laws against vice was not a secular usurpation of the Church's rights, but a prelude to their recovery . He denounced the first reformers, and the Church of England ever since, for failure to introduce a proper Christian discipline of excommunication. Cranmer's commination service deplored the absence of such a discipline, but this lament, renewed in the liturgy of every Ash Wednesday, was rank hypocrisy, for the Church had systematically "opposed and suppressed those who have desired it, and instead thereof retained only a popish relict and abuse of it".[81] The need for reformation of manners on a voluntary basis sprang from the failure of the Church and the Crown to fulfil their covenanted obligations to a God who had manifested his saving providence to the nation again and again.

Support for the movement for reformation of manners was at first widespread among devout members of the Church of England, including many and perhaps most members of the religious societies, but its wider appeal was doomed by the very fact that it presented itself as a response to a godly agenda patronized by the Crown, and by Queen Mary in particular.[82] William's victory at the battle of Aughrim on 11 July 1691, for example, was attributed by the *Athenian Mercury* to the adoption in a proclamation the day before of the cause of reformation of manners by the Middlesex justices of the peace, and by September 1691 Edward Stephens was denouncing opponents of reformation of manners as Jacobites.[83] For the many church men with queasy consciences about the deposition of James II this was a problematic pedigree, and reformation of manners became a party issue, with a consequent division of the godly, if only for prudential reasons. Most members of religious societies withdrew overt support as party tensions heightened, and it was probably in the wake of their departure that Dissenters were first recruited, to take their places.

It has been generally recognized that the movement did command a good deal of high-placed church support, notably that of Archbishop Tillotson and, to begin with at least, Archbishop Sharp of York, and of a good many other Revolution bishops – Gilbert Burnet, Edward Fowler, Richard Kidder, Simon Patrick, Humphrey Humphreys, Nicholas Stratford, John Hough. These men are often described as "Latitudinarians", and Mark Goldie has characterized support for reformation of manners, along with comprehension and Latitudinarianism, as forming a nexus, distinct from "High-Church preoccupations".[84] What the word "Latitudinarian" is in danger of concealing here is the "godly" origins of some of the key figures in these Revolution disputes. Tillotson himself had succeeded Fairclough as vicar of Kedington, and he retained a good deal of sympathy for the religious programme of those driven into Nonconformity. He was the funeral eulogist of Thomas Gouge, and an admirer of the practical holiness preached by Nonconforming clergy. Similarly, Kidder, the biographer of Anthony Horneck, had himself been ejected for Nonconformity in 1662, Fowler was the friend, patron and employer of William Smythies whose awakening preaching had begun the religious societies, and he was to lend Stephens his city church for daily communion services later in the reign. Many of the clergy who supported the reformation societies did so because, like the archdeacon of Durham, Robert Booth, who had 25 people in a single day clapped in the stocks for sabbath-breaking, they saw in the societies a revival of the aspiration for a godly nation which had lain at the heart of Protestant mission to England for a century and a half.[85] The programme of the movement for reformation of manners, with its attacks on sabbath-breaking, profanity, public drunkenness and prostitution, has many similarities, even down to the institution of professional informers, with the programme of legislation against profaneness and for reformation which Richard Baxter was advocating in the late 1650s.[86] The links were not lost on opponents, and Henry Sacheverell denounced the movement for reformation of manners as a "mongrel institution" designed to "insinuate an insufficiency in the Church's discipline", to "betray its power into the hands of a lay-eldership and fanaticism".[87]

The religious societies and the reformation societies sprang, therefore, from the same cluster of godly preoccupations with ways and means of conversion and reformation. Their separation represents the fracture, under the pressure of late Stuart politics, of a single vision of a Reformed England, and a single programme for its achievement in the parishes. Low as well as High Churchmen came to have reservations about the reformation movement in the 1690s and early 1700s, precisely because they did not wish to see the unity of that reforming vision divided into different agencies. Tillotson's successor, Archbishop Thomas Tennison, veteran of a distinguished slum ministry at St Martin-in-the-Fields which had the approval and support of Richard Baxter, thought that bishops should not support the societies for reformation of manners, but instead proposed "the doing of something ourselves, it being, I thought, most absurd for the college of bishops to be led in such a manner".[88] He wrote in

April 1699 to the other bishops deploring the "sensible growth of vice and profaneness in the nation", and urging the clergy to combat it by meeting together in local groups "to consult and advise", by enlisting the support of magistrates and the laity "of the greatest esteem and authority in their parishes", by suppressing vice and encouraging virtue, and above all by diligent catechising" to "lay the foundations of piety and morality".[89] His letter, decidedly reminiscent of the expedients of the clergy of the Association Movement of the 1650s, came within a month of the founding of a reform agency which was to dominate much of the eighteenth-century Church of England's practical work, the SPCK.

The SPCK was the brainchild of Thomas Bray, an unpleasant but phenomenally active clerical educator, dedicated to the propagation of orthodox Protestantism in England and the colonies. He envisaged his Society for Promoting Christian Knowledge as a Church of England response to the Roman Catholic *Congregatio de Propaganda Fide,* but it was also designed to combat Dissenters and Quakers in the interests of the "pure and primitive Christianity which we profess".[90] Originally intended as a clerical initiative, and, despite firm support for the Hanoverian succession, retaining the support of a broad-based clerical constituency, it quickly became an essentially lay agency, promoting Anglican reform in all its manifestations – charity schools, catechizing and the distribution of edifying literature, defence of Church principles, encouragement of more frequent attendance at the sacrament, patronage of the religious societies. It was also a vigorous patron of the reformation societies, however, publishing epitomes of the legislation against vice, issuing advice to constables and magistrates, and using its network of book distributors to disseminate blank warrants for use in the war against the ungodly. It embodied, then, most aspects of the awakened piety which had characterized the godly tradition we have been considering, and represented not merely the response of churchmen to the crisis of the 1690s, but the continuation of a long-term preoccupation with the conversion of the nation. Yet once again, the political environment in which it was born, and the concern of its directors to secure the widest possible base within the Church of England, turned it into an instrument against the Dissenters, and therefore a stumbling stone for many of the inheritors of that same godly tradition.

The ambivalences within the pedigree of the SPCK were recognized by contemporaries, and reflected in the early response to its work. The coincidence of the founding of the SPCK and the appearance of the archbishop's invitation to the clergy to associate to promote reformation, led many to identify the SPCK as an official episcopal instrument of reform. A group of thirteen Berkshire clergy told the secretary of the SPCK in 1700 that they had established a clerical association, "out of a true zeal . . . for the salvation of the souls of our poor brethren, and out of a just concern for the true interest of that truly primitive and apostolical church whereof we are members; as also in obedience to our most reverend metropolitan's circular letter, and . . . in compliance with the reasonable request of the society". But the clergy of Kent, perhaps alert to the overtones of the word "association", took a different view, judging the SPCK to be "a reviving of presbyterian classes . . . an usurpation of the rights of convocation and an inlet to division and separation".[91] The reception of the society in Wales, that long-standing focus of missionary zeal, illustrates these ambivalences. The society's objectives were easily recognized as part of a long tradition of godly reformation. One Welsh supporter listed the remedies for the "corruptions of the age", "discipline must be restored, catechizing seriously applied to and the magistrate be vigorous and resolv'd in punishing vice". This was an agenda in which Richard Baxter would warmly have collaborated. But although many clergy welcomed the help of an external agency in tackling the "reigning diseases" of "ignorance and unconcernedness" among the vulgar, and the SPCK was to play a crucial role in the stabilising of Welsh Anglicanism in the eighteenth century, in the last years of the Stuart monarchy its pan-parochial, extra diocesan character was a cause of suspicion. It was reported that there too, "some cavil at the word association", and there were fears that the activities of the society might erode the Church's distinctive jurisdiction.[92]

John Spurr has recently criticized the Restoration religious societies for having undermined the integrity of the parish. The voluntary piety of the societies, he suggests, was ultimately elitist because it needed a clerical and liturgical apparatus which "was simply not available outside London", and the societies, designed, as Woodward said, as mutual support for the godly, "to maintain their integrity in the midst of a crooked and perverse generation", were in fact a retreat on sectarianism, an abandonment of the claims of the Church of England to be the church of the whole nation. This led some Anglicans, he believes, to recognize that they had no monopoly on holiness, and that among the Nonconformists there were many who might have been "instruments of reforming the parochial churches by example, admonition and assisting the exercise of discipline". Such admissions were "straws in the wind blowing from the eighteenth century", precursors of a world "where the zealous of different denominations might have more in common with each other than with the lukewarm of their own communion".[93]

But historical winds don't blow backwards, and the limitations he ascribes to the Restoration and Revolution religious societies were precisely the limitations of the godly tradition in general. The religious societies were not the forerunners of modern-day religious voluntarism. They were, rather, part of the wreckage of the English Reformation's attempt to bring together and hold together the routinization of religion in the parish, and the personal conversion and zeal which were the essential marks of the godly. It is not clear that so difficult a bonding could ever have been perfectly achieved. The Counter-Reformation may be judged to have made a better stab at it, but with the help of three inestimable advantages. The first of these was the presence of the religious orders, and in particular of orders like the Jesuits, Lazarists, and Redemptorists, operating alongside the parish ministry and supplementing it with the specialized professionalism of the missions. The second was, within those missions, a hospitality to ritual and drama – the use of dramatic penitential gestures, the wearing of hoods, torchlight processions, the dramatic display of life-sized crucifixes, the use of *tableaux vivants* and costume to represent sacred truths, the encouragement of emotional and emotive devotional practices, all of which enabled Catholic missions simultaneously to attack the profane dimensions of popular culture, yet to put up some plausible rival attractions, and to become itself an aspect of popular culture – in David Gentilcore's words, meeting popular culture half way.[94]

The third, and arguably the decisive advantage, was the harnessing of the centuries-old obligation of confession into the service of a newer and more demanding style of Christian commitment. The confessional was the ultimate weapon of the Counter-Reformation, the perfect forum for the meeting and integration of routinization and the zeal of conversion, and Protestantism had nothing to rival it.

Yet up until the Restoration, the godly tradition in England did at least present a coherent front to the society it sought to convert and subdue, its vision of a godly nation pursued simultaneously through the pulpit, the catechism class, the house visit, the prayer meeting and the magistrate's bench. Cromwellian Kedington or Dursley, Alcester or Kidderminster would not have been to modern taste, with constables and ministers combing the pubs during service time, the sound of psalm-singing in every street no compensation for the powerful dryness of those long hot Sunday afternoons. But they were at least a serious attempt to embody the central dream of the English Reformation. The dream persisted, and was still a powerful one in the eighteenth century: it is one of the foundation stones of the Evangelical Revival. But after 1662 it was never viable as a possibility for the whole nation, and the ejection of the majority of the clergy most committed to that dream, and best equipped to pursue it, signed its death warrant. The Church of England entered the eighteenth century with all the elements of that Protestant dream of a Christian nation intact – parochial conformity, suppression of public vice, the cultivation of serious personal religion. But they were beads without a string, forces whose individual impact was fatally weakened by their lack of a common focus. The transformation of England into a godly nation remained a concern in the Hanoverian Church. As a realistic project, however, it died in 1662.

Notes

1. An earlier version of this chapter was given as the Neale Lecture on 19 January 1996.
2. J. Delumeau, *Le Catholicisme entre Luther et Voltaire* (Presses Universetaires de France, Paris, 1971): English translation, with an introduction by John Bossy, *Catholicism between Luther and Voltaire* (London, 1977): quotation from the Foreword (unpaginated).
3. J. Bossy, *Christianity in the West 1400–1700* (Oxford, 1985), p. 91.
4. D. Gentilcore, " 'Adapt yourselves to the people's capabilities': missionary strategies, methods and impact in the kingdom of Naples, 1600–1800"

(hereafter "Missionary strategies"), *Journal of Ecclesiastical History* **45**, 1994, p. 272.

5. M. Aston, *The fifteenth century: the prospect of Europe* (London, 1968), p. 167: I. Origo, *The world of San Bernardino* (London, 1963): F. Oakley, *The western church in the later Middle Ages* (Cornell, 1979), pp. 261–70: L. Chatellier, *La religion des pauvres* (Paris, 1993), pp. 17–21.

6. Delumeau, *Catholicism between Luther and Voltaire*, pp. 189–94; Chatellier, *Religion des pauvres*, pp. 51–121 and passim; J. W. O'Malley, *The first Jesuits* (Harvard, 1993), pp 126–7: F. M. Jones, *Alphonsus de Liguori* (Dublin, 1992), pp. 246–61; Gentilcore, "Missionary strategies" pp. 269–96.

7. H. Joly, *Life of St John Eudes* (London, 1932), pp. 59–62: the witness here was Baron Gaston de Renty.

8. K. Wrightson & D. Levine, *Poverty and piety in an English village: Terling 1525–1700* (New York, San Francisco, London, 1979), pp. 12–3: the classic exposition of this view is that of Christopher Haigh, "Puritan evangelism in the reign of Elizabeth I", *English Historical Review* **92**, 1977, pp. 30–58.

9. P. Collinson, "Shepherds, sheepdogs, and hirelings: the pastoral ministry in post-Reformation England", in *The ministry, clerical and lay*, W. J. Sheils & D. Wood (eds) (Studies in Church History **26**, 1989), p. 220.

10. J. Gregory, "The eighteenth-century Reformation: the pastoral task of Anglican clergy after 1689" in *The Church of England c. 1689–1833*, J. Walsh, C. Haydon & S. Taylor (eds) (Cambridge, 1993), pp. 67–85.

11. For a tentative essay in that direction, see my paper, "The godly and the multitude in Stuart England", *The Seventeenth Century* **1**, 1986, pp. 31–55.

12. J. Foxe, *The acts and monuments*, S. R. Cattley & G. Townsend (eds) (London, 1837), vol. 4, p. 636.

13. S. R. Wabuda, *The provision of preaching during the early English Reformation, with special reference to itineration, c. 1530–1547*, (PhD thesis, Cambridge University, 1991).

14. G. E. Corrie (ed.), *Sermons by Hugh Latimer* (Parker Society, Cambridge, 1844), p. 208.

15. The essential source is George Carleton, *The life of Bernard Gilpin* (London, 1629): there is a helpful modern assessment by D. Marcombe, "Bernard Gilpin: anatomy of an Elizabethan legend", *Northern History* **16** 1980, pp. 20–39, which, however, oversimplifies Gilpin's religious positions in the reigns of Edward and Mary.

16. Carleton, *Gilpin*, p. 19.

17. Carleton, *Gilpin*, pp. 27–8: Gilpin's preaching was characterized by a particular emphasis on the reconciliation of feuding factions in the Marches, a preoccupation which also characterized Lazarist and Eudist preaching in upland France and Italy. Joly, *St John Eudes*, pp. 61, 64: P. Coste, *The life and labours of Saint Vincent de Paul* (London, 1935), vol. 3, pp. 45, 50–1.

18. J. Raine (ed.), *Ecclesiastical Proceedings of Bishop Barnes* (Surtees Society **22**, 1850), pp 81–91: Marcombe, "Gilpin" p. 32.

19. Carleton, *Gilpin*, p. 21: Marcombe, "Gilpin", pp 31-4: W. Gilpin, *The life of Bernard Gilpin* (London, 1753), p. 223: M. James, *Family, lineage and civil society*, (Oxford, 1974), pp. 63, 97, 99.

20. C. Hill, "Puritans and the 'dark corners of the land'", in *Continuity and Change in Seventeenth Century England* (London, 1974), p. 5.

21. P. Collinson, *The religion of Protestants* (Oxford, 1982) pp. 257–64: S. Clarke, *The lives of sundry eminent persons in this later age* (London, 1683), p. 4.

22. Collinson, *Religion of Protestants*, pp. 242–4.

23. The phrase comes from a 1592 order of the Northern High Commission: R. W. Hoyle, "Advancing the Reformation in the North: orders from the York High Commission, 1583 and 1592", *Northern History* **28**, 1992, p. 225.

24. Clarke, *Lives of eminent persons*, p. 5.

25. W. Hinde, *A path to pietie, leading to the way, the truth and the life, Christ Jesus. Drawn upon the ground, and according to the Rule of Faith* (London, 1626), Epistle Dedicatorie.

26. P. Collinson, "'A magazine of religious patterns': an Erasmian topic transposed in English Protestantism", in *Renaissance and renewal in Christian history*, D. Baker (ed.) (Studies in Church History **14**, 1977) pp. 240–2.

27. W. Hinde, *A faithfull remonstrance of the holy life and happy death of John Bruen of Bruen Stapleford, in the County of Chester, Esquire* (London, 1641), pp. 216–7.

28. W. Harrison, *The difference of hearers* (London, 1614), p. 93.

29. A. Dent, *The plaine man's path-way to heaven* (London, 1601), pp. 285–7.

30. J. Rogers, *The doctrine of faith* (London, 1634), pp. 97–9.

31. Rogers, *Doctrine of faith*, pp. 185–6.

32. M. Sylvester (ed.), *Reliquiae Baxterianae* (London, 1696), p. 3: for the treatise in question, B. S. Gregory, "'The true and zealous service of God': Robert Parsons, Edmund Bunny, and The First Booke of the Christian Exercise", *Journal of Ecclesiastical History* **45**, 1994, pp. 238–68.

33. I. Green, "'For children in yeeres and children in understanding': the emergence of the English catechism under Elizabeth and the early Stuarts", *Journal of Ecclesiastical History* **37**, 1986, pp. 397–425. Unfortunately, Dr Green's magisterial *summa* on the subject, *The Christian's ABC: catechisms and catechizing in England c. 1530–1740*, (Oxford, 1996) appeared too late for me to make more than glancing use of it: pp. 580–751 are devoted to a finding list of the catechisms Dr Green has identified.

34. Hinde, *Path to pietie*, pp. 1–3.

35. W. Perkins, *The foundation of Christian religion gathered into sixe principles* (London, 1627), Epistle "to all ignorant people that desire to be instructed", sig. A4.

36. F. E. Hutchinson (ed.), *The works of George Herbert* (Oxford, 1967), p. 255.

37. Green, "Emergence", p. 417.

38. Hutchinson, *Works of George Herbert*, p. 257.

39. Clarke, *Lives of eminent persons* pp. 165–82.

40. For a more tentative although not contradictory discussion of the nature and development of ministry in England than is here implied, see P. Collinson. "Shepherds, sheepdogs, and hirelings: the pastoral ministry in post-Reformation England", in *The ministry, clerical and lay*, W. J. Sheils & D. Wood (eds) (Studies in Church History **26**, 1989), pp. 185–220: see also, in the same collection, I. Green "'Reformed pastors' and *Bons Curés*: the changing role of the parish clergy in Early Modern Europe", pp. 249–86.

41. Clarke, *Lives of eminent persons*, pp. 83–92; E. Calamy, *The nonconformists' memorial*, S. Palmer (ed.), (2nd edn, London, 1802–3), vol. 1, pp. 343–4.

42. For which see Hill, "Puritans and the 'dark corners of the land'", *passim*, and A. M. Johnson, "Wales during the Commonwealth and Protectorate" in D. Pennington & K. Thomas (eds), *Puritans and revolutionaries* (Oxford, 1978), pp. 233–56.

43. Clarke, *Lives of eminent persons*, pp. 140–4; Calamy, *Nonconformists' memorial*, vol. 3, pp. 208–11.

44. Calamy, *Nonconformists' memorial*, vol. 2, pp. 234–44.

45. Clarke, *Lives of eminent persons*, p. 180.

46. Clarke, *Lives of eminent persons*, pp. 203 ff.

47. This account of Wadsworth's ministry is based on Richard Baxter's prefatory "to the reader", prefixed to Wadsworth's posthumous *Last warning to secure sinners, being his two last sermons* (London, 1677); see also Calamy, *Nonconformists' memorial*, vol. 1, pp. 138–42: for Wadsworth's pastoral indebtedness to Baxter, N. H. Keeble and G. F. Nuttall (eds), *Calendar of the correspondence of Richard Baxter*, vol. 1, (Oxford, 1991) pp. 200–1, 203–4.

48. *Christian concord: or the agreement of the associated pastors and churches of Worcestershire. With Rich. Baxter's explication and defence of it* (London, 1653).

49. N. H. Keeble, *Richard Baxter, Puritan man of letters* (Oxford, 1982), pp. 81–2: K. Wrightson, *English Society 1580–1680* (London, 1982), p. 216.

50. W. Orme (ed.), *The practical works of the Revd. Richard Baxter*, vol. 14, (London, 1830), (*Gildas Salvianus*), pp. 266–7.

51. Duffy, "The godly and the multitude in Stuart England", pp. 38–40; Orme, *Practical Works of Richard Baxter*, vol. 14, pp. 401–594.

52. For Baxter's discussion of the place of these publications in his overall evangelistic scheme, Keeble, *Puritan man of letters*, pp. 74–6.

53. *Baxter correspondence*, vol. 1, p. 88.

54. *Ibid.*, pp. 112, 126.

55. *Ibid.*, pp. 145–8, 222–6.

56. Clarke, *Lives of eminent persons*, p. 169.

57. Clarke, *Lives of eminent persons*, pp. 6–7.

58. Calamy, *Nonconformists' memorial*, vol. 2, p. 258.

59. *Reliquiae Baxterianae*, pp. 84–5.

60. For lesser success with the same methods elsewhere, see, for example, the rueful and envious comments of T. Wadsworth: *Baxter correspondence*, vol. 1, p. 204: see also I. Green's remarks on the "rose-tinted glass colouring

Baxter's view of the wider success of the movement by 1659", in *The Christian's ABC*, pp. 222–7, esp. p. 226. For a discussion of similar moves in Warwickshire, and their limitations, see Anne Hughes, *Godly Reformation and its opponents in Warwickshire, 1640–1662*, (Dugdale Society Occasional Papers **35**, 1993).

61. *Reliquiae Baxterianae*, p. 85.
62. See below, notes 74–8.
63. Calamy, *Nonconformists' memorial*, vol. 3, p. 386.
64. M. R. Watts, *The Dissenters*, vol. 1 (Oxford, 1978), pp. 221–62.
65. *Baxter correspondence*, vol. 1, p. 160.
66. For a complete list of works to which Baxter provided prefaces, see Keeble, *Puritan man of letters*, pp. 170–2; on non-conformist involvement in the publication of such converting works, see Duffy, "The godly and the multitude", pp. 46–9.
67. S. Patrick, *The parable of a pilgrim: written to a friend* (London, 1679), pp. 138–43.
68. J. Eachard, *Some observations upon the answer to an enquiry* (London, 1671), p. 140; cited in J. Spurr, *The restoration church of England 1646–1689* (New Haven & London, 1991), p. 283.
69. Keeble, *Puritan man of letters*, p. 38.
70. Trinity College Cambridge, Wren Library, shelfmark K 4 13.
71. Duffy, "The godly and the multitude", p. 48.
72. Clarke, *Lives of eminent persons*, pp. 203–5; Calamy, *Nonconformists' memorial*, vol. 1, pp. 184–8; Watts, *The Dissenters*, vol. 1, p. 281.
73. G. V. Portus, *Caritas Anglicana* (London, 1912); D. W. R. Bahlman, *The moral revolution of 1688* (New Haven, 1957); E. Duffy, " 'Primitive christianity reviv'd': religious renewal in Augustan England", in *Renaissance and Renewal in Christian History*, D. Baker (ed.) (Studies in Church History **14**, 1977), pp. 287–300: F. W. B. Bullock, *Voluntary religious societies 1520–1799* (St Leonards on Sea, 1963); T. Isaacs "The Anglican hierarchy and the reformation of manners, 1688–1738", *Journal of Ecclesiastical History* **33**, 1982, pp. 391–411: A. G. Craig, *The movement for the reformation of manners 1688–1715* (PhD thesis, Edinburgh University, 1980): J. Spurr, "The church, the societies and the moral revolution of 1688", in J. Walsh, C. Haydon, S. Taylor (eds), *The Church of England c. 1689–1833* (Cambridge, 1993), pp. 127–42.
74. E. Duffy, "Wesley and the counter-reformation", in J. Garnett & C. Matthew (eds), *Revival and religion since 1700: essays for John Walsh* (London, 1993), pp. 2–5: see also Baxter's letter "to the reader" prefacing James Janeway, *Invisible realities demonstrated in the holy life and triumphant death of Mr John Janeway* (London, 1690).
75. J. Woodward, *An account of the rise and progress of religious societies in the city of London*, D. E. Jenkins (ed.) (Liverpool, n.d.) pp. 32–3; Spurr, "The church, the societies and the moral revolution of 1688", pp. 135–42 is the only

account known to me which does justice to the "godly" pedigree of the societies.

76. Spurr, "The church, the societies", p. 133: Woodward, *Account*, pp. 45–6.

77. J. Woodward, *The duty of compassion to the souls of others, by endeavouring their reformation* (London, 1698), pp. 14, 29.

78. Woodward, *Duty of compassion*, p. 27.

79. A study of Stephens is badly needed: see Craig, "Reformation of manners", pp. 13 ff:, Portus, *Caritas Anglicana*, pp. 37–39.

80. E. Stephens, *The true English government, and misgovernment of the four last Kings . . . Briefly noted in two little tracts* (London, 1689), "To the King" pp. 4–5, "A caveat against flattery", pp. 8, 24–5.

81. *Ibid.*, p. 23: many of the same points are made in his *The beginning and progress of a needful and hopeful reformation in England* (London, 1691), and *A seasonable and necessary admonition to the gentlemen of the first society for the reformatio of manners* (London n.d. but *c.* 1700).

82. M. Goldie, "John Locke, Jonas Proast and religious toleration 1688–1692" in *The church of England c. 1689–1833*, Walsh, Haydon & Taylor (eds), p. 164.

83. Craig, "Reformation of manners" pp. 29–30, 42.

84. Walsh, Haydon & Taylor (eds), *The church of England c. 1689–1833*, p. 167.

85. Craig, "Reformation of manners", p. 230: Portus, *Caritas Anglicana*, pp. 124–5.

86. *Baxter correspondence*, vol. 1, pp. 222–6.

87. H. Sacheverell, *The character of a low churchman* (London, 1702), pp. 11–12.

88. Tennison to Archbishop Sharp, 7 April 1699, quoted in Craig, "Reformation of manners" p. 268.

89. E. Cardwell, *Documentary annals of the reformed Church of England* (Oxford, 1839), vol. 2, pp. 347–52.

90. On the founding of the SPCK, see E. Duffy, "The SPCK and Europe", in *Pietismus und Neuzeit*, **7**, 1981, pp. 28–42, and C. Rose "The origins of the SPCK 1699–1716", in Walsh, Haydon & Taylor (eds), *The church of England c. 1689–1833* pp. 172–90; on the international protestant context, E. Duffy, "Correspondence fraternelle": the SPCK, the SPG, and the churches of Switzerland in the war of the Spanish succession", in *Reform and reformation: England and the continent c. 1500–1750*, D. Baker (ed.) (Oxford, 1979), pp. 251–80. Much of the devotional ethos, and a survey of the various types of activity promoted by members of the SPCK, is provided in the "Representation of the several ways and methods of doing good" included in a book by one of the leading lay supporters of the society: R. Nelson, *An address to persons of quality and estate* (London, 1715), pp. 100–16.

91. Duffy, "The SPCK and Europe", p. 31.

92. M. Clement (ed.), *Correspondence and minutes of the SPCK relating to Wales, 1699–1740* (Cardiff, 1952), pp. 7–9 and *passim*.

93. Spurr, "The church, the societies", pp. 141–2.

94. Gentilcore, "Missionary strategies", p. 274.

3

Comment on Eamon Duffy's Neale Lecture and the Colloquium

Patrick Collinson

The Colloquium held at University College London in January 1996 has strengthened and lengthened a growing sense among historians of the English Reformation that (like the "Long Seventeenth Century" and the "Long Eighteenth Century", ideas to which they may be in debt) it was a "Long Reformation". We are already removed by a generation or so from those historians who confined the essential history of the English Reformation to the thirty years from 1529 to 1559, a manageable three-course meal preceded by a few late medieval apéritifs and rounded off with a small cup of Elizabethan coffee with one or two dissenting digestifs ("Puritanism" and "Recusancy"). Once upon a time, T. M. Parker's little book *The English Reformation to 1558* (not even 1559!) almost despatched the topic between the soup and the fish,[1] while even A. G. Dickens thought that everything which happened after 1559 could be attended to (in 1964) in 38 out of 340 pages, and more recently (in 1989) 38 out of 396.[2]

To limit the Reformation to the concreteness of the politically motivated and publicly executed events of three remarkable and earth-shaking mid-Tudor decades (separating the 44 years from 1485 to 1529 from the 44 years between 1559 and 1603) has some advantages besides symmetrical periodization, as more than one participant in the Colloquium observed. This was, beyond all dispute, *the* Reformation. To spread the concept over two or three centuries is, in effect, to jettison the definite article and to trade an almost timeless principle of religious history, if not of human affairs more generally, "reform" and "reformation", against the specificity which must

71

always be the historian's limiting concern, surrendering to a diffuse generality.

Yet 1529–1559 embraces a very narrow definition of the Reformation, as primarily legislative and administrative. History is more than that. What about that "premature Reformation", the Wycliffite overture, to which Professor Anne Hudson has devoted a book of 556 pages?[3] Was anything "settled" by the so-called religious "settlement" of 1559? Not much, and not yet. The confining dates for a Reformation more generously defined would have to be not the 1520s to the 1550s, but the 1380s, (when orthodoxy was first challenged and when that challenge first received significant political support) to the 1680s, the last time that Roman Catholicism promised, or threatened, to regain its historic ascendancy.[4] The original contribution of the Neale Colloquium was to add to the long Reformation yet another century, as it were a new wing, rather like Penshurst, a rambling house extended over many generations, but always and ever Penshurst.

The announcement that the Neale Colloquium of 1996 would be devoted to the long Reformation aroused in at least one invited contributor, namely myself, the expectation that we should be paying attention to both ends of this very long piece of string, beginnings as well as ends. The committing of the first part of the proceedings, the Neale Lecture itself, to Eamon Duffy, author of *The stripping of the altars*,[5] promised an opportunity to discuss where the Reformation came from; and it was in anticipation of that opportunity that a historian more at home in the first than the second half of this three-century epoch agreed to be Dr Duffy's respondent. In fact, a moment's reflection might have suggested that what *The stripping of the altars* asks us to believe is that the Reformation came out of a clear blue sky, the consequence of contingent and unpredictable events and circumstances. Is it a contribution to Reformation studies? On its own terms, perhaps not. To speak of the calm before the storm would not be entirely appropriate, since the analogy suggests a meteorological relation between calm and storm which Duffy's account of the pre-Reformation Church and religious scene implicitly denies. Few contributors to the Colloquium, and not even Dr Duffy, could have supposed that the Reformation came literally from nowhere. But for better or worse, the Colloquium concerned itself not at all with where it came from but only with where it was going, and how long the journey took.

Those who know Eamon Duffy mainly from *The stripping of the altars* may find it surprising that he insists, in these pages, that the English Reformation was a "runaway success", echoing a phrase used by his critic and sparring partner Dr Diarmaid MacCulloch (in a review), "a howling success". They will notice the very considerable difference between this verdict on the Reformation and that of Dr Christopher Haigh in the last two, dismissive, words in his book *English Reformations*: "some Reformations", meaning, almost, "what Reformations"?[6] But they should not be surprised. For one thing, so far as confessional leanings are concerned, over and above disinterested scholarship, there is no reason why Dr Duffy should want to draw a veil over the unequivocally Protestant character of the seventeenth- and eighteenth-century Church of England, or to make a case for the Anglo-Catholic myth. For another, before the motor car took Dr Duffy out of the libraries and into East Anglia in search of what Professor John Bossy might have called "Christianity in the East"[7] and the story of the strange death of Catholic England, he was engaged in a major study of seventeenth-century Christian spirituality, Catholic, Protestant, Quaker. If we had momentarily forgotten, this Neale Lecture reminds us that its author knows at least as much about Richard Baxter as he knows about early sixteenth-century rood screens and how the ploughman learned his Paternoster. Queen Victoria was surprised when C. L. Dodgson (Lewis Carroll) sent her his next book. There is no reason why we should have made that mistake.

But this is one reason why this contributor, who has scarcely passed the time of day with Baxter, was not best qualified to comment on Dr Duffy's lecture, and why the reader will find more effective responses elsewhere in this volume, in the chapters by Dr Jeremy Gregory and Dr Jonathan Barry. The other reason why I am not necessarily the best choice for this role is that a historian who has spent forty years arguing that so-called Puritanism represented the mainstream, ongoing thrust of the Protestant Reformation, its long-term fruition, is not likely to disagree when Dr Duffy makes the same point and attaches it to Baxter in the 1650s and to his late seventeenth- and early eighteenth-century successors. When Duffy writes that the devout Protestant culture of the early seventeenth century (above all, gadding to sermons) was "too widespread and in many places too dominant to be called a sub-culture", Collinson can only say Amen, which is not a very interesting response.

The Colloquium set its own agenda; "*c.*1500" appears to mean "about 1550", and "1800" is not a misprint. However, we ought not to let *The stripping of the altars* slip out of the frame altogether, if only because it is a long time since a book on any aspect of English religious history captured such a large slice of public attention. Right or wrong, it embodies the new orthodoxy. Among the criticisms which its more censorious readers have levelled against this remarkable book are these two: first, that the "traditional religion" which is its subject, in its naturally flourishing and unnaturally dejected states, is made too consensual, without much in the way of a pathology, and too traditional. Duffy's model allows for a measure of evolutionary development, but perhaps not enough. "Traditional religion" is for the most part unexplained by Duffy (and his understanding of what religion is restricts the explanatory scope which some other historians of the subject might wish to exercise, explanation on their terms being tantamount to reductionism on his). Moreover, the concentration on the religious life of parochial communities disguises the diversity, often an adversarial diversity, of late medieval religious life. The second of these criticisms is that the politicization of religion, its appropriation and manipulation by the state and other political interests, together with the reactive responses which such appropriations and manipulations provoked, is represented in *The stripping* as something inaugurated by the politically, dynastically inspired Reformation of Henry VIII, rather than having its roots in the earlier Lancastrian period, the era of *De heretico comburendo*, a piece of history which Duffy never mentions. Henry VIII and the reformers whom he let off the leash are in *The stripping* unexplained *dei ex machina*. There is no hinge to connect the two wings of a diptych of a book.[8] One notes in the present paper a comparable interest in the arbitrary contingency of another essential political *deus ex machina*, rather than in any longer-term tendencies and processes which may have been logically implicit in it: in this case 1662, called "a parting of the ways as momentous as any event since the break with Rome".

However true to life Eamon Duffy's representation of pre-Reformation English Christianity may be, and it is surely much truer to life than any account supplied by pre-revisionists in the Protestant–Whig tradition, it makes it harder rather than easier to explain the Reformation; how, to quote eleven of my own words, "one of the most Catholic countries became one of the least", which, as Christopher Marsh remarks, is a problem still haunting us.

Several of the papers presented in the Colloquium go some way towards exorcising the ghost and making it a little easier to understand how such a profound religious change can have happened. This is managed partly by questioning how profound a change it really was. Recent scholarship as various as Tessa Watt and Alex Walsham on popular prints,[9] Ian Green on catechisms,[10] Mark Byford on Elizabethan Colchester,[11] Judith Maltby on Prayer Book Anglicanism:[12] all can be invoked to suggest that pre-Reformation and post-Reformation English people, if not sharing what was fundamentally the same religion, did inhabit the same moral universe. If this were the whole truth, which it is not, there would be, of course, no problem. But the Protestant appropriation, not to say, plagiarization, of an awakening treatise by the Jesuit, Robert Parsons (itself plagiarized from another author), which, as Dr Duffy tells us, converted Baxter, suggests that this is at least part of the truth.[13] Meanwhile, Jeremy Gregory, like Christopher Haigh before him,[14] thinks that it was an easier task to make the English people anti-Catholic, Jeremy Black's "major ideological determinant", than good Protestants; or, at least, that we need to continue to scrutinize what the credentials for being a good Protestant may have been. The concept and recognition that the Reformation was a protracted and of its nature and of necessity a never-to-be-complete process, the "Rome was not built in a day" line, is also helpful. But, it must be said, the longer we make this particular piece of string, extending it into the eighteenth and even the nineteenth century, the less useful and meaningful it becomes as a tool of measurement and as a piece of periodization. *Ecclesia semper reformanda*, like the motto of the Church of Scotland, *consumat nec consumebatur*, may contain an important truth about the dynamics of religious systems, but it does to church history what the farmers have done to Bedfordshire: rooting out the hedges and other landmarks, turning a once subtly varied landscape into a featureless prairie.

75

In the third place, several of the papers offered to the Colloquium suggest that religious changes and religious differences which, in principle, should have split communities asunder, destroying that bedrock of society which was religious unity and with it society itself, in practice did nothing of the sort. One tiny incident can furnish us with a paradigm. A vicar choral of Chichester, who at first denied that he was a Catholic, but then admitted that he believed in purgatory, transubstantiation and the papal supremacy, could hardly stay on in his post in the Elizabethan cathedral. The dean and chapter had to let him go but they gave him thirty shillings to help him on his way.[15] Muriel McClendon tells us that it was precisely because the ruling magistrates of Norwich were not of one mind in religion that they were usually careful not to put the interests of the city at risk by the proactive prosecution of religious dissidents and troublemakers. Whether "toleration" is the appropriate name for their socially judicious pragmatism some contributors to the Colloquium publicly doubted.

Christopher Marsh suggests that the uncompromising confrontation with the radically sectarian Family of Love, favoured and engineered by fiercely orthodox writers such as John Knewstub, was less typical of the response of the Elizabethan Church to this phenomenon than that of easy-going latitudinarians such as Andrew Perne, or even perhaps Queen Elizabeth herself; and that the moderate accommodation of Familism encouraged those tendencies within Familism itself which were non-confrontational and which skilfully balanced internal, endogamous, sectarian integration with a sensible measure of exogenous integration with the wider community. Ultimately, that proved detrimental to the very survival of the Family of Love as an ongoing concern, for the Family seems in its second and third generations to have succumbed to the attractions of both conformity and exogenous marriage. Alex Walsham tells a similar story about the eventual, long-term absorption of church papists into the parochial fabric of the Church of England.[16]

But the work of Margaret Spufford and her team of Spuffordians (and especially that of Bill Stevenson on the Independents, Baptists and Quakers of late seventeenth-century West Anglia) appears to demonstrate that good neighbourhoods could co-exist on a stable, ongoing basis with a distinct sectarian identity which did have a future.[17] King George VI, receiving a delegation from the Society of Friends in 1945, and being quietly told by an equerry that most people knew them as Quakers, said "Oh! I didn't know that there were any of them left!" But of course there were and are, to the confusion of those sociological typologists of sects and denominations, who believe that by rights the Quakers should have turned into something else long ago. The treaty which Quakers, in their second and third generations, made with the rest of society, and society with them, indicates that the Reformation, and post-Reformation religious disequilibrium, did not necessarily have the drastic consequences which it ought to have had, if we take too literally what was said, in sermons, in the literature of complaint and elsewhere in print.

Finally, Ronald Hutton, like a rather more folkloristic Keith Thomas, suggests that the calendrical rites and customs which were so firmly built into the pre-Reformation Church displaced only a small distance outside it into homes and open spaces. It appears that not all traditions are relatively recent, invented traditions. A fashionable idea ought not to be allowed to get out of hand. Traditional religion, or some bits and pieces of it, Candlemas lights and hot cross buns, lived on in altered settings and circumstances.[18] This is Haigh's "some Reformations".

It is time to address the substance of Eamon Duffy's lecture, and in particular two central contentions. The first is shared with several other contributors to the Colloquium, and especially with Jeremy Gregory and Jonathan Barry. It is that the Reformation was indeed a very long-drawn-out business and its essential programme persistently evangelical, or an evangelism (a term we are learning to extend beyond its original terms of reference – witness the Lake & Questier paper), in continuity with the agenda of the godly in the two, three or four generations succeeding the politically managed Reformation(s) of the 1530s, 1540s and 1550s. 1662 was a moment of frustration and fragmentation, but not even 1662 called a halt to a reformation which persisted for the remainder of the seventeenth century and invaded Dr Jonathan Clark's "long eighteenth century", eventually catching up with Professor W. R. Ward's Methodists: an "ongoing project", the achievement of a Christian society by an active ministry aiming at conversion, the language of conversion and of new birth being "an ubiquitous feature of Protestant discourse", a persistent, shared godly culture. The Church of England entered the eighteenth century with all the elements of the Protestant dream of a Christian nation intact. Jonathan Barry tells us that early eighteenth-century Bristol still cherished intact the ideal of a Protestant, godly city on a hill. But as a realizable project, Dr Duffy suggests that the dream was actually dead in the water, as a consequence of what happened to the godly tradition, divided and partly expelled into an involuntary sectarianism, after Bartholomew Day 1662. To be sure, the themes of conversion and of the reformation of manners refused to go away, but as a consequence of the Restoration religious settlement, they would no longer arouse consensual and national resonances. (Had they ever?)

The second contention arises at the beginning and end of Eamon Duffy's lecture and is not shared with other contributions to the Colloquium. It is that in the absence of the full panoply of resources and strategies available to the post-Tridentine Church in the Counter-Reformation (missionary orders, the theatricality of Catholic revivalism, the confessional, characterized as the ultimate weapon of the Counter-Reformation, "the perfect forum for the meeting and integration of routinization and the zeal of conversion") the ongoing enterprise of a converting Protestant Reformation was obliged to function for the most part in parochial units which were better suited to religious routinization (the absorption and internalization of the Prayer Book) than to conversion. However, there was success at places such as Ketton in Suffolk in the 1620s and 1630s, or at Kidderminster in the 1650s, where it proved possible to sustain a dynamic and transforming ministry on parochial footings. I shall respond briefly to these two main contentions.

First to the master principle of all our proceedings: the Long Reformation. If the Reformation, apparently in a primal, not to say primitive, sense was as long-lasting as we now all seem to think it was, is that something simply to be acknowledged, or do we need to explain its persistence as arising from special factors? Was the Long Reformation perhaps part of the pathology of the English Church and the religious scene, and does it invite us to exercise diagnostic skills? If we put the history of (largely) Protestant England in the later sixteenth, seventeenth and early eighteenth centuries into its European context, as I was obliged to do at an Anglo-German conference in Munich in October 1995, then I think that we have to attempt some explanation of what looks like an unusual state of affairs. Our German colleagues have much to say about a Second Reformation, and about a process called confessionalization. Léonard called the second, seventeenth-century volume of his history of European Protestantism *L'Établissement*.[19] The implication is that the religious forms of Protestantism had gelled and congealed into orthodox systems of largely uncontested doctrine and into an institutionalized and regulated economy of teaching, pastoral care and discipline, which some historians see as highly relevant to the early modern process of state formation, or (better?) state perfection. Now was there ever in England a Protestant *établissement*?

If the concept of a Second Reformation has any applicability in England, a question addressed in Munich, then it seems to mean more of the same, or regularly repeated doses of primary reformation. However, we may choose whether to emphasize continuity, as Dr Duffy does, or disjunctive episodes of deliberately renewed, reactivated, redirected reformation: the enterprise of reforming the Reformation itself, as in 1640, but also in the 1580s, and in the late 1680s. Why was this? Why can we not simply take the Long Reformation for granted?

One answer is the fact of royal supremacy and the royal nature of the post-Reformation Church of England: a very obvious fact of life, on which Dr George Bernard was properly insistent in a recent article, and which is perhaps unduly neglected in Duffy's lecture.[20] Royal supremacy and monarchical interests frustrated more than they furthered the cause of Reformation, until we get to William III. To make a rather obvious point concrete, Elizabeth I's idea of what a church, her church, was for was not Archbishop Grindal's idea. Although both regarded obedience as a valuable commodity, the Queen did not believe it was to be promoted by a converting, preaching ministry.[21] John Guy in a recent essay on the 1590s, Julian Davies in a book on the 1630s, have in different ways drawn our attention to the symbiotic interests of Crown and Church, which had little to do with an "awakening" evangelism.[22]

Generally, this means that what we need have no inhibitions in calling Protestant orthodoxy was less likely to work towards state formation, or to become simply an instrument for that purpose (as allegedly in Protestant Europe), and more likely to pursue its own rather different agenda for individuals, local communities, towns, the nation: converting, reforming, often, in favourable circumstances, with the socio-political grain, but as often against it: the story of English religion from Elizabethan Puritanism to the Tractarians and the Nonconformist Conscience.

Specifically, the failure of the state church to define and underwrite Protestant orthodoxy had momentous consequences with which we are all familiar. They included at one and the same time an inconclusive battle for theological definition ("Calvinism" versus "Arminianism") and an equally confused struggle over the material, liturgical symbolics of religion (surplices and altar rails), which had the effect of releasing much of the social energy which fuelled our Long Reformation.

For the energy generated by religious competition and conflict, with the nineteenth century providing our best example, is often as much functional as dysfunctional, ecumenism by contrast a tell-tale sign of morbidity in religious bodies. A further consequence was a process of doctrinal formulation which was referred downwards to all those hundreds of godly preachers in their pulpits, and in their studies, as they composed their own catechisms. We are talking not about some hundreds of distinct catechisms but about more than a thousand, the most successful running into scores of editions.[23] In effect, the seventeenth-century Church of England was subject to a collective *magisterium*, which was remarkably self-disciplined (or so Dr Ian Green seems to be telling us) but which was by no means an instrument of state religious policy.

Next, the failure, or, if you will, disinclination of the state church to deal decisively with the two greatest practical problems in the perception of the godly, Popery and sin, was a further reason for the regular re-energizing of the evangelistic and reforming impulses of the long Reformation. Peter Lake's and Michael Questier's remarkable account of the bipartisan exploitation of the opportunities of the prison and the gallows, sustaining at a dramatic and heightened level a competitive and mutually exacerbating dialogue of conversion, is a particularly vivid demonstration of this point. So far as sin was concerned, we may, as a piece of shorthand, refer to the Book of Sports, and in particular to Charles I's renewed promulgation of these orders, which Hugh Peter thought was more responsible than anything else for giving the world America, or at any rate New England.[24] And America is another branch of the Long Reformation which we ought not to ignore. If Jeremiads and Hoseads about declension (which is to say, national sin) dominated the national pulpit in England from the 1580s to the 1620s[25], and again in the early 1640s, this mode was famously revived in late seventeenth-century New England, to the extent that American historians ignorantly suppose that it was invented there and at that time, a piece of American "exceptionalism". These are some of the reasons why the Long Reformation should be represented not as the natural functioning of a healthy, unrestrained organism, but as a sustained series of responses to the constraints of a Reformation never whole-heartedly embraced and promoted by the centres and sources of ecclesiastical and political power. Here is a grand paradox which makes it possible for Diarmaid MacCulloch to write an article called "The myth of the English Reformation", from which we learn that the myth is that there was no English Reformation.[26]

I turn to the second contention of Dr Duffy's Neale lecture, consisting of a comparison between an institutionally shackled Protestant evangelism and the revivalist, converting machinery and methodology of the forces of the Counter-Reformation, as they confronted and opposed the inertia of what John Bossy calls the Moral Tradition.[27]

I should want to make more even than Duffy does of the restrictive consequences of a religious system which, in principle, was more parochial than ever before; but which starved almost a majority of parishes of essential resources: the unreformed scandal of impropriation, compounding the natural incidence of inadequate endowment within poor and marginal communities. We are putting our finger not only on the state–church insistence on the legally enforced norm of regular and uniform parish church attendance (while noting in passing that these were further factors which released religious energy in kicking over these traces in nonconformity, in gadding to sermons, and in the voluntary sustenance of preachers and lecturers); but also on the Calvinist principle that itinerant ministry, "roving apostles", was a bad thing. What had to be striven for, against all the odds, was a godly preaching ministry in every parish. This was a party line admittedly ameliorated and modified by such arrangements as early preaching itinerancy, and, later, prophesyings and combination lectures[28]: a tradition which, Dr Duffy tells us, came to something like an apotheosis in the 1650s, in Baxter's association movement.

Dr Duffy knows that there was no substitute within Protestantism for the Catholic religious orders, Jesuits, Lazarists, Redemptorists, and this must be right. But I would make the point more emphatically than he has done, because he may have exaggerated the success of the English Reformation in making the parish an effective instrument of evangelism as well as of routinization. To put it bluntly, I think that he has found the narratives of Samuel Clarke too seductive, and has come dangerously close to suggesting that the wonderful world of Clarke's godly lives was typical and a norm. Other participants in the Colloquium shared these misgivings, charging Dr Duffy with over-looking the polemical rather than descriptive purposes of Clarke's post-Restoration compilations.

But, conversely, Dr Duffy overstates his second point of critical comparison between Protestant, English evangelism and Counter-Reformation mission: what he calls a Catholic "hospitality to ritual and drama", a matter of gestures, processions, *tableaux vivants*. We are moving rapidly towards an enhanced recognition of the cultural and even popular–cultural potentialities of the Protestant religious scene. It appears that we have exaggerated the static non-demonstrative, anti-theatrical, wordy nature of the Protestant religious "exercise", partly because we have formed most of our impressions of the Protestant sermon from printed sermon texts.[29] We need to take more account of the whole business of going to and coming from the sermon, which was a demonstrative form of processional; and of psalm-singing, in these and other circumstances. Puritan fasts were a displaced form of pilgrimage and involved, like pilgrimage, the almost ritualized offering of money: not, perhaps, a theatrical gesture, but still a gesture. The Puritan form of exorcism, practised by semi-professionals such as John Darrell, was nothing if not dramatic.[30] And then there were those scaffold scenes, described by Lake & Questier. Dr Walsham's providentialist studies suggest that a religion of conversion and progressive sanctification was not as alien to the imaginative and emotional lives of the "multitude" as we once thought.[31]

The *locus classicus* of Protestantism as emotionally charged and popular culture is now Leigh Eric Schmidt's book *Holy fairs* (a phrase borrowed from Robert Burns), from which we learn how revivals came out of mass communions, celebrated as the climax of prolonged religious festivals or fairs. These seem to have attracted all sorts and conditions of men and women, including not especially "religious" hangers-on, for whom the occasion was an opportunity for some drinking and wenching, but who were in mortal danger of being sucked into the spiritual epicentre by a series of arresting and converting experiences, like moths to a flame.[32] There are parallels here to the often disorderly scenes at Glendalough in the Wicklow Mountains in nineteenth-century Ireland; and Dr Duffy tells me that it sounds rather like the rallies organized by St John Eudes. Admittedly, Schmidt's data is Scottish, Irish and American. I strongly suspect the prevalence of English phenomena tending towards "revivalism", as in the fiery preaching of John Rogers at Dedham. But they are poorly documented, except, for example, in Father William Weston's famous account of certain goings-on at Wisbech towards the end of Elizabeth's reign.[33]

But as for Dr Duffy's third point, the penalty borne by a Protestant religious undertaking which lacked the confessional: I could not agree more, and offered the same argument in the conclusion of an essay of 1989 called "Shepherds, sheepdogs and hirelings: the pastoral ministry in post-Reformation England"; where I suggested that if we want to pick one reason why, eventually, the Church of England, as a pastoral agency, found itself ministering to a largish sect rather than to a nation, we might well select the loss of confession on the Catholic model, without the gain of effective Protestant discipline.[34] It was William Perkins who wrote: "The want of this is a great fault in our churches", "the cause why a minister cannot discern the estate even of his own flock". As for discipline, the enterprise was evidently fatally compromised by the failure to reform the abuse of excommunication as a formalized legal penalty, the cause of Josiah Woodward's bitter complaints in the late seventeenth century. It was, I suggested in 1989, as if the multitude, the great unwashed, said to the pastors and evangelists: "Don't call us, we will call you." However, attendance at the 1996 Neale Colloquium taught this, among other valuable lessons: that the loss of confession as part of a sacrament did not necessarily mean the lack in post-Reformation England of an effective pastoral, rather than simply a preaching, ministry. It was, it must have been, that pastoral ministry, not expounding sermons to the empty air or to unwilling hearers, which made the Long Reformation the "howling success" which even Eamon Duffy believes it to have been.

Notes

1. T. M. Parker, *The English Reformation to 1558* (Oxford, 1950).
2. A. G. Dickens, *The English Reformation* (London, 1964; 2nd edn, London, 1989).
3. A. Hudson, *The premature Reformation: Wycliffite texts and Lollard history* (Oxford, 1988).
4. P. Collinson, "England", in *The Reformation in national context*, B. Scribner, R. Porter & M. Teich (eds) (Cambridge, 1994), pp. 80–94.
5. E. Duffy, *The stripping of the altars: traditional religion in England c.1400–1580* (New Haven & London, 1992).
6. C. Haigh, *English Reformations: religion, politics and society under the Tudors* (Oxford, 1993).
7. See Bossy, *Christianity in the west 1400–1700* (Oxford, 1985).
8. These remarks reflect, in part, the views of Duffy's most serious and hostile critic, Professor D. Aers, in "Altars of power", *Literature and History*, 3rd series **3**, 1994, pp. 90–105. In a subsequent debate in the same journal (**4**) 1995, pp. 86–9, Duffy protests, rather surprisingly, that *The stripping* was "a contribution to the history of the Reformation, not of the age of Langland and Chaucer", defends his concentration on orthodoxy rather than on marginality and "stress lines", and insists that "the political and social dimensions of cult . . . are spelled out in the opening pages, and are a recurrent theme of the book". But Aers complains that Duffy continues to ignore the role of the state in the formation of late medieval orthodoxy.
9. T. Watt, *Cheap print and popular piety, 1550–1640* (Cambridge, 1991); A. Walsham, *Aspects of providentialism in early modern England* (PhD thesis, Cambridge University, 1994); and Dr Walsham's " 'The fatall vesper': providentialism and popery in late Jacobean London", *Past and Present* **144**, 1994, pp. 36–87.
10. I. Green, *The Christian's ABC: catechisms and catechizing in England, c.1530–1740* (Oxford, 1996).
11. M. Byford, *The price of Protestantism: assessing the impact of religious change on Elizabethan Essex: the cases of Heydon and Colchester*, (DPhil thesis, Oxford University, 1988); and his "The birth of a Protestant town: the process of

Reformation in Tudor Colchester, 1530–1580", in *The Reformation in the English towns*, P. Collinson and J. S. Craig (eds), (Basingstoke, forthcoming).

12. J. Maltby, " 'By this Book': parishioners, the prayer book and the established church", in *The early Stuart Church, 1603–1642*, K. Fincham (ed.) (Basingstoke, 1993); and Dr Maltby's *Approaches to the study of religious conformity in late Elizabethan and early Stuart England*, (PhD thesis, Cambridge University, 1991).

13. B. S. Gregory, "The 'true and zealous service of God': Robert Parsons, Edmund Bunny and *The First Booke of the Christian Exercise*", *Journal of Ecclesiastical History* **45**, 1994, pp. 238–68.

14. Haigh, *English Reformations*, pp. 280, 292–5.

15. West Sussex Record Office, MS Cap 1/3/1, fo. 55r. I owe this reference to James Saunders.

16. C. Marsh, *The Family of Love in English society 1550–1630* (Cambridge, 1994); C. Marsh, "The grave of Thomas Lawrence revisited, (or the family of love and the local community in Balsham, 1560–1630)", in *The world of rural dissenters, 1520–1725*, M. Spufford (ed.) (Cambridge, 1995), pp. 208–34; A. Walsham, *Church papists: Catholicism, conformity and confessional polemic in Early Modern England* (Woodbridge, 1993).

17. Spufford (ed.), *The world of rural Dissenters*, especially pp. 332–87.

18. R. Hutton, "The English Reformation and the evidence of folklore", *Past and Present* **148**, 1994, pp. 89–116.

19. É. Léonard, *Histoire générale du protestantisme*, vol. II (Paris, 1961).

20. G. W. Bernard, "The Church of England c.1529–c.1642", *History* **75**, 1990, pp. 183–206.

21, P. Collinson, *Archbishop Grindal, 1518–1583: the struggle for a reformed church* (London, 1979).

22. J. Guy, "The Elizabethan establishment and the ecclesiastical polity", in *The reign of Elizabeth I: court and culture in the last decade*, J. Guy (ed.) (Cambridge, 1995), pp. 126–149.

23. I. Green's 767-page *The Christian's ABC*, which tabulates all surviving catechisms, updates his " 'For children in years and children in understanding': the emergence of the English catechism under Elizabeth and the early Stuarts", *Journal of Ecclesiastical History* **37**, 1986, pp. 397–425.

24. H. Peter, *A dying fathers' last legacy to an only child* (London, 1660), pp. 101–2.

25. Walsham, "Aspects of providentialism", pp. 239–79.

26. *Journal of British Studies* **30**, 1991, pp. 1–19.

27. See the forthcoming published version of Professor Bossy's 1995 Birkbeck Lectures in the University of Cambridge.

28. P. Collinson, "The Elizabethan Church and the new religion", in *The reign of Elizabeth I*, C. Haigh (ed.) (Basingstoke, 1984), pp. 169–94.

29. See forthcoming work by Arnold Hunt, of Trinity College, Cambridge.

30. P. Collinson, "Elizabethan and Jacobean Puritanism as forms of popular

religious culture", in *The culture of English puritanism 1560–1700*, C. Durston & J. Eales (eds), (Basingstoke, 1996). pp. 32–57. For Darrell and exorcism, see P. Collinson *The Elizabethan Puritan movement* (London, 1967), pp. 437–8; K. Thomas, *Religion and the decline of magic* (London, 1971), pp. 483–6.

31. Walsham, "Aspects of providentialism", and Dr Walsham's forthcoming monograph, *Providentialism in early modern England*.
32. L. E. Schmidt, *Holy fairs: Scottish communions and American revivals in the early modern period* (Princeton, 1989).
33. *The life of William Weston, SJ*, in *The troubles of our catholic forefathers related by themselves*, J. Morris (ed.), 2nd series, vol. II (London, 1875), pp. 240–1.
34. In *The ministry: clerical and lay*, W. J. Sheils & D. Wood (eds) (Studies in Church History **26**, 1989), pp. 185–220.

4

Religious toleration and the Reformation: Norwich magistrates in the sixteenth century

Muriel C. McClendon

In the historiography of religious toleration in Europe, the sixteenth century is considered to have been a dark period. With the splintering of the "universal church", prejudice and persecution marked much of the era's religious history. In England there was no shortage of expressions of religious bigotry: Henry VIII's execution of the Carthusian monks who refused the Oath of Supremacy, the burning of approximately three hundred Protestant heretics under Mary Tudor and Queen Elizabeth's execution of Catholic priests on charges of treason. Although toleration of dissenting religious groups was favoured by a few intellectuals in Europe such as Sebastian Castellio, the professor of Greek at Basel, and actually extended in France, albeit temporarily, there was little similar support for it in England.[1] Queen Elizabeth declared her intention not to make windows into men's souls where religion was concerned, but her government never extended anything resembling official toleration to those outside of the Church of England. The potential danger to the state was deemed too great to relax the requirement for religious uniformity. It would take almost a century after the Queen's death for a measure of religious toleration to be enshrined in the Toleration Act of 1689.[2]

That principled toleration found few, if any, champions at England's political centre during the Reformation era does not shut the door on the issue entirely. There is evidence that outside of Westminster toleration of religious diversity was not unknown. The purpose of this chapter is to explore the course of events in the city

87

of Norwich and in particular the activities of city rulers, in order to show that through much of the sixteenth century they extended some form of *de facto* religious toleration to religious dissidents in their jurisdiction. Whilst Tudor governments deemed toleration for those who did not adhere to their official religious policies too perilous, some local communities found it too hazardous not to tolerate some spiritual diversity among their inhabitants.

The point has been argued that when toleration was formally proffered to dissenting religious groups across early modern Europe the motive was often, if not always, a practical and political one and not a product of principled compassion for religious difference. In the case of England, Jonathan Israel has recently shown William III to have been a *politique* whose support for religious toleration was motivated by pragmatic concerns for his position in Europe and not by any such empathy with religiously marginalized groups.[3] In all likelihood similarly practical considerations informed *de facto* toleration in sixteenth-century Norwich. The civic elite probably thought it better to overlook religious differences among their neighbours than to risk the dislocation of the community that would result from unbridled religious conflict. In the sources on which this study is based – chiefly records generated by Norwich's civic government – there is no explicit articulation of support for religious toleration. But they do reveal a largely consistent pattern of behaviour among the city's rulers in which such toleration is implicit.

The existence of religious toleration in sixteenth-century England has important implications for historians of religious toleration and for historians of the Reformation also. It reminds the former that the almost complete lack of learned justifications for religious toleration and the unwillingness of Tudor governments to endorse it did not mean that toleration was absent in English society. The Toleration Act of 1689 may have enshrined a practice that had become common in many communities. That some people in England were willing to countenance religious division in their midst also suggests that the changes to religious doctrine and practice made during the sixteenth century may not have been the source of as much conflict as some historians of the Reformation have argued.[4]

Norwich, the regional centre of East Anglia with a population of about 8500 in the 1520s, was the second city in sixteenth-century

England.[5] It was also the seat of the diocese of the same name, one of the largest in the country. Richard Nix, who served as bishop from 1501 until his death in 1535, had in a letter of 1530 lamented the spiritual condition of his see. It was being contaminated, according to him, by "erroneous books in English" and by heretical religious opinions maintained chiefly by "merchants and such that hath their abiding not far from the sea", and by clerical graduates of Gonville Hall, Cambridge.[6] If Nix included his cathedral city in the description of the unorthodox complexion of the diocese it must have come as a bitter disappointment to him, a spirited opponent of religious novelty. During most of his episcopate and even before, there is scant evidence that the inhabitants of Norwich participated in unorthodox religious movements. This evidence may not reflect the survival or extent of heresy in the city and in the rest of the diocese, as it seems implausible that Norwich would have harboured no Lollards, given its connection with the London mercantile world.[7] That so few residents of the city figured in the Lollard trials of the fifteenth century or the flurry of episcopal activity against heresy in the 1510s is perhaps indicative of the toleration of religious difference for which there is clearer evidence later on.[8]

However unblemished Norwich might have previously been by heterodoxy, during the closing years of Nix's episcopate there were signs that new religious ideas were circulating in the city and that they were dividing the population. From the 1530s, the lion's share of religious conflict was handled by the mayor's court in Norwich.[9] The study of these records reveals a distinct pattern concerning the prosecution of religious infractions. The mayor and aldermen who presided over the mayor's court were generally reluctant to punish religious offenders harshly and only rarely turned them over to ecclesiastical or central government authorities. When the central government mandated severe penalties for religious nonconformity, such as after the passage of the Six Articles in 1539 or during the persecution of Protestant heretics between 1555 and 1558, cases concerning religious conflict all but disappeared from the mayor's court. While there were instances that did not conform to this pattern, it seems clear that overall civic leaders in Reformation Norwich tolerated a measure of religious diversity in their jurisdiction.[10]

It is difficult to know precisely how and when new religious ideas began circulating in Norwich, as the available records reveal only hints of such activity. Robert Necton, the brother of a Norwich alderman, was one of the distributors in the city of some of the "erroneous books in English" of Bishop Nix's description. He had been imprisoned in the Fleet in 1528 and then in Newgate in 1531 for his endeavours.[11] Thomas Bilney preached throughout the diocese of Norwich, including the cathedral city, inveighing against the veneration of images and invocation of saints, and distributing copies of Tyndale's New Testament and *Obedience of a Christian man* before his execution in 1531.[12] At Norwich Cathedral, John Barret, former prior of the Cambridge Carmelites and an early convert to Protestantism, was appointed to a lectureship in about 1536.[13] After the passage of the Six Articles in 1539, the Protestant preacher Thomas Rose was in and around Norwich denouncing auricular confession, transubstantiation and other theological tenets supported by the Act.[14]

While questions concerning the dissemination of the Protestant message in Norwich remain, it is clear that by the mid-1530s that message had begun to have an impact. In 1535 the mayor's court was confronted with the consequent problem of religious conflict.[15] Parliamentary legislation of 1534 had stripped church courts of much of their authority and may explain why the mayor's court began to hear cases concerning religious unorthodoxy at that time.[16] Other urban governments took action against religious nonconformists in the sixteenth century as well. In London for example, the Court of Aldermen often adjudicated matters concerning religious dissension.[17] In addition to the weakened condition of the church courts, urban governors' constant concern for the maintenance of public order provided an impetus for their courts to discourage the escalation of religious conflict.

At the court sessions held on 10 and 14 July 1535, the mayor's court heard testimony against a local capper, Thomas Myles. The record does not indicate how the case came to the attention of city authorities, a common feature of the court books. It seems most likely that the witnesses involved in this and in many other cases concerning religion initiated their particular complaints, as neither city constables nor aldermen appear to have been involved. In the case against Myles, a half-dozen witnesses appeared on those two days. They all related how on the Friday following the feast of St

John the Baptist, a "very drunken" Myles had apparently staggered from shop to shop loudly denouncing the saints, and the Virgin as well as some traditional religious ceremonies. Adam Smyth noted that Myles had declared before him that "St. Peter and St. Gregory were knaves." Harry Everard told the magistrates that before him and three others, Myles had announced that "the sacrament of the altar was as well on the Castle ditch as in the church," referring to Norwich Castle and also that "if I had any more children they should not be confirmed". Myles had also "rebuked the priesthood and spake against images and saints [and] pilgrimages". Despite the inflammatory, yet somewhat confused, remarks Myles apparently was not punished by the court. There is no record of any judgment rendered against him and his name never appeared in the court records in connection with this incident again.[18]

In November of the same year William Thakker, a Norwich "marbiller", appeared in the mayor's court where he asserted "that a cartload of bread shall or cannot stop the mouths of them that hath called Mr. Dr. Barret apostate and worse within the city". Thakker added that "certain preachers at London hath been plucked out of the pulpit for making of their sermons", a claim for which he could offer proof, he assured the mayor and aldermen. Perhaps Thakker's comments were meant to intimidate the priest into revising the controversial opinions expressed in his sermons or to compel city officials to prevent him from preaching. Whatever their aim, there is no evidence of any action taken against Thakker and his case disappears from the record.[19]

Not all entries in the court books concerning religious conflict were so opaque. In May 1536, the court examined one Gilmyn, a surgeon, "concerning the having of books suspected", giving credence to the late Bishop Nix's anxiety about the circulation of proscribed books. The record offers no details about the books or their provenance, the queries put to Gilmyn or his responses. After having questioned Gilmyn the court was sufficiently satisfied to decide that "upon trust of amendment" he would be "set at large", only to reappear there a decade later.[20] In September 1537, Harry Niker confessed in the mayor's court that on the previous Saturday, "being one of [the] Ember days", he "and Roger Annell did break their fast at one John Sterlyng's house with bread and butter and herring broiled". The three men consumed more broiled herring on the following day, which was "contrary to the ordinance of the holy church", as the court record noted. Niker was committed to prison. Nothing further is recorded about Niker's case, making it unlikely that he spent a considerable time in jail, if indeed he went there at all.[21]

Local clergymen were not immune from appearances in the mayor's court when they were involved in religious strife, even though clerical discipline should have been left to the church. On the eve of Pentecost in 1540 for example, Robert Spurgeon, the priest of St Michael at Plea, came before the magistrates. He possessed a mass book from which the name of Thomas Becket had not been stricken.[22] A recognizance was entered in the court book that bound Spurgeon to appear at the next session of the Norwich Assizes and a local tailor, John Pettons, stood surety for him. Yet the priest was never called. At the feast of St Bartholomew of the same year, the parish priest of one of the city's wealthiest parishes, St Peter Mancroft, was also in court. Bachelor Newman, three witnesses testified, had denounced Martin Luther, the recently executed Thomas Cromwell and Robert Barnes. There had been other outbursts, also. Despite his inflammatory remarks, Newman does not appear to have been punished by the mayor and aldermen.[23]

Although the offences leading to appearances in the Norwich mayor's court for religious-related infractions were varied, the outcomes tended to be much the same. City magistrates were disinclined to take punitive action against such offenders. When the magistrates sent a defendant to jail, it was probably for a very brief time. Some were required to find sureties for their good behaviour or be ready to reappear in the court, but the mayor and aldermen rarely followed up on these decisions. Others were simply released after questioning. Taken together these cases point to a degree of *de facto* religious toleration exercised by Norwich's mayor and aldermen. It made no difference whether those appearing before them were motivated by conservative religious sentiments, as William Thakker's comments were, or by reformed ones as Thomas Myles and Harry Niker's actions very well may have been. The magistrates made no effort to enforce religious homogeneity. Their response to religious strife suggests a greater regard for silencing public and potentially explosive expressions of religious sentiment than for its doctrinal substance. Norwich magistrates were willing to suffer religious differences among their constituents as long as they could prevent them from erupting into open conflict.

Not all religious contentions in the city resulted in an appearance before the mayor's court. In 1535 the prior of the Norwich Blackfriars, Edmund Harcocke, came close enough to denouncing the royal supremacy in a sermon that Cromwell directed Sir Roger Townsend, a local gentleman, to arrest him. Sir Roger did not carry out his orders as originally outlined, but instead struck a deal with the mayor upon his arrival in Norwich. The prior would remain in the city and the mayor would guarantee his availability to Cromwell indefinitely. Harcocke thus managed to survive his imprudent sermon and subsequent changes in Tudor religious policy, dying uneventfully in 1563.[24] Even outside the mayor's court, Norwich magistrates opted to resolve religious disputes quickly and quietly with little regard for official religious policies and with as little intervention from outside authorities as possible.

It was this aversion to enforcing Tudor religious policy strictly that must help to explain the virtual disappearance of religious conflict from the pages of the mayor's court books between 1540 and 1547. The Six Articles of 1539 had mandated a death sentence for the denial of transubstantiation and felony punishments for other transgressions. It set up commissions to seek out and punish religious unorthodoxy, but also gave power of inquiry to a wide variety of officials including mayors and sheriffs.[25] Around the country hundreds were imprisoned and some burned as heretics. In the City of London, the mayor spearheaded a persecution that led to the indictment and imprisonment of hundreds of suspected heretics. Citizens reported on their evangelical neighbours and juries of the religiously orthodox committed them to jail.[26] But at Norwich, there was not a single charge from a citizen or arrest by the magistrates made resulting from the Six Articles.

In fact, there was only one case concerning any kind of religious conflict that came before the court between 1540 and 1547.[27] Ironically, the defendants were not even residents of Norwich. In the spring of 1546, the mayor's court imprisoned Edward Breten, a shoemaker of East Bergholt, "for that he openly read upon the Bible in Christ's Church [Norwich Cathedral] to Alen Gifford and William

Grey contrary to an act thereof made".[28] The magistrates had not uncovered Breten's activities themselves, nor had another inhabitant of the city levelled an accusation. Rather, Sir Roger Townsend had sent the trio to the Norwich mayor's court for punishment. After the three confessed their offence, the magistrates characteristically decreed that they should be "dismissed out of prison whereunto they were committed".[29]

What led the magistrates to ignore Henrician religious legislation so studiously? The surviving evidence suggests that at least part of the answer lies in their own religious disunity. The chief source for a consideration of magisterial religious sentiments in sixteenth-century Norwich is wills. The use of wills as indicators of particular religious beliefs has been shown to be highly problematic.[30] Yet if the surviving wills of Norwich aldermen are read carefully and without an attempt to divide them into traditionalist, reformist and Protestant categories, the results are suggestive.

Most of the wills written by aldermen in the 1530s and 1540s were much like that of Robert Hemmyng who composed his testament in April 1541 shortly before his death. Hemmyng committed his soul to "Almighty God, to Our Blessed Lady Saint Mary Virgin, Saint Margaret mine advocate and to all the holy company of heaven". He asked that "an honest secular priest" sing and pray for his soul as well as those of his parents, friends and benefactors for a year after his death. He also requested the parson of the parish of St Swithin to instruct the parishioners to say a *Paternoster* and an Ave Maria for him. Hemmyng directed his wife Ann to dispose of goods not specifically named in his will "in deeds of piety and charity and mercy to the most pleasure of God and health of mine soul".[31]

Also among the wills written by aldermen during these years were a very small number such as that of William Rogers, penned in 1542 and proved in 1553. Rogers opened his testament with a long preamble in which he committed his soul to Christ alone and renounced "all my good works" as well. He left money for a preacher to give sermons in and around Norwich for five years following his death, while receiving room and board from Rogers' widow.[32] John Trace, who died in 1544, tendered his soul to Christ in his will, left no money for masses, but did leave a sum for sermons to be preached around the city for two years after his death. Among those who witnessed Trace's will was the ex-Carmelite and early Protestant John Barret.[33] Barret also served as a witness to two other aldermanic wills made between the mid-1530s and Kett's rebellion in 1549.[34]

The evidence from wills, while not definitive, suggests that there was not complete agreement in religion among the aldermen of Norwich. Such divergence would continue to characterize the ruling body until the beginning of Elizabeth's reign, but the magistrates never permitted it to hamper the conduct of civic government.[35] There is no evidence that the mayor's court ever divided along religious lines or that the court was ever subject to periodic purges. And as the magistrates did not allow religious difference to destroy their rule, the practice of tolerating religious dissent helped to prevent the deterioration of the city's social fabric.

Shortly after the Breten episode, Henry VIII was dead. During the first year of Edward VI's reign, the new government began to dismantle the Henrician religious settlement and, somewhat haphazardly, move towards a Protestant one. In Norwich, the religious innovations of Edward's reign provoked a variety of responses, and incidents of conflict over religion resurfaced in the pages of the mayor's court book as the draconian legislation of the previous reign was repealed. The pattern of prosecution was much the same as it had been under Henry VIII, although the number of cases that came before the mayor and aldermen increased substantially.[36] The court did not mete out severe penalties to those who came before them no matter what kind of religious sentiments they had expressed. Nor did the magistrates uphold Edwardian religious policies rigorously. Thus toleration of religious diversity in the city still seemed the order of the day.

The majority of cases of religious conflict that came before the court during Edward's reign were the result of provocative public statements. In May 1547 Ralph Gilmyn, the same man who had been examined for possessing "books suspected" in 1536, was back in court. There he confessed to believing that "there is not in the sacrament of the altar the very body of our Saviour Jesus Christ that was contained in the Virgin Mary, that it is a signification and a commemoration of it". His admission was consistent with a conversation that he had had the previous day in a local tavern with a witness who testified against him before the magistrates. A recognizance was entered into the record for Gilmyn, but he was never called before the court again.[37] In the autumn of the same year the court took no action when William Tyller reported Edward Greene's comment that "the Bishop of Norwich and Doctor Parker were idols and hypocrites and that the same Parker a blasphemer of the word of God". Greene denied the words attributed to him and the case ended there.[38]

Incidents of inflammatory public speech about religion mounted, but the magistrates continued their practice of avoiding punitive action. One reason for the rise in such occurrences was the return to Norwich of the Protestant preacher Thomas Rose. In June 1548 Nicholas Gegle and John Barker informed the court that Thomas Bedys had said "that Mr. Rose is a false knave and here like a false preacher". The mayor and aldermen committed Bedys to ward, but on the following day decided that "upon trust of amendment he is this day discharged".[39] Five others appeared in the court around the same time to answer charges about similarly hostile remarks concerning Rose. Only Robert Barman, who had declared in the parish church of St Gregory that "he had rather go to a bear baiting as to Mr. Rose's sermons and that he should find C [one hundred] to say the same", was bound to good behaviour. He was never called.[40]

Explosive speech was not the only expression of religious discord in Norwich. The alterations to religious doctrines and practices introduced by the Edwardian regime compelled some residents of the city to take action and the court had to contend with such cases as well. Still the mayor and aldermen did not change their customary responses to that conflict. In September 1547, they discussed and denounced a recent wave of iconoclasm in the city. Edward's government had issued injunctions in July which had, among other things, prohibited the veneration of images and enjoined the destruction of those so abused. In London, that order was carried out with such enthusiasm that the Privy Council attempted to reverse the process.[41] In Norwich, city leaders took no such steps to curtail the problem. Informed that "divers curates and other idle persons" had gone into city churches "pulling down images" and taken them away, they merely called upon Thomas Conyers, the parish priest of St Martin at Palace and Richard Debney, a Norwich beer brewer, to "surcease of such unlawful doings".[42]

This warning did not quell the iconoclastic impulse among residents of Norwich completely. In early 1548 two men, Doubleday and Young, confessed to having broken windows at St Andrew's church. In March 1549, Robert Osbern of nearby Kirby told the mayor and aldermen that he had heard three men declare that they had broken windows at the church at Bramerton and had pulled down a cross there and pulled down one at Rockland also. Two months later in early May Thomas Hardy, a Norwich shoemaker admitted that he "did throw a stone at the glass window of the parish church of St Julian". Later the same month, the court heard the case of William Stampe, the parish priest of St Augustine, who had gone into the church one night with a group of "adherents" and broken down the altar.[43]

In none of these cases did city magistrates impose long or harsh sentences. The iconoclast Young was committed to prison, after which his case disappears from the record, making it unclear that the sentence was served. Doubleday, a servant, was not similarly punished; his master was ordered to pay twelve pence in compensation instead. The magistrates took no action against the Bramerton and Rockland iconoclasts. The priest William Stampe was simply directed to rebuild his church's ruined altar, although there is no indication that the magistrates took steps to ensure that he completed the task. The shoemaker Thomas Hardy received the most extensive consideration from the court, perhaps because at the time of his offence, there had been "like trespasses within the city". He was jailed for two days, and then bound to appear again.[44] While most defendants bound in recognizance for religious offences in Norwich were never called again, Hardy was summoned to the Guildhall in June 1549. His good behaviour since his release from prison was noted and he was told that if he continued such good conduct until Michaelmas he would be released from recognizance. After that decision, the court never summoned Hardy again.[45]

Iconoclasm was not the only outrageous behaviour that followed the introduction of religious change in Edwardian Norwich. In December 1547 the court heard a case concerning the mistreatment of holy bread and water that had taken place at St Peter Mancroft church. On 11 December, "a variance" had erupted among nine parishioners that had resulted in the court appearance. Some had taken holy bread and water, "casting" and "dealing" them as the record recounts. Others had become offended at the defilement and an altercation ensued. The mayor and aldermen debated a course of action and decided that each man was to "bear his goodwill and favour to others accordingly as God's law". A tenth man was committed to ward for his role in the incident. Harry Swetman had not been among those mishandling the sacraments but he had said during the incident, among other things, that "one Sir Thomas Rose which preached at St. Andrew's was a knave". He was bound to appear at the next Norwich Sessions, which took place three days later. Two more witnesses gave depositions at that meeting, but Swetman himself was not present and his name never appeared in city records again.[46]

The progress of the Edwardian Reformation continued to provoke conflict that required judgment from the mayor and aldermen. In late 1548 or early 1549, they committed two city priests to ward for "using certain ceremonies contrary to the king's [order]" and for "using the communion contrary to the book sent . . . by the king's majesty". The clerics had probably violated recent proclamations banning some traditional ceremonies and the new Order of Communion that had introduced communion in both kinds and English prayers into the Latin mass.[47] Shortly afterwards in March 1549, the court listened to evidence that five men had flagrantly broken the Lenten fast. William Goose admitted to the magistrates that he and four others had gone to an alehouse in Kirby where they "did eat upon a Friday a swine's cheek [and] a cold pie". Goose and another man were bound to appear before the mayor again (which they never did), while the other three were simply released.[48] In June 1549, after the passage of the act permitting the marriage of priests the magistrates had to warn one Thurston to keep silent after he had been heard to declare that "all priests' wives were whores".[49]

The catastrophe of Kett's rebellion, during which the city was invaded by insurgents and the government overthrown, was probably responsible for the marked decline in cases of religious conflict that came to the mayor's court after the summer of 1549. After civic government had been restored, the magistrates had to devote much of the court's time to disciplining those who were publicly voicing their support for the uprising and its adherents.[50]

Only three defendants appeared before them in connection with religious disturbances during the remainder of Edward's reign, one of whom was John Dyxe. In June 1552, the curate of the parish of St Martin at Oak charged that on the previous Sunday when he had commanded "the feast of St. John Baptist to be holden and kept holy day and the even to be fasted", Dyxe had "moved and stirred the people there to dissension saying that the curate had not done well therein". For his outburst, Dyxe was sentenced to jail until he could find sureties, but a final outcome was never recorded.[51]

John Dyxe's 1552 case was the last one of Edward's reign for a religious offence. The instances of religious conflict that resulted in a court case during those years reveal much about the impact of the early Reformation in Norwich and about the concerns of the civic elite to whom the responsibility of coping with that conflict fell. The outbursts and actions that brought defendants before the mayor and aldermen indicate that the Edwardian Reformation elicited a variety of responses among the city's residents: there was neither a general acceptance or rejection of religious change. Moreover, the magistrates were willing to intervene in a wide variety of religious disputes, from ones in which a defendant demonstrated overt hostility to the Edwardian settlement to those in which it was clear that the accused was anxious to accelerate the pace of religious change. That the court intervened in all of these controversies but meted out relatively mild sentences when they rendered a decision at all, highlights their continued willingness to countenance religious heterogeneity. Their chief concern when they intervened in these cases was to suppress and defuse conflict, but not to enforce religious uniformity. This was particularly evident, for example, when the mayor and aldermen disciplined the two priests in 1548 or 1549 for failing to conduct their services properly. The court records did not indicate the nature of the clerics' divergence from the prescribed rituals, making it impossible to know their religious outlook. The magistrates were less interested in the religious sentiments of the defendants that came before them than in making sure that religious conflict did not escalate out of control.

The death of Edward VI in the summer of 1553 brought his half-sister Mary to the throne and the restoration of Catholicism as the official religion of England. In Norwich Catholicism was restored in the parishes, more slowly in some, and mass was celebrated there once more. While the potential for religious tumult was serious enough in the nation's capital for the Privy Council to summon the City's mayor and aldermen before it, trouble over religion in Norwich early in Mary's reign appears to have been of lesser magnitude.[52] And when the price for religious dissidence became death from 1555 when heresy laws were revived in England, such cases all but disappeared from the records, much as they had under Henry VIII after the passage of the Six Articles. Once again, city magistrates proved unwilling to punish those in their jurisdiction for religious unorthodoxy as seriously as official religious policies dictated.

While most of the cases that came before the mayor's court in the early part of Mary's reign were characterized by magisterial desire to suppress religious conflict before it attracted extramural attention, two incidents during this period deviated conspicuously from this customary pattern. In October 1553, before the new government had begun the repeal of Edwardian religious legislation, the mayor's court had apparently reported the activities of one of the cathedral prebendaries to the Privy Council, an initiative that it rarely, if ever, took. John Hallybred had spoken against one of the Queen's proclamations, perhaps one that the Council had sent to Norwich diocese that prohibited preaching without express licence from the crown.[53] A letter from the Council to the mayor dated 31 October is all that survives of the incident. In it, the Council thanked mayor Henry Crook for having sent the examinations of the "misordered talk of John Hallybred", which was not detailed, and noted its decision to return the priest to Norwich. There, the Council directed, the mayor was to keep the priest in safe ward for five or six days and then compel him to confess his offence at some suitably public occasion. There is no indication, however, that the magistrates ever carried out those orders, despite their role in bringing Hallybred's transgressions to the attention of the central government.[54]

Several months later, in February 1554, the court examined Robert Watson about his failure to attend mass. Having recently arrived from London to stay at the home of the alderman Thomas Beamond, Watson had attended matins and evensong at St Andrew's, a parish known for its progressive religious complexion.[55] When asked why he had neglected the mass, Watson asserted that "he intendeth not to be at any mass, for his presence at the mass is against his conscience and intendeth never to hear mass while he liveth by the grace of God". The magistrates committed Watson to jail where he was to remain "until further order be taken", but his case did not conclude there. A letter from the Privy Council to the magistrates that arrived in Norwich later the same month suggests that city leaders had informed Westminster about Watson's activities. The Council instructed the mayor and aldermen to deliver Watson to the diocesan chancellor who kept him imprisoned for over a year, after which he fled to the continent.[56]

There is no direct evidence to suggest why Norwich magistrates, who had usually recoiled from contact with the central government over religious matters, sought it out in these instances. One reason might have been the return to East Anglia of the third Duke of Norfolk, who had recently been released from his confinement in the Tower.[57] The Duke was a religious conservative and it is possible that city leaders were concerned that he might intervene in local matters.[58] They may have been willing to hand over Hallybred and Watson to show the Duke that he had no reason to scrutinize their affairs. In the case of Robert Watson, a known Protestant trouble-maker, the magistrates might have thought it best to remove him from their jurisdiction before he caused more difficulties.[59]

Apprehension about the Duke's potential for interference in religious matters cannot explain all of the actions taken by the magis-trates against religious transgressors. On the sole occasion when the Duke did intervene, the magistrates resorted to their usual course of taking little or no action in the matter of religious controversy. In March 1554, the Duke wrote to the mayor and aldermen to complain about the conduct of John Barret, who was then rector of the parish of St Michael at Plea.[60] The Duke had been informed that Barret "should omit either to preach the word of God . . . or to come to his divine service, to the evil example of such other as have him in credit and estimation". Having recently been at Norwich, the Duke continued, "I cannot a little marvel that at my late being among you, you would not declare the same unto me". He concluded the letter by demanding that the magistrates secure the priest's compliance or else commit him to ward. The magistrates answered the Duke's missive almost immediately and their response combined an effort to deflect conflict with an outside authority of the Duke's stature with a defence of the clergyman and their oversight of his activities. They promised the Duke that the allegations against Barret were untrue and that he served his cure, preached at the cathedral and in his own parish all according to the Queen's wishes. They had even examined some of Barret's parishioners who confirmed that the priest conducted his duties properly. This answer must have satisfied the Duke as there was no further correspondence on the matter.[61]

The question about John Barret was the only time that the Duke of Norfolk inquired into religious matters in Norwich before his death in the summer of 1554. When matters of religious conflict were left to the magistrates alone, they were most often handled in what had become the usual fashion. In November 1553, Thomas Swanne reported John Wagstaff's words about Thomas Tedman, a religiously conservative cathedral prebendary and parson of Acle. "Doctor Tedman had lain in his den this last vii [seven] years", Wagstaff, a servant, complained, "and now did preach upon Sunday last past, and for his preaching had like to have been pulled out of the pulpit. And if he cometh and preacheth so again he shall be pulled down indeed". Wagstaff had continued that "Mr. Mayor was like to have been pulled down at the time of preaching. And said, 'you have mass up now, God save it. How long it shall hold God knoweth'". Wagstaff, along with George Walden, the master he served, were bound to good behaviour and to appear before the mayor and aldermen again, but they were never called.[62]

Similarly, Richard Sotherton was twice bound in 1554 to good behaviour, each time with a £20 bond, once concerning unflattering remarks about Thomas Rose and again to prohibit him from trading in seditious books. He was never called.[63] The most extensive disciplinary action that the mayor and alderman took during the first year and a half of Mary's reign over a religious matter came in November 1554. Three men were accused of eating sausages on a Friday and were sentenced to prison. While it is not clear that this verdict was carried out, they were compelled to acknowledge their offence publicly, wearing papers on their heads.[64]

From 1555 when the central government began the persecution of Protestant heretics, religious conflict all but disappeared from the mayor's court.[65] The magistrates neither heard cases involving religious controversy, nor assisted local church authorities in the apprehension of religious nonconformists. Lay authorities were instrumental in the capture and arrest of many of the nearly three hundred who went to the stake during the two and a half years of the attempt to extirpate Protestantism. In the Essex town of Colchester, borough authorities gave substantial aid to church authorities in the apprehension of heretics. Norwich stands in marked contrast to the experience of many other communities in two important ways. First, only two residents of the city went to the stake and one other was taken into custody and forced to abjure.[66] By contrast 32 people were executed in London, which was probably four or five times Norwich's size.[67] Secondly, the magistrates' role in the three cases was minimal. It comes as no surprise that city magistrates were disinclined to become involved in the deadly persecution of religious dissidents and in effect shielded them from execution by so doing.

Still, in 1557 Elizabeth Cooper was put to death as an obstinate heretic at the Lollard's pit outside Norwich's Bishop's Gate. Cooper had previously renounced her Protestant beliefs, but was "greatly troubled inwardly" by it and one day interrupted a service at St Andrew's parish church to forswear her recantation publicly. An irate member of the congregation demanded that sheriff Thomas Sotherton place Cooper under arrest. From that imprisonment she went to the stake on 13 July along with Simon Miller of King's Lynn.[68] In the crowd that attended Cooper's execution was a young woman, Cicely Ormes, who exclaimed that "she would pledge them of the same cup that they drank on". In response, a Master Corbet, from the nearby village of Sprouston, took Ormes before the Chancellor of Norwich diocese. Ormes was confined in the bishop's prison after she denied transubstantiation during an examination. After subsequent interrogations Ormes was condemned to death, turned over to city sheriffs Thomas Sotherton and Leonard Sotherton, and incarcerated in the Guildhall prison where she languished for over a year. She died in September 1558 before a crowd of two hundred, according to Foxe.[69]

Although these two incidents occupy little space in Foxe's extensive accounts of the Marian persecution, they provide important evidence about tolerance of religious heterogeneity in Norwich.

Elizabeth Cooper and Cecily Ormes came to the attention of authorities in Norwich diocese and were eventually put to death because of their own public actions. Philip Hughes' analysis of the circumstances of arrest for victims of the Marian persecution for whom that information is available reveals that the majority had been pursued and then captured by lay authorities.[70] While sheriff Thomas Sotherton had placed Cooper under arrest and he and Leonard Sotherton had imprisoned Cecily Ormes, neither they nor any of the other civic officials had initiated proceedings against them. Ralph Houlbrooke has pointed out while Norwich diocese suffered the sharpest persecution it had even known under Mary, diocesan authorities there "seem to have been remarkably reluctant to grasp the nettle of urban dissent". In the case of Norwich, so too were urban authorities.[71] While there is evidence that municipal officials sometimes attended interrogations, sentencing and abjurations, it is also clear that Norwich magistrates did not offer the co-operation in apprehending heretics that was so common among lay officials elsewhere.[72]

The cases of Elizabeth Cooper and Cecily Ormes also strongly suggest that during the Marian period, reluctance to prosecute religious unorthodoxy did not reside solely among Norwich's magistrates. If the action of lay officials was the most common way in which heretics were apprehended according to Hughes, the next most common was the result of betrayal by a suspect's friends or family. Neither Cooper's nor Ormes' case fit this pattern and there is no evidence that there were any such betrayals in Norwich.[73] By Mary's accession, Norwich was one of the communities in England where Protestantism was strongest,[74] thus offering ample opportunity for religious traditionalists to expose their evangelical friends, neighbours and family members. They apparently declined to exploit that opportunity. In fact, sheriff Thomas Sotherton had not wanted to arrest Elizabeth Cooper for her outburst at St Andrew's. They had been "servants" together and friends, and he also shared Cooper's religious sentiments, as he later told Foxe. But he had been compelled to take her into custody, an action he deeply regretted. Although Sotherton's comments reflect only his own motivation, it is plausible to conjecture that they reflected a more widely-held feeling. City residents were willing to tolerate religious differences rather than condemn their neighbours to death.

In the history of the Marian persecution, the experience of Norwich clearly stands outside the mainstream. Neither the lay magistrates nor other members of the city's population sought out the unorthodox for punishment. Only blatant self-incrimination, which accounted for very few martyrs overall, resulted in a death sentence in Norwich. With the attention of diocesan authorities focused chiefly on Suffolk, the lack of co-operation from the laity goes a long way in explaining how the city escaped significant persecution.[75] Yet Norwich's experience was consistent with earlier patterns of handling religious dissidence there.

If the restoration of Catholicism did not prove to be an occasion for seeking vengeance in Norwich, neither was the re-introduction of Protestantism under Elizabeth. In the 1559 visitation of Norwich diocese, not a single priest serving a city cure was deprived of his living, nor were there any recorded acts of retribution, as there were elsewhere.[76] Neither did the mayor's court serve as a venue for settling old religious scores, even though by 1560 the magistrates were probably more religiously unified than they had been since the 1530s.[77]

Thus, the long custom of disregarding religious difference in Norwich continued. While there were a few cases of religious conflict that required the attention of the mayor and aldermen at the beginning of Elizabeth's reign, such instances of conflict disappeared largely from the record after the mid-1560s, with only sporadic recurrences afterwards. Even in the mid-Elizabethan years when, at the nation's political centre, parliament passed increasingly draconian penal legislation against Catholics, the magistrates of Norwich did not seek to enforce them. When the ministry of Puritan clerics in the city provoked contention, the mayor and aldermen handled that too in what had become the conventional way.

During the first five years of Elizabeths's reign, three complaints came to the attention of city officials, which hinted at the continued existence of religious division among city residents. In June 1561, Laurence Hodger declared to another man that despite the many "rebels' hearts" in the latter's parish of St Peter, the rood loft there would soon be demolished. A month later Edward Boston testified that John Seman had referred to the new Bishop of Norwich, John Parkhurst, as a fornicator, whoremaster and adulterer. Three years later in May 1564, Richard Tanner told the magistrates how Jeremy Gardener had threatened cathedral prebendary Nicholas Smith with a bow and arrow, intending to rid the world of an "old Papish knave". Tanner's intervention saved Smith from serious injury or worse. No action was taken against any defendants in the three cases.[78]

After 1564, the incidence of such religious disputes that resulted in a court case declined dramatically, probably reflecting both the attenuation of the Catholic community in Norwich and magisterial unwillingness to seek out Catholic nonconformists.[79] Outside of Norwich, the central government also declined to root out and punish Catholics, although it by no means advanced an official policy of toleration.[80] But such leniency towards Catholics tended to evaporate in the aftermath of the northern earls' revolt of 1569, the papal bull of the following year and subsequent discoveries of plots against the Queen's life. Parliament passed increasingly severe statutes against Catholics aimed both at the laity and seminary priests arriving from abroad.[81] Yet, in Norwich, city rulers did not participate in the official upsurge of hostility to Catholics.

It is not always clear how suspected recusants were apprehended, as some of the documentation from these cases survives in the form of correspondence with the central government. In January 1583 the mayor and five JPs penned a letter to notify the Privy Council of their recent arrest of a number of "suspected persons", who allegedly had heard mass, absented themselves from church and wore "hallowed beads". The magistrates had bound some to reappear before them and were writing to the Council to ask for mercy for the others who "seem to be penitent". No reply from the Council survives, but there was no further account of any of these recusants in city records.[82] A few dealings with recusants appeared in the court books. In 1585 it was noted that two city clerics, responding to a letter from the Privy Council, had scrutinized "certain books, papers and other popish stuff" belong to the gentleman Henry Hubbard. They then burned some of those objects "openly . . . in the market". It does not appear any civic officials participated in the investigation or destruction of Hubbard's goods. Nor did they detain or otherwise punish him.[83] Some years later, in June 1612, Frances Clapham appeared at the mayor's court where she was to take the oath of supremacy, the reason for which was not noted. Clapham, however, "refused to take the same, saying that she hath been told by divers priests of her religion that she shall be damned if she take it". Not bound over or sent elsewhere for examination, Clapham was released.[84] Recusants who attracted the notice of the Norwich authorities came to little or no harm.

Religious conflict in Elizabethan and Jacobean Norwich did not centre solely on Catholic recusancy. Norwich was also an important centre of Puritanism, the emergence of which was a source of tension among some of the inhabitants. When confronted with evidence of such strife, magistrates worked to defuse it. In August 1589, six men complained to the court that a local minister named Yould had asserted that "the preachers be dolts . . . and that the said preachers as Mr. More and others are not worthy to carry their books". "Mr. More" was John More, the curate of St Andrew's parish and leader of the city's Puritan clergy. The court decided to commit Yould to prison until he found surety for his good behaviour but there is no indication that the sentence was ever carried out.[85] Similarly, Robert Munford's case disappeared from the record after the court bound him to good behaviour in June 1610 for, among other things, "using many reviling speeches against Mr. Wells, preacher, in disgrace of him and his ministry".[86]

Separatists were also active in Norwich. Among the most notable were the so-called "Brownists", whose church was established there in the early 1580s by Robert Browne and Robert Harrison. The church outlasted the hasty departure of its founders to the continent after Browne had been imprisoned on several occasions during preaching tours around East Anglia. It was still known to be in existence at the death of Elizabeth.[87] But the activities of the Brownists and of other separatists have left no traces in Norwich city records. The persecution and executions that they suffered did not originate with Norwich city governors. Diversity of religious opinion continued to be implicitly tolerated by the magistrates into the seventeenth century.

It has often been said that the sixteenth century was "an age of religion", an age when "God mattered". Religious belief lay at the core of late medieval personal and communal identity. In the Holy Roman Empire for example, the town was not "a purely utilitarian association but was rather the place to which the life of each citizen was bound", a "sacred society". Consequently at the Reformation, "division in religion was inevitable, because everyone agreed that anyone not of their church was against it, heretic and schismatic".[88] The notion of tolerating that division in religion would not gain widespread currency until the next century when Europe emerged from long and bloody religious wars.

Yet the example of Norwich's magistracy demonstrates that the experience of the Reformation was not always characterized by intense conflict and prejudice. From the 1530s, city leaders tacitly tolerated the fragmentation of opinion that was emerging among the local population by neglecting to uphold the letter of Tudor religious law. They did not track down the religiously unorthodox and the overwhelming majority of such defendants received the same lenient treatment at their hands, no matter what their religious convictions. This practice prevented religious discord from escalating and potentially destroying the civil community. It probably originated as a solution to the civic leadership's own lack of religious unity at the outset of the Reformation, a situation that continued until the early Elizabethan years. By refusing to engage in such ideological struggles, Norwich avoided the internecine battles and purges that debilitated other communities.[89]

If the Reformation was not the occasion of constant and violent religious quarrels in Norwich, it was not because God did not matter there. There is nothing to suggest that religious feeling among city magistrates was not as deep as it was elsewhere in England or that religious differences among them were trivial. Rather, Norwich magistrates in the sixteenth century accepted that communal harmony was more important than religious uniformity and that religious unity need not be the most important criterion for the successful conduct of civic life, a principle that continued to inform city politics into the seventeenth century.[90]

Notes

1. On Castellio and his work *De haereticis an sint persequendi*, his most well-known tract on religious freedom, see Hans R. Guggisberg, *Basel in the sixteenth century: aspects of the city republic before, during and after the Reformation* (St. Louis, MO, 1982), ch. IV.

2. O. P. Grell, J. I. Israel & N. Tyacke (eds), *From persecution to toleration: the glorious revolution and religion in England* (Oxford, 1991), introduction.

3. J. Israel, "William III and toleration," in *ibid.*, pp. 129–70.

4. Compare for example, J. J. Scarisbrick, *The Reformation and the English people* (Oxford, 1984) and C. Haigh, *English Reformations: religion, politics and society under the Tudors* (Oxford, 1993).

5. J. Pound, *Tudor and Stuart Norwich* (Chichester, 1988), p. 28.

6. British Library (hereafter BL), Cotton MS Cleopatra E V, fo. 389r–390v. The question of Gonville Hall graduates is discussed by J. Venn, *Biographical history of Gonville and Caius College*, vol. 1, (Cambridge, 1897) p. xviii.

7. R. Houlbrooke, *Church courts and the people during the English Reformation 1520–1570* (Oxford, 1979), p. 225 and D. MacCulloch, *Suffolk and the Tudors: politics and religion in an English county 1500–1600* (Oxford, 1986), pp. 148–49.

8. According to R. Houlbrooke, in "Persecution of heresy and protestantism in the diocese of Norwich under Henry VIII", *Norfolk Archaeology* **25**, 1972, pp. 322–23, none of the eight people so apprehended were residents of the city. However, Norman Tanner notes one of them, the priest Thomas Ayers who was burnt at Eccles in 1510, as having been from Norwich. See his *The church in late medieval Norwich 1370–1532* (Toronto, 1984), p. 163, where he also discusses the fifteenth-century trials.

9. Houlbrooke, *Church courts*, p. 230.

10. See for example, *n* 15 and *n* 27 below.

11. On Robert Necton see J. A. Guy, *The public career of Sir Thomas More* (New Haven & London, 1980), pp. 108, 168; J. F. Davis, *Heresy and Reformation in the South-East of England, 1520–1559* (London, 1983), pp. 45, 54, 59–60, 64 and J. Fines, *A biographical register of early English Protestants and others opposed to the Roman Catholic Church*, pt. 2, unpublished typescript (West Sussex Institute of Education, 1985), N1. Copies are available at the Institute of Historical Research, London, and Stanford University's Green Library. See also S. Brigden, *London and the Reformation* (Oxford, 1989), pp. 115, 118, 121–122, 180, 196.

12. Most historians agree that Bilney was not a heretic strictly speaking. J. F. Davis, "The trials of Thomas Bylney and the English Reformation," *Historical Journal* **24**, 1981, esp. pp. 787–89 and *Heresy and Reformation*, pp. 41–66 and MacCulloch, *Suffolk and the Tudors*, pp. 149–55; Tanner, *Late medieval Norwich*, pp. 164–5; E. M. Sheppard, "The Reformation and the citizens of Norwich," *Norfolk Archaeology* **38**, 1981, p. 48; Haigh, *English Reformations*, p. 67.

13. L. P. Fairfield, *John Bale: mythmaker for the English Reformation* (West Lafayette, 1976), pp. 39, 186 n. 35. See also BL Cotton MS Cleopatra E V fo. 365r; Haigh, *English Reformations*, p. 189.

14. J. Pratt (ed.) *The acts and monuments of John Foxe*, vol. 8 (Religious Tract Society, London, nd), p. 583.

15. Religious conflict was not unknown before 1535 however. In June 1534,

alderman Reginald Littleprowe wrote to Thomas Cromwell to report on the activities of the rector of Norwich's St Augustine parish, William Isabells. Isabells had appeared before the mayor and aldermen on account of reckless speech and had also spent a short time in jail. Littleprowe wrote to say that he was sending to London depositions taken at Norwich and to ask what to do with the priest's goods, worth about £40. Isabells appeared before the Norwich Quarter Sessions where he was bound in recognizance to keep the king's peace. He was never called before any branch of the city government again. He later became rector of a parish outside Norwich and died about 1540. See G. R. Elton, *Policy and police: the enforcement of the Reformation in the age of Thomas Cromwell* (Cambridge, 1972), pp. 136–7; J. Gairdner (ed.) *Letters and papers, foreign and domestic of the reign of Henry VIII*, vol. 7 (1883, rpt. Vaduz, 1965), p. 298 #779, p. 304, #796 and Norfolk Record Office (hereafter NRO) Quarter Sessions Minute Book 1511–1541, fos. 139v–r, where the year of Isabells' appearance is erroneously given as 37 Henry VIII (1545–46). Two identical wills were proved in the NRO Norwich Consistory Court for William Isabells. The first, 302–305 Hyll in February 1540 and the second, 245 Whytefoot, in February 1544.

16. I owe this suggestion to Dr Ralph Houlbrooke. See his *Church courts*, pp. 216–17, 222.

17. Brigden, *London and the Reformation*, pp. 275, 290, 300, 312.

18. NRO Mayor's Court Book (hereafter MCB) 1534–40, pp. 13–15. Ralph Houlbrooke has pointed out that Myles' remarks about the sacrament probably represent his misunderstanding of new eucharistic doctrines that may have been taught in the city around this time. See "Persecution of heresy," p. 312.

19. NRO MCB 1534–40, p. 21 and MCB 1534–49, fo. 8r where the case is recorded again with only minor variations.

20. NRO MCB 1540–49, p. 320; see above pp. 95–6.

21. NRO MCB 1534–49, fo. 22r.

22. NRO MCB 1534–40, p. 156. Becket's feast day had been abrogated in 1536 and in 1538 a royal proclamation had dictated that his name be deleted from all books. See D. Cressy, *Bonfires and bells: national memory and the protestant calendar in Elizabethan and Stuart England* (Berkeley, Los Angeles, 1989), pp. 4–10 and P. L. Hughes & J. F. Larkin, (eds) *Tudor royal proclamations*, vol. 1, (New Haven & London, 1964) pp. 270–76.

23. NRO MCB 1540–49, p. 21.

24. Elton, *Policy and police* pp. 16–18. See also NRO, REG (Bishops' Registers) 30, Tanner's Index, and Public Record Office (hereafter PRO), Prerogative Court of Canterbury (hereafter PCC) 13 Chayre, for Harcocke's will, which was proved in March 1563.

25. 31 Henry VIII, c. 14, reprinted in H. Gee & W. J. Hardy, (eds) *Documents illustrative of English church history compiled from original sources* (1896; reprinted London, 1921), pp. 303–319, esp. p. 316.

26. Brigden, *London and the Reformation* pp. 320–40.

27. However, the Protestant reformer John Bale claimed that in 1545 his wife Dorothy was apprehended and examined by Norwich mayor Robert Rugge (brother of the bishop) and former sheriff John Corbett. There is no record of this incident in the mayor's court books, suggesting that Rugge and Corbett acted in an unofficial capacity. See Bale's *The actes of Englysh votaryes*, The English experience: its record in early printed books published in facsimile, n. 906 (1560; reprinted Amsterdam, 1979), pt. 2, sigs. o3v–o5r.

28. The 1543 Act for the Advancement of True Religion, 34 & 35 Henry VIII c. 1, restricted access to the English Bible among women and the lower orders, although women of gentle or noble status were exempt from its provisions.

29. NRO MCB 1534–49, fo. 51v; MCB 1540–49, p. 323; Houlbrooke, "Persecution of heresy," p. 311; C. E. Moreton, *The Townshends and their world: gentry, law, and land in Norfolk c.1450–1551* (Oxford, 1992), pp. 34–35.

30. This has most recently and convincingly been done by Eamon Duffy in *The stripping of the altars: traditional religion in England c.1400–1580* (New Haven & London, 1992), ch. 15.

31. NRO Norwich Consistory Court (hereafter NCC) 127 Hyll.

32. PRO PCC 12 Tashe.

33. PRO PCC F 16 Pynnyng.

34. See the wills of Leonard Spencer, written and proved in 1539 (PRO PCC 16 Crumwell) and Edmund Wood, written and proved in 1548 (PRO PCC F 19 Populwell).

35. Again most of the evidence comes from wills. In 1548, Thomas Grewe discreetly committed his soul to God alone but also bequeathed to his daughter Alice "a pair of beads of coral with pater nosters silver and gilt". The preamble of the 1551 will of Grewe's colleague Richard Suckling was almost identical but Suckling left a bequest so that John Barret and Thomas Rose (and two other clergymen) would "preach three godly sermons to the edifying of the people". In Mary's reign, there are still hints of religious diversity on the aldermanic bench. Thomas Cock who died just months before the Queen committed his soul to "God omnipotent and to Our Blessed Lady Saint Mary and to all the holy company of heaven" and provided for a priest to say Mass for his soul for a year. His colleague Thomas Gray, who had died about a year before him left no obit bequests, but willed £3 6s. 8d. to John Barret "to pray for me" and asked that "mine executrix shall give and dispose in true preaching and setting forth of the word of God in the city of Norwich ten marks". See NRO NCC 342 Wymer (Grewe), NCC 185 Lyncolne (Suckling); NRO MC 16/1 390 X 1, "Rev. J. F. Williams' notes on ACT Books 1544–55, 1577–92, 1595–1602" and Houlbrooke, *Church courts*, pp. 70–71 (Leche); NCC 290 Jerves (Cock).

36. Between 1535 and 1547 nine cases of religious conflict were heard in the mayor's court and a tenth, that concerning the priest William Isabells, was

heard before the city's Quarter Sessions. During Edward VI's reign, there were 29 such cases (with two defendants appearing more than once).

37. NRO MCB 1540–49, p. 374.
38. *Ibid.*, pp. 403–4.
39. NRO MCB 1540–49, pp. 454–55.
40. *Ibid.*, p. 432. See also pp. 433, 467, 468.
41. Brigden, *London and the Reformation*, pp. 429–30.
42. NRO MCB 1534–49, fos. 52r–53v and MCB 1540–49, pp. 402–3. Neither man took the court's warning to heart. Debney was later involved in incidents at Rockland and Bramerton noted above, and Conyers went on to preach and conduct Protestant services for Kett's rebels. On Conyers, see A. Fletcher, *Tudor rebellions* (3rd edn London, 1983), p. 66; J. Cornwall, *Revolt of the peasantry 1549* (London, 1977), pp. 149–150.
43. NRO MCB 1534–49, f. 53r, which is repeated in MCB 1540–47, p. 427; NRO MCB 1534–49, f. 54 (a) r; MCB 1534–49, fo. 58r; MCB 1534–49, fo. 59r.
44. NRO MCB 1534–49 fo. 59v.
45. *Ibid.*, fo. 62r.
46. See NRO MCB 1540–49, p. 417 and Norwich Sessions Depositions, Book 1A, fos. 108v–109r.
47. NRO MCB 1540–49, p. 538.
48. NRO MCB 1534–49, fo. 54(a)r. There were reports from around the country at this time of the abandonment of this traditional rite. See for example, Brigden, *London and the Reformation*, p. 435 and R. Whiting, *The blind devotion of the people: popular religion and the English Reformation* (Cambridge, 1989), p. 71.
49. NRO MCB 1534–49, fo. 63v.
50. For examples of these cases see: NRO, MCB 1549–55, pp. 3, 82 and Walter Rye (ed.) *Depositions taken before the mayor and aldermen of Norwich 1549–1567* (Norwich, 1905), pp. 18–22. Rye suggests, in Appendix II, that the depositions extracted in this volume were probably taken preliminary to a session in the mayor's court.
51. NRO MCB 1549–55, p. 192.
52. Brigden, *London and the Reformation*, pp. 526–30. Between Mary's accession and the end of 1554, there were ten incidents involving religious conflict that definitely came before the court. One defendant, Richard Sotherton, appeared twice. See above, p. 102. Two other episodes are recorded in a loose bunch of depositions; see Rye (ed.) *Depositions*, pp. 39–40 and 56–58.
53. P. L. Hughes & J. F. Larkin, (eds) *Tudor royal proclamations* (New Haven & London, 1969), vol. 2, p. 390.
54. NRO MCB 1549–55, p. 294.
55. R. Houlbrooke, in *Church courts*, p. 166, has observed that St Andrew's was singled out in December 1554 in the drive to enforce re-equipment of city parish churches.

56. NRO MCB 1549–55, p. 319; J. R. Dasent *et al.* (eds), *Acts of the privy council of England* (London, 1890–1907), *1552–1554*, p. 394.

57. N. Williams, *Thomas Howard fourth Duke of Norfolk* (London, 1964), pp. 19–21, 27–31.

58. Perhaps such a concern helps to explain why William Mason and Robert Gold were set on the pillory in late May and early June 1554, respectively, for "devising unfitting songs against the queen's majesty". The pair were the only two so treated by the magistrates for religious offences to that date. D. Galloway (ed.) *Records of early English drama: Norwich 1540–1642* (Toronto, 1984), pp. 33–35.

59. Watson had challenged Bishop Rugge on a sermon the latter had preached in 1539, had himself preached to Kett's rebels and had most recently served as a steward to Thomas Cranmer. See Elton, *Policy and police*, pp. 138–41; Houlbrooke, *Church courts*, pp. 230–31; J. Bale, *Scriptores . . . catalogus* vol. 9 (London, 1557), pp. 729–30; J. Strype, *Memorials of Cranmer* in *Works* (Oxford, 1840), pp. 450, 610; *Dictionary of national biography* (hereafter *DNB*); J. Foster, *Alumni Oxonienses, 1500–1714* vol. 4 (Oxford, 1892), p. 1583; C. H. Garrett, *The Marian exiles: a study in the origins of Elizabethan puritanism* (1938: reprinted Cambridge, 1961), pp. 322–23; B. L. Beer, " 'The commoyson in Norfolk, 1549': a narrative of popular rebellion in sixteenth-century England". *Journal of Medieval and Renaissance Studies* **6**, 1976, pp. 73–99; Fines, *A biographical register* , pt 2, W8.

60. Barret had been the rector of that parish since 1550; see the DNB and J. & J. A. Venn (eds), *Alumni Cantabrigiensis: Part I, from the earliest times to 1751* vol. 1 (Cambridge, 1922), p. 96.

61. NRO MCB 1549–55, pp. 332–4.

62. NRO MCB 1549–55, p. 295.

63. NRO MCB 1549–55, pp. 314, 382. Sotherton was a member of a prominent civic family; see T. Hawes (ed.) *An index to Norwich city officers 1453–1835*, Norfolk Record Society, vol. 52 (n p., 1986), p. 142.

64. NRO MCB 1549–55, pp. 392, 394.

65. In February 1557 the court set Richard Vere, a resident of Strabroke, Suffolk, on the pillory for having circulated a treasonous letter. The sentence was carried out at the explicit command of the Privy Council. See NRO, MCB 1555–62, pp. 113, 134.

66. The martyrdoms of Cecily Orme and Elizabeth Cooper will be discussed below. Thomas Wolman, a Norwich grocer, abjured the belief that the martyr William Carman had "died well for that he did affirm and say that he did believe that Christ was not present in the sacrament of the altar" and his declaration to one George Redman "that the sacrament should be his God and not mine"; BL, Harleian MS 421, fo. 154.

67. Brigden, *London and the Reformation*, pp. 608–12.

68. Pratt (ed.) *Acts and monuments*, vol. 8, pp. 380–81.

69. Pratt (ed.) *Acts and monuments*, vol. 8, pp. 427–29.

70. According to Hughes, Foxe identified 273 Marian martyrs. Hughes found that 102 of those cases described how the victims had come into the custody of the authorities. Sixty (58.82%) had been apprehended through the actions of justices, constables or through a sworn inquest, while 13 (12.74%) were turned over by friends or family. Twelve (11.76%) had already been in prison before the revival of the heresy laws, eight (7.84%) were seized through their own public actions, and seven (6.86%) detentions were a result of clerical initiative. One (0.98%) person had been turned in by someone hoping for a reward and another's (0.98%) arrest had been directly ordered by the Privy Council. P. Hughes *The Reformation in England*, vol. 2 (London, 1953), p. 274.

71. Houlbrooke, *Church courts*, pp. 231, 233.

72. *Ibid.*, p. 233; "Rev. J. F. Williams' notes," pp. 13–14, 25, 69, 75, 81, 85.

73. The circumstances of Thomas Wolman's apprehension are not known.

74. A. G. Dickens, "The early expansion of Protestantism in England, 1520–1558," *Archiv für Reformationsgeschichte* **78**, 1987; Haigh, *English Reformations*, p. 197.

75. Suffolk, where there were a large number of persecuting JPs, provided over two-thirds of the victims from the diocese of Norwich. Houlbrooke, *Church courts*, p. 237.

76. At Exeter, Catholics were forced to destroy images by throwing them into a fire before the cathedral. See Haigh, *English Reformations*, p. 243 for this and other examples. See also H. Gee, *The Elizabethan clergy and the settlement of religion 1558–1564* (Oxford, 1898), pp. 252–269 for a list of clergy deprived between 1558 and 1564.

77. In the epidemic that swept Norwich in 1558–59 ten aldermen died, among whom were some of the city's most senior and Catholic aldermen. On the dead, see F. Blomefield, *An essay towards the topographical history of the county of Norfolk*, vol. 3 (London, 1806), pp. 277–278.

78. Rye (ed.) *Depositions* pp. 65–67, 78. If indeed these depositions were preliminary to an action in the mayor's court, in each instance the case was never heard by that body.

79. In 1569, however, an episopal visitation revealed that the rood loft still remained intact in the parish of St Gregory. A group of parishioners protected it from demolition for at least another four years. NRO, VIS 1/3 (Parkhurst's 1569 visitation), n.p.; Houlbrooke, *Church courts*, p. 168; R. Houlbrooke, (ed.) *The letter book of John Parkhurst bishop of Norwich compiled during the years 1571–5* (Norfolk Record Society **43**, 1974–75), p. 212.

80. Haigh, *English Reformations*, p. 262.

81. P. McGrath, *Papists and puritans under Elizabeth I* (London, 1967), chs 8, 10, 12.

82. J. L'Estrange (ed.) *The eastern counties collectanea: being notes and queries on subjects relating to the counties of Norfolk, Suffolk, Essex and Cambridge* (Norwich, 1872–73), pp. 79–80. For other dealings with the Privy Council

about recusants that left no other trace in city records, see Dasent *et al.* (eds), *Acts of the privy council of England, 1587–1588*, p. 368; *1591*, p. 144.

83. NRO MCB 1582–87, p. 387.

84. NRO MCB 1603–15, fo. 363r.

85. NRO MCB 1587–95, p. 308; see also pp. 540, 576. On J. More, see P. Collinson, *The Elizabethan Puritan movement* (Berkeley & Los Angeles, 1967), pp. 141, 186–87, 203–4.

86. NRO MCB 1603–15, f. 295r. On Wells see NRO Assembly Minute Book 1585–1613, fo. 137v.

87. On the Brownists see, for example, McGrath, *Papists and Puritans*, pp. 304–7; B. R. White, *The English separatist tradition: from the Marian martyrs to the Pilgrim Fathers* (Oxford, 1971), Ch. 3; M. R. Watts, *The Dissenters*, vol. 1 (Oxford, 1978), pp. 266–34.

88. Haigh, *English Reformations*, p. 285; B. Moeller, *Imperial cities and the reformation: three essays*, ed. and trans. H. C. Erik Midelfort & M. U. Edwards, Jr. (Philadelphia, 1972), pp. 43–44; Brigden, *London and the Reformation*, p. 378.

89. P. Clark, "Reformation and radicalism in Kentish towns *c.*1500–1553," in W. J. Mommsen *et al.*, (eds) *Stadtbürgertum und Adel in der Reformation: Studien zur Sozialgeschichte der Reformation in England and Deutschland* (Stuttgart, 1979), pp. 115–22 on Canterbury where, in the 1530s and 1540s, radical and conservative factions vied for control of town government.

90. There is evidence from other communities in England and on the continent that the Reformation was not always disruptive and the source of fierce conflict. See R. W. Scribner, "Civic unity and the reformation in Erfurt", in Scribner, *Popular culture and popular movements in Reformation Germany* (London, 1987), pp. 185–216; M. Konnert, "Urban values versus religious passion: Chalons-sur-Marne during the wars of religion", *Sixteenth Century Journal* **20**, 1989, pp. 387–405; and J. P. Ward, "Religious diversity and guild unity in early modern London". I am grateful to Dr Ward for allowing me to read his unpublished manuscript. The separation of religion from other aspects of life in the early modern period has been most recently addressed in C. J. Sommerville, *The secularization of early modern England* (Oxford, 1992). On Stuart Norwich, see J. T. Evans, *Seventeenth-century Norwich: politics, religion, and government, 1620–1690* (Oxford, 1979).

5

From Catholic to Protestant: the changing meaning of testamentary religious provisions in Elizabethan London

David Hickman

In September 1563, nearly five years after the accession of Elizabeth I, William Dane, alderman of the City of London, drew up his will. He bequeathed his soul to God,

> the which hast made me and given thy only son to become man and die for my sins, and the third day he rose again for my justification, and opened the kingdom of heaven to all true believers. Also I bequeath my body to the earth to be buried in Christian burial according to the order of Christ's church. This I believe whether I live or die; I am our Lord's. I hope that I shall find both grace and mercy for my sins of God the Father, even for Jesus Christ's sake, in him I believe, he my redeemer, he liveth for ever and ever. This my faith and hope I lay up in my mind, the mind of my soul, trusting only to be saved through the merits of Jesus Christ, God and man, which is in heaven on the right hand of God the father. He shall in the end of the world be judge over all the quick and the dead, to whom with God the father and the Holy Ghost be all honour and glory, for ever, world without end, amen.[1]

Over the past two decades the value of such will preambles as a guide to the personal religious inclinations of the testator has attracted increasingly sceptical attention. Since the first systematic work on wills as a source for lay religious belief was undertaken by Professor

Dickens, much emphasis has been placed upon the preamble, and the significance of the diminishing place of the Virgin and saints in this context. Together with the increasing frequency during the middle of the sixteenth century of a form of preamble bequeathing the soul to God and Christ alone, this shift in the pattern of formulae employed by testators has been linked to a corresponding spread of disillusionment with traditional Catholic beliefs and a growth in the number of testators espousing evangelical opinions.[2] Yet as Dr Duffy and others have shown, the correlation is by no means so clear-cut.[3] By the middle of the sixteenth century testators of diametrically opposed religious opinions were employing identical preamble formulae. Indeed, for J. D. Alsop "in a large number of testaments the preamble was merely a formula, unrelated to the beliefs of the testators". He further notes that without supporting evidence from the religious bequests contained in the main body of a will, the preamble alone must be discounted as "what may well be a ritualised or impersonal statement of questionable utility".[4]

Nevertheless some preambles exist which, taken together with the religious bequests in the will, do demonstrate a fully Reformed conception of predestination and limited atonement, such as that of Peter Simmonds, Mercer and common councillor of London, drawn up in April 1586:

> First I here pronounce and believe in the almighty God my heavenly father, who without beginning of his gracious goodness in time made me and all the world, and in his said mercy, when we were not, *chose and elected before the creation of this mortal world all such as in Christ shall receive the fruition of his glorious kingdom*, whereof I say and hope I am one, so that in conclusion *all things is done [sic] in his majesty's providence and foreknowledge*, both heretofore present and in the end. Secondly I do believe in Jesus Christ . . . who in his mercy hath redeemed me in his glorious death and *all others God's chosen* from sin, death and hell, and now, sitting at the right hand of God the father, doth make intercession for us his people; renouncing and forsaking all other mediation or redemption besides him . . . so that all other means brought in by man and his invention contrary to this our faith, I account it to be most

blasphemous unto the precious blood of this our saviour Christ. Thirdly I do believe in God the holy ghost, which, as he is without beginning, so doth he of his gracious goodness sanctify me and all the other elect people of God.[5]

However, such clear statements of Reformed belief are relatively rare, even among the longer, less formulaic testaments of the wealthy. Hence the religious bequests contained in the body of the will assume much greater significance, particularly in view of Dr Haigh's suggestion that a substantial proportion of the English laity in effect remained devoted to a form of "works" religion, quite alien to the style of piety disseminated by Protestant preachers, and having rather more in common with older Catholic notions of good works and salvation.[6]

Some aspects of late medieval forms of piety certainly did survive in lay devotional practice after 1558. Yet it is not necessarily the case that such survivals or apparent continuities bore an unaltered religious meaning, or that their presence implies that the English Church of the later sixteenth century failed to meet the religious needs of the majority of the faithful. Ephemeral printed matter from London has been employed to suggest that the gradual modification of traditional pious forms of expression enabled the emergence of a post-Reformation lay religious culture that was clearly different from that of the Catholic past.[7] Similarly the religious calendar was adapted to meet the new religious context. Many of the former saints' feast days were abrogated, but the remainder received a Protestant facelift, and new ones such as Elizabeth's accession day were instituted in celebration of the triumph of a Protestant nation.[8]

At the political and commercial centre of that nation lay the City of London whose ruling class, composed in the main of middling to wealthy merchants, represents one of the special interest groups that Christopher Haigh regarded as unusually susceptible to the calls of early evangelists for the overthrow of papal and clerical authority, albeit for essentially worldly objectives.[9] Yet scrutiny of the testamentary material generated by this body suggests that at the Protestant heartland of England the survival of certain older patterns of pious behaviour and the continuity of some will formulae in an altered religious context, far from weakening the impact of the

Reformation, in fact greatly aided in the establishment of a committed Protestantism among the powerful mercantile class of the capital.[10]

In the sixteenth and early seventeenth centuries the City of London, excluding the rapidly expanding suburbs to east and west and the City of Westminster, was governed by an oligarchic corporation headed by the Lord Mayor. His chief executive arm was provided by the court of aldermen, twenty-six strong after 1550, while the legislative body of the City comprised the court of common council, whose members were elected annually from each of the wards of the City. No firm figures can be established for the number of commoners at any one time before the latter part of the seventeenth century, but in Elizabeth's time the number seems to have stood at around 200, rising to perhaps 250 or more by the 1590s.[11] There existed a clear division between commoners and aldermen: the latter had been required to have property and good debts to the value of £1000 since 1469, were entitled to wear distinctive red robes as a mark of office, and perhaps as significantly, regularly described themselves as aldermen of London in their wills. Commoners do not appear to have used their office as an indicator of personal status in this manner, nor do they seem to have been subject to any formal property qualification. In practice, however, the great majority of aldermen served for at least some time as commoners before rising to higher rank, and it would be a mistake to draw too firm a line between the members of the two bodies in terms of social and economic class.

The rulers of the City also provided London's parishes with most of their churchwardens and local officers,[12] and the pious provisions made in their wills reflect the centrality of the parish community and the celebration of the eucharist in their religious lives throughout the period of the Tudor Reformation. With very few exceptions, the wills dating from the earlier sixteenth century all contain token bequests to the high altar of the testator's parish church in symbolic reparation for unpaid tithes, and often for the health of the testator's soul.[13] Many testators bequeathed money to provide for tapers to burn on the high altar at the celebration of high mass; thus in 1540 William Cauntwell, fruiterer and a common councillor, left such a taper "in the honour and worship of the blessed sacrament of the altar".[14] Intramural burial was not only a mark of social status, but intimately bound up with the continued bestowal of God's grace upon the soul of the testator after his earthly death. Consequently we find a marked preference among elite testators for burial near the high altar, before the rood that stood between nave and chancel, or beneath the altar or image of a favourite saint.[15]

It is clear that these portions of the church building retained considerable funerary significance for testators long after the Reformation changes. The chancel and choir, and connecting chapels, remained prestigious sites for burials; Thomas Colsell, Mercer, requested in 1593 a burial in the chancel of his parish church "between the communion table and the wall of the south side of the same chancel".[16] A favoured place of burial, in losing the connotations of salvation through proximity to the sacrament and altar, came to reflect the importance of regular attendance at divine service in a Protestant church. The rationale for the location of a burial was thus adapted in the course of Elizabeth's reign to accord with altered religious priorities.

Hence we also find numerous requests for burial near the pew in which the testator had customarily sat for the service.[17] In 1568 John Nashe, Draper, requested burial in the chancel of his parish church, St Martin Orgar, "against or near the seat where I used commonly to sit", and a year later William Andrews, a member of common council in the mid-1560s and free of the Vintners' Company requested burial "in the parish church of St Dunstan in the East of London in the north chapel over against my pew there",[18] while in April 1586 Peter Simmonds, Mercer, requested burial in the newly-built churchyard at Bethlem, outside Bishopsgate, "right before the pulpit". Simmonds' request, indeed, reflects a significant translation of an old custom into a specifically Protestant context.[19] The spital sermons, conducted at St Mary of Bethlehem, better known perhaps as Bedlam, had long been part of the calendar of civic events attended by the City elite, in the same manner as the Paul's Cross sermons.[20] Since Edward Dering's interment, however, the burial ground had become popular with Puritans since it was easier to perform funerals there in accordance with Genevan practice.[21]

Following the dismantling of the Marian religious infrastructure at the beginning of Elizabeth's reign, and the consequent abolition of the doctrine of purgatory and the requiem masses attendant upon a burial, considerable changes may be observed in the rationale under-pinning funerary practice. Traditionally testators had sometimes requested that their funerals be performed "without pomp and vainglory", and had prescribed limits to the quantities of money handed out as doles to the poor, and to the number of mourners in black to attend the service.[22] Such deprecation of worldly display became increasingly apparent over the Elizabethan period, partly as a direct result of religious reform, although to some extent this also represented a more general trend in Western European mortuary practice.[23] Emmanuel Lucar's detailed provisions for his own funeral, drawn up in March 1573, may serve to illustrate the nature of a commoner's funeral obsequies in the later sixteenth century:

> I will my body to be wrapped in linen cloth, and to be put in a coffin, and to be buried in the vault which at my cost and charge was and is made in the church yard of the parish church of St Butolph next Billingsgate in London . . . And I will that so many scutchions of my arms and also of my wives' arms be made, painted upon paper as shall be requisite, and that the same scutchions shall be fastened and fixed upon the hearse cloth and ornaments used at my burial. And I will my body lying in the said coffin to be borne at the day of my burial from my said house with six poor men to the parish church . . . And that a godly and well learned preacher be appointed then and there to preach. And I desire the said preacher then and there to instruct and persuade the audience well to consider and know that all flesh shall die and turn to earth, the time uncertain. And I will, the sermon and ceremonies being done there for me, that the said six poor men shall bear my body from the said church unto the said vault, and the priest and clerk of the same parish church, having said the prayers accustomed at the burial of the dead, that the said poor men . . . shall put and lay my body forthwith in the said vault . . . And concerning the ringing of bells at the day of my burial I refer it to the discretion of mine executors.[24]

Lucar provided black mourning gowns for his wife, his children and their spouses and his servants to wear at the funeral, and requested the livery of his company to attend the burial. This is the typical form of burial for an Elizabethan common councillor anxious to keep pomp and expense to a decent minimum. Indeed, the fact that the funeral of a prominent citizen was as much a public as a private occasion imposed certain obligations beyond private considerations. Thomas Polle, Cordwainer, willed his body to be brought to the church "with priests and clerks convenient, so that thereby neither any law or ordinance be infringed, or any just cause to the people given to be offended". Common councillor Henry Viner, in April 1571, simply required burial "according to the use of the Church of England", and Richard Whitehill, Merchant Taylor, exhorted his executors "that eschewing all vain and superfluous charges on my said burial or dinner, they will chiefly relieve the poor".[25] However such restrictions were beginning to acquire a specifically non-Catholic interpretation. As Thomas Sares, Haberdasher, expressed it in 1587:

> forasmuch as sumptuous burials neither pleaseth God nor profiteth the soul of him as it is made for or done, but rather doth breed and increase malice and hatred amongst allies, friends and neighbours for that all of them receiveth not, nor hath legacies and bequests to them willed and bequeathed alike of their ally and friend departed, which malice and hatred much displeaseth God.[26]

Others made even stronger denials of the spiritual utility of the usual customs. Richard Peter, Brewer, made an earnest request of his wife Anne "that, in respect of singing and jangling of bells and wearing of black gowns and black coats, which my conscience beareth me witness is altogether superfluous and vain, and neither good nor profitable to my soul" she keep them to a minimum.[27] George Dodd, Vintner, in 1586 ordered that "no black gowns or other garments shall be given at my burial, nor other old ceremonies then used but Christian manner",[28] while Thomas Wade, Ironmonger, who left 40 shillings in his will to the Puritan Percival Wiburn, requested that the children of Christ's Hospital were not to sing at his burial "for I account it but a vainglory". He left mourning gowns to none but his wife, children and executors.[29]

Even the funeral sermon, an indispensable element of the funerary process, might be regarded as suspicious; in 1588 Richard Walters, Girdler, refused to permit the preaching of a funeral sermon:

> not for that I do not allow of preaching, for I am fully persuaded it is the only way declared in the Word whereby we must attain to faith, without the which we cannot be saved, but for that the funeral sermons are commonly used for custom, which in time my grow to superstition rather than for any profitable edification.[30]

Ultimately, however, nothing could be more unchristian than popery:

> there shall be no blacks or such like vain pomp or ceremony used, that in mine own opinion do rather agree with popery and paganism than with the rule of the gospel of God; but I will that my body be comely and in Christian manner, according to the same gospel, committed to burial as seed sown to happy springing up and rising again to a joyful resurrection.[31]

In the same spirit, in April 1604, alderman Richard Goddard refused to provide a distribution of alms at his burial, "for I conceive that to be but a popish imitation of such as were desirous after their death to have their soul prayed for".[32] In this way earlier practices which had carried little confessional religious significance beyond a general acceptance of the vanity of worldly things in the face of God might come to represent the righteous practice of the true Church, defined in opposition to the Church of Rome, and the popular customs increasingly denigrated as pagan.[33]

The desire, however, for a lasting memorial, while it might be denigrated as vainglorious, also assisted in translating certain patterns of pious benefaction from a purely Catholic context into a distinctly Protestant one. The perpetuation of a testator's memory had traditionally been associated with requirements for post-mortem intercession, and often obliged the recipients of a testator's alms to perform certain acts of piety on behalf of their benefactor's soul. Thus in 1544

Robert Palmer, Mercer, left a weekly dole of four pence to four poor men of three parishes in Sussex. The poor men were to "pray for my soul, and for the soul of Bridget, my late wife deceased, and for the souls of my father and mother, and all Christian souls". Every feast day the same men were to congregate at Palmer's tomb, and "kneeling devoutly upon their knees together at mass time there, in the honour of the five wounds of our lord Jesus Christ" were to say "five Ave Marias and one credo, humbly and devoutly desiring him to have mercy upon my soul and the souls aforesaid, and that we may be partakers of the joy everlasting".[34] As late as 1570, John Long, Clothworker, demonstrated what appears to be a Catholic conception of the rôle of charity in ensuring post-mortem intercession when he requested his wife to bestow the disposable residue of his estate "for my soul's health in deeds of pity and charity amongst all such as she shall see cause".[35]

Yet the Reformation made itself felt in dissociating the desire for the perpetuation of a testator's memory from the concept of post-mortem intercession for the soul. Peter Simmonds, Mercer, in 1586 requested that his portrait hang in Haberdashers' Hall and in Winchester Town Hall, "although this may seem to smell of vainglory, yet being better construed it may be thought to a better purpose". His provision for a weekly dole of bread to the poor in his London parish and in Winchester Cathedral closely followed Palmer's arrangements, but within a rather different religious context. Simmonds' loaves of bread were to be set upon a table at Winchester Cathedral, standing beneath the stone memorial slab bearing a representation of the benefactor kneeling in prayer, and were to remain there throughout the service and sermon which the poor were required to attend. After the service and sermon they would receive their gift.[36] In 1591 Thomas Ware, Fishmonger, endowed a weekly payment of twelve pence to the collectors for the poor children of Christ's Hospital, provided that "the said collectors from time to time forever write my name in their book of collection . . . for good example that others thereby may be the more moved to give liberally to that godly collection forever".[37] Early in James I's reign Thomas Hunt, Fishmonger, endowed a perpetual weekly dole of two pence for two poor men and two poor women. Like Simmonds he provided a table to stand in the church, on which the money was to rest during the service before it was handed to the designated recipients. They in turn were to attend divine service every Sunday, and kneeling at the grave slab of Hunt's father were to say the Lord's Prayer and pray to God for the King and Queen. The pivotal rôle of the mass had been replaced by the Protestant service, and expectation of regular edification with the lively Word of God.[38]

The Reformation did not, therefore, change the nature of almsgiving as an essentially religious duty: John Godd, Merchant Taylor, left his residual estate to his wife Elizabeth "well and soberly to use it and the rest, to God's honour and her own comfort", and alderman Sir Thomas Leigh in 1570 left alms to the poor "in the honour of Christ Jesus, our lord and saviour".[39] Likewise the disapproval of indiscriminate charity that had existed before the Reformation in the distinction between the deserving poor and the thriftless,[40] continued, strengthened by the succession of Elizabethan poor laws. In 1563 John Essex, Haberdasher, left two shillings each to twenty poor householders of his parish of St Margaret New Fish Street "such as be honest, and to none such as go from door to door", but to "such as be honest poor householders and live in the fear of God".[41] John Mabb the elder, chamberlain of London, left £50 in 1578 for the "poor, sick, sore, lame and comfortless people inhabiting within the City of London . . . provided always that no notorious swearer, adulterer or drunkard shall have any part of this my legacy in any wise", and his son left a weekly dole of eight pence to a poor man and woman of the Goldsmiths' Company "provided always that the said poor man and poor widow be poor indeed, and be of honest behaviour and good conversation, and no drunkard nor swearer".[42]

Yet by the late 1560s testators were already lending the charitable impulse an unmistakably Protestant flavour; the deserving poor must demonstrate not merely moral probity but, as a necessary corollary, adherence to the true religion. In 1568 alderman Henry Beecher left £100 to the three Royal Hospitals "for their better maintenance and relief so that the poor in the same houses be kept, continued and maintained in such godly order as they now presently are, and for certain years past have been". Henry Campion, Mercer, left an annual dole in perpetuity to "the good, godly and religious poor people" of his parish, Allhallows Thames Street, in 1588.[43] By 1612 alderman Sir Thomas Cambell was ordering that of his bequest to poor widows in his parish of St Lawrence Jewry, his executors were to give none above twenty shillings or below ten, "wherein the godliest as nigh as they can discern shall have the greatest portions".[44]

The will of David Smith, Embroiderer to the Queen, clearly reflects this linking of moral rectitude with religiosity among the poor. In April 1587 he left six new almshouses to the City; their occupants were to be widows

> such as shall love to serve God above all other things. Also they shall be no swearers nor blasphemers of the name of God, nor no drunkards nor scolds, nor disquieters of other people, but shall be of good and godly conversation to the better example of others. Also they shall most usually use the parish of St. Bennet's near Paul's Wharf and especially upon the sabbath, except they go to a sermon in some other place. Also I would have them to be of good and sound religion, lovers of the gospel of Jesus Christ.[45]

Indeed, by the later sixteenth century the ranks of the undeserving poor had expanded to include Catholics. Thomas Audley, Skinner, in 1590 left £100 capital in order to provide loans to aid young members of the company in setting themselves up in business, provided that

> good choice be always made of every of the said young men . . . that they may be honest and godly Christians, and such as are like to thrive . . . for my meaning and will is that no unthrifty, prodigal spender, papist nor dishonest person shall be admitted to have the use or occupying of any part of the said sum.[46]

The same year James Hewishe, Grocer, left real estate to his heirs male "which then shall be of such profession and religion as the Church of England doth now profess", but "if he be a papist in profession or religion" he should be excluded as if dead "so that the next heir male, being a professor of the gospel according to the profession of England or Geneva may receive", and alderman Richard Gourney's bequest of alms to London's prisons, drawn up in

1596, was conditional on the provision that none of the recipients be wilful debtors, or in prison for adherence to "superstitious or heretical doctrine".[47]

At the same time certain new forms of bequest became established which from their inception reflected a thoroughly Protestant religious motivation. Certain members of the City elite, exiled for their religious convictions during the reign of Mary, returned to public life after 1558 with strong attachments to their former foreign hosts. Thus Thomas Heton attended the first election of elders for the French Church in London, and John Bodley, once an elder of John Knox's English congregation in Geneva, held that post in the French Church in 1571.[48] Indeed, the endemic hostility of the London populace towards foreigners, particularly those skilled in high-quality textile manufactures, and the fears of the government that the Genevan-style churches might lead its subjects astray, meant that the patronage of the City elite was essential to the wellbeing of the stranger congregations.[49] By the late 1560s, against the backdrop of the threat to Protestantism in the French wars of religion and the Spanish campaigns in the Netherlands a small number of London's more zealous rulers such as alderman Francis Barnham in 1575, were taking an active rôle in supporting the poor of the stranger congregations. Barnham left £20 "to the poor afflicted people for the gospel's sake, in the French Church and Dutch Church in London".[50]

Yet if some of the rulers were funding religious causes that might seem to undermine the cohesion of the traditional parish community, that was not the case with the most common form of pious provision in the later sixteenth century, the sermon. Nearly a third of the surviving elite wills after 1558 contain some provision for a sermon or series of sermons and, aside from those provided specifically for the funerary context, the great majority of such bequests focus upon the parish and its rôle as a religious community.[51]

Protestants had never held a monopoly on the preaching of sermons, and the necessity of providing for preaching after one's death certainly led a number of Catholic rulers of London to expend considerable sums upon preaching. In 1565 alderman Sir Martin Bowes, a man of highly conservative religious opinions, nevertheless endowed a weekly sermon for a year to be delivered by Robert Crowley, John Philpot and John Gough, who at that point were emerging as the leading lights in London's early Puritan movement. Bowes, an alderman since 1536, was clearly performing the public ritual duty expected of a longstanding member of the City government, and employing the best qualified preachers available regardless of their particular religious stance. In this regard it is perhaps significant that he should be one of the very few elite testators to lay down specific intructions for his preachers: they must exhort "the people to flee from sin and to fall to repentence, and so to lead a new life".[52] Yet Bowes seems to have been an exception in several ways, and remains the only certainly identified Catholic among the City rulers to leave funds for more than a funeral sermon under Elizabeth.

In place of the former provisions for requiem masses and the recitation of the Ave Maria, the wills of London's Elizabethan rulers reveal an increasing emphasis upon preaching of the Word in an ever more clearly Protestant context. Alderman William Dane, whose will preamble we have noted above, provided in 1563 for a sermon every Sunday for thirty weeks "to the edifying of the people of God", and alderman William Beswick in 1567 provided for twenty sermons after his death in parish of St Lawrence Pountney, ten of which were to be given by the returned Marian exile Thomas Becon. Similarly John Baker, Mercer, willed his executors in 1568 to give "to certain ministers and preachers as you may conveniently get them, such as can edify the people best with preaching of God's Word, first at my burial 6s. 7d. and every Sunday and holiday the whole year following, 5s. for every sermon".[53] For some testators the provision of sermons and lectures also became inextricably linked with the survival of Protestantism as represented by the Elizabethan Church. In November 1580 John Rowe, Merchant Taylor, parishioner of Allhallows London Wall, and an associate of John Bodley, provided for a lecture in his parish "so long as the gospel is truly preached even as at this day, otherwise to end",[54] and a year later Cuthbert Beeston, imprisoned in 1554 for selling prohibited books imported from exiled Edwardian ministers,[55] left twenty shillings a year for ten years to provide quarterly sermons in his parish of St Stephen Coleman Street;

if the gospel of our saviour Jesus Christ shall be at the said time and space truly and sincerely preached within this realm of

England, as it is now . . . and if at any time during the said ten years (as God defend) the gospel should cease and not be truly and sincerely preached as now it is, that then during that time only the same twenty shillings . . . shall be given and distributed yearly to and amongst the poorest people dwelling in the said parish of St. Stephen.[56]

The will of the Puritan alderman Sir Thomas Smythe, dated 1622, provides a concise summary of the integrated Protestant conception of charity, church and sermon which emerged during Elizabeth's reign. Smythe provided a bread dole to the poor of three parishes in Kent, "provided that none shall be partakers of the said gift of bread but such as shall usually frequent the church to hear divine service and the preaching of God's word, and shall receive the blessed sacrament of the lord's supper". The churchwardens were to "appoint convenient pews or seats wherein the poor people that shall be thought fit to receive the said gift of bread may sit together to hear divine service and sermon every sabbath day at the least".[57]

Indeed it is clear that the pattern of pious provision which emerged after the establishment of the Elizabethan Church of England grew out of longstanding forms of religious behaviour focused upon the parish as a religious community. For both Puritan and non-Puritan the parish church remained the natural focus for pious provision. In May 1592 the Puritan alderman Sir Wolstan Dixie of the parish of St Michael Bassishaw left an annuity to the Skinners' Company, of which £10 was to be used every year to provide a lecture twice weekly in the parish. In 1580 alderman John Haydon provided £13 6s. 8d. yearly to the Mercers' Company to fund a weekly divinity lecture in perpetuity in his parish church of St Michael Paternoster, the preacher "to be elected and chosen by the good discretion and appointment of those which do choose to elect him that readeth the lecture for the Clothworkers in the same church".[58] But such endowments were not the exclusive preserve of the godly. Alderman Sir Hugh Offley had acted as a government informer upon the exiled English community in France during Mary's reign, yet when he made his will in 1594 he requested four sermons "for the edifying of the people" in his parish of St Andrew Undershaft, by whoever should happen to be the parson or minister at the time, while he also beqeathed £10 to the parishioners for a divinity lecture to last for a year after his decease.[59] In many respects Offley exemplifies the transition in the religious culture of London's rulers. Buried near his Catholic elder brother Thomas, he appointed his younger Protestant brother Robert an overseer, together with his Protestant son-in-law James Deane.

Equally the endowment of sermons, and the traditional bequest of funds to divinity scholars at Oxford and Cambridge, came to be regarded as essential tools in the evangelization of the countryside outside London and the south east. In August 1581 Anthony Cage of the Salters' Company bequeathed

> unto some godly preacher to be appointed by my son Anthony Cage £10 for thirty sermons to be made in those parish churches within the county of Suffolk, at the discretion of my son Anthony Cage, where the gospel hath been least preached since the queen's majesty's reign.[60]

Similarly alderman Sir William Elkin left properties to the mayor and commonalty of London in 1592 to maintain a reader "to read service and teach children to read, as also the principles of their faith and sound religion in a chapel called Ore Chapel in the county of Salop, and in the parish of Mickleston". Elkin had been born in the village of Ore, and this form of bequest represents merely a development of the traditional practice whereby successful London citizens born outside the City remembered their places of birth, providing charity or religious services to their ancestral communities. Anthony Calthorp, Mercer, was following the same pattern in funding a lecture for five years, to take place on market day in the town of North Walsham in Norfolk, his place of birth, "for the better instruction and edification of the people there".[61]

The expectation that testators would aid in the propagation of true religion by supporting the training of preaching clergy had been present throughout the early sixteenth century; alderman Sir Christopher Ascue in 1534 had left funds to support two "famous graduate men, used to preach, and preach according to mother Church". The custom continued throughout the sixteenth century, adapted after the Reformation to meet the needs of an altered religious context. In

1577 Henry Elsing left properties in London to the Bakers' Company, to support "two young men, scholars, that shall be of honest disposition and of good report and behaviour to profit in learning; which young men shall study and labour in the knowledge of divinity that they may be able, meet and profitable members to teach and instruct God's people in the knowledge of his truth and verity, sincerely, truly and faithfully".[62]

In some cases testators, usually Puritans, made efforts to channel funds towards scholars of a particular religious complexion. Alderman Anthony Gamage made his will in December 1571, leaving a total of £60 to six poor scholars in each university. At Oxford he charged Thomas Sampson with nominating the recipients of the exhibition, while for Cambridge he requested Percival Wiburn to perform the same function.[63] Sampson had refused a bishopric in 1559, largely because of his doubts regarding the vestiges of the Roman Church in the ceremony and discipline of the English Church, and by the time Gamage wrote his will had been deprived of the deanery of Christ Church, Oxford in the wake of the vestments controversy. Wiburn, the "apostle of Northampton", was equally recalcitrant in his opposition to "popish" vestments, and unlike most of the London clergy suffered deprivation of his benefice in 1566 rather than submit to wearing the offensive apparel. Indeed, he was in the process of introducing a severely Reformed discipline in Northampton, based upon that of Geneva, at the time Gamage named him in his will.[64] It is clear that Gamage was trying to direct his funds towards scholars of a strongly Reformed style of churchmanship.

Certain colleges were known for their Puritan connections, and attracted the benefaction of several prominent Londoners concerned to increase the supply of a particular kind of Protestant preacher. The two most commonly referred to by name by the London rulers were Emmanuel, founded in 1584, and Sidney Sussex, founded in 1595. Both were regarded as "Puritan seminaries", headed by a succession of distinguished Puritan clergy, whose presence attracted the donations of London Puritans.[65] After the foundation of Emmanuel and Sidney Sussex godly testators tended to channel their educational funds through those colleges,[66] although the absolute number of such testators was never very great and the majority of non-Puritan testators failed to distinguish any particular college above any other.

These elements of the religious culture of London's rulers represent the external manifestations of broadly accepted concepts of social duty and social status underpinned by a fundamentally religious rationale. Such forms of pious behaviour could accommodate and permit the articulation of a wide spectrum of religious belief. Above all, the widespread acceptance of this pattern of piety became possible because it involved a modification of the context and rationale of established customs, rather than the invention of wholly new forms. In this light the continuity of certain devotional patterns, far from demonstrating the survival of a system of belief essentially Catholic in nature, in fact seems to represent the accommodation of traditional social and religious rôles to an essentially Protestant understanding of customary devotional practice. Thus the choice of the chancel in a parish church for burial retained its communal significance as the focus for interments of the parochial and civic elite, but lost its rôle in ensuring continued intercession for souls in purgatory through proximity to the sacrament of the altar. Charitable benefaction remained a pivotal social and religious duty, but the benefactor no longer expected to shorten his days in purgatory; rather it was the poor who were expected to demonstrate their worthiness by leading lives of exemplary piety and ultimately by following the correct form of religion. Stripped of its purgatorial element, the commemoration of the testator which remained closely linked to charitable benefaction served to provide exempla of virtue and helped to maintain the parochial social order in highly visual fashion.

In the same way the provision of sermons took on greater significance. The dead might no longer benefit from prayer, but the living could profit, in a different manner, from hearing the lively Word of God preached by a minister of the Protestant Church of England. Ex-alderman William Thorowgood, living in retirement in the country after twenty years of faithful service to his City, and concerned for the state of his fellow parishioners' souls, provided for six sermons a year in perpetuity in the Hertfordshire parish of Broxbourne,

> for the advancement of the glorious gospel of Jesus Christ, and of God's true religion now set forth and established within this realm by public authority, and for the better instruction and erudition of the people of Broxbourne aforesaid in the true

knowledge thereof to their eternal souls' health . . . for and during so long as God's true religion now established and used within this realm as afore shall continue and be used within the same (which I hope will be forever).[67]

The City elite retained their traditional social and religious rôle as leaders of their parishes, and their wills, less formulaic than the shorter wills of their humbler contemporaries in town and country, offer an insight into the manner in which the Reformation altered the religious landscape of the sixteenth-century laity. It seems possible that continuity in the forms of religious practice may conceal relatively rapid shifts in the basic conceptions which informed them with meaning. In effect, the continued repetition of traditional rôles through a period of dramatic religious change, eased rather than hindered the transition to Protestant modes of thought. Protestant preachers might bewail the persistence of popular customs which signified popery and paganism to them, yet where the laity found a meaningful channel of spiritual expression in the rites and devotions of the Church of England, as alderman William Dane clearly did, one may doubt that they can be reduced to an unthinking mass trapped in a spiritual limbo between recusancy and Geneva-style Calvinism.

Notes

1. Public Record Office (hereafter PRO), PROB. 11/55, fo. 216v; p. 129 above.
2. A. G. Dickens, *The Marian reaction in the diocese of York*, (pt. 2) (Borthwick Institute of Historical Research **12**, 1957), pp. 21–2; A. G. Dickens *Lollards and Protestants in the diocese of York* (Oxford, 1959), pp. 171–2, 215–18; A. G. Dickens *The English Reformation*, (2nd edn, London, 1989), pp. 214–15, 325–6; P. Clark, *English provincial society from the Reformation to the Revolution: religion, politics and society in Kent 1500–1640* (Hassocks, 1977), pp. 58–9; G. J. Mayhew, "The progress of the English Reformation in East Sussex 1530–1559: the evidence from wills", *Southern History* **5**, 1983, pp. 38–67; C. Cross, "Parochial structure and the dissemination of Protestantism in sixteenth-century England: a tale of two cities", in *The Church in town and countryside*, D. Baker (ed.) (Studies in Church History **16**, 1979), pp. 269–78; C. Gross "The development of Protestantism in Leeds and Hull, 1520–1640: the evidence from wills", *Northern History* **18**, 1982, pp. 230–38.
3. M. Spufford, "The scribes of villagers' wills in the sixteenth and seventeenth

centuries and their influence", *Local Population Studies* **7**, 1971, pp. 28–43; *Contrasting communities. English villagers in the sixteenth and seventeenth centuries* (Cambridge, 1974), pp. 320–34; M. L. Zell, "The use of preambles as a measure of religious belief in the sixteenth century", *Bulletin of the Institute of Historical Research* **50**, 1977, pp. 246–9; E. Duffy, *The stripping of the altars. Traditional religion in England c.1400–c.1580* (New Haven & London, 1992), pp. 511–15; C. J. Litzenburger, *Responses of the laity to changes in official religious policy in Gloucestershire, 1541–80*, (PhD thesis, Cambridge University, 1993).

4. J. D. Alsop, "Religious preambles in early-modern English wills as formulae", *Journal of Ecclesiastical History* **40**, 1989, pp. 23 & 27.

5. PRO, PROB. 11/71, fo. 82 [my italics]. Simmonds' will, to which attention is drawn later in this chapter, places great emphasis upon the importance of the Protestant service as the context for his charitable benefaction, and upon the training of preaching ministers at the universities.

6. C. Haigh, "The Church of England, the Catholics and the people", in *The reign of Elizabeth I*, C. Haigh (ed.), (London, 1984), pp. 195–219; "The continuity of Catholicism in the English Reformation", in *The English Reformation revised*, C. Haigh (ed.) (Cambridge, 1987), pp. 176–208; "The English Reformation. A premature birth, a difficult labour and a sickly child", *Historical Journal* **33**, 1990, pp. 449–59; *English Reformations. Religion, politics and society under the Tudors* (Oxford, 1993), pp. 268–95. See also A. Walsham, *Church papists: Catholicism, conformity and confessional polemic in early-modern England* (Woodbridge, 1993), pp. 100–119.

7. T. Watt, *Cheap print and popular piety, 1550–1640* (Cambridge, 1991).

8. D. Cressy, *Bonfires and bells: national memory and the Protestant calendar in Elizabethan and Stuart England* (London, 1989). For survival of pre-Reformation elements in folklore and custom, and changes in the meaning of such material during and after the Reformation, see R. Hutton, *The rise and fall of merry England. The ritual year 1400–1700* (Oxford, 1994), pp. 69–110, 153–199; "The English reformation and the evidence of folklore", *Past and Present* **148**, 1995, pp. 89–116.

9. C. Haigh, "Anticlericalism and the English Reformation", in *The English Reformation revised*, C. Haigh (ed.) pp. 59–62.

10. D. J. Hickman. *The religious allegiance of London's ruling élite, 1520–1603*. (PhD thesis, University of London, 1995), pp. 211–240.

11. E. Jones, *The corporation of London: its origin, constitution, powers and duties* (London, 1950); V. Pearl, *London and the outbreak of the Puritan Revolution: city government and national politics* (Oxford, 1961), pp. 45–68; F. F. Foster, *The politics of stability. A portrait of the rulers in Elizabethan London* (Woodbridge, 1977), pp. 12–28; I. Archer, *The pursuit of stability: social relations in Elizabethan London* (Cambridge, 1991), pp. 18–20, 180–83; R. M. Benbow, "Limning the London councillors: the index of common councilmen for 1550–1603", unpublished paper (Institute of Historical Research, London, 1993).

12. Foster, *Politics of stability*, pp. 54–60.

13. For a comparative account of pre-Reformation testamentary religious provision among an urban population see C. Burgess, "'By quick and by dead": wills and pious provisions in late medieval Bristol", *English Historical Review* **102**, 1987, pp. 837–858.

14. PRO, PROB. 11/28, fo. 46. For further examples see PRO, PROB. 11/28, fo. 29 & 11/24, fo. 81.

15. Burial by high altar, e.g. PRO, PROB. 11/21, fo. 103; 26, fo. 37v; 32, fo. 104r. Burial before rood e.g. PRO, PROB. 11/24, fo. 22v;' 25, fo. 182v. Burial near patron saint, e.g. PRO, PROB. 11/22, fo. 241v; 23, fos. 33v, 119r; 27, fos. 130v, 201r, 214r, 270av; 29, fo. 159r; 31, fo. 307r. Such burial sites were not necessarily available to those lower in social status: V. Harding, "Burial choice and burial location in later medieval London", in *Death in towns. Urban responses to the dying and the dead, 100–1600*, S. Bassett (ed.) (London & New York, 1992), pp. 119–135.

16. PRO, PROB. 11/85, fo. 172v.

17. E.g. PRO, PROB. 11/42b, fo. 447v (John Whitepayne, Merchant Taylor, 1559); 57, fo. 291v (William Bowley, Fishmonger, 1575); 65, fo. 304v (William Barnard, Draper, 1583); 66, fo. 270r (John Best, Haberdasher, 1584); 74, fo. 346v (John Rogers, Grocer, 1587); 116, fo. 118r (Robert Cambell, Ironmonger, 1609).

18. PRO, PROB. 11/50, fo. 45v; 51, fo. 33v.

19. Cf. burial of Alderman Sir John Rudstone, buried under the pulpit cross he had built in the churchyard of St Michael the Archangel in 1531; J. Stow, *The survey of London*, H. B. Wheatley (ed.) (London, 1956), p. 178.

20. Stow, *Survey of London*, pp. 150–52.

21. PRO, PROB. 11/71, fo. 82r; P. Collinson, *The Elizabethan Puritan Movement* (London, 1967), pp. 370–1.

22. E.g. PRO, PROB. 11/23, fo. 90v (Stephen Lunne, Haberdasher, 1528); 24, fo. 175r (Ellis Draper, Haberdasher, 1527); 25, fo. 116 (Alderman Sir Thomas Baldry, Mercer, 1534); 30, fos. 41r (Thomas Trappes, Goldsmith, 1543), 96v (Robert Palmer, Mercer, 1544); 37, fo. 219r (Robert Warner, Draper, 1555); 38, fo. 150r (Humphrey Packington, Mercer, 1555).

23. P. Ariès, *The hour of our death* (London, 1981).

24. PRO, PROB. 11/56, fos. 125r–v.

25. PRO, PROB. 11/51, fo. 147r (Thomas Polle, 1569); 54, fo. 316v; 48, fos. 351–352r (Richard Whitehill, 1565).

26. PRO, PROB. 11/72, fo. 446r.

27. PRO, PROB. 11/85, fo. 59r. Cf. Richard Reynolds, Draper, "I will that there be no ringing for me but a knell": PRO, PROB. 11/61, fo. 79r (3 February 1579).

28. PRO, PROB, 11/69, fo. 353v. Cf. will of Alderman Humphrey Weld, dated May 1610, requiring burial "without any superstitious ceremonies": PRO, PROB. 11/116, fos. 350v–353r.

29. PRO, PROB. 11/98, fos. 89v–92v.
30. PRO, PROB. 11/72, fo. 156r.
31. Will of Walter Fish, Merchant Taylor, 1578: PRO, PROB. 11/68, fo. 421v.
32. PRO, PROB. 11/103, fo. 272v.
33. Descriptions of the Church of England as the true, Catholic Church appear from the mid-1560s. Alderman William Beswick left his soul to

> almighty God in Trinity, and trusting in the merits of the precious death, passion and resurrection of his only son Jesus Christ, and other his works for my whole redemption, by the which, through his mercy, I trust to be saved from death, hell and sin, according as it was promised to every true member of his Catholic Church, of the which I do trust by his grace assisting, I shall depart this present life, a true member of the same.

   PRO, PROB. 11/49, fo. 107r, April 1567.
34. PRO, PROB. 11/30, fos. 96–97r. Cf. PRO, PROB. 11/25, fos. 42v, 312v; 31, fo. 55r.
35. PRO, PROB. 11/52, fo. 265r.
36. PRO, PROB. 11/71, fos. 83r–85r.
37. PRO, PROB. 11/82, fo. 51r–v.
38. PRO, PROB. 11/129, fo. 63v. See also will of John Riley, Haberdasher, 1577, providing a weekly dole of 1d. and a penny loaf to twelve poor persons of his parish "betwixt the reading of the epistle and the gospel in the service time": PRO, PROB. 11/59, fo. 234r. See ff. PRO, PROB. 11/58, fo. 23r (Thomas Metcalf, Goldsmith, 1576); 68, fo. 448r (Stephen Scudamore, Vintner, 1585); Corporation of London Record Office HR. 268 (22) Membr. 10v (John Lute, Clothworker, 1585); PRO, PROB. 11/84, fo. 185v (Anthony Calthorp, Mercer, 1593).
39. PRO, PROB. 11/60, fo. 179v; 53, fos. 346r–347r.
40. Duffy, *Stripping of the altars*, pp. 313–27, 357–62.
41. PRO, PROB. 11/47, fo. 60r–v. Thomas Brown, Scrivener, likewise excluded "all such poor as go a-begging from door to door" from his alms-giving: PRO, PROB. 11/65, fo. 8r–v, dated September 1581.
42. PRO, PROB. 11/65, fo. 7r; 71, fo. 71r.
43. PRO, PROB. 11/53, fos. 74v–75r; 73, fo. 103r. For similar bequests see ff. PRO, PROB. 11/69, fo. 325v (John Marden, Merchant Taylor, 1586); 72, fo. 157v (Richard Walters, Girdler, 1588); 79, fo. 313r (Hugh Henley, Merchant Taylor, 1592); 89, fo. 439r (John Fox, Goldsmith, 1596); 96, fo. 329r (Richard Platt, Brewer, 1600); 117, fo. 223r (Abraham Campion, Clothworker, 1611).
44. PRO, PROB. 11/123, fo. 180r. Similarly Thomas Wade, Ironmonger, of St Matthew Friday Street, who left 40s. to the Puritan divine Percival Wiburn in 1600, left alms to the poor "that are poor indeed and well given in religion, as near as they may be found out": PRO, PROB. 11/98, fo. 89v.

45. PRO, PROB. 11/71, fo. 129r–v. See also William Lamb, Clothworker's will, 1580: his domestics would be supported for six months after Lamb's death until they found a new master, provided that "they during all the time that they shall remain without service do repair to the church and sermons, and spend their time in other godly exercises": PRO, PROB. 11/62, fo. 157v.

46. PRO, PROB. 11/80, fo. 132av.

47. PRO, PROB. 11/76, fo. 185r–v; 89, fo. 269v.

48. A. Pettegree, *Foreign Protestant communities in sixteenth-century London* (Oxford, 1986), pp. 271–2; P. Collinson, "The Elizabethan Puritans and the foreign reformed churches of London", *Proceedings of the Huguenot Society of London* **20**, 1964, pp. 528–55.

49. Pettegree, *Foreign Protestant communities*, pp. 133–44, 262–95.

50. PRO, PROB. 11/58, fo. 77r. See ff. PRO, PROB. 11/49, fo. 98v (John Mynors, Draper, 1567); 51, fo. 145r (William Coxe, Haberdasher, 1569); 60, fo. 18v (John Quarles, Draper, 1577); 65, fo. 309r (Alderman Sir James Harvey, 1583); 81, fo. 30v (Thomas Danser Girdler, 1590); 83, fo. 1v (Alderman Sir Wolstan Dixie, 1592); 103, fo. 273r (Alderman Sir Richard Goddard, 1604); 105, fo. 210v (Alderman Sir Henry Anderson, 1605); 117, fo. 336r (Alderman Sir William Romney, 1611); 133, fo. 114v (William Quarles, Mercer, 1592).

51. Hickman, *Religious allegiance of London's ruling élite*, chs. 4 & 5.

52. PRO, PROB. 11/49, fo. 21r. For Bowes' conservatism see J. Foxe, *The acts and monuments*, S. R. Cattley & G. Townsend (eds) [8 vols] (London, 1837–41) vol. 5, pp. 538–39; *Narratives of the days of the Reformation*, J. G. Nichols (ed.) (Camden Society **77**, 1859), pp. 40–41; *The diary of Henry Machyn, citizen and merchant taylor of London, 1550–1563*, J. G. Nichols (ed.) (Camden Society **43**, 1848), pp. 68, 70–71; *The House of Commons 1509–1558*, S. T. Bindoff (ed.) (London, 1982), s.n. Bowes, Sir Martin.

53. PRO, PROB. 11/55, fo. 216v; 49, fo. 108r; 51, fo. 42r.

54. PRO, PROB. 11/64, fos. 264v–265r.

55. J. Foxe, *Acts and monuments*, vol. 6, p. 561.

56. PRO, PROB. 11/64, fo. 53r.

57. PRO, PROB. 11/147, fo. 38r–v.

58. PRO, PROB. 11/66, fo. 108r; 83, fo. 2v.

59. PRO, PROB. 11/84, fos. 295v, 297r.

60. PRO, PROB. 11/66, fo. 33v.

61. PRO, PROB. 11/82, fo. 241r; 84, fo. 185r, dated April 1593.

62. PRO, PROB. 11/27, fo. 239; 63, fo. 206r.

63. PRO, PROB. 11/61, fos. 355v–356v.

64. Collinson, *Elizabethan Puritan Movement*, pp. 46–9, 73–83, 141–2.

65. J. Morgan, *Godly learning: Puritan attitudes towards reason, learning and education, 1560–1640* (Cambridge, 1986), pp. 232–3, 247–56; P. Lake, *Moderate Puritans and the Elizabethan Church* (Cambridge, 1982).

66. PRO, PROB. 11/83, fo. 1v (Alderman Sir Wolstan Dixie, 1592); 82, fo. 242v (Alderman Sir William Elkin, 1592); 103, fo. 3r (Alderman Sir John Harte, 1604); 108, fo. 317v (Alderman Sir Henry Billingsley, 1606); 112, fo. 404r (Roger Owfield, Fishmonger, 1608); 119, fo. 37r (Randall Manning, Skinner, 1612).
67. PRO, PROB. 11/101, fos. 63r–64r, dated August 1603.

6

Piety and persuasion in Elizabethan England: the Church of England meets the Family of Love

Christopher Marsh

The argument that the majority of English men and women were content with the late-medieval church seems to be emerging as a consensus amongst historians. As a result, however, the popular motives behind mass compliance with the disruptive process of Protestant reform are surfacing as a serious problem. If the English did not need, want or like the Reformation, why did they accept it? Several possibilities deserve consideration. Some might wish to look for the answer in the Tudor state's brute power, if such it was. Or we might explore the contemporary culture of obedience in its relation to religious matters. Was compliance perceived as one of the primary spiritual duties, binding almost without reference to the nature of the system being implemented? Alternatively, it can be argued that many people only conformed outwardly, while doggedly retaining an older set of beliefs in the privacy of their own heads. Another possibility might be that the Reformation, in practice if not in theory, turned out to be more a negotiated modification of popular piety than an outright imposition of something innovative and alien. This was not, of course, the mainstream Protestant strategy. But in the circumstances of Elizabethan England, where a deeply conservative Protestant ruled over a basically Catholic people, it may have emerged as the most workable alternative. It is the last of these suggestions that will occupy us here.

The limelight has been dominated, naturally enough, by those with a more zealous attitude to the task of religious persuasion: iconoclasts, martyrs, recusants, separatists and Puritans. As the militant Protestant, Philip Nichols, put it, "God's word is never spread abroad without contention, strife and much trouble".[1] Gentler souls have consequently been neglected, and it is arguable that our perspective on sixteenth-century religious change has been distorted as a result. Can we really solve the compliance conundrum without investigating the possibility that many reformist clergy and laity were prepared, in practice, to allow compromises with the wider population and with the past? This chapter takes a sideways look at these questions. It explores the nature of the encounter between the reformed Church of England and that troublesome fellowship of mystics, the Family of Love. It is hoped that, by examining the prevalent attitudes to religious persuasion on both sides of this meeting, something worthwhile can also be said about the progress of Protestantism in general.

It may, at first, seem misguided to propose that the Family of Love can be treated as a symbolic substitute for the traditionalist religion of the majority. The Familists' spiritual allegiance was, after all, strange and intensely specific: they were the followers of a mid-century Dutch visionary who preferred to be known only as 'HN' (his real name was Hendrick Niclaes). His message – a mixture of mysticism, perfectionism and messianism – was disseminated in England during the 1560s and 1570s. It attracted a small but deeply committed following, a network of Familist cells spread across ten southern counties. As far as we can now tell, a few hundred people had come to believe with considerable conviction that HN was directly inspired by God, that Scripture was to be interpreted allegorically, that non-Familists could not be saved, that humans could rise to perfection by a process of spiritual "illumination", and that the true godly did not necessarily have to tell the truth when under pressure. This amounted to a potentially dangerous creed.[2]

Although these people were clearly not typical of the population at large, there are several reasons for methodological optimism. Puritan opponents of the Family frequently associated its members with Catholic traditionalism, and even regarded them as a sort of test case for the wider Reformation. The frustrations of the Protestant godly with a reluctant population and a "heretical" fellowship were clearly related in their own minds. If the Familists could be won over, then there was hope. Other connections between HN's followers and their

142

more orthodox contemporaries might be found in the perceived reluctance of them all to stand up boldly for their beliefs, and in their alleged practice of a shallow, perhaps hypocritical, ecclesiastical conformity. Puritan writers also complained that the Familists, like most of their neighbours, were far too ready to judge the spiritual purity of others on the inadequate basis of visible actions.[3] HN's disciples and their co-parishioners were very different, but they also shared some important common ground.

The Family of Love's own approach to religious persuasion forms an intriguing study in itself, and also provides some vital context within which to address the issues outlined above. HN gave his followers a great deal of highly contradictory advice concerning the task of dissemination. At times, he commanded them to be bold and open with their faith, and he prophesied global expansion. In other passages, however, HN was far quieter, advising his followers to operate a policy of caution and discretion in their attempts to persuade the world. Members were warned to avoid contact with the hostile, making discreet approaches only to those thought already to be sympathetic. The harvest was not to be hurried. The Familists were told to display love, tolerance and obedience in their contacts with wider society. HN's extravagant promises of worldwide success were modified by a belief that the service of love would be incorporated *within* existing religious systems, rather than obliterating them. There were other passages again in which this mood of quietness gave way to one of virtual silence. HN told his followers, "Let your forth-going be in stillness, with few words". Known enemies were to be greeted with absolute taciturnity: "be now by them . . . even as-though ye were dead". While HN was in this mood, the expansive prophecies degenerated into a rather glum prediction that "there shall few come".[4]

It was the responsibility of the English Family of Love to interpret and apply this rather bewildering set of instructions, to make their choices from HN's varied menu of commands. The history of the fellowship between 1560 and 1630 provides evidence of attitudes both aggressive and gentle, but it was overwhelmingly at the quieter end of the spectrum that the activities of members were concentrated. The Family devoted much more energy to consolidation than to expansion, as a short survey of their practices will reveal.

HN's disciples certainly came together in groups from time to time, but their "parlour meetings" were small, secretive, intimate and domestic.[5] The same impression of collective introversion and extreme quietness is created by evidence of the numerous ways in which members of the Family supported one another in their dealings with the world. As far as was possible, they maintained a close-knit community through intermarriage, shared economic enterprises, and assistance with the bringing up of one another's offspring. The Family's precious and exotic books were distributed with great discretion and secrecy, to the exasperation of John Rogers who complained, "for except one will be pliant to their doctrine and show good will thereto, he shall hardly get any of their books".[6]

The Family did make approaches to outsiders, but always it seems with great care and circumspection. Sympathetic neighbours were occasionally provided with copies of HN's more accessible works, but Familists generally took as few risks as possible, "for they say love must not be awakened before the time".[7] This amounted to an opt-out clause of considerable scope. There is also evidence of a more ambitious, but equally selective, policy of courting those who occupied positions of particular influence. Familists, it appears, won a measure of sympathy, if not actual allegiance, from individual governors great and small. These ranged from a local magistrate in Ely at one end right up to Queen Elizabeth at the other. One "apology" written by a member of the fellowship was dedicated to the Earl of Leicester, and was said to have been "penned by one of her Majesty's menial servants, who was in no small esteem with Her, for his known wisdom and godliness".[8] It is doubtful, however, that such approaches reflected a serious bid for the fulfilment of HN's expansionist prophecies. Instead, they were primarily a request for the continuation of a basically peaceful situation that had allowed the Familists to pursue their less disruptive goal of what we might call *inward* growth.

The impression of an emphasis on careful and very selective evangelism is further reinforced by an examination of the work of HN's "illuminated elders", a vital group of itinerant Familists who successfully prevented the fellowship from becoming a disparate collection of disconnected cells. The English elders are as elusive now as they were at the time, but they can sometimes be glimpsed for a moment in the surviving sources, caught like rabbits in the headlights of history. It has been possible to identify a handful of these dedicated individuals, but only rarely can their activities be traced in any great detail. They travelled around within their regions, ensuring that the Family retained its cohesion. They wrote letters of comfort and advice; they supplied books and supervised meetings, and they co-ordinated the secretive and effective efforts of the Family to defend itself in print.[9] It seems clear, however, that the elders did little to carry HN's message to the Elizabethan masses, despite the deep anxieties of their critics.

Ordinary members of the Family were generally prepared to comply with the requirements of their earthly governors. They regularly held local offices, paid their taxes, and attended their parish churches. As far as we can tell, the Familist attitude of compliance amounted to a thorough and enthusiastic endorsement of the values and moral expectations of the communities within which they lived. They played their parts in the regulation of local social life, made generous gifts to the local poor, and were often entrusted by their neighbours with considerable responsibility. In short, the Family's members were archetypal good citizens, and there is plentiful evidence to suggest the respect with which most – but not all – of their neighbours regarded them.[10] It was exceptionally rare for members of the Family to find themselves presented to the church courts for their religious affiliation, and their appearances in the records of those courts were much more likely to be as witnesses to the wills of other parishioners than as suspected heretics. Several of HN's followers even made testamentary bequests to their local clergymen and parish churches.[11]

The persuasive value of such behaviour was another of those grey areas for the Family. Its members may well have believed that, by revealing themselves as upright citizens, they could hope to impress their neighbours and create a gradually widening pool of potentially sympathetic onlookers. Alternatively, the Familists were hoping to throw the authorities off the scent with their display of enthusiastic subservience and service, while simultaneously sneaking up on their neighbours and "taking them aside".[12] It is, nevertheless, difficult to avoid the conclusion that these were theoretical strategies rather than an actively implemented programme for expansion. In most circumstances and most Familist minds, compliance was surely a tactic permitting the survival and internal development of the fellowship, and it probably reflected a genuine commitment to the smooth running of society. It was not really a bid for global success, and in its most exaggerated form – the obedient and public recitation of explicit diatribes against HN – it must actually have exerted a negative persuasive influence. Such cases were not very common, and were criticised from within the Family, but they did occur.

Overall, the mild-mannered approach of the Family to the task of persuasion is clear. We should also ask, however, what its members did with the more radical, aggressive and expansionist urges that must periodically have affected all enthusiastic readers of HN's work. There were, in fact, occasions upon which Familists adopted a far more defiant stance, showing that they did not treat the duty (or ploy) of compliance as absolute and without limits. When the Wisbech Glover, John Bourne, was called before Bishop Cox and the ecclesiastical commissioners in 1580, his behaviour during the early stages of his ordeal was anything but submissive. Under interrogation, several of his answers were insolent in the extreme. He explained, for example, that he could not "deny HN" because these letters were liberally distributed through the Bible, and he was reluctant to denounce "the most part of the scriptures".[13]

More commonly, the expansive instinct may have found displaced expression in the Family of Love's prophecies. These, arguably, provided something of the "buzz" of evangelical endeavour and success, but without the stress. The Wisbech brethren were reported to believe "that there should come a time shortly when there should be no magistrate, prince nor palace upon the earth, but all should be governed by the spirit of love".[14] Along similar lines, it can be argued – speculatively, of course – that the Familists' expansionist urges were often suppressed, only to find expression in a variety of other forms. In several instances, members of the fellowship made gestures or statements which appear to have been carefully coded. They sometimes employed unusual, but not necessarily unorthodox, phrases in the preambles to their wills. Occasionally, they used such expressions even as they submitted humbly to hostile clerical investigators. The memorial inscription of one Familist gentlewoman opened with the words "Here lies God's love".[15] In all such cases, individual Familists created for themselves an opportunity to register their beliefs in official or public forms, but in such a way as to prevent accurate interpretation by any persons other than their co-religionists. The technique was brilliant, and probably quite satisfying, but it was designed to persuade only the persuaded. It may have felt bold, but in truth it was nothing of the sort.

The frustrated urge to expand may also have found expression, very occasionally, in behaviour considerably more outrageous. Now and again, members of the Family conducted themselves with supreme arrogance, even an air of untouchability. Such incidents attract the attention of the historian (and of the amateur psychologist) because they seem to reveal instincts running directly counter to those around which the Familists generally based their actions. They perhaps demonstrate the outburst of mutated desires which, though voiced in the works of HN, were nevertheless suppressed during the daily lives of his followers. In the summer of 1580, for example, the courtier Familist Robert Dorrington was busy felling and misusing trees on a Huntingdonshire estate that was temporarily under Privy Council management. He defied the officers of Sir Francis Knollys and boasted openly of the friends he had at court. Dorrington acted as if invincible, and conducted himself with a measure of bluster that seems out of keeping with the Family's public declarations of obedience and its generally impeccable social morality.[16]

Thirty years later, in Balsham, Cambridgeshire, an episode of even greater complexity occurred. Following the death of an aged Familist named Thomas Lawrence, his friends apparently took it upon themselves to appropriate a prestigious and ancient grave that lies close to the chancel wall in the churchyard. Archaeological research suggests that they removed the former occupant, a medieval priest, before lining the grave with six hundred bricks and installing their obviously beloved companion. Their action was, to some extent at least, arrogant and provocative. The story has been told elsewhere and cannot be repeated here. Most importantly, it has been argued that this extraordinary burial amounted to a symbolic religious statement of some complexity, the inner meanings of which would be better explored in a novel than a work of history. The Familists revealed some sort of urge to publicize and defy, but an even stronger urge to encode and conceal. This was the central paradox of Family membership. Intriguingly, the key players placed the original thirteenth-century gravestone back over Lawrence's body so that the full statement was, quite literally, buried underground.[17]

It is clear that the Family of Love generally opted for the quieter side of Niclaes' advice, concentrating on consolidation rather than expansion and keeping a lid upon their more extravagant desires. They chose the milder flavours on HN's menu. The fellowship did not, therefore, conquer the world, and its exuberant prophecies still await fulfilment. The eventual fate of the Family does not appear to have been a glorious one. As far as we can tell, it eventually faded out of existence during the second half of the seventeenth century. It seems, therefore, that the reformed Church of England achieved a modest and very gradual success. It did not obliterate the Family in one fell swoop, but this potentially dangerous fellowship was certainly contained, and somehow persuaded not to evangelize. It remains to explain the choices that were made, and the pattern that emerged.

Part of the explanation lies within the Family itself. Put simply, introversion came naturally to mystics. An equally important factor, however, must have been the treatment the Family received from "outsiders", clerical and lay. The Familist pattern was a response to a response. Those who accepted a duty to confront heresy approached their task in a wide variety of ways. For the sake of analytical clarity, we can divide this array of attitudes into two basic tendencies, each represented by an individual Elizabethan clergyman.

The spotlight falls first on John Knewstub, a hero of the "militant tendency" and a Puritan by anyone's definition. Knewstub, who was mentioned glowingly in the Marprelate tracts, sought a reformation that was both rigorous and rapid. He remained within the established church throughout his life, and was vicar of Cockfield in Suffolk from 1579 until 1624, but he was far from happy with the Elizabethan settlement. In 1582, for example, an assembly of Puritan clergy from three counties reportedly met in Cockfield church to discuss the inadequacies of the Book of Common Prayer, and in 1604 Knewstub was one of the Puritan representatives at the Hampton Court Conference. His close links with Presbyterianism had made relations with the church government of the 1580s and 1590s decidedly prickly, and it is hard to imagine that his dealings with the bulk of his flock in Suffolk were entirely harmonious.[18] Knewstub's published work shows him to have been rigidly principled on topics related to religious persuasion. He criticized other members of the clergy for their "sleepiness" in defending the truth against its enemies. He insisted that ordinary Christians had a responsibility to "be the chief doers in the death and execution" of all heretics, even those amongst their friends and relatives.[19] There was little or no justification for flexibility and accommodation, and the idea of gentle piece-by-piece reformation was anathema. On the progress of the gospel by 1579, Knewstub conceded that many people were "content to speak to it, and take knowledge of it", but insisted that this simply was not enough: "they are but a few, that so friendly do entertain it, as that their hearty goodwill and affection may be seen to appear thereby towards it."[20]

Knewstub was also the Family of Love's most ferocious enemy, and he built his early career on a vigorous campaign against its members. He pressed tirelessly for official action against the fellowship in the years between 1576 and 1582. He preached at Paul's Cross, published *A confutation of monstrous and horrible heresies taught by HN*, lobbied the Privy Council, sought fierce parliamentary legislation, helped secure a royal proclamation commanding arrests and book burnings, led personal examinations, extracted confessions from suspects, advised bishops on how to proceed, encouraged other eminent Protestants to write against the Family, and generally revealed himself as one of the busiest of all the "busy controllers". He cared deeply about the task of Protestant persuasion, and evidently viewed the Family as a test case of some import. Knewstub despised their secretive approach, and obviously considered the threat posed to church and society to be very serious indeed. He urged the Queen to see to it that the Family's leaders, along with those members who resisted cure, were "quite cut off". This was the religious urge to persuade or, failing that, to destroy, presented in a particularly extreme version.[21]

A vital part of the strategy was to demand and extract "confessions" from Familist suspects, either in the form of recantations of past heresies or damaging declarations of current belief. Knewstub used both methods, and very probably exerted extreme psychological pressure as he confronted his worst enemies. In 1580, for example, he was almost certainly the chief examining officer when three of the courtier Familists – quite probably the most sophisticated in England – provided "The confession of Sele, Ely and Mathew, being of the family of love and of her majesty's guard". This was a radically reduced and incriminating account of their beliefs. They stated that the Day of Judgement had already occurred, that they had risen to perfection, that the Scriptures were not to be taken literally, that dissembling was justified, and that there should be no magistrates among Christians. This short and fascinating document, written in an inexpert (or frightened?) hand and presenting some bizarre spellings, tells us much more about the tense circumstances of its production than about the beliefs of the Family of Love. It makes use of both first and third person plurals in revealing its heresies, but the ratio of four "theys" to one "we" surely indicates the domineering presence of Knewstub. Several of the beliefs expressed in this and other confessions can also be related directly to passages in Knewstub's printed *Confutation*. There is no question of the Familists being offered any kind of platform upon which to explain and justify their unusual faith. Instead, such "confessions" were desperate attempts at persuasion or destruction through fear and force, even if they were sometimes dressed up for posterity as exercises in "gentle" and "friendly" Christian admonition.[22]

Knewstub insisted that he was not alone in his intense hostility to the Family of Love, although he clearly did feel somewhat isolated. A selection of other divines and magistrates approached the problem with similar tactics, and it can be argued that the anti-Familist campaign of 1576–81 revealed an acute crisis of confidence amongst England's Puritans. They felt that the people were slow to learn the gospel, that many officers in state and church were lukewarm in their persuasive energies, and that the existence of the Family somehow proved the validity of both feelings. They asked for religious passion, insisting that the truth should be published "not in corners, but on the house top".[23] They argued that people should not conform to the requirements of the established church merely for form's sake, and that outward actions were no proof of inward righteousness.

These frustrated militants turned their attentions to the Family of Love. The fellowship's investigators included the MPs who spoke in favour of the Knewstub-backed bill against the Family, the godly

Suffolk gentlemen who urged the Privy Council to take action, and the other authors – William Wilkinson, John Rogers and Lawrence Thompson, for example – who put pen to paper in angry opposition to HN's disciples.[24] At a lower social level, they also included the unnamed locals who circulated "sinister reports" about the activities of the Cambridgeshire Familists, the church officers from Downham in the Isle of Ely who "vehemently suspected" one of their neighbours, and the Balsham churchwarden who, many years later, took action against the local brethren. The newborn son of this man had recently received the tell-tale Christian name, Jeremiah.[25] Finally, we should also mention the members of some of the special commissions established in 1580. The commissioners who visited Wisbech, for example, were hand-picked for their persuasive Protestant zeal, and their investigative tactics were, overall, unsympathetic and deeply intimidating.[26]

The evidence left to us by the militant tendency is conspicuous and compelling – a collection of fiery tracts, bitter court cases, and painfully extracted "confessions". It would, however, be an error to rush towards a conclusion that the Knewstub strategy was clearly responsible either for the quiet, non-expansive style which the Family subsequently adopted, or for the fellowship's apparently peaceful demise. It must have been a factor, of course, but the fierce persuaders also ran the risk of driving the Familists into serious subversion, of activating the more radical and evangelical instincts that were also present somewhere in their make-up. The Family's apologist of 1580, feeling the strain of persecution, pleaded with God to "behold our misery: let us not now, be driven away from our dutiful obedience . . . for any manner of fear, tyranny, and false bruits, of such as live not under thy law".[27]

It is noticeable that most of the episodes in which members of the Family behaved themselves arrogantly, insolently or provocatively also involved the presence of men such as Knewstub. When Bishop Cox of Ely found the Familists in his diocese "arrogant", "obstinate" and "wilful" in their "blindness", he did so against a background of arrests, tense examinations and enforced denunciations of deeply held beliefs.[28] John Bourne's insolence before the Wisbech commissioners was born out of a similar atmosphere. Phases of persecution also provide the context for the extreme behaviour of Robert Dorrington

151

in 1580, the symbolic gravestone affair of 1609, and a bizarre incident in the 1570s when one of the courtier Familists apparently assisted in the abduction of a wealthy twelve-year-old heiress.[29] Is it possible that the policy of aggressive persuasion on the part of Knewstub and company in fact *increased* the potential threat from the Familists? It certainly must have driven them further into secrecy, but did it actually reduce their will to make headway in society by surreptitious means and to cause damage to their enemies? Probably not.

There was another way of addressing the problem, although it was rarely, if ever, articulated with clarity and depth in the surviving records. We can say with certainty, however, that Dr Andrew Perne was one of its leading exponents. Perne, best known to posterity for the way in which he trimmed his sails under successive Tudor monarchs, had very few points of temperamental or ecclesiological contact with John Knewstub. If Knewstub bordered on nonconformity at the Puritan pole of the church's spectrum, then Perne looked more likely to drop off the other end. By nature he was a moderate and conservative man, and can certainly be classified as one of the most gentle of religious persuaders. He is credited with having eased the persecution of Protestants under Mary, and with having persuaded a fiery young John Whitgift to soften his act and stay out of the flames. Radical Puritans despised his temperate nature, and Perne's appearance in the Marprelate tracts – one of the few locations in which he and Knewstub came together – was as "Old Andrew Turncoat", a figure of mockery. His admirers, nevertheless, ranged from secret Catholics to some of the most convinced of Protestants.

A question mark hangs over Perne's theological convictions, for the signals are contradictory. He came to an early and momentarily defiant rejection of transubstantiation and bequeathed a Geneva Bible in his will, but he never accepted the most vehement and fundamental Protestant denunciations of the Church of Rome. Professor Collinson has suggested that Perne displayed "an openness to conflicting tendencies" and "many features of what would later be called Anglicanism".[30] In addition, Perne was a great servant of Cambridge University, the owner of an immense and fine library, dean of Ely for many years, and – most importantly for us – the rector of two parishes, one in Cambridgeshire and one in Huntingdonshire.

We know little of his role as a rector, although the hints are that he executed his responsibilities with more dedication than many other pluralist absentees, and always ensured the presence of curates. In 1588 Perne's will, which opened with an expressively solifidian preamble, registered careful legacies to his Cambridgeshire parish. The testator provided for a visiting preacher to deliver an annual Lenten sermon, and to catechize the poor folk, "both old and young". This specification, according to Ian Green, was characteristic of catechists who took their educational duties particularly seriously.[31] The sum of three shillings and four pence was to be distributed amongst them, and those capable of saying the Lord's Prayer, Creed and Ten Commandments "in the English tongue" were also to receive one sixth of a "barrel of white herrings". Perne noted that he himself had catechized the poor "every time that I did preach there". These were the persuasive techniques of a committed, though hardly zealous, servant of the new church. The Protestant Reformation in the hands of such a pastor was likely to be a gentle, sympathetic (and perhaps incomplete) thing, built around coaxing and nudging rather than fire and thunder. Even a sworn enemy said of Perne, "he had such a patience, as might soften the hardest heart".[32]

One of Perne's parishes was in fact Balsham in Cambridgeshire, home to more Familists than any other village in the region (and probably the world). He had held the living since the start of Elizabeth's reign, generally leaving the daily duties of spiritual care to his curates. In 1574, it was brought to Perne's attention, through parties unknown, that a group of his parishioners had been holding conventicles and was rumoured to espouse unorthodox religious opinions. So, like Knewstub a few years later, Andrew Perne launched an investigation. We do not know how this was conducted, but the resultant document, yet another of the so-called "confessions", offers us several clues. Unlike the declaration Knewstub wrested from the courtiers, the Balsham example is essentially a statement of orthodoxy, conformity and obedience. The signatories were being given a chance to assert their acceptance of the status quo, rather than pressured into making radical and deeply incriminating admissions.

The Balsham men pronounced their allegiance to the Book of Common Prayer; they presented themselves as "good faithful and obedient subjects"; they denied involvement in clandestine ceremonies; they agreed, thenceforth, to restrict their meetings to members of their own households; they accepted the godliness of giving alms to the poor; and they stated that they did not belong to the Anabaptists, Puritans, Papists or Libertines. In addition, they made statements on several theological matters, all of prime importance to the Family: the perfectability of humans; the proper interpretation of the resurrection; the possibility of divine revelation "in these our days"; and the right "to speak one thing with the mouth, and think the contrary with the heart". In each case, the Familists were able to portray themselves as thoroughly orthodox, but they never quite condemned explicitly the beliefs they certainly held.[33] They created for themselves, or were offered, a formula designed to clear their names without requiring them seriously to endanger their consciences. There was no mention of the Family of Love, nor of HN, and no oaths nor public purgations were demanded. Dr Perne was satisfied with the statement, and he took no further action. He seems, however, to have known exactly what he was dealing with, for the copy he sent to Archbishop Parker was filed by the primate as a "Subscription by certain of the family of Love before Dr Perne".[34]

We can only presume that, following discussion, Perne was convinced that the individuals involved were neither subversive nor arrogant, although they were certainly unusual. Perhaps he deliberately did not probe too deeply, believing instead that a little unorthodoxy need not be targeted vigorously in persons who attended services in Balsham church more regularly than he did, served the community in a variety of ways, and were prepared to endorse publicly a document declaring their obedience. This looks very much like a negotiated settlement that left both parties feeling reasonably satisfied. Perne would doubtless have preferred that his parishioners had not been disciples of a Dutch messiah, but he perhaps felt that a diet of Church of England services and sermons might, in time, lure them from their strange obsession. He did not force the issue, and adopted a characteristically gentle stance in the task of persuasion. Intriguingly, the quiet and sober men of Balsham were to metamorphose into the wilful, arrogant monsters who confronted Bishop Cox and his commissioners just six years later. Had they really changed so much, or did the different inquisitorial approaches simply activate conflicting impulses within the Familist mind? The investigators of

1580 were angered to find that the Balsham men now cited their encounter with Perne, somewhat cryptically, as evidence that not all learned men considered them to be deadly heretics.[35]

It is possible to detect in the surviving records the faint imprint left by a more direct confrontation between Ely's fierce and gentle persuaders. When Cox recruited his team in 1580, Andrew Perne might have seemed to uninitiated observers an obvious candidate for inclusion. He had already examined some of the Familists, and was more familiar than most with their ideas and activities. He was very well known within the diocese, serving regularly as the university's vice chancellor and continuously as dean of Ely. A few years later, he was to be one of the commissioners appointed to examine evidence of Catholicism in Cambridgeshire. Yet, his name was noticeably absent from the puritanical panel appointed to combat the Family.[36] We know that he continued to take an interest, for he placed copies of the anti-Familist tracts by Wilkinson and Knewstub in his library.[37] At this time, Perne looks rather like one of those dejected but righteous TV detectives who finds himself taken off the case at a crucial juncture by a misguided superior, but who continues to pursue his enquiries behind the scenes. Sadly, if Perne returned, Morse-like, to set matters straight, he did not do so within the historian's restricted field of vision.

Further evidence of the Perne tendency is not difficult to find. Bishops Aylmer and Freke appear to have been similarly accommodating. From their viewpoint, Knewstub was less convincing as the self-appointed identifier of deadly threats to the church than as a conspicuous example of the main threat itself. While he pointed a quivering finger at the Familists, the bishops pointed a somewhat steadier one straight at him. Aylmer agreed to examine several of the courtier Familists in 1578, but found them "very sound" in religion. The same men would be assessed quite differently when they met Master Knewstub. Aylmer, like Perne, was probably satisfied with a show of conformist piety, and saw fit to delve no further. It seems that the Queen herself followed the same line; she was content for the Familists to return to her service even after Knewstub had done his worst.[38] Visible conduct was, for the moderate persuaders, a sufficient guide to the spiritual state of individuals. It was counterproductive, in their view, to insist that suspects turn their insides out.

Less famous churchmen were often just as mild in their dealings with the Family. In fact, it seems certain that the Perne perspective was considerably more widespread than the Knewstub tendency. Ely's ecclesiastical court judges, for example, tended to deal with the very rare accusations of Familism that came before them with considerable tact and flexibility. When two old Balsham men, both veterans of the earlier investigations, were presented in 1609, Judge Gager quietly postponed judgement, and the matter was not raised again. When more vigorous persuaders, like Bishops Woolton and Cox, reported their investigations to the Privy Council, they often sounded like men on the defensive, under pressure to justify their rigorous dealings. Cox, for example, was at pains to explain why he had required the Wisbech men to make public recantations.[39] As William Wilkinson watched the progress of the Family in 1578, he lamented that "the withstanders are not many". Rogers agreed, referring to "the negligence of our ministers, which either can not, or will not impugn their error in country towns where it is embraced". Another inveterate anti-Familist, writing in 1606, alleged that members of the fellowship were content to live with the religion of their parish clergymen, "provided that they hold them still, and suffer the Familists to be quiet". This was precisely the settlement negotiated by Perne in Elizabethan Balsham. And in 1648 the Presbyterian Samuel Rutherford looked back on the religious history of earlier decades, and argued that the Family had been tolerated by prelates, courtiers and the multitude alike, on account of the conformist, anti-Puritan and flexible attitudes of its members.[40] As we have seen, he was right to add the majority of the common people to his list.

It seems more convincing, on balance, to portray the containment and private death of the Family as primarily the result of its contact with persuaders such as Perne. They may not have convinced the Familists of the need to abandon their faith on the spot, but they did procure an unwritten agreement that HN's disciples would concentrate on persuading one another while leaving their neighbours in peace. In an age of evangelism, this was a significant concession. The agreement, as it was implemented out in the parishes, had several positive features. Most importantly, it established a climate in which the Familists could perceive themselves as existing comfortably *within* the Church of England, rather than as an alienated sect of spiritual outsiders. This was to activate one of the milder behavioural options from HN's comprehensive menu. Such a policy, it could reasonably be anticipated, would minimize any destructive instincts whilst maximizing the possibility of eventual reabsorption. As early as 1580, Familist apologists insisted strenuously on their support for the church, and they and their successors were willing to quote the official Homilies and Prayer Book in debate.[41] It is within the context of this negotiated settlement that the bequests made by Familist testators to their vicars should be seen. Members of the Family, it was alleged in 1622, even felt comfortable with the prospect of careers as ministers of the established church.[42]

In contrast, the dangerous potential of Knewstub's approach can be seen in the shadowy development of radical groups displaying some of the features of the slanderous Familist stereotype he and others had done much to create. In a sense, his dire warnings may have become a kind of self-fulfilling prophecy which ran exactly counter to the ongoing repercussions of the Perne perspective. In the middle decades of the seventeenth century, there were religious radicals known as "Familists", who may have read HN but whose connections with the Elizabethan fellowship were extremely tenuous.[43] They were the descendants of a hostile stereotype, rather than of the first English disciples of Niclaes. If these later "Familists" really did argue in justification of the resistance of authority and in favour of sexual freedom, they owed as much to Knewstub as to HN. It is true that some of the direct descendants of the original Family of Love probably joined the Quakers, rather than being gently reabsorbed into the Church of England, but we should note that they did so at a time when the established church was being transformed by zealots who traced their spiritual ancestry to John Knewstub. Once again, it seems that fierce persuasion drove moderate dissenters into forms of nonconformity that were far more alienated and threatening. Mid-century Quakers pinned their tracts up boldly and openly in market towns. Members of the Elizabethan Family of Love, following consultations with Andrew Perne, had never done anything of the sort.

What, in conclusion, can the encounter between the Church and the Family tell us about the promotion and reception of reform more generally? It has been argued that the majority of England's clergy addressed the potential dangers of HN and his followers in a flexible, gentle manner, and that, in so doing, they prevented those dangers from intensifying. This was a success of some significance, even if it was partial and did not bear its final fruits – the fading of the Family – for many decades. Should we perhaps develop a parallel analysis of the English Church's progress within a wider society whose members, in the mid-sixteenth century, were generally traditionalist in their religious outlooks?

These decades, as everybody knows, were for the majority of people religiously disturbing, disorientating, and potentially disenchanting. For Christian persuaders on all sides there was felt to be a real possibility that violence or indifference would develop on a massive scale. Into this fragile ecosystem marched our fierce persuaders, shooting from the hip. According to one current view, militant Protestants were reacting aggressively against the flexible but overwhelmingly popular attitudes that had characterized medieval Christianity. New rigour and new vigour were thought to provide the answers: the people should be shaken violently out of their spiritual malaise, and shown a better way, the only way. But, according to this view, Protestantism was inherently divisive and deeply unpopular: it removed comforts, published doctrines which few could understand, and did so through a tedious programme of intellectual sermons, colourless services and books which, of course, were of little use to the illiterate majority. It offered nothing to the person in the pew, and polarized many communities as they had never been polarized before. The Protestant persuaders themselves were aware of their disastrous failure by the 1580s, and regularly lamented that the truly godly were lonely figures amongst the laity. The basic compliance of the majority is explained in terms of blind obedience to authority or growing indifference to religion as a result of reform.[44]

It is essential to ask just how widespread and how representative of Elizabethan reforming attitudes such fierce persuaders were. The case of the Family of Love suggests that they, like their lay followers, were thin on the ground. Martin Ingram has been unable to find a single Wiltshire parish dominated by the self-styled "godly" in the manner of Terling in Essex.[45] Contemporaries did not make the mistake of equating the terms "Puritan" and "Protestant", as modern commentators have often tended to do. The need to distinguish between them was perceived from the middle years of Elizabeth's reign, and one Jacobean rector criticized the Puritans for singling themselves out as "brethren", "as if none had brotherhood in Christ, none had interest in goodness, none made profession of the Gospel, but themselves".[46] Gentle persuaders are not conspicuous in the archives because they did not behave themselves in ways guaranteed to find a place in a historical record that privileges militancy over moderation. When they are encountered, however, they should be attended to with care. Many invisible clerics doubtless shared the sympathetic attitude of the catechist who argued that, although lay people often had difficulties recalling what they had learnt, they "did yet understand the matter, and were therefore not to be despised or discouraged".[47]

Perne became the target of posthumous Puritan satire not because his soft-pedal attitude and his readiness to accommodate differences were considered exceptional, but because they reflected the attitude of a great many Elizabethan and Jacobean clergymen. The reflection was not, of course, precise, for Perne was an intellectual of rare calibre. Nevertheless, he can stand as an exalted example of common instincts. This was precisely how his critic Gabriel Harvey saw him, remarking that Perne's readiness to comply with sharp theological changes was not unusual amongst the ordinary clergy, though it was found less frequently in the higher ranks of church and government.[48]

Evidence of gently persuasive attitudes is widely distributed through the sources, despite the fact that it was inherently less likely to be recorded for posterity than that of more pungent perspectives. The "Perne tendency" surely informed the opinions of many of Ian Green's catechetical authors, who explained the theology of salvation in as upbeat a tone as possible, avoided contentious issues such as predestination, and accepted that reformation needed to be gradual.[49] It also lay behind the attitude of the Northamptonshire vicar who, arriving at a new parish in 1605, regretted the mutual hostility of Puritan and Catholic factions there and saw his role as one of gentle mediation between the two.[50] And it was to clerics of the Perne school that Bishop Freke of Norwich referred when he drew a distinction between the undesirable Puritan element amongst his clergy and "the staid and wiser sort of preachers".[51] We might also mention the personnel of the ecclesiastical courts who, according to Martin Ingram, adopted a careful approach to the task of raising standards of religious observance, "marching slightly in advance of popular attitudes so as to effect gradual improvement".[52] Elizabethan Catholic propagandists were more aware than certain modern historians of the gradually Protestantizing impact of such clergy, and scorned the traditionalist laity who explained that they attended the services held by their Church of England vicar "because he is a gentle person forsooth, and his wife a very honest woman".[53]

Government programmes of reform were also sensitive to the dangers of pushing too hard. Repeatedly, official acts, injunctions and homilies urged people to avoid religious controversy and to refrain from delving too deeply into spiritual questions. In 1580, the Privy Council advised one bishop "charitably to tolerate them (that esteem wafer bread) as children, with milk". This may sound to us rather patronizing, but a readiness to accommodate attachment to old symbols was also flexible and shrewd. It is not particularly fashionable nowadays to commend the texts of the Elizabethan settlement for the way in which – whether through accident or design – they permitted continuities, softened the Protestant blow, and provided a climate in which an attachment to something new was not only imposed by statute but encouraged slowly to generate. Initially, it was not so much a battle for hearts and minds as a battle for bottoms on seats; but the settlement left space for a deeper sense of devotion to follow. As Alexandra Walsham has put it, "The Church of England was to be a nursery in which the masses were gently weaned, not roughly snatched, from popery."[54] Fashionable or not, this analysis of the Prayer Book, the Thirty-nine Articles and the Homilies still has much to recommend it.

These were approaches that fitted well with the habits and expectations of a wider religious culture. Sixteenth-century Christians were accustomed to blending bits and pieces of belief that, to us, may look contradictory.[55] Protestant reformers, we are often told, set about the wholesale eradication of this tendency. But they may not all have done so. Both Susan Brigden and Ian Green, for example, present us with reformist clergymen who clearly implied that charitable efforts would bring spiritual rewards, despite the contempt in which Protestants are supposed to have held any such connection.[56] The same persistence of the old within the new is found, less surprisingly, in cheap print of the period.[57]

Milder, more sympathetic attitudes to Protestant persuasion should be viewed as part of a religious culture that was considerably more flexible and accommodating than is often assumed. Significant examples are encountered occasionally in the historical record, but probably occurred with much greater frequency. One parish constable under Mary attempted to protect a suspected Protestant by advising her to go to mass and, if called upon by magistrates, to agree to anything required, even that "the crow is white". In 1561, a dying Catholic gathered his neighbours to his bedside and said, "masters, I cannot tell of what religion you be that be here, nor I care not, for I speak to tell you the truth, and to accuse mine adversary the Devil". A year later, in a west country parish, one peace-seeking parishioner asked his neighbours to cease their quarrelling over a rood screen, the removal of which had recently been ordered: "let us agree together and have it down, that we may be like Christian men again of holy time".[58] Above all, these incidents suggest the overwhelming importance that was attached to the preservation of social harmony. It is surely wrong to portray this as primarily a secular, non-religious, instinct. Arguably, it was at the core of sixteenth-century Christianity, and was acted out every week in the mass and, later, in the Prayer Book "order for the administration of the Lords supper".

If we shift our perspective in the ways suggested here, the Protestant Reformation begins to appear in a somewhat more flattering light. The argument that it made its way triumphantly and inevitably through a landscape ready and eager for change is, one hopes, dead and buried. Recent research has demonstrated conclusively that the majority of people were reasonably content with the late-medieval church. It is therefore all the more noteworthy, given this unpromising start, that Protestant reform was achieving modest successes by the latter part of the sixteenth century. The work of a gathering band of historians substantiates this suggestion. Tessa Watt has argued that recognizably Protestant doctrines became popular in cheap printed forms, though they were frequently mixed with much that had its origins further in the past. Martin Ingram has argued, on the basis of ecclesiastical court records, that the church was gradually and effectively promoting higher, though never spectacular, standards of religious observance amongst the population. Jeremy Boulton and

Nicholas Alldridge have both commented quite positively on the capacity of the Elizabethan and Jacobean church to incorporate its lay members in the parishes. Judith Maltby has argued for the existence of a widespread and committed "Prayer Book Protestantism" from the later sixteenth century, and has denied that it was indistinguishable from "church popery". And Ian Green has encouraged us to think a little more positively about the effectiveness of the post-Reformation catechizing effort, and a little more realistically about the aims of most English clergy.[59]

It is, then, a mistake to assess the progress of Protestant reform by the standards of its fiercest and most ambitious spokesmen. It is important to read their pessimistic remarks without necessarily picking up their measuring stick. Sometimes, it should be noted, even they dropped hints that suggest the gradual development of a fairly committed form of Protestantism amongst the ordinary people. Late in Elizabeth's reign, the Puritan preacher at Wethersfield in Essex formed a covenant with a small minority of his flock, who were said to "as far exceed the common sort of them that profess the Gospel, as the common professors do exceed them in religion which know not the Gospel".[60] He may have felt compelled to discard "the common sort of them that profess the Gospel", but to us – surely – this is an intriguing and stimulating category.

This was obviously not Protestantism in anything like a pure, unadulterated form. It incorporated a variety of compromises with the past; it made its way slowly; and it was never going to satisfy the zealous persuaders. Perhaps we should think in terms of a "twin-track" Reformation, with John Knewstub losing his way after an explosive start in one lane, while Andrew Perne and his descendants jogged along slowly but robustly in the other. To clerics of Knewstub's type, the ordinary people often came to be seen as "old barrels which could hold no new wine". To those who shared Perne's perspective, they simply required patience, being more like "vessels that have narrow mouths" and that "receive not the liquor hastily poured".[61] The tiny minority that joined the Family of Love fought angrily and dangerously with Knewstub; but they compromised with Perne and ultimately – it seems – faded back into the church. Arguably, the enthusiastic traditionalism of the English majority went the same way.

Notes

1. R. Whiting, *The blind devotion of the people* (Cambridge, 1989), p. 254.
2. The fullest recent discussion of the fellowship's history is in C. Marsh, *The Family of Love in English society, 1550–1630* (Cambridge, 1994).
3. J. Rogers, *The displaying of an horrible sect* (London, 1578; 2nd edn, 1579); W. Wilkinson, *A confutation of certain articles* (London, 1579); J. Knewstub, *A confutation of monstrous and horrible heresies* (London, 1579).
4. HN, *Exhortatio I* (Cologne, *c*.1574), fos. 10, 20v, 24v, 27; *Evangelium regni* (Cologne, *c*.1574), fos. 4r, 12r, 99r–v; *Revelatio dei* (Cologne, *c*.1574), fo. 54; *Proverbia HN* (Cologne, *c*.1574), fo. 34r; *The prophetie of the spirit of love* (Cologne, *c*.1574), fo. 12v; *Epistola XI HN* (Cologne, *c*.1574), fo. B4v.
5. Knewstub. A confutation, fo. 94r; *A supplication of the family of love* (Cambridge, 1606), p. 54; Inner Temple Library, London, Petyt MS 538/vol. 47, fos. 492–3, "A declaration and confession made the xiii of December 1574".
6. Rogers, *The displaying*, fo. A4r.
7. Public Record Office (hereafter PRO), London, SP12/133, confession of Leonard Romsye.
8. *An apology for the service of love* (written, *c*.1580; published London, 1656), title page and fo. A3r.
9. See Marsh, *Family of Love*, pp. 85–9.
10. *Ibid.*, ch. 7 and pp. 68–70, 95–8, 217–18, 229–34, 249–52.
11. Cambridgeshire Record Office, Ely Consistory Court Will Register (hereafter CRO, Ely CC), C23. 47, and see Marsh, *Family of Love*, p. 187.
12. This phrase was used in Leonard Romsye's confession (PRO, SP12/133).
13. Gonville and Caius College, Cambridge (hereafter G & C), MS 53/30, fos. 126v–7r.
14. PRO, SP12/133, confession of Leonard Romsye.
15. See, for example, CRO, Ely CC, C16.465; *An apology*, p. 33; CRO, Ely CC C20.32; Wilkinson, *A confutation*, fos. 3v–A1r; HN, *Revelatio dei*, p. 54; *An apology*, pp. 18, 21, 35; British Library (hereafter BL), Landsdowne MS 921.
16. PRO, SP12/141, no. 8; SP12/140, no. 6; J.R. Dasent *et al.* (eds), *Acts of the privy council of England* (London, 1890–1907), *1580–1581*, pp. 122, 137.
17. Cambridge University Library, Ely Diocesan Records (hereafter CUL, EDR), B/2/28, fos. 17–18. This episode is reconstructed in greater detail in Marsh, *Family of Love*, pp. 218–34.
18. *Dictionary of National Biography*. See also the indexed references in P. Collinson, *The Elizabethan Puritan movement* (Oxford, 1967).
19. Knewstub, *A confutation*, fo. 8r.
20. *Ibid.*, fo. 3v.
21. See Marsh, *Family of Love*, pp. 127–36; Knewstub, *A confutation*, fos. 3v–6v.
22. BL, Harley MS 537, fo. 110.
23. Rogers, *The displaying*, fos. N4r–O5v.
24. T.E. Hartley (ed.) *Proceedings in the parliaments of Elizabeth I*, vol. I (Leicester,

1981), pp. 536, 539; Dasent *et al.* (eds), *Acts of the privy council of England, 1578–1580*, pp. 138–9; see also Marsh, *Family of Love*, Ch. 5.

25. Inner Temple Library, London, Petyt MS 538/vol. 47, fos. 492–3, "A declaration"; CUL, EDR, D/2/10a, fo. 144; CUL, EDR, B/2/28, fo. 18r–v; Cambridgeshire Record Office, Balsham parish registers.

26. G & C, MS 53/30, fos. 126–9.

27. *An apology*, pp. 55–6.

28. G & C, MS 53/30, fos. 72–3.

29. PRO, STAC 5, F3/23, F4/36.

30. P. Collinson, "Perne the turncoat: an Elizabethan reputation" in his *Elizabethan essays* (London, 1994), pp. 179–219. See also E. S. Leedham-Green, *Books in Cambridge inventories*, vol. I (Cambridge, 1986), pp. 419–23.

31. I. Green, *The Christian's ABC: catechisms and catechizing in England, c.1530–1740* (Oxford, 1996), pp. 73–4.

32. PRO, Prerogative Court of Canterbury (hereafter PCC), 46 Leicester; Gabriel Harvey, cited in Collinson, "Perne", p. 217.

33. They insist, for example, that there are no "sects" among them other than "those that doe profess . . . to learn gods word with all humility". This was not the same as denying membership of the Family of Love.

34. Inner Temple Library, Petyt MS 538/vol. 47, fos. 492–3, "A declaration".

35. G & C, MS 53/30, fo. 72v.

36. Other commissioners included Richard Greenham, William Fulke, Lord North and John Hutton, all amongst Knewstub's close contacts.

37. Collinson, "Perne"; C. Talbot (ed.) *Miscellenea recusant records* (Catholic Record Society **53**, 1961), p. 1; Leedham-Green, *Books in Cambridge inventories*, p. 444. It is just conceivable that Perne's connection with the Family of Love was stronger and more suspect than has ever been realized. He also seems to have bought copies of HN's works (which was difficult to do), and it is a striking fact that his Huntingdonshire and Cambridgeshire parishes were both home to definite or suspected Familists. For now, however, I am assuming that this was simply a strange coincidence.

38. Dasent *et al.* (eds), *Acts of the privy council of England, 1577–1578*, pp. 332, 344; BL, Landsdowne MS 29, no. 39; PRO, E351/542, and see Marsh, *Family of Love*, pp. 136–9, 164–6.

39. CUL, EDR, B/2/28, fo. 18r–v; BL, Landsdowne MS 33, no. 15; G & C, MS 53/30, fos. 127r, 129r.

40. Wilkinson, *A confutation*, dedicatory epistle; Rogers, *The displaying*, fol. E4r; *A supplication*, p. 14; S. Rutherford, *A survey of the spiritual Antichrist opening the secrets of Familism and Antinomianism* (London, 1648), pp. 170, 349.

41. *An apology*, p. 47; *A discovery of the abominable delusions of those, who call themselves the Family of Love* (London, 1622), p. 87; Rogers, *The displaying*, letter from "ER".

42. E. Jessop (alias John Etherington), *A discovery of the errors of the English Anabaptists* (London, 1623), pp. 90–1.

43. PRO, SP12, 520/85. This contains information on a variety of "Familists", some "of the Mount", some "of the valley", and some "of the Sensualists".
44. The strongest statements of this view are in C. Haigh, *English Reformations* (Oxford, 1993).
45. M. Ingram, *Church courts, sex and marriage in England, 1570–1640* (Cambridge, 1987), p. 95.
46. Examples of the Puritan/Protestant distinction can be found in J. Strype, *Annals of the Reformation*, vol. 2, pt. 2 (Oxford, 1824), p. 679; A. Walsham, *Church papists* (Woodbridge, 1993), p. 10; and *Temporis filia veritas* (Leiden? 1589). The quotation is from Robert Sanderson, cited in C. Holmes, *Seventeenth-century Lincolnshire* (Society for Lincolnshire History and Archaeology, 1980), p. 42.
47. Green, *The Christian's ABC*, p. 258.
48. Collinson, "Perne", p. 214.
49. Green, *The Christian's ABC*.
50. W. J. Sheils, *The Puritans in the diocese of Peterborough, 1558–1610* (Northamptonshire Record Society **30**, 1979), pp. 10–11.
51. BL, Landsdowne MS 33, no. 20.
52. Ingram, *Church courts*, p. 124.
53. Gregory Martin, cited in Walsham, *Church papists*, p. 35.
54. S. Brigden, *London and the Reformation* (Oxford, 1989), pp. 304, 434; Walsham, *Church papists*, pp. 8, 17.
55. See, for example, E. Duffy, *The stripping of the altars. Traditional religion in England, 1400–1580* (New Haven & London, 1992), pp. 50, 72, 184.
56. Brigden, *London and the Reformation*, p. 482; Green, *The Christian's ABC*, p. 472.
57. T. Watt, *Cheap print and popular piety, 1550–1640* (Cambridge, 1991).
58. Brigden, *London and the Reformation*, pp. 620, 631; Whiting, *The blind devotion*, pp. 183–4.
59. T. Watt, *Cheap print*; M. Ingram, *Church courts*; J. P. Boulton, "The limits of formal religion: the administration of holy communion in late Elizabethan and early Stuart London", *London Journal* **10** (2), 1984, pp. 135–54; N. Alldridge, "Loyalty and identity in Chester parishes, 1540–1640", in *Parish, church and people. Local studies in lay religion, 1350–1750*, S. J. Wright (ed.) (London, 1988), pp. 85–125; J. Maltby, "'By this book': parishioners, the Prayer Book and the established church", in *The early Stuart church, 1603–1642*, K. Fincham (ed.) (Basingstoke, 1993), pp. 115–139; Green, *The Christian's ABC*.
60. Richard Rogers, cited by P. Collinson, *The religion of Protestants* (Oxford, 1982), p. 269.
61. Josias Nichols, quoted by Walsham, *Church papists*, p. 109; I. Green, *The Christian's ABC*, p. 252.

7

"The lopped tree": the re-formation of the Suffolk Catholic community

Joy Rowe

Professor Bossy in delineating the character of English Catholicism has much that is useful to say about the geography of Catholicism, of its independent seigneurial households in the border counties, of households in the broadest sense, that encompassed kin, servants and tenantry found scattered across the face of the countryside.[1] J.C.H. Aveling's meticulous studies of Yorkshire recusancy reflected sadly on "the small, rustic, nonconformist sect of the seventeenth century . . . dominated utterly by its lay aristocracy and squireachy".[2] How far can these descriptions be recognized as true to what is known about Suffolk Catholicism? In this chapter I propose to work as close to the ground as possible. The evidence is drawn from the local records of the diocese of Norwich, from the parochial inquisitions prepared for visitations and from wills, where we may hear the echo of an individual voice. The broad sweep of Exchequer records such as the recusant rolls add little to my picture; we know who were our local gentry and their burden of fines and of the mulct. More to the point in this study is a consideration of how their fortunes affected the lives and tenancies of their dependants. One of the differences between the gentry dominated counties and Suffolk is the prevalence of freeholdings, particularly on the heavy wood/pasture lands of High Suffolk – approximating to the deaneries of Hartismere, Stow, Bosmere and Claydon. Does heavy soil breed stiff-necked independence and conservatism? Here it would seem so. In Elizabethan Suffolk yeoman freeholders struggled to retain their common rights just as they refused to join the established church; popish recusants and sectary recusants had

Distribution of Catholics in Suffolk, c.1600 and c.1800

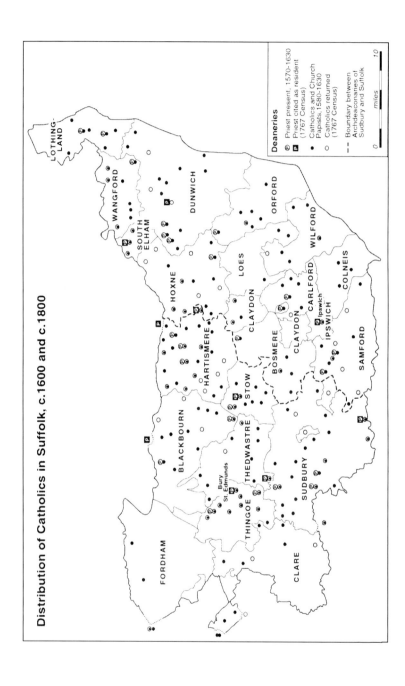

Deaneries

- Ⓟ Priest present, 1570–1630
- 🅿 Priest cited as resident (1767 Census)
- ● Catholics and Church Papists, 1580–1630
- ○ Catholics returned (1767 Census)
- – – Boundary between Archdeaconaries of Sudbury and Suffolk

0   miles   10

LOTHING-LAND

WANGFORD

DUNWICH

ORFORD

SOUTH ELHAM

WILFORD

HOXNE

LOES

CLAYDON

CARLFORD

COLNEIS

HARTISMERE

CLAYDON

BOSMERE

Ipswich

IPSWICH

SAMFORD

BLACKBOURN

STOW

THEDWASTRE

Bury St. Edmunds

THINGOE

SUDBURY

FORDHAM

CLARE

much in common. It is therefore my aim to present a couple of snapshots of Catholicism in Suffolk, at *c*.1600 and *c*.1800, in sepia rather than in black and white, certainly not in full colour.

The anonymous author of *The chorography of Suffolk* writing at the end of Elizabeth I's reign described the different areas of the county in terms that cannot be improved upon today

> The nature of it is diverse, as myself can testify having travelled in most parts of the same. That part of it which is called the Woodland and High Suffolk is exceedingly fruitful comparable to any part of England for pasture for oxen and kine, not so good for sheep. In this part of the country are made butter and cheese in exceeding great quantity of wonderful goodness comparable to any in the realm. The commodity thereof is unspeakable unto the inhabitants of the same amongst which are very many yeoman of good credit and great liberality, good housekeepers, but the ways and common roads in this country are very foul and uncomfortable in the winter time to travel in. The other parts westerly of the county are very fruitful also but the Woodland carrieth the chief credit for goodness of ground. That part of the country that is near to the sea is nothing so fruitful neither so commodious for cattle as the other but more fit for sheep and corn. The soil also about Bury to Newmarket-ward, Mildenhall, Elden [Elveden], Barton etc is mostly heathy and barren fit only for sheep and conies although in some places of the same there be some spots of good and fertile grounds at their bottoms and meadows.[3]

The description for the purposes of this chapter must be amplified by the addition of the ancient administration areas: the Liberty of St Edmund, centred on Bury St Edmunds, and made up of the ancient jurisdiction of St Edmund's Abbey, (pre-1974 West Suffolk), the Liberty of St Audrey comprising the south east of the county, with Ipswich in its south eastern corner, and the Geldable, the remaining parts of the county. The majority of the Catholic gentry houses were to be found at the time of *The chorography* in the Liberty of St Edmund and High Suffolk. Paradoxically, these areas were also the foci of earlier Lollardy, along the valley of the River Waveney forming the Suffolk–Norfolk border, and of later Puritanism in High Suffolk and around Bury St Edmunds. But this should be seen only as one aspect of the complex web of political and social interests that made up the county community in which kinship played an even more dominant role than clientage.

Although many of the Suffolk gentry had been clients of the 4th Duke of Norfolk, his disgrace in November 1569 did not greatly disturb the relationships which were the stuff of everyday life. Sir Thomas Cornwallis of Brome in Hartismere deanery, prominent among the conservative group, was summoned to appear before the Privy Council at Windsor in October 1569 "for matter of religion" and remained in the custody of Bishop Jewel of Salisbury until the following June. The matter was concerned with his conforming to the Church of England as a demonstration of his loyalty to Queen Elizabeth. He was able to exploit his long acquaintance with the Queen in her earlier years and his old friendship with Sir William Cecil to clear himself of the charge of disaffection but also to explain his dilemma in terms of conscientious non-attendance and above all, non-communicating in the Church of England. Like many of his fellow Catholics in the 1560s he was still prepared to temporize over the issue,

> to be drawn no further than to coming to church where I will use myself (by God's grace) to want offence to any man and not by device to be pressed further, which might make me either an hypocrite or desperate, but suffered without offence to any good man for a time to forbear the rest, until Almighty God (if that be His Holy Will) shall suffer me to [be] fully more persuaded of the rest.[4]

Cornwallis's stance although equivocal, marked the end of a period of indecision for the Catholic gentry of East Anglia who had hoped to achieve some degree of accommodation with the reforming Bishop Parkhurst of Norwich. Diarmaid MacCulloch, for example, has described Bishop Parkhurst's rejection of the attempt made by Thomas Kitson, Cornwallis's son-in-law, to present Thomas Atkinson, ejected in 1560 from Hollesley, to a second benefice in his gift, to be held in plurality with Fornham All Saints.[5] In defining the position of conservatives and Catholics MacCulloch quotes Lord Chief Justice Coke's dictum about emergent recusancy that "in the beginning of the eleventh year of her reign, Cornwallis, Bedingfeld and Sulyard were the first recusants, they absolutely refusing to come to our churches, and until they in that sort began, the name of recusant was never heard amongst us", and recognizes the chronology of overt recusancy as being independent of the fall of the Duke of Norfolk.[6] From the time that Sir Thomas Cornwallis returned to the county in June 1570, the influence of the religiously conservative gentry of Norfolk and Suffolk was limited to the exploitation of personal links to achieve very restricted successes in local affairs. Even as early as 1570 the stress lines were showing in any accommodation over religious policy. The replacement of Bishop Parkhurst with Bishop Freke, with his immediate aim to reduce the power and irregular conduct of Puritan enthusiasts, did not result in restoring the former confidence of the Catholic cadre. Cornwallis and his fellow conservatives co-operated fully in the anti-Puritan campaign but against a background of opposition from younger Puritan magistrates, such as Sir Clement Heigham, who had succeeded their Catholic relatives in county offices. The high ground of the new antagonisms and alignments has been explored for Tudor Suffolk by Dr MacCulloch. Similar stresses were also rising in the parishes. Ipswich and its penumbra had adopted moderate Puritanism without ascertainable strain and by the 1580s the godly town was established, with lecturers paid for by contributions from the townsfolk. The centre of religious conflict was at Bury St Edmunds where the Bishop's commissary, the archdeacon of Sudbury and the conservative members of the town's oligarchy, the Guildhall Feoffees, were in head-on conflict with Puritan gentlemen and townsmen. The intricacies of the "Bury Stirs" have been teased out by John Craig in a masterly analysis of the persons involved in this struggle for religious ascendancy and political control of the powerful institutions that governed the public activities in the town.[7] The conservative element was concentrated in the Guildhall Feoffees with their control over property in the town, extending into the countryside. A number of Catholics with local influence and interests appear on diocesan lists of papist recusants. At the same time, they formed a separate community within the town parishes of St Mary and St James.

As has been noticed, at the time of the "Bury Stirs" substantial townsmen from long-standing Catholic families were associated with the Guildhall Feoffees. As lists of names from the two parishes of Bury St Edmunds continued to be presented at the local and diocesan courts, a core of Catholic recusant families becomes apparent. In 1577, Margaret Stone alias Oliver, widow of a rich goldsmith, made a will of particular interest in the light it sheds on the network of Catholics in Bury St Edmunds.[8] After disposing of lands and tenements to her eldest son, Thomas, she bequeathed to him "all my tools and instruments and boxes belonging to the art of surgery or poticarie art". She also gave gifts "to Margaret Coppinger, widow, my best silk hat . . . to widow Godfrey, my best petticoat . . . to Mary Tebold my second best gown". These names are found on the lists of recusants through several generations of Catholics in the town. Thomas Oliver alias Stone continued his mother's calling as a physician and he and his wife, their children and grandchildren were consistently presented for recusancy, together with his sister and brother-in-law, Susanna and Thomas Rockett, and Mary and Robert Tebold, glazier. Mary Tebold, remembered in Margaret Stone's will, may have been associated with her as a midwife as she baptized two of Dr Oliver's children "privately in his house" and the child of her son, Oliver Tebold, who was an apothecary. This private baptismal ceremony was the preference of Catholics, underlining the withdrawal from the parish church and the building up of a parallel confessional body. Margaret Coppinger, the recipient of the "best silk hat", was the grandmother of the future Jesuit priest, Henry Coppinger. Educated at Bury St Edmunds Grammar School and Cambridge, he visited the priests imprisoned in Framlingham Castle in 1603 and was there converted to Catholicism by Father Ralph Bickley SJ. He was ordained in Rome in 1613 and entered the Jesuit order in the following year. Others of the "middling sort" included Thomas Willis, mason, George Fisher and Thomas Fison, innholders, Edward Hanson, keeper of the sick house, William Rich, tailor, Thomas Parker, thatcher, and many yeomen and their families. Members of the Catholic country gentry families had also settled in the town: Ambrose Jermyn, brother of the Puritan Sir Robert, and his family, Thomas Short, originally from Timworth, "no recusant in the reign of Queen Elizabeth", whose family continued as prominent

Catholic physicians in the town for several generations, Francis Moundeford (or Montford) related to many Norfolk Catholic families, and Alice Payton of Sotterley and her daughters.[9]

In the first two decades of the reign of Elizabeth, questmen, empanelled for specific inquisitions, were repeatedly required to report on the state of the parishes, from the condition of the church building and the conduct of the incumbent to the behaviour of their neighbours, with regard to their religious observance and their neighbourly behaviour. The latter included the most common failings of brawling, drunkenness and scandal-mongering as well as the more serious breaches of the fabric of village life, adultery and fornication, so often resulting in the birth of children likely to become a financial charge on the parish finances. After the statutes of 1581 and 1585 "to retain the queen's subjects in their due obedience" aimed at religious nonconformity both "papistical" and "sectary", the churchwardens' task to present their neighbours, first at the archdeacon's visitations and then, if a case was found, at the consistory court, added a responsibility with far-reaching consequences.

Among the Norwich episcopal archives is a book of presentments at the consistory court and of some indictments at the assizes which lists both papist and sectary recusants by parishes from 1593–1616. Taken in conjunction with the visitation records, these reveal the incidence of nonconformity and give a minimal indication of its strength. It is also possible to detect the number of cases pursued from the local to the diocesan courts. By the last decade of the sixteenth century it is clear from these records that the Elizabethan Church was seriously challenged at both ends of the religious spectrum. Radical Puritans were beginning to separate into communities of believers, withdrawing from their parish churches and meeting for worship in private houses. In Chattisham near Ipswich from which the vicar, James Hunt, was expelled for Brownism in 1588, Elizabeth Barker, widow, continued to lead a separatist community apparently with the connivance of the new vicar, John Baker. The latter was presented by his churchwardens at the archdeacon of Suffolk's visitation in 1606, as one that "doth impugn and speak against the rights and ceremonies established in the Church of England . . . and "doth not denounce excommunicated persons".[10]

One of the excommunicated persons was Widow Barker. "There

be often meetings at her house to confer about religion. She is a Brownist". Other excommunicated persons presented year by year from 1606 to 1616 in Chattisham were members of the Catholic gentry family and servants of Christopher Foster. He and his wife were also presented in the next door parish of Copdock. "He doth impugn the articles of religion agreed upon AD 1562. He is a recusant papist and cometh not to church". For this, the churchwardens fined him seven shillings and referred the whole family to the consistory court.[11] There their names were listed every year to 1614, but no verdicts or further penalties recorded. In 1603 the number of communicants in Copdock was 77 and in Chattisham 55. In these small parishes, the withdrawal of Catholic and sectary recusants from the Church of England established religious dissent as a significant factor in the religious demography of the county. However, it is important to give attention to those parishes further away from a gentry house. The parishes of central Hartismere Deanery had formed one of the centres of Lollardy at the beginning of the century; by its end, recusant Catholics were presented there in larger numbers than recusant sectaries. It may be, of course, that the sympathies of the parish officers lay with radical Puritans and so fewer were presented. Nevertheless, the Catholic community here does not appear to have been dependent on its proximity to gentry houses. By 1596 Father Holt, a Jesuit missioner, estimated that there were between 40 and 50 "old" priests still at work throughout the country. In Suffolk at the end of Elizabeth's reign, "old" priests were still active in addition to the secular priests who, where they can be charted, numbered between eight and 12. These seem to have been peripatetic missioners rather than chaplains resident in gentry houses.[12]

The Jesuits, always many fewer in number than their reputation gave credit for, tended to remain at a single house, giving the Spiritual Exercises to individuals and instruction and spiritual direction to Catholics who sought them out. In 1590, John Gerard SJ spent a year with Edward Rookwood at Euston before moving the 15 miles to Lawshall where he remained for a similar period with Henry Drury. On their own testimony, these enthusiastic young priests had a low opinion of the "old" priests who had been caring for the Catholics for the sixteen years before any of the seminary priests arrived. Their objective had been to sustain Catholics in the style and ground of faith in which they had been brought up, using the depleted means at their disposal. The objective of the secular priests and Jesuits was to extend the mission and to introduce the Tridentine reforms and methods in which they had been educated in the new continental seminaries. In Suffolk all priests were welcomed and given the support they needed. A system of communication was set up and apparently centred on Roger Martin's extended household in Long Melford. Among those named on the Norwich indictment lists for 1610 were Henry Thurgood, Will of Yorke, Will Rookes and Robert Rookes his son, Robert Reve and John Shepherd, "travellers, recusants and messengers for the papists". Robert Reve *gentleman* also appeared from time to time, in 1603 and 1605, and in 1606 is noted as "supposed to be a priest". In 1609–11 his name had been replaced by Henry Foster, "supposed" or "suspected to be a Popish priest". The priests imprisoned in Framlingham Castle in 1604 had John Medcalf "to run to and fro" for them. From the places in Suffolk at which the secular priests were arrested, it seems that in this county they were constantly on the move. Some of them were local men, for instance Montford Scott born *c.*1550 at Hawstead, near Bury St Edmunds, ordained in 1577, at work in High Suffolk in 1580, arrested at Hawstead in 1590 after betrayal by his cousin Richard Lacey of Brockdish, Norfolk, and executed in 1591.[13]

In the 1593 visitation of the archdeaconry of Sudbury 33 parishes returned between them 18 popish recusants, all of whom were ordered to appear at Ipswich and fined seven shillings or 12 shillings; 46 parishioners were also presented for not communicating, some for seven years past, others for six or four years, down to one year's failure. Of these, four were referred to Ipswich and one fined 7 shillings. This raises the question of who were these refusers to join in the common sign of unity with God, queen and neighbours. Using the available sources of information about Catholic and sectary recusancy from exchequer, episcopal and assize court records, it is possible to make a distinction between religious refusal and negligence without any confessional content. In the end, this often comes down to recognizing individual and family names. Sometimes Catholics, whose names appeared repeatedly as popish recusants, were removed from this category into that of non-attenders or non-communicants, and often were marked as being excommunicated.

175

Similarly, local clusters of sectary recusants, often more specifically categorized as Brownists or Anabaptists, can be identified as earlier non-attenders. This posits that there were church sectaries as well as church papists. The severity of penalties imposed on sectary recusants seems to have varied with the religious climate. In Suffolk a large degree of toleration was extended even to persistent attenders at wholly separated conventicles. The sectary recusants were largely drawn from yeoman families and, as with Catholics, there was a strong family tradition of separation building up throughout the early seventeenth century. Along the northern boundary of Hartismere deanery lie a number of parishes where both Catholic and sectary recusancy was strong. They lay within the estates of Cornwallis of Brome and Yaxley of Yaxley and Mellis; a general indulgence of nonconformity was extended to them, so much so that at Thrandeston the sectary pastor Thomas Scase, a yeoman copyholder, in 1627, had "not resorted to his parish church by the space of 20 years last past".[14] There in 1629 "omnes et singulos for holding erroneous opinions" were presented at the archdeacon's visitation, those in error including two Catholic married couples and the Catholic wife of a non-attender. In the parish of Redgrave Joan Marshe, widow, was also presented in 1627 "for leaving her own parish church to resort to a private conventicle kept at Thrandeston at the house of Thomas Scase", and with her, two other women. At the same parish visitation: "Bridget Branson cometh not; she is a papist. Andrew Branson cometh negligently", and also both were presented for "not receiving the holy communion for the space of one year". She also had Catholic neighbours, Peter Hobart, yeoman, John Sutton, Alexander Roryson and John Laws.[15]

One category of churchwardens' presentments gives particular difficulty – the non-attenders, non-communicants and the negligent. But, a lack of consistency in categorization often sheds light on an individual's convictions. Some of the non-attenders named at a visitation come from families of known Catholic antecedents. The two sons of the Catholic Rushbrooke family, victuallers in Wetherden (Hartismere deanery) moved in 1611 to Thurston where George Rushbrooke "did not receive as he is bound" and in 1627, in the next door village of Great Barton, he "stands excommunicate for not coming to church for the space of three years". William Rushbrooke, the second son, in 1609 moved five miles away to Rickinghall Superior, where he too refuses to come to church. In Bury St Edmunds, St James Parish, at the 1611 visitation a distinction is made between Thomas Short "a popish recusant", who "cometh once a month but receiveth not the communion and Anne his wife a popish recusant but goeth not at all". Their son James Short was presented for "playing cards in time of divine service in the house of Robert Mauce victualler". There is no difficulty in determining the styles of Catholicism in this family: Thomas Short a church papist, his wife Anne, a strictly nonconforming Catholic and their son James negligent but still nonconforming.[16]

The significance of church papists has until recently either been misunderstood or has received a bad press. Alexandra Walsham has very successfully teased out the different strands of contemporary as well as modern controversy that emerge from the polemics of the Elizabethan pamphleteers. Where I think she is less convincing is at the point where the sword slips between bone and marrow, at the level of the local Catholic unit, however small, within the parish. Here she seems to follow the clerical polemicists. Compromise in matters of conscience has always been a problem, involving as it does fundamental issues of divided loyalties and conflicting obligations to communities as well as to individuals. For many Elizabethan lay people, to make one's physical presence in the parish church the touchstone of loyalty to the Queen and the affirmation of solidarity with one's neighbours was to put conflict at what should have been the centre of unity. The social nature of parish life is a factor to reckon with. Walsham leaves no room for inevitable shifts and accommodations. She is aware of the impatience and unease felt by the Counter-Reformation priesthood with the initiatives taken by the laity to preserve some sense of community as well as of continuity with the past. The subtleties of the casuists provided ways of escape for those able to make use of them. They were not a great deal of use to simpler Catholics confronted by incomprehensible choices. The choice of occasional conformity may have been for some the start of the slippery slope into indifferentism, for others it may have been a temporary and expedient means of survival. When Sir Thomas Cornwallis exclaimed in exasperation over the political pamphleteer-ing of Father Robert Parsons that "they be out of the way themselves and therefore do not regard what we endure", he might equally well have been referring to Parson's *Brief discourse containing reasons why Catholics refuse to go to church.*[17]

Church papists among the gentry felt able to attend their parish church from time to time to avoid the financially crippling cumulative fines for non-attendance but drew the line at receiving holy communion. In spite of the attempts of the continentally-trained priests to discourage this semi-conformity and to withdraw the Catholic community into an uncompromising separation, out-and-out recusancy proved too costly for many. Their wives remained openly Catholic, bringing up their children and ruling their households as models of domestic piety and running the risk inherent in harbouring and sheltering priests. The penalty of excommunication from the Church of England did not lie heavily on Catholic women and few went to the trouble of a journey to Ipswich or Norwich to be absolved. Occasionally, consistory court and visitation records notice absolutions being granted for nominal payments and various private arrangements could be made. In 1606 Richard Poley of Boxted, gentleman, is recorded as "a recusant who hath sometimes privately reported unto his parish priest". The principle of withdrawal resulted in a separated ecclesial body, lacking the vitality of Protestant dissent and marked by an intense private spirituality. The complaint levelled at priests in plush Oxfordshire manor houses, neglecting the pastoral care of more spiritually and physically deprived parts of the English mission perhaps should be redirected at the heads of the households who looked no further than outside their own gates.[18]

By the end of Elizabeth's reign a pattern of Catholic community had been established in Suffolk, scattered across the county but with the greatest concentration in High Suffolk and the Liberty of St Edmund. Some adherents were rich enough to sustain the weight of fines and well enough connected by family ties and old friendships to keep out of serious trouble so long as they did not obtrude their convictions. Nevertheless, one cannot convincingly dismiss the whole community as a socially uniform gentry circle with their servants and tenants and so far as people of lower social status were concerned, essentially seigneurial in character. If this had been the case, the failure of a Catholic gentry line for any one of a variety of reasons such as through conforming to the Church of England (Waldegrave), through death without a direct Catholic heir (Hare) or through giving so many sons and daughters to the priestly and religious life that it became impossible to sustain the blood line (Foster of Copdock), the consequent loss of the house with its facilities for harbouring a priest and welcoming neighbours to receive the sacraments from time to time would have meant the disappearance of that community. A second strand in this new, evolving Catholic network was provided by a substantial stratum of lay people sufficiently well-grounded in the theology as well as the practice of their faith to be able to transmit it to their own families and associates. The gentry made their own arrangements for the education of their children, either in schools or convents abroad or at home. In 1599 at Euston "the children of the said Mr Edward Rookwood (obstinate recusant) be brought up in popery but be under the age of 16 years as is informed". In 1606 at Hintlesham, near Ipswich, "Charles . . . teacheth school in Mr Timperley's house" and in the same year, Mary Barney, widow, living in Michael Fuller's household at Mickfield was fined 7 shillings for not coming to church and the churchwarden noted that "she keepeth at Mr Fuller's house and traineth his children up in popery". This bringing-up of children in the Catholic faith however was not confined to the gentry. At Stanningfield, John Garnet, yeoman, and his wife were presented and fined 7 shillings. "They instruct William and Dorothy their children in popish religion". The will of John Gooderich, yeoman, of Bacton, proved 4 November 1631, attached a proviso to a bequest intended to ensure the continued family adherence to Catholicism.[19] It may also reflect the benefits of rubbing shoulders with neighbours in a strongly Puritan parish. His whole estate was left to his niece Mary, wife of Robert Spencer. On her decease her husband was to have £10 per annum out of the estate provided that "he shall read every day two chapters of the sacred word of God and that he shall bring up his son to learning, and both his son and his daughter in the Catholic religion". If these children died without issue "then this my land shall return to the nearest of my blood and name that is of the Catholic religion, after the death of their father Robert".[20] The Gooderich family had many branches with members throughout the central part of Hartismere. In addition to their Catholicism they had a family tradition of practising medicine. Another Robert Spencer, in

1662, witnessed the will of Susan Gooderich of Haughley, widow of Thomas Gooderich, in which she left "to my son John the case of instruments of chirurgeon and one silver syringe which was his father's". This dynasty of surgeons continued in the practice of their faith and their craft in Ipswich and in Sudbury but above all in their native parishes. The family name appears repeatedly in the earliest Catholic registers of the Bacton Mission which date from the late eighteenth century.[21] Thus the link between the earliest Catholic community of post-Reformation days and the more formalized establishment can be linked as directly through this line of yeomen freeholders in High Suffolk as it is through the surviving gentry, most of whom continued to live in the Liberty of St Edmund.

One neglected source for the sustaining of isolated and poorer Catholics was the dominance in the family of women recusants, the well-to-do grounded in a sense of responsibility to feed the hungry and clothe the naked and to teach the rudiments of faith to their children and dependants. Many girls from gentry families and their personal servants felt that the only place for them to follow their religion was in one of the observant communities of exiled English nuns in France or Flanders. The English Ladies, first recruited by Mary Ward in 1609, were struggling to establish themselves at St Omer on the pattern of the Jesuits, with the intention of being able to return to England to teach and to work, through visiting the sick, and isolated Catholics and those in prison. One lay sister was at work in 1621 in the Suffolk countryside. Known only as Sister Dorothy she was closely associated with Anne Markham, wife of the recusant Sir Nicholas Timperley of Hintlesham near Ipswich. She sent an account of her work to an unnamed superior, describing her visits to the sick and poor in the villages, teaching and catechizing children and adults in their own homes, whenever possible persuading church papists to return to a more regular practice of Catholicism and preparing them and her other converts to receive the sacraments. She complained of the shortage of priests in the Suffolk countryside although she was able to make contact at Hintlesham with Father Cuthbert Parker OSB and Father Edward Bedingfeld SJ whom she knew by his alias of Silsdon, and with an unnamed secular priest living about ten miles away. Judging by the distance she had to travel to meet this priest he was possibly living with the Sulyards at Haughley or the Mannocks at Wetherden. Thus something recognizable as Catholic corporate life was still present, though deprived of the vivacity of the cycle of liturgical life in the parish to which older Catholics could look back with nostalgia. It was with something of this regret that Robert Southwell, once of Horsham St Faith, Norfolk, poet and Jesuit missioner, son, nephew and cousin to many East Anglian gentry families wrote, from his prison in the Tower as he awaited execution. He had not experienced the days to which conservatives and traditionalists looked back, but he lived in the faith that eventually all would be well.

> The lopped tree in time may grow again,
> Most naked plants renew both fruit and flower;
> The sorriest wight may find release of pain,
> The driest soil suck in some moistening shower.
> Time goes by turns, and chances change by course,
> From foul to fair, from better hap to worse.[22]

In the absence of much contact with fellow Catholics outside their immediate circle and deprived of the sacraments except on rare occasions, what resources could Suffolk Catholics draw on for spiritual nourishment? There were, of course, the proscribed blessed rosaries which priests carried with them for distribution. In April 1584 two friends of Father Montford Scott were indicted at Norwich for receiving beads from him.[23] Charles Yelverton in 1601 described his life travelling through High Suffolk before arrival at the English College in Rome, spending some time with Dr Thomas Gooderich in Winston near Debenham, then with Mr John Bedingfeld at Redlingfield where he stayed for a year.

> Then Sir Thomas Cornwallis, knight, sent for me and invited me to stay with him and there for three or four months I repeated the breviary with him to whom at my first arrival I told my intentions and whither I wished to go.[24]

Primers and Manuals were still circulating among Protestants as well as Catholics. Fr Augustine Baker OSB (1575–1641) looking back on his childhood wrote of his Protestant father that

181

he did daily at least, whensoever he could get vacancy from his employments and solicitudes spend much time in recital of vocal prayers and that out of Latin Catholic authors, whereof by some means or other he had gotten some variety. In the English tongue there were then no prayer books save some few Catholic ones whereof he had gotten some. And of these books one after another, walking in the garden in his way to and fro thither, he would recite to himself, yet so audibly that others could not but hear somewhat . . . nothing troubled his mind either one way or other concerning Catholic and Protestant beliefs, yet still persevered in daily vocal prayer.[25]

It was possible, although dangerous, to circulate copies of Catholic books from the illegal presses. Manuscript versions were also available. Peter Mowle of Attleborough, a scrivener presented for recusancy from 1590 to 1611, travelled among the Catholic houses of south Norfolk and north Suffolk distributing his copies, sometimes as New Year's gifts with fulsome dedicatory prefixes. He was with "old" Lady Lovel at East Harling, Norfolk close to the Suffolk border where her chaplain Thomas Moore wrote his name on the final page of the collection. Father Moore had been instituted as vicar of East Harling in March 1558; he was deprived for popery in 1568 and may have made his home with the recusant Lovel family. Peter Mowle described the collection as his Commonplace Book; it seems likely that the individual items, written at different times, were the master copies from which he was able to make up different compilations for his various clients. Interspersed with miscellaneous items such as "of the earthquake 24 December 1601 between 10 and 12 of the clock and the terrible crack of thunder with flash of lightning which happened on the 25 day of the same month" are copies of Vaux's Catechism in the 1583 edition; A Manual of Prayers 1583 "copied out by me Peter Mowle of Attleborough the year of our Lord God 1589 and in the 35 year of my age, desiring all good Catholic readers to remember me and all such other sinners"; the Jesus Psalter; prayers of Sir Thomas More; *Desiderius or the ready way to the love of God written in dialogue wise, under learned and pleasant allegories first put forth in the Spanish tongue and after translated into Latin and now lately into English for the behoof of the devout of our nation by I*

G *prisoner* (John Gerard SJ). Perhaps the most poignant items are Robert Southwell's St Peter's Complaint and his Epistle to his Father. The whole Commonplace Book is full of references to the Catholic gentry families of East Anglia: Sulyard, Wodehouse, Yaxley, Daniell among others, on whom their dependants relied to keep alive their links with the Catholic Church.[26]

In laying this emphasis on the self-help measures to sustain individual and corporate Catholic life it must not be assumed that the rare ministrations of the priests, both "old" priests and those trained in the seminaries overseas, were less than lifegiving, for it was the mass that all longed for and for which such heroic sacrifices were made. The penal legislation was aimed at destroying Catholicism, root and branch, as a system of belief of which the guarantee was the succession of orthodoxy through the apostles and the see of Rome. This appeal to a power beyond local sovereignty was the source of a centuries old struggle, exacerbated by the pressures to reform a church grown corrupt. The sixteenth century was as conscious as our own of the dangers of the baby-and-bathwater syndrome. The problem over the church papists occurred, and occurs still for some, exactly at this point: could those who put first the survival of property and the means of supporting a Catholic recusant wife and family, who attended the parish church but refused to receive holy communion but who, when the rare opportunity occurred, came to mass, be regarded as too compromised to be counted as part of the Catholic community? The Ecclesiastical Census of 1603 and the Canons of 1604 solved the problem for the government by including on lists of recusants all "half recusants" and those who refused to receive communion. The numbers recorded for the archdeaconry of Sudbury and for the episcopal visitations of 1606 and 1611 show a general rise in designated popish recusants where there had previously been appreciable numbers of non-attenders and non-communicants. It is not possible to give precise or percentage figures as the parishes returning answers differed on each occasion.

Some sixteen Jesuits were at work in the Suffolk area, in the first quarter of the seventeenth century, some as chaplains as before, but most constantly moving about so as not to compromise their harbourers. They administered the sacraments, made converts and collected alms for the relief of poor Catholics. The secular seminary priests were not in such a happy position. Many of them had been imprisoned from 1580 in Framlingham Castle. The prison regime allowed them a degree of liberty to receive visitors and to exercise their calling as priests. Grace Nuthall and Christian Bedingfeld from the neighbouring parish of Swilland were indicted at the consistory court in July 1601. "These repair to Framlingham Castle to the popish priests there". In the same year, amongst the papists known to be living in the castle, was the keeper's converted wife. At least four of the many visitors from Cambridge were converted by Fathers Robert Bickley SJ, Robert Woodruff and Thomas Bramston, the converts themselves in their turn becoming priests. Serious disputes arose between the seculars and the few Jesuits confined with them. The Appellant and Archpriest controversies continued to poison relations between the two sides long after they were sentenced and sent into exile from Framlingham in 1603, when the prison was closed. As the political manoeuvrings surrounding the Spanish and French marriages led to a reduction in non-fiscal pressures on Catholics, so it became possible for the Jesuits to organize themselves into area colleges and residences. Suffolk became part of the College of the Holy Apostles, together with Essex, Norfolk and Cambridge-shire. In coded messages, this college was always referred to as "Mrs Suffolk".[27]

The problems of rural Catholicism so clearly understood by J.C.H. Aveling were also reflected in East Suffolk in the late seventeenth and early eighteenth century. This is the setting for my second snapshot of the Suffolk Catholic landscape. Although the Jesuits were able to maintain a discreet presence, there was a shortage of suitable mass centres in the countryside as a consequence of the giving up of many Catholic gentry houses. The Everards of Linstead Magna and Parva and the Fullers of Chediston had sold up and returned to their family roots in Norfolk and Yorkshire. The Warners at Parham and the Fosters at Copdock had made over their estates to religious orders and had themselves entered religion. Only the Jetters in Lothingland and the Tasburghs at Flixton maintained chaplaincies that also served the surrounding areas. The Registry of Papists' Estate, of 1717, is a useful source for tracing the movements and property transactions of families who once figured so conspicuously on the recusant rolls and among those presented for popery. As the century drew on, so more and more of the gentry consolidated their properties; for example the Bedingfelds of Redlingfield and Wingfield gradually contracted their Suffolk interests, concentrating on their estate at Oxburgh in Norfolk.

Although Suffolk Catholics had not manifested any Jacobite tendencies, the justices for the borough of Bury St Edmunds summoned all papists either reputed or suspected to be, to appear personally on 30 September 1745 to make, repeat and subscribe to the anti-Jacobite declaration and take the oaths of allegiance. This provides a very accurate picture of the Catholic community, their social status and occupations. Children were not included. Of the 118 Catholics who were summoned, 16 were gentry, two doctors and their wives, 34 were shopkeepers, three farmers and yeomen, 15 gardeners and labourers, 13 servants, six widows and wives and 14 spinsters. On the next day the constables were directed

> to search for all arms, weapons, gunpowder or ammunition which shall be in the houses, custody or possession of the several persons undernamed . . . and to seize and take for the use of his Majesty and his successors . . . and to search for and seize . . . all horses above the value of five pounds to be sold.

Thirty eight people were named, the gentry and the most substantial of the tradesmen.

> The constables . . . have made diligent search . . . and have taken and seized to his majesty's use . . . of Mr Dillon one fowling piece, a brace of pistols and two swords without hilts, of Sir William Gage, a brace of pistols and three swords, of Mr Bond a sword and no more. But have not taken or seen on such search any horse of the value of five pounds in our judgment.[28]

The Bury St Edmunds' Catholics formed a comprehensive cross-section of a generally prosperous and law-abiding town. There were significant names among the families represented on the summons, first to be found on lists of recusants from the 1580s: in particular Stone alias Oliver and Godfrey, Short, Tildesley, and Rookwood and

Gage of Coldham, Euston and Hengrave. The names of Emmanuel Christmas and his wife Susan form an interesting connection with an earlier Emmanuel Christmas, who had entered Douai on a burse, a scholarship boy. He was ordained in 1710, remaining as prefect of the scholars until 1718 when he became chaplain to the Blue Nuns at Paris. He died in 1748.[29]

The Jesuits were firmly established in the archdeaconry of Sudbury. The Mannock house of Gifford's Hall, Stoke by Nayland, had as chaplain, Father Sir George Mannock SJ, the 9th and last Baronet, who not only said mass in the chapel adjoining the house but also visited Catholics along the Stour valley. The chaplaincy was so extensive that a properly constituted register of baptisms, confirmations, marriages and burials was kept from 1783, with notes of the visits of the vicar apostolic of the Western Region to administer confirmation, and the numbers of Easter and Christmas communicants. The Martin family chapel at Long Melford appears to have been closed about 1760 and Catholics were expected to attend either at Gifford's Hall, as did "old" Lady Martin and her companion, or at the chapel of Coldham Hall, Stanningfield. Father John Gage SJ, son of Sir William Gage (2nd Baronet) of Hengrave and Elizabeth Rookwood, heiress of Coldham, lived in a house belonging to his mother

> in Southgate Street, Bury St Edmunds . . . in which divine service was performed in secret, and which was afterwards tenanted by a Mrs White who was a friend of the Gages though a Protestant and from whom the lane which there branches off from the street is still called Madam White's Lane.[30]

The chapel was and is approached by a separate outside door, leading to a back staircase in the house and was able to accommodate about 50 people. This was inadequate for the numbers of Catholics in the town and during the years 1760–1 properties in Westgate Street were bought and demolished to build a double-fronted house for the priest with a chapel attached behind, costing £2,000 to construct and furnish. This became the centre of the mission and the priests stationed there rode out to administer the sacraments wherever there were groups of Catholics. The register of 1757 makes clear that although *de jure* Catholicism was proscribed, *de facto* a quantifiable Catholic community within the town was a reality. The number of Easter communions provide a guide to the effective core of the congregations: at Bury St Edmunds an average of 110 from 1756 to 1790; at Stoke by Nayland about 30 and in the scattered High Suffolk area about 30.[31] The chaplaincies had indeed done much to keep Catholicism alive but it was the tenacity of the laity to hold on, even in extremes of isolation, that provided the congregations for these new public chapels, the congregations socially disparate but with a single sense of loyalty.

In one sense it was easier to create this sense of corporateness in a small and flourishing town than to bring Catholics together in the much less accessible countryside of High Suffolk. The few remaining Catholic gentry houses were in a strong position still to dominate a landscape of scattered settlements. From Thelveton, just over the Norfolk border, to Stradbroke, Redlingfield and south to Haughley, there were opportunities for travelling priests as well as household chaplains, to build up a coherent body of Catholics. Marriages between Catholics and Protestants were becoming increasingly common and by no means invariably led to conversions in either direction. Buttlesea Hall, the Fox family home, was the setting for the baptisms by Thomas Havers' chaplain from Thelveton, of all the children of Joseph Fox. When their father died in 1778 the children's names were inscribed in their Protestant mother's Church of England baptismal register at Worlingham, accompanied by a memorandum that they had all been previously baptized by a Popish priest.[32] Francis, the eldest son's name, (baptized 1759) is omitted from the register, as it is from his mother's will, since he had entered a Catholic seminary before his father's death. The Fox family chapel at Buttlesea Hall with its altar rails still in place remains today in the attic of the house, the furnishings, including a fold-away pulpit and the great retable having been transferred after many vicissitudes to the nearby parish Church at Thornham Parva.

In 1767 every Anglican incumbent was required to make a return of papists in his parish to the bishop of the diocese. The original list for Norfolk and Suffolk with individual names noted, has survived, unlike the majority of local returns, and presents an accurate picture of the Catholic community in the two counties. In all, Suffolk returned 512 Catholics.[33] Bury St Edmunds' two parishes contained 150 Catholics, Ipswich's few parishes that sent in returns, just 12. The distribution of Catholics persisted around remaining gentry houses. Where the mass was available, there the community remained however feebly, but still replacing itself when losses occurred. This is the perdurable story of the *bekennende kirche*, the confessing church. The mass was the cohesive force that held together isolated congregations. High Suffolk remained a comparatively strong Catholic area in spite of its relative isolation from the towns.

But by 1767 the old network of chaplaincies in Hartismere deanery was in the process of being transformed as traditional houses were no longer available. The last Yaxley died in 1782; Cornwallises of Brome had removed a hundred years before; Bedingfelds had returned to Norfolk from Redlingfield but had left provision for the partial maintenance of a priest to travel the area, saying mass in different locations and drawing the balance of his stipend from the congregations he visited. The benefactress, Mrs Mary Maire, was born a Bedingfeld. She died in 1784 having completed the formalities for the foundation of the mission, with a stipend of £40 per annum for the priest and the obligation to remember in prayer members of the Bedingfeld and Maire families. The memorandum book of the mission is prefixed by the following explanation "The following are true copies of untied pieces found scattered about at Bacton congregation". Chronologically the two earliest entries, although not first in the book, are "February 10 1768: the baptism of – Wilson, daughter of Edward and Frances Wilson, and James Pike received into the Church: witnesses James Panton and Anne Lilly", both certified by J Wyke. Father Wyke was living in Coulsey Wood House, Stoke Ash, a former house of the Bedingfelds, which had remained in Catholic occupancy since their departure, first rented by James Farrell who in 1768 had sold his furniture and moved into Bury St Edmunds and then by Francis Gostling, who continued to support the mission. Father Wyke remained at Coulsey Wood until 1796 when he was succeeded by a French émigré priest, August Henry Joseph Joly.[34] Coulsey Wood proved an excellent centre for worshippers to attend from a seven-mile radius. Bishop Talbot in 1778 and Bishop

Berington in 1786 confirmed ten candidates from five families and 18 from eight families. The southern end of the mission was served from Haughley Park, still the home of the Sulyards, that most faithful of recusant families, until the death of the last representative, Edward Sulyard, in 1799. In spite of this, the chapel at Haughley Park remained available for regular masses, confirmations and weddings. Another émigré priest, Louis Gilles de La Fontaine, lived there, sharing the duties with Father Joly from 1799. He opened a new Register, "Libellus Memoriales Catholici Congregationis vulgo dicta BACTON CONGREGATION inceptus a me Ludovici Gilles cognomine De la Fontaine 19 Maii AD 1799". Another centre was at an unidentified house in Cotton, seven miles from Coulsey Wood and Haughley Park. The Easter communion numbers for 1793 were 43 at Cotton and 22 at Haughley Park; in 1795, 31 at Bacton (another unidentified house); in 1797, 36 and in 1798, 34, both at Bacton when communicants came from Thelnetham, Thornham Magna, Walsham le Willows, Thwaite, Woolpit and Elmswell, distances of seven to ten miles. Among the names of the parishioners is that of the Gooderich family, now with several branches but still living in the ancestral parishes of Bacton, Wyverstone and Haughley. Another branch had migrated as far as Bury St Edmunds and figures in the register of 1757.[35]

The Relief Act of 1791 legitimized the freedom to meet for worship that Suffolk Catholics had already enjoyed for some years. The transition from a small enclave, its circumstances necessarily self-regarding, to an engaged part of a wider community, was a challenge that not all were ready to take up. Father John Baptist Newton, chaplain at Coldham Hall, with responsibility for Catholics south of Bury St Edmunds, in 1786 wrote to his superior

There was formerly a chapel in these parts (Long Melford) . . . but as things are at the present, I must ride forty or fifty miles east, west, north and south, where nothing is to be met with but ignorance, stupidity and sometimes a total neglect of religion, attended with such indifference as one would not expect to meet with even in a Canadian who had once learned the truth taught in the Gospel.

189

On another occasion he lamented

> Will you believe it? I carry the blessed sacrament twenty or thirty miles to people as full of health as I am myself, and only because they do not think it worth their while to wait upon Almighty God at Coldham.[36]

In 1794 a brick "Emancipation" chapel was built onto Coldham Hall and remained for public use until 1823 when the Rookwood Gages sold the estate and other arrangements for a substitute chapel were made.

The indifference complained of by Fr John Baptist Newton was a prevailing problem but one that was vigorously addressed by the Jesuit fathers in Bury St Edmunds. They not only shared in the social, intellectual and cultural interests of their better-off parishioners but also kept before them the needs of the less fortunate. In 1794 a "Friendly and Charitable Society of persons professing the Roman Catholic religion . . . for the relief and maintenance of the several members thereof, in sickness, old age and infirmity" was established. The stewards or treasurers, committee men and supervisors were all laymen, respected tradesmen in the town. The sickness and old age benefit of 7 shillings per week for six months, reduced to three shillings and sixpence for the remainder of the time and £4 6s. 0d. for funeral benefit was financed by members' entrance fee of two shillings and sixpence and weekly contributions of two pence. Fines of two pence were imposed for non-attendance at meetings, funerals and the annual mass for benefactors. In addition "Every member . . . shall observe the precept for attending chapel on Sundays and holidays . . . and every member shall observe the precept for Easter".[37] A free school, open to all denominations, was also established. This liberal approach to the concern for the education of the poor, shared by all the churches in the town did much to break down the traditional prejudice and suspicion against the once feared and demonized Jesuit priests.

For the Catholic Church to be visibly involving itself in social welfare and education for all was both a reminder of what its role had been in the past and a hopeful sign of growth in the future. In addition, its contribution to the intellectual and musical life of the town was recognized by contemporaries, who enjoyed the soirées of the Jesuits, at which a string quartet, made up of the resident priests, performed with great effect. Here is an engaging picture with which to end this consideration of the developing Catholic community in Suffolk but is it apt? The church of the early nineteenth century may have also been pausing *"pour mieux sauter"*, to gather strength to deal with the new challenges of industrialization and immigration. In this context Robert Southwell's image of the lopped tree, pruned of old wood, a thing of utility as well as of beauty, is surely more appropriate.

At the beginning of the nineteenth century Catholicism in Suffolk, as elsewhere, differed in several respects from what it had appeared to be two hundred years earlier. Any suggestion of survivalism had been shed but a just sense of the value of tradition had been maintained; the imbalance due to the dominant patronage of the gentry over the deployment of priests was being corrected by the activity of the vicars apostolic. The growth in numbers of prosperous tradesmen and artisans in the towns and yeoman farmers and wage earners in the countryside provided another source for the financing of chapels and mass centres. Although the Church of England, with its political apparatus, still dominated town and country, there was also a deeply rooted counter-culture of separatism, of scepticism over the limits to which power should be exercised. Professor Bossy, reflecting on the place of Catholicism within the English religious tradition, sets it firmly within the context of nonconforming, "non-Protestant" dissent, in empathetic community alongside Quakers and Unitarians.[38] This was a position in which re-formed Catholicism felt itself at home, within the good fellowship that Sir Thomas Cornwallis had described as "the plain old English manner".[39]

Notes

1. J. Bossy, *The English Catholic community 1570–1850* (London, 1975).
2. J. C. H. Aveling, *The handle and the axe* (London, 1976), p. 19.
3. D. N. J. MacCulloch, *The chorography of Suffolk* (Suffolk Record Society **19**, 1976), pp. 19, 20.
4. P. McGrath & J. Rowe "The recusancy of Sir Thomas Cornwallis", *Proceedings of the Suffolk Institute of Archaeology* **XXVIII** (3), 1961, pp. 226–271.

5. D. N. J. MacCulloch, *Suffolk and the Tudors* (Oxford, 1986), p. 194. For Atkinson's ejection see C. W. Field, "*The province of Canterbury and the Elizabethan settlement of religion*" (Privately produced, 1972), p. 217.

6. MacCulloch, *Suffolk and the Tudors*, p. 192; T. B. Trappes-Lomax, "Catholicism in Norfolk 1570–1780", *Norfolk Archaeology* **XXXII**, 1961, p. 27.

7. J. S. Craig, "The Bury Stirs revisited", *Proceedings of the Suffolk Institute of Archaeology* **XXXVII** (3), 1991, pp. 208–224.

8. Suffolk Record Office (West) (hereafter SRO(W)), IC/AA1/37/235.

9. Norfolk Record Office (hereafter NRO), DN/DIS9/1a; NRO, DN/VIS 4/2/3/1606; G. Anstruther, *The seminary priests. A dictionary of the secular clergy of England and Wales, 1558–1850*, vol. II (Ware and Great Wakering, 1968–77), p. 72.

10. NRO, DN/DIS9/1a; NRO, DN/VIS4/3/3 for Chattisham.

11. NRO, DN/VIS4/3/3 for Chattisham; NRO, DN/VIS4/3/2 for Copdock.

12. Return of recusants and non-communicants together with numbers of communicants in the parishes of the archdeaconries of Sudbury and Suffolk 1603, British Library (hereafter BL), Harleian MS 595, no. 26, in *Proceedings of the Suffolk Institute of Archaeology* **VI** (3) p. 366 and **XI** (1) pp. 1–46. Figures for priests have been calculated from Anstruther, *Seminary priests*.

13. Anstruther, *Seminary priests* vol. I, p. 303.

14. NRO, DN/VIS5/3/3.

15. NRO, DN/VIS6/1; NRO, DN/VIS4/3/2.

16. NRO, DN/VIS4/3/2.

17. A. Walsham, *Church papists. Catholicism, conformity and confessional polemic in early modern England* (Woodbridge, 1993); McGrath & Rowe, "Recusancy of Cornwallis".

18. NRO, DN/VIS4/2/3; C. Haigh "From monopoly to minority", *Transactions of Royal Historical Society*, 5th series; **31**, 1981, pp. 145–6.

19. SRO (W), IC/AA1/56/74.

20. SRO (W), IC/AA1/62/400.

21. Roman Catholic Diocese of East Anglia Record Office (hereafter RC DRO), St John's Cathedral, Norwich, Bacton Register.

22. H. Peters, (tr. H. Butterworth), *Mary Ward* (London, 1994), pp. 356–361; R. Southwell, *Saint Peter's complaint* (London, 1595).

23. Anstruther, *Seminary priests*, vol. I, p. 303.

24. H. Foley, *Records of the English province of the Society of Jesus* vol. I (London, 1877), p. 142.

25. J. McCann & H. Connolly (eds), *Memorials of Father Augustine Baker* (Catholic Record Society **33**, 1933) p. 18.

26. Peter Mowle's Common Place Book (1583–1605) Oscott College MS, Shelf RZZ3. I am grateful to the Rector of Oscott College and Mr George Every who drew the manuscript to my attention. See also N. P. Brown, *Paperchase: the dissemination of Catholic texts in Elizabethan England*, English Manuscript Studies 1100–1700 (Oxford, 1989) vol. I, pp. 120–143.

27. J. Booth, *The prisoners of Framlingham* (London, 1930); NRO, DN/DIS9/1a; Ex. Archives Society of Jesus, Farm Street, London W1. Collegium SS. Apost. MSS.
28. SRO (W), D8/1/3, Bundle 2.
29. Anstruther, *Seminary priests*, vol. III, p. 34.
30. Ex. Archives Society of Jesus, Farm Street, London W1. Collegium SS. Apost. MSS.
31. St Edmunds Roman Catholic Church, Bury St Edmunds Parish Archives. For Stoke by Nayland see Withermarsh Green Register RC DRO. For High Suffolk see Bacton Register RC DRO.
32. Suffolk Record Office (East), Worlingham Baptismal Register.
33. NRO, DN/DIS 9/1b.
34. D. Bellenger, *The French exiled clergy* (Bath, 1986), p. 206. The Bacton Register contains his signature in the form given here and not as listed in *The French exiled clergy*. His successor Father L. G. de La Fontaine does not appear in Dr Bellenger's list.
35. RC DRO, Bacton Register.
36. Foley, *Records*, vol. V, pp. 543–4, *n*.10.
37. St Edmunds Roman Catholic Church, Bury St Edmunds Parish Archives.
38. Bossy, *The English Catholic community*, pp. 398–401.
39. PRO, SP 11/7, no. 33.

8

Prisons, priests and people

Peter Lake and Michael Questier

Recent writing on post-Reformation England has constructed a very pessimistic picture of the consequences of both Catholic and Protestant attempts to evangelize or convert "the people". On both sides of the confessional divide, it has been argued, there was an effectual barrier between the elite world of the clerical would-be proselytizers and the people whom they were trying to convert. On this view, because of the word- and doctrine-based nature of Protestantism, along with Protestantism's heavily iconoclastic attitude to the vast assemblage of symbolic image and ritual practice in which the holy was shadowed forth and manipulated in the late mediaeval Church, it was almost inevitable that "the people" would be turned off by the interminable sermons and improving books through which the godly tried to transform the religious condition of England. On the Romish side, things might well be thought to have been rather different. There the attachment of the majority to the old ways surely offered the Catholic clergy a head start as they sought to turn the conservative religious proclivities of the people into a self-consciously Catholic community, a launching pad for the re-Catholicization of the whole country, should the political tide turn in their favour. Even here, it has been argued, that the, if not cowardice, then at least prudential passivity of the seminary priests in the face of official persecution, along with a social and cultural elitism that was inherent in the nature of "the mission", conspired to alienate the Catholic clergy from "the people" and to consign the bulk of post-1570 Catholic "missionary" activity to the houses and spheres of influence of the Catholic gentry. There the priests stayed, preferring to associate with their social equals and to disseminate their own forms of rigorist practice amongst a captive, literate and elite audience rather than to proselytize among the unlettered and superstitious multitude. In the process, of course, the priests were only too happy to avoid too direct an acquaintance with the general nastiness of government officials, privately-run prisons and Tyburn. In so doing, it has been argued, they removed themselves from the popular sphere and the affections of the people as effectively as did their Puritan enemies who alienated their audiences more directly by long and boring sermons and a *dirigiste* attitude to religious belief and observance. Perhaps the only real difference between these two groups was that while at least the Puritan evangelists tried to evangelize, the inadequately-trained seminarists scarcely made the attempt. Thus Christopher Haigh has pictured both formal, recusant Catholics and Protestants/Puritans as differently embattled minorities confronting audiences they neither liked nor understood.[1]

This version of the cultural, social and religious shifts wrought by the sixteenth-century Reformation relies on an arguably very one-sided reading of the sources which record Catholic/Protestant confrontation during this period. We want to look at the dynamics of some of these confrontations as they occurred in the place where Catholics and Protestants were most often brought together, before a (both socially and confessionally) mixed, i.e. "popular" audience, in public disputations, confrontations and trials of spiritual strength – the prisons. For it was the prisons which provided the venue for the most exciting and imaginative battles between the two sides. Prisons, and particularly the public executions which they assisted in staging, attracted large crowds. They thus provided an arena where both sides could make a pitch to a wider public. The drama of conversion from sin and degradation via repentance to salvation often started in interviews and debates within the prison and ended in spectacular public performances on the gallows. Where Catholics were involved the drama of conversion took on an overtly confessional aspect, as Catholics and Protestant ministers competed to convert felons to their brand of evangelical Christianity. Still more spectacularly, when priests or Catholic activists were the victims of the law, the rites of state violence were appropriated by Catholic martyrs to turn a celebration of state power and demonstration of Catholic treason into a public showing forth of the power of true Christian faith to triumph

196

over tyrannical persecution and cruelty.[2] In the prisons we can watch both Catholics and Protestants posing in front of, and making their pitch for, popular audiences and attention, and it is this which provides the subject of this chapter.

I

Let us start by describing the prisons, the site of so much of this evangelical activity. The extraordinary laxity, corruption and inefficiency which some historians have professed to see in Tudor and Stuart government was, apparently, displayed in an extreme form throughout the semi-privatized prison system on which the regime relied to maintain some measure of control over its political enemies. Sean McConville argues that "the criterion for success in gaol management was not . . . the reform of criminal offenders, or even the financial sobering of reckless debtors", but "quite simply the ability of the gaol to prevent escapes", to keep suspects, debtors and rebels on remand until somebody decided what to do with them.[3] Though it seems some prisons did not work particularly well even as holding areas, this may explain why there was such an extraordinary combination of brutality, filth and yet relative freedom in places such as the London prisons (Newgate, Fleet, Marshalsea, King's Bench, the Tower and so on), York and Wisbech Castles. In the absence of "official" archives for these institutions (consolidated bodies of administrative records), the conditions of the prisons have to be reconstructed in large part from the accounts of the various politico-religious engagés who went or were taken there. Such material must naturally be treated with caution, subject as it is to confessional, indeed martyrological, hyperbole and distortion. In what follows we try to read some of this material against the martyrological grain, collating a variety of such accounts, including many asides about the prisons gleaned from narratives, the prime focus of which was often not on the condition of the prisons at all, with other, more "official", Protestant records and comments.

On the one hand we are confronted with the gruesome accounts of stench, gaol fever and victimization by the psychopaths who were entrusted with the control of these places. In many accounts the dire consequences of imprisonment were pictured as fully as bad as the torments of those Catholics who met a traitor's death on the gallows. Even allowing for a considerable element of martyrologically-motivated exaggeration, incarceration was often no cakewalk. Priests, in particular, might be tortured, kept in loathsome solitary confinement and subject to all kinds of mental cruelty and intimidation.[4] But, on the other hand, the privatized and decentralized nature of the prison regime also served to ensure that it was sometimes possible for those with means to live in prison much as they would elsewhere. Such people frequently enjoyed the liberty of the prison, as did the suspect Jane Shelley in the Fleet in November 1593, when Sir Robert Cecil wrote to the warden instructing him to end her close confinement. That Cecil felt the need to explain that "my meaning is that she should be so kept that she may not escape" spoke volumes for the prison regime with which he was dealing.[5]

Close confinement was relatively rare, and servants or relations could visit or reside virtually unsupervised. Stephen Vallenger, the Catholic printer, had his own library with him during his imprisonment.[6] Largely because most prisons were run as a private enterprise there was no connection between the economics of prison administration and the maintenance of security. In other words, the keeper of the prison was interested primarily in profits while those who were responsible for ensuring prisoners stayed incarcerated were paid very badly. Brutality was not unusual but nor was bribery of the underpaid prison staffs.[7] Sir John Horsey and George Trenchard reported from Dorchester to Sir Francis Walsingham in October 1586 that "the common gaols are rented by persons of no credit, that lives [sic] only upon the gain thereof" and so "all justice is subverted, and papists live at ease, and have their conventicles in despite of us".[8] During the 1580s the York sheriff's sergeant was allowing the recusants in the New Counter prison to visit their friends and various seminary priests in York.[9] Prisons, then, might often be "a nurse of roguery, and an earthly hell"[10] but for Catholics, whose activities on the outside were heavily restricted by statute law, they might sometimes facilitate rather than confine religious activism. At times of crisis Catholic priests might be very closely confined, tortured and generally maltreated. Equally, at other times, when the government's attention was elsewhere and as bribery and familiarity took hold, the same men might enjoy a prison regime of, by modern standards, almost farcical laxity.

Thus imprisonment (though not exactly luxurious) was not inevitably detrimental to priests' general well-being. In May 1596 John Mush wrote to his clerical friends in Wisbech concerning the recent escape of the priest Francis Tilletson: "Could none of you dissuade him from this perilous attempt? If you knew what difficulties we daily suffer abroad, you would account yourselves happy to be where and as you are. It is a great misery in man's nature, not to know or not to be content when he is well. If it so might please God, many of us would be right glad to change places with you".[11] The Benedictine political activist, Thomas Preston, found that the Clink prison made a good base for his operations during James's reign, and he had no intention of leaving (especially when it seemed that if he were known to be at liberty he might be recalled to Rome to be questioned by the Holy Office about some of his political and religious views).[12] In late 1613 when the departing French ambassador was petitioning the government to allow him to take some Catholic priests from the prisons, Richard Broughton reported that "few I think will give their names, for that they find so cold entertainment in foreign countries, that they had rather live in prison at home".[13] Imprisoned priests tended to escape only when they found it difficult to carry out their ecclesiastical functions there. The clerical breakout from the Gatehouse prison in 1597 occurred because the priests concerned were not prepared to be sent to the less commodious prison at Ely. William Medeley, the Wisbech keeper, told Sir Robert Cecil in August 1597 that the priests there were bound to start escaping soon because of "their so slender maintenance". William Ward reported in November 1615 that there was only one priest left in Newgate, "the rest that were there are lately escaped. They can not do as they were wont by reason of some malicious Puritans and other offenders which of purpose are placed in Justice Hall to hinder their devotions".[14] Indeed, on occasion, the Catholicization or spiritualization of the gaols became so complete that a priest's escape could come to be viewed by other Catholics as a sign of serious moral and spiritual weakness. In March 1597 Sir Robert Cecil received a report that the secular clergy's complaints included that "if any secular escape prison, they [the

Jesuits] pretend he is a spy [for the regime], and thus make him odious".[15]

The extent of the relative autonomy ceded to imprisoned priests by the authorities shows through clearly in the "Wisbech Stirs", the well-publicized quarrels among the Catholic clergy shut away in Wisbech Castle. The accusations thrown up in the course of the dispute confirm the impression gleaned from other sources of an astonishing laxity in the prison system. Giles Archer reported that the Wisbech cell of the notorious Jesuit-hater Thomas Bluet "was like a public tavern" where the anti-Jesuits "used to hold banquets with splendid provision" and that Bluet's habitual inebriation was common knowledge. Of Edmund Calverley, one of the anti-Jesuit Bagshaw-Bluet group, it was said that he lost vast sums by gambling, as well as being addicted to wine and women.[16] Later on, John Colleton, an anti-Jesuit but a priest who had tried his vocation with the Carthusians in the 1570s, objected strongly to the modish dress and frequent theatregoing of some of his clerical colleagues in the Clink prison (though they soon retaliated by having his day-release privileges stopped).[17]

But, and this is the crucial point, official complaisance or corruption might lead as much to Catholic evangelical rigorism (and a wide broadcasting of it) as it did to moral laxity. Protestants might profit from disputes and feuds among imprisoned Catholics but the public display of grace, and, indeed, of exemplary austerity of life under pressure, might also redound to the polemical and evangelical advantage of the Catholics. It was reported, for instance, that William Fitch, the Capuchin, made his prison "a cloister for the austerity of his profession". With the imprisonment of William Davies in 1592, Beaumaris Castle became a centre for Catholic worship. Davies said mass daily and people came from up to forty miles away to enjoy his services, while Davies himself and four other priests were able to establish a spiritual regime within the prison of an almost monastic severity. It is hardly surprising in such circumstances that lay zealots such as Margaret Clitherow came to regard the gaols as substitutes for religious houses. When the aura of sanctity lent to these places by the intermittent martyrdom of some of the inmates is factored into the equation the extent of the spiritual power generated by Catholics in and through the prisons becomes clear.[18]

In short, the prisons served as a series of semi-permanent detention centres but often approximated to a species of clerical lodging house. For Catholics this system provided a number of centralized locales where many priests were gathered together, to which other Catholics could resort and upon which a considerable public attention might intermittently be concentrated. And the prison became a privileged arena for a variety of Catholic pastoral and propaganda activities. In the 1580s an informer related that in Newgate "the papists have recourse, the one to the other" and say mass in the keeper's house in secret (though openly in Latin in the common gaol).[19] Thomas Bell the zealous northern seminarist invaded York Castle in 1582 with three other priests and various York Catholics; he had already entered the prison once before and remained for a fortnight, offering mass every day, hearing confessions and preaching. Now he brought rein-forcements. He sang high mass there with deacon, subdeacon and music.[20] Benjamin Beard, a knowledgeable and reliable informer, told Lord Keeper Puckering in 1594 that mass was being said in the Marshalsea every Sunday.[21]

The priest William Spenser voluntarily made himself a prisoner in York Castle so as to serve the Catholics there.[22] Prisons were the obvious sites for confession, which included, of course, sacramental reconciliation to Rome from schism and from heresy. Thus, when John Rigby was troubled in his conscience by his conformity to the Church of England, it was to an incarcerated priest "who had the liberty of the prison" that he turned for solace. Occasionally Catholic parents sent their children to reside in prisons where priests were kept so that they could receive an appropriately Catholic religious training. Catholics even resorted to prisons to be married.[23]

Since one ran far less risk encountering a seminary priest in prison than outside it the relative laxity of the prison regime offered many Catholics a sort of *de facto* immunity from prosecution as they sought out the services of the imprisoned priests. Robert Page confessed in 1593 that before he was arrested he had resorted to many seminary priests in prison but, to get round the statute, denied that he had assisted or relieved them. In James's reign, a charge of being treason-ably reconciled to the Church of Rome was thrown out on the grounds that the converted individual had gone to the prison intending to convert the priest who ended up converting him.[24]

As one might expect under these circumstances, Catholic visitors flocked to the gaols. Once the regime at Wisbech had been relaxed in 1593, William Weston could say that the flow of visitors was unceasing. Nor was this merely hyperbolic Catholic whistling in the dark; from the opposite end of the ideological spectrum Richard Topcliffe confirmed Weston's claim, reporting that there was "access to them . . . from all the parts . . . of England" and that "they have infected the greatest part of the town" of Wisbech.[25] It was therefore no rhetorical excess for Robert Parsons to say that "by the supreme providence of God it happens that . . . priests who are shut up in prisons are sometimes of more use to us there than if they were at liberty. For these men, being always definitely in the same place, make possible the visits of many people who are unable to discover the whereabouts of other priests".[26] John Gerard wrote that in the Clink prison he was able to perform "all the tasks of a Jesuit priest, and provided only that I could have stayed on in this prison, I should never have wanted my liberty again in England".[27] Nor did the mountain always have to come to Mohammed; sometimes Mohammed even got to visit the mountain. Cardinal William Allen wrote in March 1583 that the priests were on permanent day release in London; "hence the salvation of many is incredibly promoted, no less indeed than if the priests were at liberty".[28]

Of the 471 seminary priests who operated in Elizabethan England, 285 were imprisoned at some time or other (although the ministry of 116 of them was terminated by execution). The distribution of such priests was wide. At least 50 prisons contained priests at some point. Between 25 and 30 priests were imprisoned in the Marshalsea at any one time, and at different times Newgate had 55 and the Clink 51.[29] In view of all this it seems reasonable to claim that close attention to Catholic activity in the gaols is crucial if the true extent and nature of the priests' evangelical activities is to be properly gauged. Certainly, on this evidence, the propensity of priests newly arrived from the continent to repair to the London prisons seems less like the neurotic courting of martyrdom, censured by Dr Haigh, and more like an entirely natural attempt to touch base with one of the symbolic and practical centres of Catholic activity in England.

Of course, the regime made intermittent efforts to combat this Catholic infestation of the prison system. As one might expect, so long as these measures were located in the administrative rather than the ideological or spiritual sphere they proved largely ineffectual. Efforts were made to restrict the number and types of visitors to prisons, and raids were launched to confiscate Catholic books and artefacts. The authorities tried sporadically to isolate priests (by sending them out of London), and, notably in a purge of the Clink and Newgate in 1615, to separate lay prisoners from clerical ones. After John Chrysostom Campbell, a Scottish Capuchin, had preached a sermon in the Marshalsea prison before an audience of 48 in February 1600, he was committed to a closer confinement and the keeper was commanded to remove his "friar-like weeds".[30] People such as Richard Topcliffe raged against what they took to be the total anarchy in the London prisons.[31] But when the regime relied on people such as Robert Redhead, the keeper of York Castle, anarchy was inevitable. It was said that he allowed a notorious felon "to be out of the Castle whole nights playing at dice, and to have the company of a gentlewoman to be his harlot".[32] He sent criminals out of the castle to work on his estates, or to act as his rent collectors, and frequently they escaped. In fact, two of them had simply been given the keys to the place in order to make everyone's life easier![33] But at least Redhead did not much like Catholics. Other prison keepers, such as Simon Houghton of Newgate apparently did (his wife was an obstinate recusant). He facilitated contact between London Catholics and the clerical prisoners in Newgate.[34] In December 1594 Lord Buckhurst was informed that a Sussex gentleman had been appointed as a sub-warden at the Fleet, and he "purposes to animate the recusants (being of his own sort)".[35] Even in the technically secure prison of the Tower there was the potential for mayhem; at a politically sensitive time (1588) it was reported that priests were saying mass there, mainly for the benefit of the Earl of Arundel, and that the officials were in receipt of numerous bribes (and that many of them "were by persuasion, and otherwise, fallen . . . unto popery").[36]

Every now and again a particularly flagrant abuse of the system would bring angry letters from the Privy Council demanding reform and probity but with as much effect as most early modern attempts to reform government.[37] In the 1590s it appears that Winchester gaol (which held some notably high-risk prisoners) was actually being run by leading Hampshire recusants. Priests were allowed in and out to say mass. Recusant prisoners were let loose and received warnings to return only when higher authority was coming to find out who was still there. From the early 1580s the prison was stuffed with altars, vestments, candles, liturgical and polemical books. Nothing was done about it and the lax administration of the prison culminated in the escape of the priest Edward Kenyon early on 2 October 1599 (the day on which he would have been tried for treason). The officials who had been "at their uttermost peril" charged with keeping Kenyon in custody did not seem to think it incongruous that the subject of a projected major treason trial should have free run of the prison, be visited by large numbers of recusants, and be acting as personal domestic chaplain to the prison keeper's wife![38] So, while intermittent crackdowns might make conditions more difficult in the short term, over the long haul this was not an administrative system or prison regime able really to control, or even effectively to constrain, the religious activities of imprisoned priests.

II

The prison's status as a site of religious activity and conflict might thus be seen to be a product of the peculiar relationship between Catholicism and the state in post-Reformation England, as that relationship was refracted or mediated through the complicated administrative, social and financial arrangements through which that same state ran the prisons. Here the maladministration of the state and the pertinacity of the imprisoned priests conspired to produce a place to which Catholics could resort to receive the sacraments or to confer with a priest. But there was more going on here than the mere servicing by incarcerated priests of the disgruntled conservative-minded Catholicism that lies at the heart of so much recent revisionist writing on Elizabethan religion. For Catholicism in the prisons came to be characterized by an evangelism both more urgent and more populist than can easily be accommodated within the terms and assumptions of much revisionist writing on the Catholic "mission".

Ironically this was in part due to the actions of the Protestant regime. Unable to control the activities of Catholics in the gaols by a tightening up of the prison system, the authorities turned instead to ideological and polemical weapons. As we have argued elsewhere, this was entirely typical of the way in which the Elizabethan state reacted to the Catholic problem. Thus rather than tut-tut at the "inefficiency" and "corruption" of the prisons (although, even by contemporary standards, they were both inefficient and corrupt, as the complaints and reproofs cited above amply demonstrate) we should locate what happened in the prisons in an overall picture of the symbolic and ideological means by which Catholicism was contained and confronted by the Protestant state.[39] The result was a form of complicity between the authorities and their Catholic enemies and captives whereby the ideological means used by the state to combat Catholic activism in the gaols also served to heighten rather than to suppress the status of the prisons as centres of religious debate and conflict, sites where the spiritual power and charisma generated by controversy, conversion, evangelically charged death and more rarely martyrdom could be deployed for overtly confessional purposes. For the Protestant authorities connived at the process whereby the gaols served as public stages for religious debate between Catholics and Protestants. Here perhaps the most famous example is the series of debates between Edmund Campion and a whole battery of Protestant divines held in the Tower in 1581. But other examples of the same syndrome abound. The notable Catholic recusant Thomas Pound, cousin of the second Earl of Southampton, was confronted and challenged in the Marshalsea by the Puritans Tripp and Crowley. The disputes over recusancy and attendance at sermons went on for over a year (1599–1600) in York Castle as the authorities compelled the Catholic prisoners there to listen to a series of Puritan sermons delivered by the Yorkshire godly. Acting as a front man for the Jesuits, Paul Spence, a Marian deacon and a seminary priest, became involved in a long-running debate with Robert Abbot in Worcester gaol during the early 1590s.[40] William Fitch disputed at Wisbech with various Protestants, while some of John Percy's incessant challenges to the London godly were issued from prison. One of them was answered by George Walker, the Protestant polemicist, who confronted Percy in a London prison in 1621.[41] Prisons, in fact, were the obvious place for Protestant activists to challenge their Catholic popish adversaries. There the normal constraints, in particular the difficulty of priests appearing in semi-public, and the suspicion attaching to anyone who associated with papists, were largely nullified.

Official Protestant connivance at, and exploitation of, the prisons as sites of religious conflict were not, however, limited to formal theological debates between Protestant and Catholic divines. The authorities also went out of their way to create the conditions within the prisons for intra-Catholic debate, hoping thereby to exacerbate the ideological and personal divisions and rivalries which increasingly came to characterize the Catholic community. In the prisons, of course, Catholics of very different persuasions were thrown and kept together with inevitably disruptive results for the unity and coherence of the Catholic cause. It did not take long for the Protestant authorities to try to foster and exploit this phenomenon. For while it might be impossible to prevent contact between Catholics and priests in the gaols, it was possible to influence which priests they saw. Thus in July 1615 the nuncio Bentivoglio reported that the non-loyalist clergy were being removed from the London prisons, apparently with the intention that Catholics in the capital would have to receive the sacraments from loyalists, and that this would promote greater acceptance of the Jacobean oath of allegiance.[42] A similar strategy dictated that Catholics and priests should be assigned to different prisons depending upon their opinions about the oath.[43] In 1588 when the seminary priests Anthony Tyrrell and William Tedder began to show themselves conformable, they were both removed from the Romanist milieu of their London prisons to another place of imprisonment where, deprived of the moral support of other priests, they could be expected to show themselves more favourable to the regime's demands.[44] Recantations were frequently staged by the authorities in the prisons where they would have most impact on Catholics. Men such as John Nichols, Anthony Major, William Hardesty, Miles Dawson, Thomas Bell and James Bowland were directed to preach to Catholic prisoners,[45] while Archbishop Abbot used the prisons systematically to shield loyalists such as Thomas Preston from the attacks of their Catholic enemies and to prevent their authorship of loyalist books becoming public knowledge. At one point Abbot attempted to obtain redress for the loyalist priests in the Clink against the effects of a pursuivants' raid which had occurred after an information was laid, as he thought, by "a disciple of the Jesuits".[46]

Thus it was almost as much the activities of the authorities as those of the Catholics which rendered the prisons centres of religious dispute, propaganda and evangelism. This was a tendency compounded by a distinct yet linked set of practices surrounding the "last dying speeches" of executed felons. As a number of scholars have shown these were performances of considerable cultural resonance and import. The executions of notorious offenders, murderers or, in the case of Catholic priests, alleged traitors and/or martyrs, attracted large crowds. The more gruesome or famous offenders were described in cheap pamphlets. There was a distinct sub-genre of martyrological news and rumour circulating amongst Catholics about the fate and conduct on the scaffold of priests which in turn was answered by cheap pamphlet accounts of the same events written from a mocking and sceptical Protestant point of view.[47]

Of course, what ended on the scaffold had started in the prison, as felons were worked on by a variety of ministers, all of them seeking to bring the offender to a proper sense of repentance and contrition for his or her offence. Much was at stake in these exchanges. On the one hand, given that the stakes were so high, nothing short, in fact, of eternal salvation, felons who went to their death insisting on their innocence could raise popular suspicions concerning the justice of the verdict. Why else risk hellfire through an obstinate refusal to repent, unless one were genuinely innocent? From the point of view of the secular authorities, therefore, if the spectacle of public execution were to do its proper task in reaffirming order through the overt punishment of publicly acknowledged sin, the victim must accept the justice of his or her fate. To bring this about the authorities would often stay executions to allow a variety of ministers to work on the victim in prison, in the words of one pamphlet allowing "worthy ministers" to "exhort them to clear their consciences and confess their faults with true penitence". Often whole troops of ministers were involved. One particularly stubborn group of murderers, convicted of the slaying of one Mr Tratt, curate of Old Cleave, were visited in gaol by "Dr Goodwin, Dr Slaier, Mr Morley, Mr Vaughan and other worthy ministers", although in this instance to no avail for the felons in question "died obstinate and unrepenting sinners".[48]

One pamphlet of 1608 praised the London authorities to the skies for their care for the spiritual condition of Elizabeth Abbot who, despite her obvious guilt and conviction for the murder of one Mistress Killingworth, persisted in her professions of innocence. The case was notorious in London and when Abbot had been led back to the city from Gravesend whence she had fled after the murder, she attracted a great crowd. "As she was being carried through the streets the people that came to behold her were infinite, some cursing her, all reviling her and the most desirous to have had her presently torn to pieces as a creature not worthy to continue to her trial". Clearly, that a case so notorious should be denied satisfactory closure by the convicted felon's stubborn refusal to confess was totally unacceptable to the authorities. Abbot's pertinacity had prompted serious doubts amongst the populace about the justice of the verdict; doubts that the magistrates (and later the author of the pamphlet) rushed to efface. First they sent a "grave doctor of divinity" to interview her in prison, but he got nowhere. She was then taken to the place of execution and shown the gibbet, whereupon the two sheriffs them- selves "began of their own charitable disposition to persuade her to disburden her conscience, showed her how near death she was, pointed her towards the house where Mistress Killingworth [her victim] dwelt" so that the scene of the crime might itself "be a remembrance to have her cleanse her soul". For all that the sheriffs managed to get Abbot on "her knees then in the cart to offer her prayers to God" they still could not prevail on her to confess. So seriously did the authorities take this continued obstinacy in the very face of death that they caused the lord mayor to delay the execution and removed Abbot to Katharine Cree church where they reas- sembled "all those who gave evidence against her, first charging them upon the love they bare to their own souls to view her well whether she were the woman or no". The witnesses, however, stuck to their story and Abbot was executed still professing her innocence, an event the author of the pamphlet glossed as a sure sign that "the devil whom she served had fully hardened her heart".[49]

On other occasions, however, these stories had a happier or, at least, from the authorities' perspective, a more convenient, end. Here the intercession of ministers and others in the prisons led the felon to a properly edifying display of repentance on the gallows. As is clear from the Abbot pamphlet such notorious cases often attracted consid-erable crowds to the execution, but popular interest was not limited to the gallows. The process of edification and exhortation in the gaol also took place in something like semi-public and often drew a crowd. John Dilworth, a dreadful drunkard, wife-beater, and ulti-mately murderer, admitted his guilt yet refused utterly to repent for his crime "but in graceless and godless sort justified the doing thereof, saying he had done God and the world good service in sending so unquiet a creature out of it". This clearly would not do and he was visited in gaol by "many poor men and women, divines and others" who finally prevailed upon him at the end "to look into the foulness of his offence and to ask forgiveness both of God and the world".[50] The spectacularly efficacious repentance of one Elizabeth Caldwell attracted even more attention. Caldwell herself became evangelically active in the gaol, exhorting to repentance her fellow prisoners, her visitors and, indeed, even her husband – the intended victim of her crime whom she had tried to dispatch with poisoned pies, only to kill her neighbour's daughter by mistake. According to Gilbert Dugdale, the author of the pamphlet which described her fate, this miracle of God's grace was visited in prison by as many as 300 people a day.[51] The protracted prison conversions of two London apprentices convicted of murder in the 1650s and 1660s respectively were wrought by whole batteries of Presbyterian and subsequently Nonconformist divines whose evangelical activities were attended by considerable crowds who gathered to watch the young men being prayed over and preached at in the prison.[52]

As the Caldwell narrative shows, then, there was far more at stake in these exchanges in the prisons and performances on the gallows than merely the restoration of social order and control, or the vindi-cation of secular justice. Souls were at stake and the power of true religion and God's grace was on display, even in some sense, on trial. Thus, from the perspective of the clergyman labouring to save the soul of the felon, what greater sign could there be of the efficacy of his ministry, the truth of his particular style of religion and the power of God's grace than the conversion of even the most desperate sinner on the very steps of the gallows? William Perkins was famous for his prison evangelism as were later Nonconformist divines.[53] The capacity to bring even the most recalcitrant felon to repentance redounded much to the minister's credit. Spiritual power and personal charisma were created and distributed by such transactions between minister and felon and the ensuing scaffold performances. On hearing of the imminent execution of the gentleman Humphrey Stafford for buggery, one "lame Master Paget", "a reverent preacher of God's word", rushed off to the prison where "Master Stafford reaping much joy by his ministering" desired Paget's "company to his death". At the execution, "where the press of people to behold his [Stafford's] death" was great, Paget proceeded to take the starring clerical role, thus in effect displacing "Master Cartwright, minister of St George's church" who had up to that point been in charge of the struggle for Stafford's "soul's health".[54] There may, therefore, have been an element of competition amongst the various ministers visiting particularly notorious, recalcitrant or charismatic felons like Elizabeth Abbot or Humphrey Stafford to see who could have the most startling effect on them and thus preside over the affecting scenes at the gallows. That certainly seems to have been true in the case of the deranged axe-murderer Enoch ap Evan who was visited in prison by upwards of 14 ministers all eager to bring him to repentance and to put their own polemical and spiritual spin on his crime and demeanour.[55]

One pamphlet of 1577 told the story of the murder of a London merchant at the hands of a servant suborned by his wife Ann Sanders and her friend, one Mistress Drewry. The case attracted much attention and the executions of the principal figures drew a vast crowd composed of

> so great a number of people as the like has not been seen there together in any man's remembrance. For almost the whole field and all the way from Newgate was as full as could well stand by one another and besides that great companies were placed both in the chambers near about (whose windows and walls were in many places beaten down to look out at) and also upon the gutters sides and tops of the houses and up[on] the battlements and steeples of St Bartholomew's.

The assembled multitude was edified by decently repentant scaffold performances from the principal felons. But this was not an effect wrought by the authorities without effort. At her trial Mistress Sanders had stubbornly maintained her innocence to such effect that "some were brought in a blind belief that either she was not guilty at all or else had but brought herself in danger of law through ignorance and not through pretenced malice". The result, as with Elizabeth Abbot, was a delay of sentence while the "parties condemned were brought to Godward . . . and the willing confessing of the things for which they had been justly condemned and which as yet they obstinately concealed". Unfortunately, one of the ministers who attended Mistress Sanders in gaol, one Mell, "a minister that had heretofore been suspended from his ministry", became infatuated with her and consequently convinced himself of her innocence. He proceeded to persuade her accomplice Mistress Drewry to take all the blame on herself and, planning to marry Sanders, Mell set off to get her a pardon. Mell's activities thus undermined the efforts of the dean of St Paul's and other ministers to bring Sanders to true repentance. It was only the collapse of Mell's plan before the perspicacity of the Privy Council (who not only denied his request for a pardon but also consigned him to the pillory for his pains) combined with the prospect of imminent execution, that brought Mistress Sanders round. Then, under the influence of a battery of ministers, including the dean of St Paul's, Mr Cole, Mr Charke and Mr Young, Mistress Sanders confessed her guilt and embraced her fate in a properly repentant and pious way.[56]

There could scarcely be a better example of the complicated web of secular and religious, temporal and spiritual, issues at stake in these gaol conversations and pulpit performances. Doubts about the justice of the verdict and a variety of ugly rumours about the role of witchcraft and the unchastity of a number of other merchants' wives, that had attended the proceedings, were all dispelled by the last dying speeches of the condemned, all of whom dutifully embraced their fate and confirmed the official version of events. This happy outcome vindicated the official evangelism of the dean of St Paul's and his respectable Puritan helpers at the expense of the fond and fanciful activities of the suspended and lovesick Mr Mell.

At times the variant readings of such events in circulation could take on an overtly political or factional tinge. Thus in July 1627, when one Joshuah Purchas was convicted and executed for rape, the notoriously eccentric Puritan divine and erstwhile judaiser John Traske inserted himself into the proceedings. According to George Montaigne, the bishop of London, Purchas was "a professor as they now call them, that is, a violent puritan". Purchas continued to broadcast his innocence of the charge throughout the proceedings, admitting that while he died under a just law he was the victim of an unjust accusation and beseeching God "at his execution to forgive his accusers". On Montaigne's account "the faction laboured much for his life and spoke . . . as if he fared the worse for his religion". Traske had interviewed Purchas in Newgate, preached before him "and some other condemned prisoners there", prayed with and over him at his execution and had been slated to preach a funeral sermon for him at St Sepulchre's. According to Montaigne,

> it was reported he would have justified him and have censured the proceedings against him, and I believe it, for the church was so full of the faction that I dare say the assembly was unlawful, whereupon I forbade the sermon to be preached by Traske and commanded the curate, an honest man, to preach that sermon, which he did but he no sooner appeared in the pulpit but they all went out and left him almost alone.

As for Traske, he was accused of acting without official authority or permission and of praying at the execution that God would "show . . . some token upon all atheists and profane heretics and others that came there to see his death and rejoice in the same".

For his part he replied that he had exercised his ministry in the prison with the full permission of the ordinary, Henry Goodcole, and that, far from attempting to justify Purchas's fault, he, along with two other ministers, had dedicated all their efforts to working a true confession and repentance in the condemned. The most he would admit to was that, even under the most vociferous encouragement of both Traske and his fellow ministers, Purchas had continued to protest his innocence, taking the sacrament and making "a good profession of his faith" on the scaffold itself without once breaking down into a confession of guilt. At the execution, "by the leave and with the advice of the minister that attends the prisoners", Traske admitted that "he prayed with the poor dying soul amongst other petitions . . . that if yet anything did lurk in the heart of that man he might now reveal it and so have cheerful passage out of this life". He also conceded that he had prayed that

> the true religion might not be scandalised by the death of that delinquent and said that it was just with God that if any came thither to scoff at our religion by reason of the death of that man to show his judgment upon them.[57]

Here, then, as with the cases of Mistress Sanders and Elizabeth Abbot, we have an alleged miscreant who refused to follow the official script. Where, in the instance of Sanders, the ministerial help afforded to the felon stemmed from mere infatuation, with Purchas the affair took on an overtly ideological tone with the accused's protestations of innocence producing rumours that cast the prosecution case as an anti-Puritan conspiracy. While conformist, indeed, Arminian, authority, in the persons of Montaigne and Laud, sought to describe the case as a confirmation of the immorality and hypocrisy of the godly, Traske sought, even on the gallows, to cast doubt on Purchas's guilt and to call down the wrath of God on all those in the gawping crowd who might be tempted to use Purchas's fate as a stick with which to beat true religion.

Even amongst Protestants, therefore, prison evangelism and the gallows performances scripted and choreographed by that evangelism could be spiritually charged and potentially divisive events. They could also attract the attention of the people. As the examples cited above show, executions attracted crowds and particularly shocking or controversial cases generated rumours and interest, drawing visitors and spectators to the gaol to interview or stare at the accused or condemned. Here, then, was another sort of spiritual power, another area of religious struggle centred on the prisons. But it was when the social and spiritual forces and energies released by these occasions intersected with the presence in the prisons of large numbers of Catholic priests that their full potential to generate and dramatize overt and polarized religious conflict was realised.

For storing Catholic priests in the prisons ensured that they were exposed on a regular basis to large numbers of desperate people, condemned felons who, staring certain death in the face, were ripe for conversion and spiritual solace. Confronted with this opportunity to combine evangelism with propaganda, some Catholics at least did not confine their activities to servicing the spiritual needs of the already convinced Catholics who flocked to the gaols for sacraments and succour. On the contrary, they set to with a will to exploit this unintended consequence of official policy for their own confessional ends, demonstrating the truth and spiritual power of their religion through the conversion of the lost souls they met in the gaols to a true (Catholic) faith and repentance.

The Jesuits, in particular, never ceased to emphasize in their correspondence how successfully they induced a true sense of repentance in such people. In one notorious case of a mercenary soldier condemned in 1610 (for killing another mercenary soldier), the Jesuit-oriented brigade in Newgate prison schooled him in the things he should say from the scaffold, and so he died, "a professed papist". The same faction worked a similar miracle of grace on two poisoners in Newgate in 1615. Their public proclamation of their newly discovered Catholic impulses was broadcast in advance.[58]

Like Puritan ministers, Catholic priests were not above seeking out the most notorious and prominent of felons. When the gentleman and rake-about-town Humphrey Stafford was condemned for buggery and awaited execution in the King's Bench prison, he was approached by Catholic recusants. "Being a gentleman of good descent", Stafford would constitute quite a catch. The Catholics "studied much" to turn him, arguing that there was no salvation in the Church of England and that "he should not admit of any of our ministers to confer with him but that he should be confessed by some seminary priest". Stafford rebuffed them and died a Protestant death[59], but on other occasions the Catholics were more successful. Pirates and highwayman were spiritually waylaid and persuaded not just towards an internal resolution against sin but also an outward rejection of the Protestant ministers who came to them for much the same reason as the Catholics had approached them. During the 1580s George Nichols presided over the conversion of a highwayman in Oxford gaol and James Fenn did the same for a pirate. Both felons lay in desperation before the enormity of their sins but were effectually converted. The pirate adamantly refused the ministrations of Protestant ministers on the gallows and professed that "he died a

Catholic, and blessed the providence of God that had brought him to a place where he had met with such holy company as taught him to be a Christian". The highwayman professed under the gallows "that if he had a thousand lives, he would joyfully part with them rather than renounce the Catholic Roman faith". The structure of these accounts is remarkably similar to that of Puritan narratives of the same process which presumably made Catholic propaganda of this sort all the more threatening.[60]

The significance of these activities was heightened by the authorities' tendency, very prevalent after the early 1580s, to execute priests in the company of a group of common criminals. The regime did this in order to combat the priests' pretensions to martyrdom by associating them with the more general run of depravity. But such tactics allowed the priests to combine their everyday evangelical functions with the more intermittent but testing role of martyr for the faith. Many managed to do so with remarkable *élan* and effect, converting some if not all the felons with whom they died not merely to a repentant acknowledgment of their fault but to an overt profession of an expressly Romish faith.[61] When retold by Catholics, stories about felons repenting through the agency of Romish priests and sacramental confession echoed the salvific activities of Christ (who died with criminals) and pointed to central differences between Catholic and Protestant attitudes to conversion (in several cases the priest converted all but one of the felons who awaited death with him, and this lone figure for Judas also emphasized the universalism of grace under the Romish dispensation and the Calvinist restriction of it to the elect).[62]

Thus Catholics twisted the conventions of the last dying speech and the providentialized crime pamphlet. The "chain of sins" that led the unfortunate felon first to murder and then to the gallows played a central explanatory role in many of the pamphlet narratives and the last dying speeches they claimed to record. This theme allowed the extreme crimes and punishments of the murderer to be linked to other more everyday sins and moral failings. The providential means by which many murderers were brought to book were often presented as punishments for sin, but also, if the felon repented properly and made a good end, they were perceived as divine interventions in a life of sin and depravity which, if left uninterrupted,

215

would surely have led straight to hell, but which now, having been disrupted by the inscrutably merciful providence of God, led via the gallows to heaven. As one of the Puritan ministers attending on John Barker in 1637 opined, it was better to go to heaven from the gallows than to hell from a down bed.[63]

Given their exiguous control over the prisons, the Protestant authorities were unable physically to constrain such displays of Catholic evangelism and piety either in the prisons or still less on the gallows. Rather, as with their use of the prisons for polemical debates, they were forced to fight fire with fire, and confront the Catholics with their own spiritual, evangelical and performative weapons. As with the scaffold and the conventions of the last dying speech, the prisons and the procedures of prison evangelism represented an arena and a genre that were open to manipulation by more than one party. Admittedly, the forced residence of so many Catholic clerics within the prisons gave these Romanists an initial advantage. One senses that in this period there was something of a struggle among Protestant evangelicals to make their presence felt. Although the cleric Phineas Hodson, a member of the York Chapter, might provide £25 a year (via a rent charge from his Yorkshire properties) to institute weekly preaching in York Castle, formal provision for the discharge of such spiritual duties was scarcely ubiquitous.[64] Thus Charles Richardson told the London magistrates in 1616 that in prison many wicked persons

> die like dogs, for want of knowledge and for want of grace. It is a lamentable thing, that in so great a place as this, there is not some godly and sincere minister appointed to instruct them better, and to prepare them for their ends.

He urged his auditory

> that a competent maintenance may be allowed to some faithful and skilful minister, who may take care of these poor wretches. It were to be wished that there were in every prison such a man maintained. For we see by experience, that they are nurseries of all ungodliness, and men that once come in prison, learn more villainy, than ever they knew before.[65]

Interestingly, Richardson's complaints inverted the earlier observations of Robert Parsons who claimed that "owing to the loose habits engendered by heresy, the youth of England fall into many faults and crimes, for which not seldom they are cast into prison by the magistrates" and encounter the priests from whom "in the space of one month in that school they learn more virtue, self-control, and habits of discipline than they had learnt in many years whilst at liberty".[66] We should, of course, beware of taking this combination of complaint literature and polemic at face value. What this mixture of Protestant jeremiad and Romanist triumphalism does unequivocally show, however, is an area of conflict and anxiety centred on the prisons as sites of evangelical and polemical activity. It was an arena where, for all Richardson's complaints, Protestants as well as Catholics had long been active. While it was not until 1620 that a full-time chaplain or "ordinary" was appointed for Newgate, that role had been filled intermittently before by a number of London ministers who made a name for themselves attending on and disputing with both Catholic priests and notorious felons and, as the story of Traske and Purchas related above shows, even after the appointment of Henry Goodcole at Newgate his efforts continued to be supplemented on an *ad hoc* basis by other London ministers.[67]

Certainly, throughout the period, Protestants were able to exploit the prisons just as effectively as Catholics. They arranged sermons and disputations at which Catholic prisoners were compelled to attend. In Salford gaol in the early 1580s Sir Edmund Trafford and Robert Worsley organized the reading of Scripture and petitioned the Privy Council for the appointment of a preacher there. Although the recusants in York Castle strenuously resisted the efforts of the authorities to make them listen to the Puritan preachers who swarmed there, it nevertheless provided a magnificent setting for the confrontation of two opposing theological systems, with Catholicism, for once, very much on the defensive. The same was true of Wisbech. In February 1584 it was proposed that the priests there might be disputed with and preached at by various divines, Lancelot Andrewes amongst them. Earlier, in 1580, the Puritan divine and anti-Catholic controversialist William Fulke had been sent to preach there by Richard Coxe, Bishop of Ely.[68]

Triumphs of Catholic evangelicalism could be met with a variety of responses. Gallows conversions always involved trafficking with dubious, and often desperate, characters. As the unfortunate Mell found out to his cost, the most earnest prison evangelist could end up being duped by his criminal charge. In other rhetorical and polemical contexts, clerics of all ideological persuasions spent a good deal of time warning against the veracity or trustworthiness of last-minute repentance. Certainly, one stock Protestant response to the profession of Catholicism, evangelical or otherwise, by condemned criminals was simply derision. William Sherwood had been convicted of killing another Catholic imprisoned with him in the Queen's Bench in an argument over money. The crime itself was taken as a comment on the bloodthirsty nature of all papists

> because opportunity offers not itself to let them delight their eyes with beholding our channels, running and reeking, with the warm blood of Protestants, rather than they will want this delight they will wash their hands in the blood of their own brethren, in their own chambers.

Sherwood's scoffing retorts to the efforts of "certain devout Christians" who tried to win him over to repentance all came as no surprise to the author, "for scoffing, mocking and mowing, licking of chalices and all manner of toying is the life of their religion". Another Catholic murderer, Humphrey Lloyd, was similarly mocked for his ungodly concept of repentance and his belief that he had been absolved from his crime by the seminary priest Robert Drury, himself condemned for treason and who refused to take the oath of allegiance.[69]

A report on the general disorder in Newgate in 1588 noted that unsavoury characters were becoming Catholics, adding treason to their catalogue of crimes; one had taken to tearing up all the "books as he could come by, set out by her Majesty for the advancement of the gospel".[70]

Not that, given the opportunity, Protestants were shy in turning the tables on the Catholics and trumpeting the conversion of notorious Catholic felons (to Protestantism) in cheap and lurid murder and conversion narratives. Henry Goodcole converted the forger Francis Robinson whose descent into capital crime had been assisted by a concomitant fall to popery. His redemption through the expert spiritual assistance of Goodcole was a dual confession of felonious guilt and a rejection of his popish companion who had persuaded him towards the crime.[71]

The famous murderess Margaret Vincent was a woman converted to popery by "the devil's enticement". Having failed to convert her husband, who insisted on bringing up their two children as Protestants, she decided to kill them in order to protect them from the soul-destroying effects of her husband's heresy. She proceeded to strangle them with a garter, then tried to hang herself with it, and, when this failed, to drown herself in a pond. She was prevented in this by the chance return of her maid, a deliverance presented in the pamphlet as providential, since through it God was able to give her more time to repent. This at first she refused to do, remaining convinced that her deed had been "meritorious and of high desert" since it had made her children "saints in heaven that otherwise might have lived to destruction in hell". When first she was presented with an English bible, "she, with great stubbornness, threw [it] from her" and refused for a long while "to look upon any Protestant book . . . affirming them to be erroneous and dangerous for any Romish Catholic to look in". In Newgate she was visited by many people "as well of her acquaintance as others", all of whom tried to reason with her but with small success. Then, through the "good means" of "certaine godly preachers . . . her heart by degrees became a little mollified and in nature somewhat repentant" until at last she expressed the earnest belief that "she had eternally deserved hell fire for the murder of her children". In court she received her "judgment and execution" with a "patient mind", and at the close the author felt enabled to consign her soul to heaven. Throughout, popery was presented as the sole cause for the crime. She was a "gentlewoman, who if popish persuasions had not been, the world could not have spotted her with the smallest mark of infamy", let alone the "witchcraft begot by hell and nursed by the Romish sect" that had led her to kill her children. The Romish sect, of course, blamed the unfortunate episode on a persecutory state but, significantly, did not challenge the Protestant account of her change of religion.[72]

III

What we are seeing here is the playing out, for evangelical and polemical purposes, in the most public of settings, of two basic Christian dramas – those of conversion, and of the good death. The second was, or certainly could be portrayed as a function of the first. In the dramatically compressed form in which these stories were acted out in the prisons and on the gallows, the two stories were habitually collapsed into one another. Again there were a variety of forms of Christian conversion; from unbelief to belief, from sin to grace, false to true faith. But all of these could be mapped onto and indeed sometimes collapsed into a more straightforward transition from one confessional allegiance to another.[73] The basic story lines at work here, the starkly polarized categories or spiritual states in play, were very simple. Sin, death, false faith or unbelief, the world, the flesh and the devil, were lined up on one side, and grace, repentance, true faith, Christian profession and salvation were lined up on the other. The trick for the Catholic or Protestant polemicist was to get his version of the true Church on the right side of those dichotomies and that of his opponent on the wrong side. In the prisons these basic oppositions took on an even more straightforward form as incarcerated Catholic priests debated with intrusive Protestants, and felons confronted sin and death under the most controlled and appallingly predictable circumstances. The resulting tableaux, staged in the prisons and on the scaffold, were performances, in a series of stripped down, brutally powerful scenes, of doctrines and motifs taken from the very centre of Christianity.

Here, then, were a series of events and performances, locales and genres, in which the religious interests and concerns of the most humble Christians and those of the most learned clerks and casuists might meet. As Dr Watt has shown, the *ars moriendi*, the concern with a good death, as a crucial sign of and means to salvation, was almost as prominent in the cheap religious print of the period immediately after the Reformation as Dr Duffy has shown it to have been in the late Middle Ages.[74] We can assume that in staging these prison conversions and last dying speeches the prison evangelists were engaging in a game or dance, the rules, conventions and visceral emotional dynamics of which were entirely familiar and explicable to the simplest Christians. They were doing so, moreover, in arenas – the prisons and the scaffold – which held an undoubted fascination for the multitude. Here was a form of popular evangelism with a vengeance, being pursued by Puritans and Jesuits, precisely the sort of educated, elitist religious rigorists and engagés who are supposed, in certain revisionist accounts of the period, to have been neither able nor willing to appeal to the people.

But however popular and populist, simple and stripped down, these acted-out versions of conversion, repentance and the good death may have been, it would surely be a mistake to see all this activity in the prisons merely as a form of intellectual slumming; the "dumbing down" of a sophisticated evangelical message for the sake of popular applause and attention. On the contrary, in these compressed, sometimes desperate and bitter, little scenes, some of the most controversial and difficult theological and pastoral issues of the day were being expressed. Central soteriological issues – involving grace, predestination, indeed, in the case of felons who refused to confess, reprobation and free will – met an equally controversial set of ecclesiological questions about the precise nature of church membership and its relationship to salvation. Here, too, one of the central issues of evangelical Christianity, raised in heightened form by the Reformation, was confronted. How might one tell a true faith from a false one? How to cut through the potentially illusory and delusory evidence of one's own feelings and emotions to come to a settled sense both of one's own spiritual estate and that of one's contemporaries? Here, of course, the issue of the good death was central, for it was precisely the capacity of the individual to sustain a properly repentant yet confident faith in the face of the Grim Reaper that provided clinching evidence about his or her personal spiritual state, about the truth or otherwise of his or her religious profession and, indeed, of the ecclesiastical hierarchy which had framed and validated that profession. Here, some of the most intricate spiritual and theological issues of the day, issues that obsessed the rigorist doctors of the soul on both sides of the confessional divide, were being played out in public, in the prisons and on the scaffolds of England; played out, moreover, in ways that were surely entirely accessible to the most humble Christian spectator.

But if we can assume that the imagery of prison evangelism, of the last dying speech and the good (or bad) death, spoke to the sensibilities and concerns of "the people", we also need to remember that it provided a language, an idiom, through which some of the concerns and dilemmas of the clerical evangelists themselves could be articulated and expressed. It is clear, for instance, that for both Protestant and Catholic evangelicals, the prison could serve as a microcosm of both the world and the Church. It was "a little world of woe . . . a map of misery",[75] but also a place where the grace of God was active and salvation was on offer. Prison, like the visible Church, was a place where the faithful and the unfaithful were mingled together. Here was a place where the most disgusting human sin and depravity might meet the most luminous miracles of divine grace. For Catholics, it was also a place where, in post-Reformation England, the Word was preached and the sacraments administered with unrivalled openness and publicity, a place where the efficacy, truth and power of the Catholic faith was on daily public display. Moreover, those Catholics who were incarcerated there represented a sort of rigorist elite; they were in prison, after all, as often as not because of their obstinate recusancy. These were people who had rejected the temporizing conformity with the Church of England and complicity with an heretical establishment against which militant seminarist Catholicism had set its face. In that sense their conversions, envisaged evangelically as well as ecclesiastically, had already begun. They were now being tested providentially by God with affliction to try their faith and accelerate the partial separation of the wheat from the tares, a process which evangelicals tended to think should be encouraged within the visible Church. The prisons presented, therefore, a vision of the proper relation of the true Church and the visible Church, and also a model for a godly clerical ministry within it.

Prison was also a place of death where the faithful could learn to die. A common figure in evangelical discourse was a translation of the *ars moriendi* back through life, so that life becomes a preparation for death. Death is a "medicine" rather than a disease. It is the natural cure for those who "do all their lives learn to speak of amendment, and yet do never think of amending their lives".[76] For the evangelical, the worldlings were like prisoners; indeed all men are such "against whom as soon as ever they be born, in this miserable and transitory life, the severe sentence of death is pronounced. And so we all stand in this world, as the malefactor stands in prison, condemned to death and ready to go unto execution. Of whom as it is said, that he lies in prison upon his life, so of us all may it truly be spoken, that we are in this prison of the world, and lie upon our lives, which being considered: oh how much ought we to weep, and how much ought we be careful and diligent to prepare ourselves for death".[77] As the anonymous author of the pamphlet describing the fate of Humphrey Stafford observed, "a notorious general sinner dying, all the time of his riotous life to Godwards, as soon as he heartily repents him of his sins, then he begins his life with God, when he proves a dead man unto the world, and utterly mortifies all his filthy affections, so he never truly lived till death touches him and a true feeling of all his former offences. The sense and apprehension of death makes men wise, and those that have spent most follies in their youth reap most wisdom in such an hour".[78]

Through the mechanisms of prison and gallows evangelism these truths could be vividly expressed. Of course, this was done most obviously through the manipulation of the last moments of condemned felons, but it could also be done more subtly. Thus those who were drawn into the clerical web within the prisons were confronted, in the spiritual rigorism of the priests themselves, with an example of evangelical "conversation" suitable to the evangelical "conversion" which formed the basis of these priests' proselytizing activity. Although (thought the lawyer Geoffrey Mynshul) prison is "a place that will learn a young man more villainy . . . in one half year, than he can learn at twenty dicing-houses", at the same time, prison "is your prodigals *ultimum refugium*, wherein he may see himself as in a glass what his excess hath brought him to", it is "a Purgatory which doth afflict a man with more miseries than ever he reaped pleasures" and "a pilgrimage to extenuate sins, and absolve offences: for here be seminaries and mass-priests, which do take down the pride of their flesh more, than a voyage to the Holy Land, or a hair shirt in Lent". It is the "very idea of all misery and torments, it converts joy into sorrow, riches into poverty, and ease into discontentments",[79] almost an exact evangelical prescription for the life of faith!

Such attitudes and insights were in play among Protestants as well, where the experience of incarceration, condemnation and imminent death was sometimes presented as but a peculiarly startling or vivid instance of that providential imposition of affliction upon the souls of the elect through which God so often called his saints to a true faith. In a pamphlet account of a robbery that went wrong in London in 1608, the miscreants involved were pictured coming to a proper sense of their own sins only through their experience of incarceration in the King's Bench prison. Only then did they begin to "have a remembrance and a remorseful touch" of their lives. "In this", editorialized the anonymous author, "a prison to a man's life may be well compared with a glass, which looked upon, gives a man to remember the form and beauty, or blemishes and scars of his own face, which otherwise happily he should utterly forget: so a man being imprisoned, and made . . . chambermate with thieves and murderers . . . begins there like a Christian arithmetician, to number and cast up the account of his whole life past, comparing his with theirs. . ." and being

> tainted with the guilt of his own conscience, and the terror of his own sins, he there falls to unfeigned and perpetual repentance, and instead of begging daily food for the sustenance of his body, he on his knees entreats heaven's mercy to the relief of his soul.

The "inclosed prison put them in mind of their grave: the grates and locks put them in mind of Hell, which deprived them from the joy of liberty, which they saw others possess".[80] As we have seen, Mistress Sanders had been brought to repentance only after she had been deprived of all hope of a pardon, stripped, that is, of all worldly thoughts and expectations and brought to confront death full in the face – embodied in her case by the sight of the scaffold upon which she was to die the next day.

In short, the felon's journey through capture, condemnation and imprisonment, to death could be used to represent the journey that all Christians must take away from the world, the flesh and the devil, so that, brought by the inevitability of death to confront their own sin and depravity, they would come finally to rest on Christ (and his Church) for the salvation that they alone could provide. In that conversion, for Romish and Protestant evangelicals, meant a titanic struggle against the world, the flesh and the devil, the prison was both an ideal site and synecdoche for that wider spiritual struggle.

IV

The prisons, then, allow us a measure of insight into a world of popular evangelism and polemic that might otherwise remain closed to us. Far from being simple sites of official repression and constraint, the prisons became arenas of ideological contest. Their status as such was overdetermined, a product of a whole series of interlocking administrative, religious and political forces. On the one hand, prison evangelism symbolically legitimated the criminal justice system, uniting the spiritual power of the church and true religion with the secular power of the state in an integrated reaffirmation of those principles of social and indeed cosmic order that had been challenged and disrupted by the crime for which the felon in question was being dispatched and, if things went according to plan, showing a devout repentance. Such practises established the prisons and the gallows as sites for religious activity, places where the spiritual power generated by successful evangelism and conversion could be publicly displayed. Here was a source for the spirit-haunted status of the gaols that was entirely independent of the Protestant/Catholic divide. However, the resulting religious aura was certainly compounded by the presence in the prisons of large numbers of Catholic priests and, in particular, by the martyrs' and/or traitors' deaths suffered on the gallows and disembowelling block by a significant minority of those priests.[81] The gaols, however, operated as much as holding pens as condemned cells for the priests and, given how loosely they were controlled by the state, how susceptible they were to bribery and ideological manipulation by the Catholics, their status as centres of spiritual power was very rapidly compounded by the sacramental grace, spiritual counsel and saintly examples on offer to any Catholic who cared to resort there. The authorities, unable to react to these developments by exerting effective administrative or physical control over the prisons, responded by seeking to turn the status of the gaols as arenas for ideological dispute and the display of spiritual power to their own advantage. But by seeking to combat and exploit the prison evangelism of the Catholics in this way the authorities became complicit in the creation there of a privileged enclave for certain sorts of religious activism. Here Protestant and Catholic rigorists and evangelicals duked it out, staging rival displays of the power of their religion to convert sinners and heretics and to confute and face down heresy. Very similar versions of the last dying speech and the gallows or prison conversion were displayed by both sides but for utterly opposed confessional purposes. On some occasions, as with Humphrey Stafford in 1607 or the young apprentice Nathaniel Butler in 1657,[82] Catholics and Protestants might end up struggling over the same felon, each side trying to win the unfortunate over to their version of true religion, to turn his or her final agony into a vindication of their claims to truth and power.

In so doing, both sides were feeding off the very considerable popular interest in the theatre of the gallows and the prison conversion and playing to the nexus of concerns and anxieties surrounding the *ars moriendi* and the trope of the good death as the ultimate test of a true faith, and the gateway to heaven. Here the world of Dr Watt's cheap religious print met the sophisticated pastoral techniques, the subtle theological distinctions and evangelical obsessions of clerical engagés, both Protestant and Catholic. The point here is not to assert that elite and popular perceptions of these events were the same – indeed, if our analysis of the crowd's response to the execution of Catholic priests is anything to go by, they were not[83] – but merely to argue that they were integrally related, using the same idioms and narrative tropes to address what remained recognizably the same issues and anxieties.

This perhaps is not what some recent revisionist writing on the subject of Catholic and Protestant evangelism in post-Reformation England would have led us to expect. Of course, it could be argued that what happened in the prisons was not "typical". But the themes and issues at stake – the good death as the ultimate test of a true faith and conversion – were central to virtually all contemporary versions of the Christian life and, indeed, to great swathes of human experience. Thus, even if we deny them the revisionist palm of "typicality" (a category more often deployed than defined) these dreadful, bitter and sometimes farcical little scenes, played out in the prisons and on the scaffold, can advance a claim, if not to universality, then at least to a typological, symbolic resonance that cannot be gauged merely by counting them (even if such an exercise were possible, which, thankfully, it is not).

For, here, we can see in peculiarly compressed and concentrated form the actively evangelical impulses of both Protestant and Catholic clerical engagés, in urgent competition for the attention and allegiance of a variously constituted "people". Judging from what they did in the prisons, the Catholics who engaged in this sort of evangelical activity did not envisage their task as the restoration of a bygone golden age of Catholic piety and they would have been surprised if they had been told that they were avoiding or ignoring their natural constituency – the rapidly dwindling people of Catholic England. They would surely have been equally amazed to be told that there was nothing to fear from their natural enemies – the Puritans – who confronted them in the prisons. And they would have had good reason to disagree with the proposition that their brand of activism was suitable only for the houses of the gentry, where they supposedly aspired to spend most of their time. Likewise, the Puritans would have been stunned to hear that all that was required for the efficacious spread of the Gospel was a less rigorous style of communication.[84]

What is remarkable in all this are the similarities between the evangelical styles, concerns and methods of the two sides. Both knew how to skewer a soul in distress and to play to the gallery; both conceived of their evangelical role in relation to the visible church and the godly community within it in remarkably similar ways; and both remained committed to a style of evangelism pitched at what can best be described as a mass audience, exploiting common Christian tropes and narrative patterns for their own polemical and confessional ends; all of which is surely worth pondering as we come to consider the relations between priests and people in the long aftermath of the English Reformation.

Notes

1. C. Haigh, "The continuity of Catholicism in the English reformation", *Past and Present* **93**, 1981, pp. 37–69; Haigh, "From monopoly to minority: Catholicism in early modern England", *Transactions of the Royal Historical Society*, 5th series, **31**, 1981, pp. 129–47; Haigh, "Puritan evangelism in the reign of

Elizabeth I", *English Historical Review* **92**, 1977, pp. 30–58; Haigh, "The church of England, the Catholics and the people", in *The reign of Elizabeth I*, C. Haigh (ed.) (London, 1984), pp. 195–219.

2. J. A. Sharpe, "'Last dying speeches': religion, ideology and public execution in seventeenth-century England", *Past and Present* **107**, 1985, pp. 144–67; P. Lake, "Deeds against nature: cheap print, Protestantism and murder in early seventeenth-century England", in *Culture and politics in early Stuart England*, K. Sharpe & P. Lake (eds) (London, 1994), pp. 257–83; P. Lake & M. Questier, "Agency, appropriation and rhetoric under the gallows: Puritans, Romanists and the state in early modern England", *Past and Present* **153**, 1996, pp. 64–107.

3. S. McConville, *A history of English prison administration* vol. I (London, 1981), p. 5.

4. McConville, *History*, pp. 19–20; J. Morris (ed.), *The troubles of our Catholic forefathers*, vol. III (London, 1872–7), pp. 74–8.

5. *Historical Manuscripts Commission* (hereafter HMC) *Salisbury MSS* vol. IV, p. 407.

6. P. McGrath & J. Rowe, "The imprisonment of Catholics for religion under Elizabeth I", *Recusant History* **20**, 1991, pp. 415–35, at p. 422.

7. J. C. H. Aveling, *Catholic recusancy in the city of York 1558–1791* (London, 1970), pp. 60–5; McConville, *History*, pp. 12–13, showing that gaolers were notoriously unreliable and their oaths before taking office were a standing joke; the system of demanding and accepting fees extended downward to the lowest officials in the prison, turnkeys, porters and clerks.

8. Public Record Office, State Papers (hereafter PRO, SP) 12/194/32, fo. 552.

9. Aveling, *Catholic recusancy*, pp. 59–60.

10. McConville, *History*, p. 19, citing Geoffrey Mynshul, *Essayes and characters of a prison and prisoners* (London, 1618).

11. P. Renold (ed.) *The Wisbech Stirs (1595–1598)* (Catholic Record Society (hereafter CRS) **51**, 1958), p. 180.

12. W. K. L. Webb, "Thomas Preston OSB, alias Roger Widdrington (1567–1640)", *Biographical Studies* **2**, 1953–4, pp. 216–69. Preston was not the only one who benefited from the lax conditions in the Clink and the privileges of day release there, PRO, SP 14/91/20, fos. 31v–32r.

13. Archives of the Archdiocese of Westminster (hereafter AAW), A XII, p. 523.

14. *HMC Salisbury MSS* vol. VII, pp. 331, 224; AAW, A vol. XIV, p. 643.

15. *Calendar of State Papers Domestic* (hereafter CSPD) *1595–7*, p. 369.

16. Renold, *Wisbech Stirs*, pp. 333, 12.

17. G. Anstruther, *The seminary priests. A Dictionary of the secular clergy of England and Wales, 1558–1850*, vol. I (Ware & Great Wakering, 1968–77), p. 83; AAW, A vol. XIV, p. 471.

18. J. Brousse, *The life of ... Angel of Joyeuse* (Douai, 1623), p. 115; J. H. Pollen, *Acts of English martyrs* (London, 1891), pp. 137–8; Morris, *Troubles* vol. III, p. 370.

19. PRO, SP 12/165/5, fo. 23r.

20. Anstruther, *Seminary priests*, vol. I, p. 30.

21. *CSPD 1591–4*, p. 511. Bishop Aylmer in December 1583 had reported on the masses said in the Marshalsea, British Library (hereafter BL), Lansdowne MS 38, no. 57. For accounts of masses in Newgate in the 1590s, *HMC Salisbury MSS* vol. X, p. 280.

22. Pollen, *Acts*, p. 276.

23. For the education of Catholic children in the gaols, Foley, *Records*, vol. III, p. 187, vol. IV, p. 609; J. H. Pollen, *The institution of the Archpriest Blackwell* (London, 1916), p. 8; *CSPD 1598–1601*, p. 319; for marriage, *HMC Salisbury MSS* vol. X, p. 280 (the testimony of Francis Taylor who had been married in Newgate by a priest); J. R. Dasent *et al.* (eds), *Acts of the privy council of England* (London, 1890–1907), *1619–1621*, p. 153; for confession and sacramental reconciliation to Rome in the prisons, see A. J. Loomie (ed.), *Spain and the Jacobean Catholics*, vol. II (CRS **64**, **68**, 1973, 1978), p. 30; A. Kenny (ed.) *The responsa scholarum of the English college, Rome*, vol. I (CRS **54–5**, 1962–3), pp. 250, 265–6; *HMC Salisbury MSS* vol. VI, pp. 312–13; for Rigby, see Richard Challoner, *Memoirs of missionary priests*, J. H. Pollen (ed.) (London, 1924), p. 238.

24. A. G. Petti (ed.), *Recusant documents from the Ellesmere manuscripts* (CRS **60**, 1968), p. 72. Cf. PRO SP 14/72/77; Godfrey Goodman, *The court of King James the First*, J. S. Brewer (ed.), vol. I (London, 1839), p. 406.

25. McGrath & Rowe, "Imprisonment of Catholics", p. 423; AAW, A vol. V, pp. 5–6; for a similar situation at Framlingham, see Foley, *Records*, vol. I, pp. 619–22; Anstruther, *Seminary priests*, vol. II, p. 367.

26. L. Hicks (ed.), *Letters and memorials of Father Robert Persons, SJ*, vol. I (CRS **39**, 1942), p. 179. See also R. B. Manning, *Religion and society in Elizabethan Sussex* (Leicester, 1969), p. 136.

27. P. Caraman (ed.), *John Gerard* (London, 1951), p. 78.

28. *Miscellanea IV* (CRS **4**, 1907), p. 79.

29. McGrath & Rowe, "Imprisonment of Catholics", pp. 416, 420.

30. E.g. *CSPD 1591–4*, p. 253, the Privy Council's orders to the Earl of Huntingdon that visitors to Catholics should be only those that might reform them; AAW, A vol. XIII, pp. 293, 363; AAW, A vol. XIV, pp. 299, 475 (the Council's directions to the Wisbech keeper that no one might speak to the priests except in his presence); for Campbell, see *CSPD 1598–1601*, p. 398.

31. *HMC Salisbury MSS* vol. VI, pp. 311–13.

32. *HMC Salisbury MSS* vol. VI, p. 506.

33. *HMC Salisbury MSS* vol. VI, pp. 514–17.

34. PRO, SP 14/61/91, 99; G. Anstruther, *Vaux of Harrowden* (Newport, 1953), pp. 412–14.

35. Manning, *Religion*, p. 137.

36. PRO, SP 12/209/3, fo. 6r, SP 12/217/61, fo. 103r–v.

37. e.g. PRO, SP 14/61/88, 91, 92, 98, 99.
38. J. E. Paul, *The Hampshire recusants in the reign of Elizabeth I with some reference to the problem of church papists.* (PhD thesis, University of Southampton, 1958), pp. 244–6, 236–47.
39. Lake & Questier, "Agency, appropriation and rhetoric".
40. Anstruther, *Seminary priests* vol. I, p. 328; R. Abbot, *A mirrour of popish subtilties* (London, 1594), sigs. A4v, A8r–v; PRO, SP 14/14/40, fo. 95r–v.
41. BL, Harleian MS 3888, fo. 32r; P. Milward, *Religious controversies of the Jacobean age* (London, 1978), pp. 217–26; Foley, *Records*, vol. III, pp. 590–3; BL, Additional MS 34250; G. Walker, *Fishers folly unfolded* (London, 1624), p. 9; M. Questier, "'Like locusts over all the world': conversion, indoctrination and the Society of Jesus in late Elizabethan and Jacobean England", in *The reckoned expense: Edmund Campion and the early English Jesuits*, T. M. McCoog (ed.) (London, 1996), pp. 365–84, at pp. 369–70.
42. Webb, "Thomas Preston", p. 236; cf. AAW, A vol. X, no. 21; Anstruther, *Seminary priests* vol. I, p. 206; AAW, A vol. XI, p. 123. Birkhead said to the clergy agent in Rome in November 1613 that "the Clink is visited with many" and there was a surge of support in favour of Preston and the loyalist stance, AAW, A vol. XII, p. 443. Before 1615 the Clink had been divided about equally between loyalists and non-loyalists, AAW, A vol. X, p. 485; nevertheless, the non-jurors in the Clink were moderates, people such as John Colleton, and the authorities' intention may have been to influence them by putting them together with oath-takers such as the archpriest George Blackwell.
43. Thus, when two Wiltshire Catholics, Henry May and Francis Kenyon, were imprisoned in May 1611, May was sent to Newgate because he denied the oath directly, but Kenyon, answering "more moderately" was sent to the Clink. In 1607, after his arrest, Thomas Rand asked to be sent to the Clink but was refused, Foley, *Records*, vol. IV, p. 591.
44. Anstruther, *Seminary priests*, vol. I, p. 362.
45. *Miscellanea IV*, pp. 9, 11; Foley, *Records*, vol. III, pp. 762, 767–8 (Hardesty's unsuccessful attempt to deliver a sermon to the prisoners in York Castle); *HMC Salisbury MSS* vol. VI, p. 339, vol. VII, p. 404. Thomas Bell disputed with the imprisoned Jesuit Henry Walpole, J. E. Bailey, "Thomas Bell", *Notes and queries*, 6th series, **2**, 1880, p. 430. In 1599 Bell returned to the castle to deliver one of the sermons in the series organized by Lord Burghley, BL, Additional MS 34250, fo. 67r. James Bowland was terrorized into a display of conformity and directed to read his recantation before the other prisoners in York Castle, *ibid.*, fo. 28v.
46. Cambridge University Library, MS. Mm IV 38, fo. 16v; cf. BL, Harleian MS 161, fo. 93r.
47. Sharpe, "'Last dying speeches'"; Lake, "Deeds against nature"; T. Laqueur, "Crowds, carnival and the State in English executions, 1604–1868", in *The*

first modern society, A. Beier, D. Cannadine & J. Rosenheim (eds) (Cambridge, 1989), pp. 305–55; Lake & Questier, "Agency, appropriation and rhetoric"; P. Lake, "Popular form, Puritan content? Two Puritan appropriations of the murder pamphlet from mid-seventeenth-century London", in *Religion, culture and society in early modern Britain*, A. Fletcher & P. Roberts (eds) (Cambridge, 1994).

48. *The crying murder, containing the cruel and most horrible butcher of Mr Tratt, curate of Old Cleave*, reprinted in *Blood and knavery*, J. Marshburn (ed.) (Rutherford, New Jersey, 1973), pp. 56–7.

49. *The apprehension, arraignement, and execution of Elizabeth Abbot* (London, 1608), *passim*.

50. *A brief and true report of two most cruel, unnatural and inhuman murders done in Lincolnshire* (London, 1607), reprinted in *Reprints of English books*, J. Foster (ed.) (Claremont, California, 1948), pp. 13–20.

51. G. Dugdale, *A true discourse of the practises of Elizabeth Caldwell* (London, 1604), *passim*, and for the prison visitors, see sig. B2r.

52. R. Yearwood, *The penitent murderer, being an exact narrative of the life and death of Nathaniel Butler* (London, 1657); R. Franklin, T. Doolittle, T. Vincent, J. Janeway, & H. Baker, *A murderer punished and pardoned or a true relation of the wicked life and shameful-happy death of Thomas Savage* (London, 1668). See also Lake, "Popular form, Puritan content?".

53. S. Clarke, *The marrow of ecclesiastical history* (London, 1650), pp. 417–18.

54. *The arraignement, judgement, confession, and execution of Humfrey Stafford, gentleman* (London, 1607), *passim*.

55. P. Lake, "Puritanism, Arminianism and a Shropshire axe-murder", *Midland History* **15**, 1990, pp. 37–64.

56. A. Golding, *A brief discourse of the late murder of Master George Sanders* (London, 1577), *passim*.

57. The sources upon which the preceding account are based are Montaigne's letter to Laud describing the affair dated 1 August 1627, PRO, SP 16/73/7, fo. 10r, Traske's own account of the business, PRO, SP 16/72/45, fo. 71r; and the official "examination of John Traske" dated 9 August, PRO, SP 16/73/64, fo. 96r–v. We owe our knowledge of this incident and these sources to the kindness of David Como. For a parallel case involving the execution of a Puritan minister, one John Barker, for adultery and infanticide, and the Puritan attempts to defuse the propaganda impact of the case on the godly cause through the pyrotechnics of gallows conversion, see P. Lake, " 'A charitable Christian hatred': the godly and their enemies in the 1630s", in *The culture of English Puritanism 1560–1700*, C. Durston & J. Eales (eds) (London, 1996), pp. 145–83.

58. N. McClure (ed.) *The letters of John Chamberlain* [2 vols] (Philadelphia, 1939) vol. I, p. 298 (we are grateful to Michael Bowman for this reference); PRO, SP 14/53/107, fo. 157v; Foley, *Records*, vol. VII, p. 1014; AAW, A vol. XIV, p. 211; PRO, SP 14/80/84, fo. 125r.

59. *The arraignment, judgement, confession and execution of Humfrey Stafford*, sig. B2r–v.

60. Anstruther, *Seminary priests*, vol. I, p. 251; Pollen, *Acts*, p. 252; Challoner, *Memoirs*, pp. 153–4, 91.

61. Lake & Questier, "Agency, appropriation and rhetoric", p. 86.

62. Lake & Questier, "Agency, appropriation and rhetoric", p. 87.

63. Lake, "Deeds against nature", pp. 268–9, and *passim*; Northamptonshire Record Office, Isham MS (Lamport) 2570 (which reference we owe to the kindness of John Fielding).

64. York Minster Library, Lease Register, Wd, fo. 180r (for which reference we are grateful to Christopher Webb of the Borthwick Institute of Historical Research).

65. C. Richardson, *A sermon concerning the punishing of malefactors* (London, 1616), pp. 21–2. In May 1622 John Cradock, archdeacon of Northumberland, said at the quarter sessions that he was anxious for financial provision to be made for a chaplain in Durham gaol, M. Fraser & K. Emsley, "The clerical justices of the peace in the North East, 1626–1630", *Archaeologia Aeliana*, 5th series, **2**, 1974, pp. 188–99, at p. 192.

66. Hicks, *Letters*, p. 179.

67. McConville, *History*, p. 14; V. A. C. Gatrell, *The hanging tree* (Oxford, 1994), p. 44.

68. PRO, SP 12/152/48, 153/6, 45; BL, Additional MS 34250; PRO, SP 12/168/1; W. Fulke, *A true reporte* (London, 1581).

69. *A true report of the late horrible murder committed by William Sherwood upon Richard Hobson . . . both prisoners in the Queen's Bench for the profession of popery* (London, 1581), sig. A2v, A6r, A6v–7v; *A true report of the arraignment, tryall, conviction and condemnation of . . . Robert Drewrie* (London, 1607), sig. B4r–v.

70. BL, Lansdowne MS 56, fo. 14r.

71. H. Goodcole, *A true declaration of the happy conversion, contrition and Christian preparation of Francis Robinson* (London, 1618).

72. *A pitiless mother* (London, 1616), *passim*; for the Catholic view of the crime, see AAW, A vol. XV, p. 259.

73. M. Questier, *Conversion, politics and religion in England, 1580–1625* (Cambridge, 1996), ch. 3.

74. T. Watt, *Cheap print and popular piety, 1550–1640* (Cambridge, 1991), pp. 105–15, 162–5, 208–9, 227–8, 244–5, 251–2, 313; E. Duffy, *The stripping of the altars* (New Haven & London, 1992).

75. Mynshul, *Essayes*, p. 3.

76. P. de Mornay, *The defence of death* (London, 1576), sigs. Avv, Cviiv. Evangelicals such as Mornay contrasted the liberal arts, which are suitable for attaining merely earthly glory, with the art of dying well, which attains to heavenly glory; cf. *A dialogue of dying wel. First written in the Italian tongue by the reverend father Don Peeter of Luca, a chanon regular, a doctor of divinitie and*

famous preacher. Wherein is also contayned sundry profitable resolutions, upon some doubtful questions in divinitie. Translated first into French and now into English (Antwerp, 1603), fos. 2r–3r.

77. *Dialogue*, fo. 4v. For John More, all men are under sentence of death through original sin and, citing John Chrysostom,

> even as those that are condemned of the judge, although for a while (perhaps) they may be reserved alive in prison, and be reprieved, yet in effect they are accounted but for dead men ... even so our first parents, though (through the exceeding great mercy of God) after sentence pronounced they did long enjoy their lives, yet forthwith in effect they were as good as dead, for no day, or hour, or moment, did afterwards ensue that they had assurance of their life.

J. More, *A lively anatomie of death: wherein you may see from whence it came, what it is by nature and what by Christ. Togeather with the power, strength and sting thereof: as also a preparative against the same. Tending to teach men to lyve, and die well to the Lord. By Iohn More, preacher of the gospel* (London, 1596), sig. Ciiv. See also, for similar images, W. Whately, *The new birth* (London, 1618), p. 121 ("the world is your present prison"); N. Campbell, *A treatise upon death* (Edinburgh, 1635), sigs. E3v–4r.

78. *The arraignement, judgement, confession, and execution of Humfrey Stafford*, sig. C2v.

79. Mynsul, *Essayes*, pp. 3–5.

80. *The lives, apprehension, arraignment and execution of Robert Throgmorton, William Porter, John Bishop, gentlemen* (London, 1608), sigs. Bv–2r.

81. Sharpe, " 'Last Dying Speeches' "; Lake & Questier, "Agency, appropriation and rhetoric".

82. Butler was tempted to convert to Catholicism by a number of nameless Catholic women, see Lake, "Popular form, Puritan content?", p. 328.

83. Lake & Questier, "Agency, appropriation and rhetoric".

84. See also Lake & Questier, "Agency, appropriation and rhetoric".

9

"Popular" Presbyterianism in the 1640s and 1650s: the cases of Thomas Edwards and Thomas Hall[1]

Ann Hughes

Of all the possible candidates for "popular religion" in the 1640s and 1650s, Presbyterianism has been seen by recent historians as the most improbable, while the two specific subjects of this chapter, Thomas Edwards and Thomas Hall, are usually placed amongst the most unattractive of the Presbyterians, intemperate, intolerant and authoritarian. Presbyterianism's appeal, insofar as it existed, is confined to the socially respectable who looked to rigorous parochial discipline as a hedge against immorality and lower-class subversion in tumultuous times. It was thus unpopular in both of the senses historians usually use, attracting little numerical support, and gaining followers only from ambitious, university educated clergy and sections amongst landed and urban elites. In this chapter I wish to question the prevailing scepticism about the possibility of popular Presbyterianism. It would be absurd to argue that zealous Presbyterianism was a majority or even a widely supported position, but I will demonstrate that the polemical strategies of men such as Edwards and Hall reveal a dynamic relationship with a broad range of the population. Both Hall and Edwards were "extreme", or "high" Presbyterians anxious for a national church organized through classes and synods with coercive powers. But my arguments apply also to the broader groupings of orthodox Puritan clergy, more loosely termed "Presbyterian" – those who were more open-minded on details of church government, but supported a national church, Calvinist in doctrine, with an effective well-maintained preaching ministry and a rigorous disciplinary structure. As Eamon Duffy argues in his chapter, the reforming efforts of such men in the 1640s and 1650s offered the best hopes for a thorough reformation of the English church.

Broadly speaking, there are two very different stresses in the historiography of religious conflict in the Interregnum, both connected to alternative views of the English Reformation itself. From *The world turned upside down*, to *The English bible and the seventeenth-century revolution*, Christopher Hill has emphasized the radical, emancipatory and *popular* potential of the Reformation. "Popular bible-reading", the Protestant stress on the "priesthood of all believers", culminated in the "world turned upside down" of the 1640s and 1650s. With ineffective censorship, a ruling elite in disarray, and a politicized and mobile army, the radical side of Protestantism – and indeed the anti-hierarchical elements in English popular culture – came into their own. Mechanic preachers, with significant support from the common people, challenged fundamental political, social and religious hierarchies.[2] For Hill, and those working in a similar tradition such as Barry Reay, popular radicalism is the most significant, if not necessarily the most numerous, response in the Interregnum: Reay's general account of the Quakers during the English revolution is presented as "an essay in popular history".[3] This interpretation has become more difficult to sustain as historians such as Christopher Haigh and Eamon Duffy have stressed the losses of the Reformation rather than its emancipatory potential.[4] Working within this framework John Morrill has argued that zealous interregnum Protestantism, particularly in its Presbyterian form, was over-demanding in its intellectual requirements, forbidding in its high Calvinism, exclusionary and inaccessible to most English parishioners. In contrast to Hill, Morrill has argued that religious radicals too were a peculiar and decidedly unpopular minority; rather it was traditional, conservative or Anglican responses to the religious upheavals of the 1650s that were "popular".[5] Where both these frameworks meet, of course, where Hill and Morrill agree, is in pronouncing orthodox Puritanism or Presbyterianism in the 1640s and 1650s as an elitist and unpopular failure. For Hill, orthodox Puritans were an increasingly embattled and conservative minority, horrified at the excesses of the sectaries, and guiltily aware that some of their fiery preaching might have contributed to the spread of religious radicalism. For Morrill, orthodox Presbyterians had greater dynamism, but they were also elitist failures whose reforming zeal was sabotaged by a more easy-going, more accessible "Anglicanism" based on communal parochial worship, and a straightforward view of basic Christian morality as the path to salvation.

This chapter focuses on two Presbyterian polemicists, or as I shall suggest, two Presbyterian populists and popularizers, one crucial to the London agitation of the mid-1640s, the other a more obscure provincial, who published mainly in the 1650s and was a casualty of Bartholomew Day in 1662. The best known is Milton's "Shallow Edwards", Hill's "that great persecutor",[6] Thomas Edwards, the Presbyterian lecturer and pamphleteer active in London in the 1640s, remembered mainly as the author of *Gangraena: or a Catalogue and Discovery of many of the Errours, Heresies, Blasphemies and Pernicious Practices of the Sectaries of this time, vented and acted in England in these four last years*, published in three parts in February, May and December 1646 (the first part going into three editions in as many months). This notorious heresiography, with its repetitive lists of the errors of the sectaries – 176 errors in the first part, made up to 180 in a last-minute appendix – was intimately connected with the Presbyterian campaigns of 1645–7 which drew together elements in the Westminster Assembly of Divines, the City of London and the Scots commissioners living there. Edwards was predictably active in the "high" Presbyterian campaign of the summer of 1647, as the city sought to erect a rival armed force to the Independents' New Model, and violently coerced the parliament to disband the army and make peace with the King. He was a prominent preacher on the 28 July fast day as the New Model approached the city, urging his audience to violent resolve. Edwards thereafter felt himself to be a marked man and fled to Amsterdam shortly after the Army's triumphal entrance to the city with its parliamentary allies on 6 August. He was dead within the year, still aged less than fifty. Of the fourth part of *Gangraena* and the many tracts promised at the end of part three, only one volume was ever published, although ten years after Edwards' death, his old associate the Scots divine Robert Baillie was still urging his London contacts to seek out and publish Edwards' surviving manuscripts.[7]

Thomas Hall (1610–65) rates a couple of columns in the *Dictionary of national biography*, and usually described himself on title pages as "Thomas Hall BD and Pastor of Kings Norton, Worcestershire", a large chapelry on the outskirts of Birmingham, but within the parish of Bromsgrove. Educated at Oxford, partly by a "stark, staring Arminian", he spent all his career at or near Kings Norton as schoolmaster and perpetual curate, preaching there from *c.*1633 until his ejection. On his death he bequeathed a large collection of books to libraries at Birmingham and Kings Norton. Many of these, heavily annotated by Hall, are now in Birmingham Reference Library – including a copy of Edwards' *Antapologia*, and of all three parts of *Gangraena*, valued at 2s. 6d. and 10s. respectively in the early 1660s.[8]

The published writings of Presbyterians and of godly ministers in general have been widely used to support historians' arguments about the popular failure of Presbyterians. *Gangraena* has been a major source of information about "plebeian radicalism"; while broader contemporary Puritan narratives of the failure and decline of godly reform in the 1640s and 1650s have been used to bolster later analyses.[9] This chapter focuses on Edwards' and Hall's published works. Broader research on the contexts, sources and responses to *Gangraena* and on Hall's local networks will, I hope, add nuances to this more sketchy and preliminary discussion. Here I wish to stress that we cannot use the printed works of men such as Hall and Edwards as direct sources of information on religious developments in the 1640s and 1650s. Orthodox Puritan accounts of failure (or success) in this period are always artful, constructed narratives, with a particular rhetorical slant, rather than factual descriptions of reality. An examination of the aims, structure and tone of Edwards' and Hall's polemical works, as well as of their content, suggest a more complex engagement with popular religious opinion than the conventional judgement of failure.

The most obvious but nonetheless important aspect of the careers of both Hall and Edwards was their willingness, indeed determination, to compete in a lively fashion for popular support in a public arena. Edwards' *Gangraena* was in no sense a detached list of errors, but a horrified description and a call to action. It arose from the haunting sense amongst the most committed Presbyterians – the Scots representatives in London, the zealots of the Westminster Assembly, and well-placed networks, both clerical and lay, in the city of

London – that the hoped-for reformation of the church within a Presbyterian framework would be sabotaged – chiefly by the Independents. The Independents had delayed the work of the Assembly, and in the absence of settled church government, errors and division had proliferated. The Independents had acquired a wholly disproportionate influence with the parliament and its army; consequently the plans for the new church structure were extremely flawed, and, as bad, parliament was considering some form of religious liberty. The first part of *Gangraena* came out at the start of the City of London's petitioning campaign, co-ordinated with the protests of the Assembly, against the inadequacies of parliament's first Presbyterian legislation, particularly its measures for excluding the unworthy from the sacrament of the Lord's supper. It coincided also with the London authorities' renewal of their commitment to the Solemn League and Covenant with the Scots at a sombre day of humiliation.[10] The second part coincided with the House of Commons' condemnation of the Assembly's petitioning as a breach of privilege, and its declaration that its commitment to a Presbyterian system did not tie it to giving an "arbitrary and unlimited power and jurisdiction to near ten thousand judicatories . . . nor have we yet resolved how a due regard may be had that tender consciences, which differ not in fundamentals of religion, may be so provided for, as may stand with the word of God and the peace of the kingdom".[11]

The third part of *Gangraena* was published as the Presbyterians tightened their grip on City government with an overwhelming victory in the common council elections of December 1646. It was linked also to a renewed petitioning campaign in the City which, according to Robert Brenner, "set off the chain of events that resulted in the final split with the army and, ultimately, the army's invasion of London in the summer of 1647". For these new petitions called on parliament not only to establish a full Presbyterian system, and to repress errors, both religious and civil; they called also for the disbanding of parliament's army, "that the so much complained of oppression by their means may be redressed". It is no coincidence that the third part of *Gangraena* has the most material critical of the army and of the political radicalism of Overton, Lilburne and company.[12]

The Presbyterians' campaigns involved a range of connected

methods: active lobbying and organizing support; petitioning – that crucial political activity of the 1640s which attempted persuasion through a combination of action and text; and an overt battle of ideas – through public declarations, letters, tracts, and even orchestrated gossip in the city of London.[13] Within this campaign Edwards had a specialist role as Presbyterian "rough-houser" through both print and preaching, but not, significantly, through a parochial pastoral responsibility. A letter from Robert Baillie in the summer of 1644 revealed how Edwards was appointed the Presbyterians' hard man:

> Mr Edwards has written a splendid confutation of all [the] Independents' Apology [*Antapologia*]. All the ministers of London, at least more than a hundred of them, have agreed to erect a weekly lecture for him in Christ's Church, the heart of the city, where he may handle these questions, and nothing else, before all that will come to hear. We hope God will provide remedies for that evil of Independency, the mother and true fountain of all the church distractions here.[14]

This Christ Church Lecture was a rumbustious and provocative occasion: Henry Burton denounced it in a series of pamphlets attacking Edmund Calamy, while the London separatist William Kiffin hurled a written demand for a right to reply at Edwards' pulpit and later put it into print. According to Edwards himself, the sectaries

> have all the time from the beginning of that lecture by railing and wicked reports, by hubbubs and stirs, by laughing and fleering in the face of the congregation, and in the midst of the sermons, sought to blast and dash it [and] about the beginning of September, in my sermon, having some passages against the preaching of illiterate mechanic persons, one stamped with his foot and said aloud this rascally rogue deserves to be pulled out of the pulpit; upon whose words, half a dozen more who stood near him said, let's go pull him out of the pulpit. Whereupon, one Mr B. spoke to them, and the first man who railed on me, called him rascal too, and so all of them went out of the church.[15]

It was the reputation of Edward as author of *Antapologia* – which began the fightback against Independency and as the lecturer who took on the sectaries in theatrical weekly confrontations that enabled him to compile *Gangraena*. The work itself is a composite multi-authored text, constructed from a wide range of sources, and dependent on a broad network of informants. Crucially it demanded the active participation of readers, spurred into action by part one. In his first volume, Edwards urged their co-operation in the struggle against error:

> My earnest desire is to all the godly, orthodox readers, into whose hands this book shall come, who are enemies to sects and schisms, and lovers of truth, peace and order, whether gentlemen of committees in the several counties, or soldiers in the armies, or ministers in the several parts of the kingdom, or other godly Christians, that they would be pleased within this three or four months next following, to communicate to me all the certain intelligence they have, of the opinions, ways and proceedings of the sectaries.[16]

The product was a complex, ramshackle text which is very hard to sum up briefly; the title page of the third part gives some hints of what Edwards offered: "A new and higher discovery of the errors, heresies, blasphemies, and insolent proceedings of the sectaries", along with his animadversions to confute them; "many remarkable stories, special passages, copies of letters. . ." of many kinds, together with "ten corollaries from all the forenamed premises"; "brief animadversions on many of the sectaries late pamphlets. . .", defending the House of Lords, the City's authorities and their Remonstrance, and "our brethren of Scotland"; and finally "some few hints and brief observations on divers pamphlets written against me and some of my books". Edwards was very rarely brief, and in practice many of the elements isolated on the title page or in the table of contents (provided for Part III only) were jumbled together in the text, for Edwards never stuck to one organizing method for long. In the third section of Part I, for example, devoted to "certain corollaries and observations" on the errors of the sectaries, Edwards could not resist inserting some further examples of error, which had come to his attention since the main descriptive sections had been printed.[17] Some pages of *Gangraena* were long accounts of particular pamphlets; in some sections letter after alarmed letter from godly ministers and laymen were reproduced for the benefit of readers; in others a variety of sources – eye-witness testimony, oral reports, letters, official legal or administrative records, petitions and pamphlets – were used to construct a particular incident or biographical account. These usually had compelling openings. Three pages on Clement Writer of "London, but anciently belonging to Worcester," began thus, "sometimes a professor of religion, and judged to have been godly, who is now an arch-heretic and fearful apostate, an old wolf and a subtle man". More succinctly, the twenty-six page account of the career of Hugh Peter introduced him as "a great agent of the sectaries".[18]

Thomas Hall, in contrast, had parochial duties, as well as a long-lasting career as a polemicist, but he shared with Edwards a commitment to provocative debate and to a determined public competition for support. In the autobiographical prefaces to his public works and in his edited autobiography, he presented his whole career as one of struggle and "combat". In 1646, "by the good hand of providence being delivered from the plunderers of our goods [i.e. royalist soldiers], new plunderers arose that sought to plunder us of our God . . . when one storm is over, we must prepare for another. . ."; while in a 1650 preface he summed up two decades:

> so soon as I began to exercise, my refusing to read the book of sports on the sabbath endangered me. That lustre of years which I spent at Moseley, I was threatened by the episcopal party for non-conformity; since I am come to you I have suffered deeply by the cavaliering party, often times plundered, five times their prisoner, oft cursed, accused, threatened etc. And now at last I have been set upon by sectaries, who sometimes have spoken to me in the middle of sermon, sometimes after, sometimes challenge me to dispute.

At the Restoration,

> the year 1660 was a great year of combating with profane and superstitious persons; before he contended with white devils

that pretended to extraordinary sanctity, now he was to grapple with black ones, drunkards, atheists, papists, liars and the rest of those blackguards etc, with what success his labours show.[19]

Two of Hall's works of polemic, *The pulpit guarded* (a defence of the ministry) and *The font guarded* (a defence of infant baptism) were inspired by face-to-face public disputes with sectaries: the first with "a nailer public preacher, a baker-preacher, a plowright public preacher, a weaver-preacher [Samuel Oates], and a bakers' boy public-preacher", at Henley in Arden, Warwickshire; the second with a dyer, a butcher, a shoemaker and John Evans, "a scribe, yet anti-scripturist" at Beoley in Worcestershire.[20]

Both Hall and Edwards thus adopted a contentious and dynamic practice, not content to bemoan the spread of error and heresy they set themselves to defeat sectarianism through debate and denunciation. Furthermore both men adopted populist literary strategies and techniques, which are rarely credited to mainstream orthodox Puritans or Presbyterians of the Interregnum. As with popular religious belief, popular literary practices have been variously credited to royalist journalists such as John Taylor or Sir John Berkenhead and to radical pamphleteers, notably Richard Overton. But Presbyterians also could be seen as the heirs of a popularizing and radical Puritan tradition, exemplified by the Martin Marprelate tracts, or by popular anti-popish writing.[21]

Gangraena offered a melange of techniques from cheap print as well as more extended genres. Edwards offered no disciplined historical narrative beginning with the Anabaptists of Munster or with the English separatist Robert Browne, no neatly demarcated sections on different sects. Rather, he began with the confusing horrors of the present and only in passing mentioned if particular errors had also been found in the early Christian Church or during the Reformation. In more formulaic and tightly structured heresiographies such as those by Robert Baillie and Ephraim Pagitt it was obvious to the reader where any specific information would be.[22] The repetitive and disorganized *Gangraena*, in contrast, was initially harder work but perhaps more involving; both sympathetic and hostile readers had to work through it to find relevant material. Even in Part III, which included a detailed table of contents, there was extensive cross-referencing by

Edwards himself to help the reader navigate the complex overlapping text: a full account of any person or incident involved moving to and fro in the volume.[23] It was a work to pick up and browse through, not one to be read systematically from beginning to end. A browser found sensationalist and voyeuristic stories of monstrous births or sexual immorality, and vivid biographical accounts of the misdeeds of prominent sectaries echoing sensationalist genres of cheap print. There were passages based on newsbooks, and extended use of reprinted letters, while long sections drew on legal models for story-telling or truth-telling techniques. All these were coupled with more predictable lists of errors and theological discussions. *Gangraena* as a whole was a large and forbidding volume, but there was no need to take it as a whole. It could be read in small sections and many of its techniques were familiar to consumers of a variety of cheap print genres: factual or quasi-factual witchcraft and murder pamphlets, trial narratives, fictional biographical genres.[24] Furthermore, there is no clearly focused intended reader in Edwards; he clearly wanted (and expected) his enemies as well as his allies to consult his book and argue over it.

Edwards' techniques clearly owed something to popular royalist and anti-Presbyterian writers. One of the Independents attacked in *Gangraena*, Samuel Eaton, for example, was denounced in an appendix to Sir Thomas Aston's *Remonstrance against presbitery* (1641) and his activities were taken up by John Taylor in his satirical religious pamphlets of 1641; other stories of women preachers also echo Taylor.[25] One of Edwards' most notorious stories, of soldiers urinating in a font in Huntingdonshire and baptizing a horse, in order to prevent an infant's baptism is paralleled by a similar account in the royalist newsbook *Mercurius Aulicus*, 26 October 1644. In this story, soldiers of Essex's army were reported as baptizing a horse with the sign of the cross in Lostwithiel Church. The following week the London newsbook *Mercurius Britannicus* gave the story further circulation in order to attack it. Edwards' version also originated in the summer of 1644, but the details and dates he gives are attached to the evidence, not the original event. "July the third, [1646] two citizens, *honest men* related to me this story, in the hearing of another minister, and that with a *great deal of confidence*" [my emphasis]. Because it was "so sad a story" Edwards sought further corroboration and offered a letter from seven inhabitants of Yakesly, precisely dated 15 August

1646 which he had received "about ten days ago in September . . . from the hands of a godly minister". He had the original still. The elaborate accounting of the process by which the evidence was acquired; the details of time and place; the attempts to suggest the reliability of his informants – all were central to Edwards' truth-telling methods, but he was also publicizing activities which had already been made plausible by newsbook accounts.[26]

Hall's most successful works of polemic were shorter and less complex than *Gangraena*, but they too were made up of a variety of distinct sections in different formats, with poems of recommendation, multiple epistles, and several appendices. An appendix to *The font guarded*, was a vivid attack on the Baptist Thomas Collier, "the collier in his colours: or the picture of a collier where you have the filthy, false, heretical, blasphemous tenents of one Collier, an Arian, Arminian, Socinian, Samosatenian, Antinomian, Anabaptist, Familist, Donatist, Separatist, Anti-Scripturist etc", with insulting labels derived probably from Ephraim Pagitt's classification. Hall included lively, satirical verses in his autobiography, and a colleague, 'R.B.' contributed a typical poem to Hall's *The loathsomenesse of long haire*:

> Go Gallants to the Barbers, go
> Bid them your hairy Bushes mow
> God in a Bush did once appear
> But there is nothing of him here[27]

But Hall's most characteristic resort to the techniques of cheap print, was the mock trial, a favourite device also of Richard Overton's.[28] In *The pulpit guarded*, "Lay-Prophet, thou art here indicted by the name of lay-prophet of the city of Amsterdam in the county of Babel". The Independents, the Churches of France and Scotland, and the Solemn League and Covenant were amongst those called to give evidence against him.[29] Similarly in *The font guarded*, Anabaptist was indicted "by the name of Anabaptist of the city of Munster in the county of Babel" for bringing "disorder and confusion into the Church of God". Evidence against him was given by a series of divines including again the "wiser and better sort" of the Independents, and by the Directory – when it could enter the court being blocked by "a crowd of Libertines, Levellers, Ranters etc that rent and hinder me".[30]

"Flora" too was tried in Hall's 1660 attack on may games, in a fashion that indicates another characteristic of both Hall's and Edwards' polemic techniques, an incantatory style and a voyeuristic obsession with what is supposedly condemned:

> Thou art here indicted by the name of Flora, of the city of Rome in the county of Babylon, for that thou contrary to the peace of our sovereign Lord, his crown and dignity, hath brought in a pack of practical fanatics, viz. ignorants, atheists, papists, drunkards, swearers, swash-bucklers, maid-marions, morris-dancers, maskers, mummers, may-pole stealers, health drinkers, together with a rascalian rout of fidlers, fools, fighters, gamesters, whore-masters, lewd-men, light-women, contemners of magistracy, affronters of ministry, rebellious to masters, disobedient to parents, mis-spenders of time, abusers of the creature, etc.[31]

The loathsomeness of long haire and the attack on Collier show similar characteristics and also appealed to wide-ranging anxieties or tensions about sexual hierarchy and gender distinctions in a manner also found in *Gangraena*.

Both men used a variety of techniques to provoke the active engagement of readers. As I have indicated, *Gangraena* had a time-liness, an urgency, which makes it not surprising that it was never reprinted after 1646. The sense of urgency is reflected in the very structure of all three parts which are unfinished, still in the making.[32] It was an involving and a participatory text – in its solicitation of information, as we have seen; as a call to action against the sectaries and Independents, and in its aim of stimulating study and even debate. William Walwyn accused Edwards of a "base fear that plain unlearned men should seek for knowledge any other way than as they are directed by us that are learned".[33] This was not unfair, but Walwyn's judgement is more complex than it at first appears – for *Gangraena* was an encouragement to search for knowledge – albeit under Edwards' guidance. In 1641 Edwards had been amongst the London ministers to support the Stationers' Company's campaign for restrictions on the press, while in a call to action at the end of Part I, he asked that "the wicked books, printed of late years, (some whereof licensed, dispersed, cried up) should be openly burnt by the hand of the hangman.", going on to provide a convenient list, along with biblical justifications from the Old Testament. "O what a burnt offering, a sweet smelling sacrifice would this be to God?" But while calling for censorship, Edwards paradoxically was clearly dependent on wicked books for the construction of *Gangraena*, and sought them out. The account of the veteran radical Clement Writer culminated in a direct sighting of the "old wolf", "on April the 9 1645, being that day commonly called Easter Wednesday, Mr Cole book-seller in Cornhill, in his own shop (I going to him to help me to an unlicensed Book)".[34]

Without wicked books to analyze and attack, Edwards' *Gangraena* would have been a much shorter volume.[35] Moreover he was clearly challenging the sectaries to reply to him – to write more wicked books – and was cross, even humiliated, that there was so little response to *Antapologia*. To Edwards' abiding shame the main response was from a mere woman, Katherine Chidley. "Tis not unknown how the sectaries by writing and speaking have set themselves to disparage me . . . being looked upon as a man so weak that a woman can answer my writings".[36]

Indeed, whole sections of *Gangraena* were offered as reading guides to the wicked books of the sectaries; despite demanding that such works be burnt, given that they existed, Edwards wanted people to read them under his guidance rather than to ignore them altogether. One end of his work was to be "a manual that might be for every one's reading". So there were, for example, several pages on how to read *Master Peters last report of the English wars*: eleven "particulars" giving the work's "main designs and scope", followed by eight points showing the "manner and way" through which he effected his design. Edwards wanted readers to see through Hugh Peter's apparent "moderation to the Presbyterians", for the work was rather "written and calculated for the meridian of Independency and sectarianism".[37]

It might be seen as perverse to agree that a three-part work, of over 750 pages, costing approximately 7s. 6d. and valued at 10s. by Hall in the 1660s, could be a manual for everyone's reading, although it was within the means of many shopkeepers or yeomen. We should note, however, that Hall too claimed that he was writing for a broad, even poor readership:

> When I observed the *gangrene* of Anabaptism to spread in your town [Birmingham], and some of my friends elsewhere falling that way . . . I was constrained to arm myself and fell to study the point: the sum and substance whereof is here presented to you. Some men are idle and will not; others are poor, and cannot spare time or money for larger tracts. To take off their excuses, I have laboured to couch as much matter in as little room as possibly I could; knowing that those coins are best, which contain the greatest values in the smallest compass; and great books (oft-times) are but great burdens, tiring out the reader.

Furthermore, Hall's establishing of local libraries (albeit later) is a reminder that one copy could have many readers or browsers.[38] *Gangraena* provoked a range of replies and seems to have been widely available.[39] Over thirty pamphlet responses, mostly hostile, were published in 1646–7, while its impact was not confined to radical intellectuals. In May 1647, the New Model Army included *Gangraena* amongst its grievances along with the more familiar sources of resentment such as parliament's attack on their right of petitioning or pay arrears.

> That whereas divers persons have both privately and publicly laboured by aspersions and false calumnies to make us odious to the kingdom, thereby seeking to alienate their affections from us, in order to which they have published many scandalous books, such as Mr Edwards *Gangraena* and divers others of that nature.[40]

For sympathetic commentators – such as Hall – *Gangraena* was a frequently cited summing up of the dangers of religious anarchy in the 1640s.

A variety of work by literary and cultural historians has reminded us of the relatively wide spread of literacy (broadly defined) in early modern England. The printed word was at the heart of Protestant culture. Tessa Watt, for the period before 1640, has shown a culture where printed material was ever-present, not only amongst the prosperous or educated, but also in the homes and alehouses of comparatively humble people, often intimately intertwined with the oral world of poetry and song. By the 1620s rising literacy rates and falling book prices made possible the invention of a new genre, the godly chapbook, for a new audience in husbandmen's and yeomen's households who could make regular purchases of such works. On this basis, many civil war polemicists appealed to a broad and active readership, invited to decide for themselves amongst competing ideological positions.[41] Hall and Edwards were clearly part of this process, offering accessible entertainment as well as instruction to a broad readership.

Edwards himself naturally rejoiced in the wide welcome his own books received:

> The quick sale these books had being bought up by learned and judicious men of all ranks, the last book *Gangraena* being now in the press the third time within less than two months, unto which adding the greatness of the book, consisting of so many sheets, with the not being exposed to sale by setting up titles in all places of the city, at church doors, exchange, etc. like wine that needs no bush (though all ways under heaven were used by the sectaries to blast it).[42]

Here there is a very vivid appeal to the marketplace as an arena in which value and religious truth can be decided.

Hall's *Life* gave evidence for the success of *some* of his works, specifically *The pulpit guard* (his title) and *Funebria florae*. The first, "took so well that it came to a third edition in 3 months space and about 20,000 printed in less than two years space. His *Flora* also took so well, that it was printed three times within little more than the compass of one year".[43]

It is probable that both Hall and Edwards found their readership amongst prosperous households of the "middling sort" rather than amongst poorer people. But I want in conclusion to stress that the social messages of the texts themselves are complex and ambiguous.

Presbyterian authors such as Hall and Edwards constructed their relationship to the "popular" in contradictory ways, depending on the rhetorical context of particular passages. Edwards' *Gangraena* has been used by many historians as a literal guide to the heresies of plebeian radicals, and in some parts of his text Edwards clearly claims that this is what he is providing. He quoted, for example, a letter from Josiah Ricraft who complained about "illiterate persons presuming to preach" and about William Kiffin "sometimes servant to a brewer".

> This man's man is now become a pretended preacher . . . hath by his enticing words, seduced and gathered a schismatic rabble of deluded children, servants and people, without either parents' or masters' consent; (this truth is not unknown by some of a near relation to me, whose giddy headed children and servants are his poor slavish proselytes).[44]

The recalcitrance of servants who had come under sectarian influence is a recurrent theme of Edwards, while throughout Part III he attacked the radical democratic political theories emerging from sectarian circles. Another prominent complaint was about the pernicious effect of religious radicalism on social and sexual hierarchies. A series of lurid stories at the end of Part III, are magnificently introduced:

> There are divers of the dippers and mechanic preachers of the sectaries, not only shrewdly suspected for filthiness and uncleannesses, but some of them accused by women, and have been so taken as they could not well deny it.[45]

These included a man "between a cobbler and a shoemaker" from Ely, and a fiddler in London; this identification of individual sectaries through their demeaning occupations is a frequent technique in *Gangraena* – Samuel Oates, weaver, John Durant, soap boiler or "wash-ball maker", "a weaver in Somersetshire one Crab", and so on.[46] More generally Edwards complained:

> Among all the confusion and disorder in church-matters both of opinions and practices, and particulars of all sorts, of mechanics taking upon them to preach and baptize, as smiths,

tailors, shoemakers, pedlars, weavers etc, there are also some women preachers.

These included the lace-woman later identified as the notorious Mrs Attaway, but with her there was a more restrained gentlewoman, "in her hoods, necklace of pearl, watch by her side, and other apparel suitable", who acted as her foil.[47]

This is one indication that Edwards never assumed the Independents (whom he held responsible for the spread of sectarianism) were supported only by the lower orders. A key argument against the Independents was that they were a powerful minority, working like the Jesuits by stealth against the more numerous but more innocent Presbyterians, "insinuating themselves . . . into great noblemen's houses and acquaintance".[48] Indeed, in some of Edwards' stories the Independent ministers were accused of self-aggrandizement, and of favouring the rich and powerful. "I was informed for certain, that a young maiden buying in the Strand of a goldsmith a gold ring", was asked if she was to be married, but answered, "she was to be of the congregational way, and of a church where the minister was a man of precious gifts," so she was buying him one. Edwards claimed many maidservants were required to give five or six shillings a year to their ministers, and,

> that some poor godly persons who have expressed great desire
> to be of their church way, and gone to some independent
> ministers to be admitted to church fellowship, could not
> because of their poverty; that persons of great rank and quality,
> as some ladies are admitted to their churches, in a more favour-
> able way, and not after the ordinary manner.[49]

The image of disease, of "gangrene," was itself a complex one, intended to imply that Independency was both a minority position and a very dangerous one, liable to spread rapidly if not stopped. Furthermore, the complex structure of this multi-vocal, collectively-produced text, allowed for a variety of contradictory social messages. As well as the tales of sectarian servants defying their masters there was a story of a godly young maid being led astray after becoming a servant "in a family of some rank and place where the master and mistress are Independents". In this household her days were spent (typically) in a combination of "railing against the Scots and against some of our ministers", and of attempts to resist the sexual harassment of her master who predictably used antinomian arguments to support his seduction. The devil, of course, "tries all sorts of men, watches all opportunities".[50]

On occasions Edwards supports the stereotype of Presbyterians as an embattled minority, but there is usually a particular reason for this argument. When denying he wrote against the sectaries for worldly motives, for example, Edwards claimed:

> I well knew the sectaries' strength, policy, activeness, and how England was a bad air at that time and still is for zealous Presbyterians to thrive in, [and that] much might be lost by it, but nothing gained.[51]

The sectaries he claimed had "so many for them in city and in country", besides "so many friends in high places, such an influence upon our armies, counsels, etc", that it was dangerous to oppose them.

More commonly, however, there was a countervailing narrative to the story of lower class heresy, popularity and subversion, one of the Presbyterians as an oppressed majority, rather than a selective minority. Thus Edwards attacked, at length, John Goodwin's sneer that Presbyterians had plenty of time for polemic because they preached "to bare walls and pews". In a long passage he praised the Presbyterians' forbearance in putting up with sectarian attack for so long without retaliation. The Presbyterian party was

> from the beginning of the differences between the king and parliament, among those who profess to stand for reformation and for the parliament hath been, and still is (without all compare) the greater part of both kingdoms, the body of both assemblies and ministers, the body of the people in cities and counties (especially of persons eminent in place and quality).

Here Edwards presented a picture of Presbyterian support as consonant with social hierarchy (as in his call to action quoted earlier) but it was also a picture that ranged broadly through the social spectrum:

the Assembly of Divines, the representative body of the city, the court of common council, the ministry of the kingdom, thousands and ten thousands of godly well-affected persons

all supported the Presbyterian "way". In contrast the sectaries were "a contemptible number, and not to be named at the same time with the Presbyterians".[52] Hall's works were less complex in structure than *Gangraena*, but they covered a broader and more ambiguous period: there was no sense in which 1646–7 was a watershed for him. While Edwards wrote obsessively against the Independents, Hall's polemic was directed against a profanity he associated particularly with elites, and with royalism, as well as against ignorant heresies he associated with nailers and bakers' boys.[53] Like Edwards, Hall's works included conventional linkages of learning, godliness and social status. Hence he justified an English translation of a Latin tract defending the ministry: "I thought they who had so much knowledge as to understand Latin, had also more judgement than to need to be satisfied in that thing."[54] In *The loathsomeness of long haire*, he wrote that sins in "the under-sort" were less dangerous than those in the socially superior, but here he was specifically attacking the pride in hair and appearance that was found in the godly. Even "God's own people by profession" were affected, amongst them, "ministers (who should be patterns of gravity and modesty to their inferiors) . . ., appearing like ruffians in the pulpit".[55] The prefatory poem about the "gallants", quoted above, is a further indication of his main target in this work.

Hall is very difficult to fit into the pessimistic stereotype of 1650s Presbyterianism, frequently presenting conflicting views in the same text. Thus in his dedication to the godly of Birmingham, in *The font guarded*, he managed to be generally gloomy and specifically optimistic in the space of a page or two.

I have done what in me lies, to stop the flood-gates of Anabaptistic errors, which like a loathsome leprosy have overspread the face of the nation, to the astonishment of the nations round about us: And O that my head were waters and mine eyes a fountain of tears, that I could weep day and night for the sad apostasies and divisions that are amongst us.

But his view was more complex than this for Hall believed, "the times be glorious, in respect of light and excellent means, yet they are very perilous, in respect of our abuse of them to libertinism, formality, apostasy, and back-sliding". The people of Birmingham, on the other hand, were a "willing people in the day of Christ's power", dedicated to the service of parliament, "to the help of the Lord against the mighty . . . a people very loving and free to the ministry . . . an unanimous people".[56]

Hall's prevailing image was of a "tractable" populace, of the profane and ignorant transformed by zealous Puritan divinity. In *The pulpit guarded*, he claimed to his Kings Norton congregation, "I have found you also a very tractable people; few families but have submitted to examination before the sacrament, and have freely sent in some hundreds of your children and servants to that end."

The image was expanded in his (auto) biography, where Hall described how at Kings Norton he

came amongst a rude and ignorant people, amongst drunkards, papists, atheists, sabbath-profaners etc., but it pleased God to bring him amongst them in a fit juncture of time, viz when the parliament began to sit and the work of reformation began to appear, [and] . . . it pleased God so to bless his ministry that in a short time they were civilized and became in the general tractable and teachable, only some old knots and knuckles were to be hewed and squared.

The "Life" described Hall's congregation as "the best and choicest people" in the neighbourhood, a judgement that must be as much moral as social.[57] Even in 1660 he assumed his struggle against profanity had met with some success, as indeed did many of the godly discussed by Eamon Duffy.

We know that Hall was supported by some of his congregation when he was disturbed by Quakers in the 1650s; and that some members of the local gentry family, the Greaves, remembered him in wills. Further research is required, however, to assess the validity of Hall's picture of his tractable parishioners.[58] For the time being I believe it is important to stress that many Presbyterians of the 1640s and 1650s, far from writing off the mass of the people as prone to profanity or to radical heresy, spent their careers competing for public support and influence in the pulpit and in the press; some, at least, believed they had had a positive impact.

Notes

1. Research on *Gangraena* has been supported by generous grants from the British Academy and the Leverhulme Trust, for which I am very grateful. Dr Kate Peters as research assistant has made a crucial contribution through her wide-ranging understanding of the print culture of mid-seventeenth century England as well as through her exemplary research and textual analysis.

2. C. Hill, *The world turned upside down: radical ideas during the English revolution*, paperback edition, (London, 1975) *passim*; Hill, *The English bible and the seventeenth-century Revolution* (paperback edition, London, 1994), pp. 15–19.

3. B. Reay, *The Quakers and the English revolution* (London, 1985), p. 1.

4. C. Haigh, *English Reformations: religion, politics and society under the Tudors* (Oxford, 1993; 1994 edition quoted), pp. 14–18, is the latest summing up of the "revisionist" position; cf. Eamon Duffy, *The stripping of the altars. Traditional religion in England c.1400–1580* (New Haven & London, 1992).

5. J. Morrill, "The Church in England", in *Reactions to the English Civil War*, J. Morrill (ed.) (London, 1982).

6. Edwards features in Milton's sonnet, "On the new forcers of conscience under the Long Parliament": the attack on the Presbyterian clergy which ends, "New presbyter is but old priest writ large"; Hill, *The English bible*, p. 163.

7. For Edwards' career in London Presbyterianism, see Murray Tolmie, *The triumph of the saints: the separate churches of London 1616–1649*, (Cambridge, 1977), pp. 130–134; V. Pearl, "London's counter-revolution", in *The interregnum: the quest for settlement*, G. E. Aylmer (ed.) (London, 1972), pp. 29–56; Pearl, "London Puritans and Scotch fifth columnists: a mid-seventeenth century phenomenon", in *Studies in London history*, A. E. J. Hollaender & W. Kellaway (eds) (London, 1969), pp. 317–351; M. Mahony, "Presbyterianism in the City of London, 1645–1647", *Historical Journal* **22**, 1979, pp. 93–114; I. Gentles, *The New model army in England, Ireland and Scotland, 1645–1653*, (Oxford, 1992), p. 191; *The letters and journals of Robert Baillie AM*, D. Laing (ed.), vol. III (Edinburgh: 1841), pp. 302–3, for the 1655 comment.

8. Information on Hall's life and library is taken from the manuscript "Life" in Dr Williams's Library, Baxter Treatises vol. 9. Although written in the third person, it is basically an autobiography, edited and revised after Hall's death for possible publication. See also F. J. Powicke, "New light on an old English Presbyterian and bookman: The Revd Thomas Hall, BD, 1610–1665", *Bulletin of the John Rylands Library* **8**, 1924.

9. cf. A. Hughes, "The frustrations of the godly", in *Revolution and restoration: England in the 1650s*, J. S. Morrill (ed.) (London, 992), pp. 70–90; Hughes, *The godly and their opponents in Warwickshire 1640–1660*, (Dugdale Society Occasional Paper **35**, 1993). Eamon Duffy's Neale lecture discussed similar issues in the work of Samuel Clarke in particular.

10. For this, besides the material in n. 7, above, see W. A. Shaw, *A history of the English church during the civil wars and under the commonwealth* (London, 1890); A. Argent, *Aspects of the ecclesiastical history of the parishes of the city of London, 1640–49, with special reference to the parish clergy* (PhD thesis, London University, 1984) pp. 134–7; P. J. Anderson, *Presbyterianism and the gathered churches in Old and New England 1640–1662: the struggles for church government in theory and practice* (DPhil thesis, Oxford University, 1979), p. 149.

11. *Journals of the house of commons* 17 April 1646.

12. R. Brenner, *Merchants and revolution: commercial change, political conflict, and London's overseas traders, 1550–1653*, (Cambridge, 1993), pp. 478–9; I. Gentles, "The struggle for London in the second civil war", *Historical Journal* **26**, 1983, pp. 277–305.

13. For general discussions of political communication and conflict, see K. Lindley, "London and popular freedom in the 1640s" in *Freedom and the English revolution*, R. C. Richardson & R. M. Ridden (eds) (Manchester, 1986), pp. 111–150; D. Freist, *The formation of opinion and the communication network in London, 1637 to c.1645* (PhD thesis, Cambridge University, 1992). *The letters and journals of Robert Baillie AM*, D. Laing (ed.) provide vivid accounts of Presbyterian activities.

14. *The letters and journals of Robert Baillie AM*, D. Laing (ed.), vol. II, pp. 215–6.

15 Edwards, *Gangraena*, Pt I, pp. 107–8, 111; W. Kiffin, *To Mr Thomas Edwards*, dated in print November 15, 1644; a very roughly printed small 'ticket': British Library (hereafter BL): E17 (6). Edwards reproduced Kiffin's note *verbatim* on pp. 107–8.

16. Edwards, *Gangraena*, Pt I, p. 42.

17. Edwards, *Gangraena*, Pt I, p. 119. A page earlier Edwards wrote, "And for conclusion of this corollary, I say no more". The first 76 pages of Pt I were printed earlier, and separately from the rest, which enabled Edwards to respond very rapidly to new outrages from the sectaries. Extended analysis of the structure of *Gangraena* will be offered in future publications.

18. *Gangraena* Pt I, pp. 81–4; Pt III, pp. 120–46.

19. Dr Williams's Library, Hall "Life", pp. 74, 82; T. Hall, *The pulpit guarded* (London, 1650), epistle dedicatory.

20. Hall, *The pulpit guarded*; T. Hall, *The font guarded with XX arguments containing a compendium of that great controversie of infant baptism* (London, 1652), epistles dedicatory.

21. For a particularly perceptive account of this sort of writing and its potential popularity see N. Smith, *Literature and revolution in England* (New Haven & London, 1994), pp. 297–305. See also M. J. Mendle, "De facto freedom, de facto authority: press and parliament 1640–1643", *Historical Journal* **38**, 1995, pp. 322–5.

22. R. Baillie, *A dissuasive from the errours of the time*, (London, 1645); E. Pagitt, *Heresiography, or a description of the heretics and sectaries of these latter times* (London, 1645).

23. See for example, the section of *Gangraena*, Pt. III, beginning p. 185, "A relation and discovery of the Libertinism and Atheism, horrible fearful uncleanesses of several kinds", in which Edwards referred his readers to the "remarkable story of Mary Abraham" on pp. 82–85 (*ibid.*, p. 188), and to "many more instances of this kind in the Appendix of the first part of *Gangraena* and in this third part, pp. 25 and 26", for further evidence of the sectaries' "cozening and deceiving both the public and particular persons" (*ibid.*, pp. 191–2).

24. T. Watt, *Cheap print and popular piety, 1550–1640*, (Cambridge, 1991); P. Lake, "Deeds against nature: cheap print, Protestantism and murder in early seventeenth century England", in *Culture and politics in early Stuart England*, K. Sharpe and P. Lake (eds) (London, 1994), pp. 285–310.

25. T. Aston, *A remonstrance against presbitery* (London, 1641); J. Taylor, *A discovery of six women preachers* (London, 1641), BL E166 (1); J. Taylor, *A swarme of sectaries and schismatiques* (London, 1641) BL E158 (1), p. 6 for Eaton; *The Brownists conventicle* (London, 1641), BL E164 (13), pp. 3–4 for Eaton.

26. *Mercurius Aulicus*, 43rd week, ending 26 October 1644: BL E17 (60); *Mercurius Britannicus*, Monday 11 November–Monday 18 November 1644: BL E17 (11); *Gangraena*, Pt. III, pp. 17–18.

27. Dr Williams's Library, Hall "Life" p. 50, for a poem denouncing the church courts; T. Hall, *The loathsomenesse of long haire* (London, 1654).

28. Smith, *Literature and revolution*, pp. 300–302, for Overton's trial scenes in which he used Edwards' words, amongst others, to provide "voices of persecution". R. Pooley is currently working on a full study of Overton's writings. S. Achinstein, *Milton and the revolutionary reader* (Princeton, 1994), p. 43 for the drama of trials in printed works.

29. Hall, *The pulpit guarded*, pp. 36–41.

30. Hall, *The font guarded*, pp. 74–84.

31. T. Hall, *Funebria florae, the downfall of may-games* (London, 1660), p. 19.

32. In both the first and second parts of *Gangraena*, the print becomes very small in the last couple of pages so that Edwards can fit in his latest information.

33. W. Walwyn, *A prediction of Mr Edwards his conversion* (London, 1646), quoted in Hill, *The English bible*, p. 163.

34. Mendle, "De facto freedom, de facto authority", pp. 320–21; *Gangraena*, Pt. I, pp. 82–3, 171–2.

35. Consequently, as Smith points out, the radicals were as much the victims as the beneficiaries of religious radicalism, as Edwards was able to construct his hostile picture from their own writings and from newsbook accounts: Smith, *Literature and revolution*, p. 42.

36. *Gangraena*, Pt. III, preface.

37. *Gangraena*, Pt. I, p. 8; Pt. III, pp. 127–145.

38. *The font guarded*, preface, "to my beloved and approved friends in the town of Birmingham". My italics. For a very useful discussion of the ways in which Restoration nonconformists tried to make their works as cheap and accessible as possible, see N. H. Keeble, *The literary culture of nonconformity in later seventeenth-century England* (Leicester, 1987), pp. 130–4.

39. Most major libraries in Britain have several copies; for private examples, see V. F. Snow, "The Lord General's library, 1646", *Transactions of the Bibliographical Society*, **20**, 1966, p. 121, "item 55, Edwards *Gangraena*; item 64, *Gangraena*, the 1 and 2 part"; C. Hurst, *Catalogue of the Wren library of Lincoln Cathedral. Books printed before 1801* (Cambridge, 1982), for copies of parts one and two; The Cathedral Library at Canterbury has two copies, one of which apparently belonged to Henry Oxinden; John Rylands Library, amongst other editions, has three copies of *Gangraena* that belonged to the library of the Unitarian College and were clearly being used by eighteenth and nineteenth century readers: John Rylands University Library of Manchester, UCC 1701, 1702, N573.

40. *Divers papers from the Army* (London, May 1647): BL E388 (18); I owe this reference to A. Woolrych, *Soldiers and statesmen: the general council of the army and its debates, 1647–1648* (Oxford, 1987) pp. 83, 92.

41. T. Watt, *Cheap print and popular piety 1550–1640* (Cambridge, 1991); A. Fox, "Ballads, libels and popular ridicule in Jacobean England", *Past and Present* **145**, 1994, for the important reminder that print was easier to read than 'written hand" – and so published material was more accessible than manuscripts. Perhaps this is why Kiffin printed his scrappy note to Edwards; Achinstein, *Milton and the revolutionary reader*.

42. *Gangraena*, Pt. II, p. 48. Edwards' vivid appeal to the marketplace as an arena in which value and religious truth can be decided is echoed by Milton amongst other writers: Achinstein, *Milton and the revolutionary reader*, pp. 34–5.

43. Dr Williams's Library, Hall, "Life", pp. 75–76; this seems a more credible statement than a blanket claim for popularity. Others of Hall's works were said to have appealed specifically to ministers or schoolmasters.

44. *Gangraena*, Pt. I, pp. 54–55; J. F. McGregor & B. Reay (eds) *Radical religion in the English revolution* (Oxford, 1984), pp. 14–15 and C. Hill, *Milton and the English revolution* (London, 1979, paperback edition), p. 94, are examples of the endorsement of Edwards' claim to be a "catalogue". Future studies of

Gangraena by myself and Dr Peters will discuss the "accuracy" of Edwards' text.

45. *Gangraena*, Pt. III, pp. 188–9.
46. *Ibid.*, Pt. III, pp. 188–9; Pt. III, p. 95; Pt. II, p. 54.
47. *Ibid.*, Pt. I, pp. 84–6.
48. *Ibid.*, Pt. I, p. 46.
49. *Ibid.*, Pt. II, pp. 16–17.
50. *Ibid.*, Pt. II, pp. 144–5; Pt. I, p. 131.
51. *Ibid.*, Pt. III, Preface.
52. *Ibid.*, Pt. II, pp. 60–63; Pt. I, pp. 56–58.
53. In Hall's manuscript "Life" the 1640s are largely a story of Hall's resistance of the debauched royalist soldiery, who plunder the countryside, promoting drunkenness and swearing.
54. T. Hall, *An apologie for the ministry* (London, 1660), Epistle to the impartial reader.
55. Hall, *The loathsomeness of long haire*, pp. 1–2.
56. Compare T. Hall, *The beauty of holiness* (London, 1655), dedication to his parishioners:

> a gracious God … hath decreed that we should be born in this blessed age, and best of times in respect of glorious light and means (though we have made them the worst by our wretched abuse of them) and hath also allotted us the best nation in the world to dwell in, and hath given to us in special, above most people in the land, the fairest dwellings, and sweetest habitation, even a little Canaan flowing with milk and honey, enriched with many privileges, which many of our neighbours round about us want".

A marginal note added: "You have within yourselves, three ministers, a free school, a court baron, a charter, rich pastures etc".

57. Dr Williams's Library, Hall, "Life" pp. 53, 72–3.
58. C. D. Gilbert, "The Puritan and the Quakeress: Thomas Hall and Jane Higgs", *Journal of the Friends Historical Society* **57**, 1995, pp. 118–122. It is also, however, the case that Bromsgrove, if not Kings Norton, was a stronghold of early Quakerism in Worcestershire. Fragmentary evidence for "godly reformation" in the mid-1650s survives in Hall's part of the county, but its significance is hard to assess. I am most grateful to Don Gilbert for much helpful discussion and for a copy of his article. For the local gentry, F. A, Bates, *Graves memoirs of the civil war compiled from seventeenth century records* (Edinburgh & London, 1927), especially p. 179. Research on wills for Kings Norton and for Birmingham is under way.

10

Bristol as a "Reformation City" c.1640–1780

Jonathan Barry

Introduction

The recent reassessment of the sixteenth-century Reformation, to which Eamon Duffy has contributed with such distinction, is commonly associated, like other revisionist enterprises, with an emphasis on short-term contingencies over long-term trends. The English Reformation becomes a political event, not a long-term process, at least in its causation. It may therefore seem paradoxical to argue that this historiographical shift has triggered the need to re-examine the long-term religious history of individual communities over many centuries, after as well as before the central Reformation decades. Yet Dr Duffy's own career has shown the value of working back from the eighteenth century, and in particular the conditions facing both Roman Catholicism and pietism in that period, to the late medieval church.[1]

I hope that my attempt to understand Bristol between the English and American revolutions in the light of Reformation historiography will shed its own illumination on the Reformation seen not as an outcome, but rather as the interplay of a set of issues, each highly complex and prone to contingent developments yet also, at the same time, extremely long-lasting in their central importance to the identities of communities. To borrow a (paradoxical) term from John Pocock, one might call this a "Reformation moment": Pocock himself has now identified the "Tudor system of sovereignty in church and state" established in 1533, and the "roots of instability" this contained, as the key to British history until the eighteenth century, even until 1832. If this in itself may be regarded as a sufficient heuristic justification for the notion of a "long Reformation", further legitimacy is supplied by the evidence that contemporaries themselves still regarded their religious life as bound up with, and defined by, the success or failure of the Reformation process begun in the sixteenth century.[2]

For my purposes, the following issues will be defined as the central "Reformation agenda", whose continued dominance of religious affairs (and indeed civic life as a whole) in Bristol before 1775, justifies the title a "Reformation city".

1) the establishment of uniform parochial worship by the whole community as the foundation of social unity;
2) emphasis on the preaching and reading of the Word as the heart of effective worship and on a system of church maintenance able to deliver this;
3) the association of religious reformation with the reformation of manners, not only through a providentialism linking all forms of godliness, but also as an alternative to anti- or non-religious forms of recreation;
4) the assumption that goals (1–3) could only be attained and sustained through the support of secular authority, at every level from the family to the nation-state, in face of opposition from popish forces, themselves operating at every level up to the international power situation in Europe and the world;
5) a vision of the future deeply influenced by the alternative forms and fortunes of Protestantism found across Europe, as conveyed by emigrés and intellectual contacts, as well as through news of European developments.

It might be thought that this agenda merely characterizes a "Protestant city". However, there were clearly alternative Protestant agendas, both at the time and since, which can usefully be distinguished from the above. There is also a strong case for regarding Counter-Reformation Catholicism as participating in much of the agenda noted above (save, of course, for the fear of Popery and the final concern), but this will not be my subject here.

There is no space to do more than refer to the mass of recent scholarship, led by Patrick Collinson, which has reconstructed the priorities and problems of the post-Reformation church in terms of these issues and shown how the Civil War, as a British war of religion, arose out of the tensions inherent in the application of concerns 1–3 by rival authorities, each giving different interpretations and priorities to the three goals, when these tensions were then interpreted in the light of the hopes and, in particular, the fears generated by concerns 4–5.[3] It would be possible to offer an account of Bristol's pre-1640 religious experience along these lines, building on, although also considerably modifying, the work of Martha Skeeters and David Sacks.[4] There have been fewer efforts, however, either at national or local level, to extend this analysis into the next century, and it is that task which I shall attempt here, using Bristol as a case-study. I shall consider the five concerns in turn, hoping to show that they offer a fruitful, if not necessarily exclusive, means by which to understand the central issues of the period. It will be all too clear that what follows is the sketch of an argument, rather than its detailed working out. Some of the areas I have covered in essays already published and others in pieces soon to appear and readers are invited to turn to these for the supporting details, which cannot be fully referenced here.[5]

Parochial uniformity and social unity

It has now become conventional to recognize that the Reformation, far from introducing religious toleration and diversity, saw an unprecedented effort to unify religious practice around a single institution, the parish church, and a specific form of worship (*Common* Prayer), and that the simultaneous development of the parish as a secular focus of government made the post-Reformation century a high point for the fusion of religious and secular community around the parish. Historians have increasingly recognized the strengths of what has become called "parish Anglicanism", not least in explaining the established church's ability to survive the 1640–60 period and be restored thereafter, as well as the attraction of parish power to Puritan groups eager to pursue reformation before and after the Civil War years. Yet in many places and for many purposes, of course, the parish turned out to be a problematic basis on which to build a reformed society. The parish might not represent a viable community, able to support a Protestant ministry, and there was an inbuilt tension between the godly's desire to use the parish to further reform and their desire for a fuller and more demanding religious life than standard parochial provision could provide.[6]

With a few notable exceptions, however, religious historians after 1660 have failed to explore the enduring power of the parish, both as a religious institution and as a site for the fusion of secular and religious community. When they have done so, it has tended to be seen as a bastion of intolerant Tory Anglicanism or as the product of "closed" communities dominated by squire and parson. This has been contrasted with the voluntarist associational practices of Nonconformity, while the inability of the parish to meet the demands of growing and shifting populations in towns, industrializing areas and other "open" communities has been stressed.[7]

The Bristol evidence suggests that the parish retained a more central role than this historiography allows, while also showing how the ambiguities regarding the place of the parish in reformed religion continued and were intensified by the emergence of alternative Protestant religious communities.[8] Even in a rapidly growing city with perhaps the strongest Nonconformist presence outside London, the parish remained central to civic life and, moreover, remained a potent model for religious practice not just for high Tories but also for Low Church Anglicans and, in various ways, for Nonconformist groups as well. Though the parish had to compete with worship organized by and around both the civic and the cathedral authorities, as well as that of dissenting groups, it remained firmly integrated into both civic culture and ordinary social life. As Martin Gorsky's recent work on Bristol philanthropy has shown, it was not until the 1770s that endowment of parish charities began to decline. Only then did the parish lose its centrality in Bristol, both as the natural focus for secular and religious organization and, for a while at least, as a site for struggle until, in the nineteenth century, the parish structure was rightly regarded (and attacked) as the stronghold of establishment Anglicanism.[9]

The place of the parish was certainly problematic, and growing more so, during this period. The emergence of a powerful dissenting presence raised many problems about how far the parish should or could remain the focus for community organization, when so many respectable citizens no longer fully accepted its religious dimension. The parish itself became a centre for ideological strife, whether in terms of presentments for Nonconformity before 1686 or, later, the use of the parish as the basic building block of electoral organization by Whig and Tory parties in the city: the organization of poll books by parish represented starkly the continuing importance of parish residence and the variations in political allegiance between parishes. The poll books also revealed the growing disparity of populations between the smaller inner-city parishes and the growing suburban ones. The disproportionate clustering both of Nonconformist meeting-houses and, when this can be tested, of Nonconformist residents, in these large suburban parishes suggests some correlation, although whether this is primarily topographic (the large parish lacked the community identity focused on the church of smaller parishes, and meeting-houses might become alternative foci) or whether the relationship was social (the suburban parishes tended to have more of the poorer groups, though also a core of middling residents) would require detailed research to establish. As we shall see, efforts were made to adjust Anglican provision to this new social topography, but it was not easy. The only new parish to be created before 1775 was St George's Kingswood, carved out in the 1750s to meet the most pressing social problem, namely the unruly colliers. Decades of turbulent relationships between colliers and city had come to a head in the riots of 1753, while the Kingswood population were the subject of evangelization by various Dissenting and Anglican groups, most famously by the new Methodist movement from the late 1730s. It would be tempting to see the new parish as an Anglican riposte, but if so it was a nuanced one, since the first minister was himself a committed evangelical on friendly terms with the Wesleys.

The sharpest expression of the issue of the parish in civic life came over the question of responsibility for poor relief. This concerned simultaneously the social topography of poverty (the uneven distribution of need compared to wealthy taxpayers across the city) and the politics of using the parish to raise funds from non-Anglicans, both issues sharpened by the moral and political power assumed to flow from the issuing and receipt of poor relief (or, indeed, of charity).

The problem of uneven distribution had already emerged in the early seventeenth century, but became ever sharper. By the 1690s it was one of a number of justifications for the creation of a city-wide Corporation of the Poor, removing most aspects of poor relief from parish control. As I have argued elsewhere, this was in large part a Dissenting and Whig-inspired measure to replace parishioners with ratepayers (of whatever denomination), as part of a broader effort to wrest both civic and neighbourhood power from the Tories who had, to Whig eyes, so abused power in the previous decades and were now identified as potential Jacobites. This coup, however, far from settling the issue, merely intensified the politics of the parish, as successive realignments of the Corporation's membership, financing and political orientation left it, by the mid-eighteenth century, less a rival to the parishes than an ally in their struggle with a city council dominated by Presbyterian Whigs.

While these political struggles highlight the continued centrality of the parish, they may draw attention away from the ongoing appeal of the parish as a model for the unity of church and community. In their different ways the various non-Anglican movements all testified to this appeal. The Baptists and, in particular, the Quakers did so by the thoroughness with which they tried to create self-contained communities of discipline, welfare, even of kinship, which would seal their members off from parochial life. Congregationalists and Presbyterians, by contrast, sought for a long time to retain a place within the parish structure, both as occasional (or often regular) conformists and as members of parish government, entitled to a say in the secular affairs of the parish. Only when they finally lost hope of comprehension within a reformed national church after 1689, did they gradually follow the others in creating their own communities of belief, whose power structures reflected closely the parish vestry. The Lewin's Mead Presbyterians, who provided so many mid-century mayors, saw their chapel as, in effect, a further parish church of the city, attending it in civic regalia along with the regular round of civic visits to the parish churches.

Equally, the Methodist movement in Bristol, while it generated a number of new Nonconformist congregations, mostly associated with Whitefield's wing and with Baptist evangelicals, was strongly committed to the strengthening and complementing of parochial life.

This attitude, particularly associated with Charles Wesley (who made Bristol his residence), carried over into the powerful anti-separatist tradition which made Bristol the battleground when the mainstream of Methodists sought to move decisively outside the Church of England after John Wesley's death. Until then many Bristol Methodists were convinced that their movement was the rightful heir to the earlier traditions of Puritan non-separatism which had sought to build upon the basic structure of parish worship those extra elements of pietist devotion and evangelical outreach which were not catered for by the standard repertoire of Common Prayer and Sunday church sermons. While many of the Anglican clergy (like earlier Laudians) regarded this as a programme inherently subversive of the uniformity of parochial community, many (even of these critics) sympathized with the ecumenical aspects of what was presented as a renewed drive for "reformation" and renewal.[10]

The maintenance of the Word

There is nothing novel, of course, in identifying the Reformation with a new priority for the spreading of God's Word, through both preaching and reading. Yet recent work has reminded us of the complex agenda implied in this task, given widescale illiteracy and official distrust concerning how the Bible might be read by undirected laypeople. The obvious solution was an evangelical ministry of educated men who could provide a mediated access to the Word, through preaching and catechizing, yet this raised two further problems: how could the mediators themselves be directed and what was to be done regarding the lack (or at least the uneven distribution) of clerical funding to support an educated ministry. The uneasy compromises achieved in this field by the 'Jacobethan' church and the collapse of these under Charles I have been ably charted,[11] but much less attention has been directed to the continued efforts to meet these demands after 1640. The implicit assumption has been that Anglicans fell back on liturgical indoctrination, while Nonconformist laypeople took the Word into their own hands (and mouths) as a self-sufficient and educated group for whom ministerial leadership was increasingly unnecessary. However, the Dissenters' social exclusivity and tendency towards introversion meant that, by the eighteenth century at least, they were failing to cater for the general population. The ensuing vacuum of evangelicalism was not, on this model, bridged until the revivals of the mid-eighteenth century, which are widely seen as initiating a new relationship between preaching ministry and uncultured laity.[12]

Once again this version of events seems at best one of half-truths, if Bristol's experience is representative.[13] Here one can find a basic continuity in the efforts by both Anglicans and Nonconformists to support and extend a preaching ministry. As noted above, this aspect of the Evangelical Revival in Bristol attracted a lot of support, even though elements of the programme, such as field preaching, mass meetings and conversion ministry drew a lot of criticism. Furthermore, it is clear that Whitefield and Wesley were not, as myth might have it, entering a wilderness of neglect. Not only was Bristol a city well-provided with regular preaching and with a plethora of extra endowed sermons, but it had seen several earlier efforts to extend this preaching out into the rural hinterland and the poorer suburbs. It is clearly a matter of judgement whether one emphasizes the positive or negative side of the fact that such evangelical initiatives had to be constantly renewed and that they clearly failed to transform Bristol into the holy city they hoped to create. This was true for the Quaker missionaries of the 1650s, the Quaker and other prophetic messengers of the decades around 1700, the more orthodox campaigns of sermons and pamphleteering conducted by the Society for Reformation of Manners and the city clergy during the same period, and the efforts of Baptist and independent clergymen at various stages of the eighteenth century. In every case they seemed to run into a stubborn "fact" of the sociology of religion, at least in this period, namely that such movements, while temporarily garnering many hearers from across the social and geographic spectrum, normally found it hard to sustain the commitment of more than a small core, usually of the more respectable, whose piety tended to become more introspective and moralistic and less evangelistic in focus.[14] It was with this tendency in Bristol Methodism (as elsewhere) that John Wesley struggled, seeking to square the circle with the range of organizations he created, but it is hard to see that, by 1775 at least, he had been particularly successful in meeting the challenge, given the rather small core membership that had emerged from the massive evangelistic campaigns waged in and around the city.

A tension was to emerge within Methodism between the evangelical priorities of the preachers and the desire of the core among their lay flock to develop a regular community of worship, which both created and reflected a struggle for control between lay and clergy. A similar tension may also be detected, not only within dissenting denominations, but also within the Church of England. There is no neat contrast to be found between self-sufficient Dissenters and clergy-dominated Anglicans. Both groups displayed enormous respect for, and high expectations of, their learned clergy and the power of the Word they wielded, yet this never led to a willingness to relinquish control. Indeed, the heavy financial burden of supporting an educated clergy made control of the purse, which was firmly in lay hands, a crucial feature. In Anglican historiography this issue has traditionally been approached as a matter of patronage, which in turn has usually been identified with the right to appoint ministers. In Bristol almost all the livings belonged to the city council or the various cathedral groups. But, in addition to an ongoing rivalry between these two for civic leadership in religious matters, there was a more quotidian dependence of the clergy both on their vestries and on the ordinary parishioners. This arose from the obsolescence of tithes and pitiful size of the fixed endowments of Bristol's parishes, which ensured that ministerial income largely arose from the paid services performed for parishioners, from gift sermons and the like, and from parish collections and subscriptions.

From the 1640s onwards, the city's clergy sought to remedy this, partly by reform of the parish structure to create larger units able to sustain a decent living and partly by creating a system of church rating to ensure the clergy a steady income. We can learn a great deal from the debates over these proposals. It is clear from the arguments of both sides that preaching remained the priority and the mark of a Protestant city. However, it was not clear what should be the social relationship of clergy to laity in such a setting. Would an endowment allow clergy to exercise their evangelical role better, with resources to meet the pastoral demand and with the independence and social weight to preach freely to their flock about their spiritual needs? Or would it create a clerical estate above the laity, able to neglect their duties and hold sway over the people? The politics of the situation added a further dimension: shifting coalitions of Dissenters and Anglicans, who distrusted the politics of the clergy of the day, strenuously opposed the reforms and defeated all attempts except those briefly implemented by Presbyterians in the 1650s. This very success, reversed at the Restoration, created a paradoxical precedent as later Anglican clergy could be accused of following a "Dissenting" model. In the end, parish reorganization was delayed until the 1760s, when some very specific rearrangements of the city centre's smallest parishes began to occur.

Reformation of manners

The interplay between religious and moral reformation has long fascinated historians, not least because of the potentially confusing (if also highly significant) ambiguity as to which type of reformation is signified by "Puritanism". Recent years have seen a considerable backlash against the efforts to associate the reformation of manners too exclusively with Puritans and/or with an elite effort to suppress popular culture. We have been reminded forcefully by historians such as Spufford, Ingram and Walsham that moral concerns and their link with providentialist notions of judgment were common to all levels of culture, though perhaps in varied forms. Indeed, we are beginning to see that reformation of manners could take many different guises, linked with varied priorities. Common to many, if not all, of them, however, was a providentialism which linked personal, communal and national salvation with the repression of vice, and the associated assumption that religious reformation would be threatened should the sins of the community evoke God's displeasure. This anti-Catholic rhetoric of moral renewal, which showed itself remarkably adept at appropriating a range of cultural forms, from popular festivities (bonfires and bells, for short) to traditional anti-clerical and anti-court satire, helped to cement the temporary alliance of classes and interests which defeated the monarchy in the 1640s.[15]

Thereafter the historiography is somewhat ambivalent. Historians whose training focuses on the pre-1660 period, such as Hirst, have tended to regard the 1650s as both the high point and also the death throes of both the reformation of manners and national providentialism. Yet historians of the "long eighteenth century" have taken a growing interest in the continuation of such movements, notably in the war decades 1689–1715, while Linda Colley and Gerald Newman have (somewhat belatedly) identified such attitudes as the core of a "new" British nationalism in the eighteenth century. Although such concerns were nurtured by civic humanist fears about loss of civic virtue, they also drew heavily on continued providentialism, even before this was reinvigorated by the evangelical revival.[16]

It is certainly the case that the reformation of manners, as both a personal and a civic project, remained at the heart of Bristol's politics and religion throughout the period under study.[17] Far from being the preserve of a particular religious group, such as Nonconformists, it was, like uniformity and evangelism, an area both of potential co-operation across the religious divides and, often at the same time, of competition between religious groupings each eager to claim the moral high ground, and the civic legitimacy that followed. Although the sabbatarian and other reforming impulses of the 1650s succeeded in tarring such moral Puritanism with a radical brush, so that maypoles and cock-squalling became suitable symbols of popular support for restoration in 1660, it would be wrong to see reformation of manners thereafter as a Dissenting, or even a Whig, monopoly. Certainly the Dissenters and their allies lamented court vices and contrasted the zeal of their persecutors against them with their laxity against sinners, but the preachers of Anglican intolerance were not prepared to give up the high ground of moral reform, insisting that it was only through religious uniformity that the moral community could be sustained.

Such debates reached their heights in Bristol, as elsewhere, between 1689 and 1715. The social pressures and national dangers posed by warfare, the intensity of partisan conflict and the fears many felt about the future in an unknown world of open religious pluralism, all rendered the issue of moral reformation, behind which loomed the question of God's judgment on a sinful people as they responded to the providence of 1688, ever-present in local affairs. At the heart of this very complex process lay the shortlived Bristol Society for the Reformation of Manners (1700–5), which represented an effort to establish a non-denominational anti-Jacobite pressure group of leading citizens to encourage moral regeneration. It failed, probably because of the splits in the anti-Jacobites brought about by renewed Whig–Tory electoral campaigning, which intensified ongoing tensions and differences of tactic between those who wished to build reform largely on a parochial programme of education and evangelization (the SPCK model) and those who distrusted such an Anglican-led campaign. But the Society was only one expression of the concern for reformation of manners, to be understood alongside such issues as the new Corporation of the Poor (sold in part as a vehicle for reformation), prophetic calls for repentance to avert God's wrath on the city, debates over the theatre, concerns about blasphemy and oaths, both profane and perjured (for political gain), and an intense concern about the implications of a more tolerant society and media for the right education of the young and the poor, which led eventually to the sponsorship of charity schools by parishes and dissenting congregations.

Once again, the Evangelical Revival takes on an interesting new light when we see its leaders not only proclaiming their movement as one of "the reformation of manners", as Whitefield did in reaching the Kingswood colliers, but also working within a complex realignment of forces opposed to Walpolean corruption. One expression of this was the publishing output of Wesley's first Bristol printer, Felix Farley, and his widow Elizabeth, who combined a major role in Wesleyan publishing of tracts and books, with a newspaper tradition which offered a sustained critique of the national and, by implication, the local, Whig oligarchy. Like earlier Puritan traditions this could draw on the public's fascination with crime and sleaze to satisfy both public demand and moral righteousness. The boisterous anti-oligarchic movement which followed and became associated with the Wilkite movement of the 1760s and early 1770s was continued in print by Wesley's new Bristol printer, William Pine, until his relationship with Wesley was undermined by disagreements over the American War, in which Pine supported Baptist evangelicals such as Caleb Evans in seeing the British establishment, not the American rebels, as in need of thorough reformation.

The politics of religion

As the previous sections will hopefully have demonstrated, the Reformation, far from separating the religious and secular, or church and state, served instead to render them even more inseparable, not just in practice but also in the thinking of the various religious groups who recognized that, without the support of sympathetic secular authority (at every level from the family upwards), not only would the nation never be successfully reformed, a task they thought their *duty*, but their own *right* to continue to worship and believe according to God's word would be endangered. In such a world division and disunity spelled doom, especially given the looming power of Roman Catholic absolutism as it re-established an ever tighter hold on continental Europe and extinguished one Protestant community after another from 1600 onwards. As Lamont, Lake and others have shown, these fears had a deeply ambivalent effect on English Protestants up to and into the Civil War. The awareness of the need for a strong state to buttress Protestantism helped to ensure the Erastian nature of English Protestantism and could be harnessed to legitimate and enhance secular authority, whether that of monarch, parliament, civic elite, or even paterfamilias. Yet the fear of betrayal from enemies within could, in the right conditions, turn religious conservatives into radical overthrowers of the established order, whether they be Laudians (for want of a better term!) fearful of Puritan hierarchies or Puritans (ditto) fearful of popish courtiers and ecclesiastics: the double conspiracy myth now invoked to explain the origins of revolution.[18]

Far from ending with Civil War, however, I would argue that such anxieties were heightened thereafter, not least because, while the "popish" threat took on a new French and then Jacobite/French lease of life, the notion that reformed Protestantism might be undermined by internal division ceased to be the (self-fulfilling) nightmare of Charles and Laud and became the substantiated reality of the sectarian movements of the 1640s and 1650s, notably the Quakers. In religious terms, at least, the electoral fortunes of the political parties of the century 1660–1760 depended on the (fluctuating) predominance of fear in people's minds between the threat posed by popery and that posed by sectarianism. Furthermore, the very existence of rival political parties on these grounds within a reformed community itself seemed both a reproach and a threat, since it offered politicians an inducement to perpetuate and manipulate religious division for personal interest. Thus both the political and the religious pluralism which we may regard as the distinguishing feature of post-Restoration England were neither of them, until at least the 1760s, regarded by most English people as desirable, attractive as they may have been to visiting *philosophes*. Their status as necessary evils, needed to prevent all-out civil war and hence an even greater threat of popish invasion, helps to explain why toleration and political rights remained strictly rationed, certainly for Roman Catholics and to a considerable extent even for Protestant dissenters.[19]

Religion's role within Bristol politics illustrates this model, as has been shown not only by my own work but in a succession of fine studies of Bristol politics in the eighteenth century.[20] Not only did religion supply the principal grounds for political division, but in terms of propaganda among the freemen electorate and street politics it was the twin extremes of popery and republican sectarianism which shaped the myths of division and downfall around which the fiercest struggles revolved until the Seven Years' War and even, to some extent, until the American War. The fate of the nation and of the local civic community were assumed to be bound together in an association which permitted a constant transfer of images and personnel from one to the other. At the same time the complexity of Bristol's political structure and the powerful forces supporting both extremes, as well as the existence of a strong middleground drawn in both directions, prevented any decisive resolution of the battle for power in the city. Although the stakes involved, and the means employed, gradually declined in severity from 1688 onwards, the political animosity did not, and while an ethos of civic unity and restraint could be used to justify a *de facto* toleration of difference, it could equally be deployed to denigrate one's opponents as the party (still a dirty word) responsible for betraying the common good.

European models for the future

One of the most striking developments in our understanding of the English Reformation has been the intensified recognition of its European (as well as British) dimension, and the importance to the debate about the nature of the Church in England of the rival models provided by other countries and the issues raised by the need to interact with these other churches, including their members present within England. As Milton has recently shown so brilliantly, the varied responses to these challenges did much to preform, and hence to shape, reactions to the crisis of the early 1640s.[21]

Thereafter, however, historians have been less inclined to regard European models as crucial, either to the Church of England or to the varied forms of nonconformity. The major exception to this, of course, is the debate over the debt owed by the Methodists to European pietism, which has led W. R. Ward to open up, almost singlehandedly, the broader question of the interplay between Protestant churches across Europe and, indeed, the Atlantic. As he has shown, there was a vigorous and growing world of intellectual and personal communication, through letters, travel and, above all, print, often co-ordinated by religious emigres with European-wide contacts.[22]

Three crucial similarities of situation bound these groups together. The first was the threat of Counter-Reformation power and its impact in causing the migration of groups. The second was the interplay of different Protestant churches who found themselves, like the English churches, forced to live together, either when migrants brought divergent traditions into contact or in countries such as Germany and the Netherlands with several powerful variants of Protestantism (as well as entrenched Catholic minorities). In England the most important migrants were the Huguenots, although one should not forget the later Moravians (displaced at one remove), while the impact of religious pluralism was felt first through Dutch channels and then later through German pietism. Finally, there was a common concern to preserve the essentials of scriptural orthodoxy in the face of the intellectual challenges posed by "freethinking" of all sorts, without abandoning the claim to "enlightened" reason which supposedly distinguished the reformed tradition from popery.[23]

The impact of these trends on a city such as Bristol is manifest. The city played host to a considerable Huguenot influx in the decades after 1685, and was influenced, if largely at second hand, by such groups as the French prophets and then the Moravians (whose ministers were mostly European even if the small flock were largely local), quite apart from the mediated influence of Moravians and pietists on the Methodist groups.[24] The Huguenot church, as elsewhere, fell uneasily between Anglican and Nonconformist churches, but sustained its identity for many decades before losing its members gradually to both; in the meanwhile the civic authorities had helped to sustain this symbol of Protestant internationalism by granting them the civic chapel as a place of worship. Although they did not come to play the major role in mercantile and financial affairs in Bristol that they did in London, their contacts on the continent reinforced the impact that concern with trading links and patterns of warfare had in making Bristol public opinion strongly conscious of European developments.

The press in Bristol, heavily dependent (directly as well as via London) on the Dutch media and on mercantile correspondence, reported extensively on matters European, filtering their views through their own sense of the domestic implications. For example the Walpolean Whig editor, Andrew Hooke, sought to enlighten his readers with a sense of the complexities of European power relations that would undermine simple "patriotic" calls for a militant foreign policy, while seeking to portray his rival, Felix Farley, as a Jacobite for his failure to glorify George II's victory at Dettingen. In other respects, also, the growing world of print, while strongly English in focus, still had a European dimension, especially perhaps in religious publishing. Bristolian intellectuals seeking to reconcile the Scriptures with enlightenment were drawn to European syntheses old and new, such as Behmenism and Swedenborgianism. Through the SPCK and then later through Methodist publishing, the classics of European spirituality (including those Catholic authors such as Kempis, Fenelon and Guyon who had been accepted into the canon) became part of an effort to sustain and spread devotional reading, among both the educated and, in suitably simplified forms, the humbler readers. Alongside John Wesley's characteristically extensive publishing of such works we should set the lesser known efforts of Bristol figures such as the Quaker schoolmaster James Gough, the pietist accountant William Dyer and the mystic bookseller Thomas Mills (maternal grandfather of Lord Macaulay).

Conclusion: a "Reformation city"?

It might be argued that, illuminating though the particulars may be, the exercise above is largely nominal, because I have defined the

"Reformation moment" to suit what I see as the main themes in Bristol's religious history post-1640 and thus been able to justify calling it a "Reformation city". At one level I cannot respond to this except by appealing to the reader to judge the fairness of my identification of the central Reformation issues as they have appeared to recent historians and the insight that follows from assuming that they remained central until later than is usually argued.

At another level, however, I would wish to argue that the constellation of issues identified above are ones that Bristolians of the period would, could they be questioned, recognize as central dilemmas linking them historically back to the Reformation (and, of course, to "primitive Christianity").[25] Furthermore, I believe one can detect, around the 1770s, the growth of an alternative Protestantism and a different agenda of religious and civic issues, in which this "Reformation agenda" ceases to be paramount, both because the Reformation (and hence Protestantism) is itself redefined and because the need to defend the Reformation legacy no longer appears to be the crucial political, ideological or ecclesiastical priority.[26]

At one extreme there was a "Catholic" tradition within the Church of England which emphasized continuity with the medieval past and might even deplore the Reformation process and its effects on the church's autonomy and power. Alleged expressions of this viewpoint, interestingly combined with questioning of the reality of a popish plot, brought the controversial clergyman Richard Thompson before the bar of the Commons in 1680, for which he earned the deanery of Bristol.[27] By the mid-eighteenth century a nostalgia for the medieval had become more widespread and less controversial, if still heavily outweighed, even in Tory circles, by a sense of reformed progress.[28]

At the other extreme, significant groups within the Nonconformist churches, and perhaps some Anglican sympathizers, were beginning to reinterpret and re-evaluate the Reformation. The lead here does seem to have been taken, as Jonathan Clark would have us expect,[29] by heterodox figures such as the unitarian Edward Harwood, whose writings justifying his *Liberal translation of the New Testament* appeal against the standard reformed tradition to the test of enlightened reason and argue for toleration of diverse religious views as no longer a necessary evil but rather as the touchstone of a truly reformed church, by which measure Luther, Calvin and the like are tried and found wanting. Similar sentiments were expressed by Whigs of deist or like persuasions in discussions of natural theology and of such matters as witchcraft. It was views such as these that persuaded the trinitarian and scripturally orthodox (to their view) from a range of religious backgrounds to mount a common campaign to defend the traditional reformed understanding of various scriptural ideas.[30]

This formed, for example, the battleground for the lengthy and acrimonious newspaper and pamphlet exchanges between Harwood and the Baptist ministers Caleb Evans and James Newton in the mid-1760s. Yet interestingly the evangelical Evans in his other writings, including his successive sermons on 5 November, increasingly portrayed "liberty" as the essence of the reformed tradition, in line with his much publicized support for the American rebels against the likes of John Wesley.[31] While the notion of liberty had long been an anti-popish shibboleth, and Evans continued to deploy this theme vigorously, it also took on a much more positive and substantive significance as a justification for pluralism within the Protestant community than had been common in earlier Nonconformist writings. Indeed, one might argue that evangelical alliances, such as those found between Calvinist Baptists, Methodists and their sympathizers within and outside the Established Church, helped to create a new awareness of the advantages of diversity in "selling" religion to an increasingly diverse society, both culturally and socially.[32]

Historians of religion in the early modern period have long sought to rescue their subject from the labels, and especially the polarizing labels, placed on the subject by the rival nineteenth-century religious movements, notably the Oxford Movement and the Free Churches. In their different ways, both the 1540–1660 period and the long eighteenth century have been reinterpreted to reveal a complexity whose appeal doubtless owes something to the complexity of our own religious landscape. Yet, by and large, the two periods have been considered separately; it is to be hoped that the publication of this Colloquium will give a decisive impetus to mutual communication across the Restoration divide.

Notes

1. Notably, E. Duffy, "Primitive Christianity revived", in *Renaissance and Renewal in Christian History*, D. Baker (ed.) Studies in Church History **14**, 1977, pp. 287–300; E. Duffy, "The godly and the multitude in Stuart England", *The Seventeenth Century* **1**, 1986, pp. 31–55; E. Duffy, *The stripping of the altars* (New Haven & London, 1992).

2. J. G. A. Pocock, *The Machiavellian moment* (Princeton, New Jersey, 1975); J. G. A. Pocock, "Empire, state and confederation", in *A union for empire*, J. Robertson (ed.) (Cambridge, 1995), pp. 318–48, especially pp. 320, 322, 330; J. Gregory, "The eighteenth-century Reformation", in *The church of England c.1689–c.1833*, J. D. Walsh, C. Haydon & S. Taylor (eds) (Cambridge, 1993), pp. 67–85.

3. P. Collinson, *The religion of Protestants* (Oxford, 1982) is perhaps the key text, but see also J. Morrill, *The nature of the English revolution* (Harlow, 1993), Part I and, for recent scholarship, K. Fincham (ed.) *The early Stuart church 1603–1642* (London, 1993); S. Gilley & W. J. Sheils (eds) *A history of religion in Britain* (Oxford, 1994), Part II; C. Durston & J. Eales (eds) *The culture of English Puritanism, 1560–1700* (London, 1996).

4. M. Skeeters, *Clergy and community: Bristol and the Reformation 1530–70* (Oxford, 1993); D. H. Sacks, *Trade, society and politics in Bristol 1500–1640* (New York, 1985); D. H. Sacks, "The demise of the martyrs", *Social History* **11**, 1986, pp. 141–69; D. H. Sacks, *The widening gate: Bristol and the Atlantic economy* (Berkeley, 1991); D. H. Sacks, "Bristol's 'Wars of Religion'", in *Town and countryside in the English revolution*, R.C. Richardson (ed.) (Manchester, 1992), pp. 100–29.

5. Many of the essays cited below will reappear, with additional material, in J. Barry, *Religion in Bristol* (Tiverton, forthcoming).

6. S. Wright (ed.) *Parish, church and people* (London, 1988); Morrill, *The nature of the English revolution*, pp. 148–75; A. Pettegree (ed.) *The reformation of the parishes* (Manchester, 1993); J. Maltby, " 'By this book': parishioners, the Prayer Book and the established church", in *The early Stuart church*, Fincham (ed.), pp. 115–37; K. Wrightson, "The politics of the parish" in *The experience of authority in early modern England*, A. Fox, P. Griffiths & S. Hindle (eds) (London, 1996), pp. 10–46.

7. A. Everitt, "Nonconformity in country parishes", in *Land, church and people*, J. Thirsk (ed.) (British Agricultural History Society, Reading, 1970), pp. 178–99; A. D. Gilbert, *Religion and society in industrial England* (London, 1976); M. D. Watts, *The Dissenters: from the Reformation to the French Revolution* (Oxford, 1978); P. Virgin, *The church in an age of negligence 1700–1840* (Cambridge, 1989); K. Snell, *Church and chapel in the North Midlands* (Leicester, 1991); B. Short, "The evolution of contrasting communities within rural England", in *The English rural community*, B. Short (ed.) (Cambridge, 1992), pp. 19–43. But see now M. Goldie & J. Spurr, "Politics

and the Restoration parish", *English Historical Review* **109**, 1994, pp. 572–96; D. Eastwood, *Governing rural England* (Oxford, 1994); J. R. Kent, "The centre and the localities: state formation and parish government in England *c*.1640–1740", *Historical Journal* **38**, 1995, pp. 363–404.

8. J. Barry, "The parish in civic life: Bristol and its churches, 1640–1750", in *Parish, church and people*, Wright (ed.), pp. 152–78; J. Barry, "Cultural patronage and the Anglican crisis: Bristol *c*.1689–1775", in *The church of England*, Walsh, Haydon & Taylor (eds), pp. 191–208.

9. See M. Gorsky, *Charity, mutuality and philanthropy: voluntary provision in Bristol 1800–70* (PhD thesis, University of Bristol, 1995), pp. 47–72, 103–36. The role of the parish in mid- to late eighteenth-century Bristol is also explored in P. T. Marcy, *A chapter in the history of the "Bristol hogs"* (PhD thesis, Claremont Graduate School and University Centre, 1965); E. Baigent, *Bristol society in the later eighteenth century* (DPhil thesis, University of Oxford, 1984); M. Fissell, *Patients, power and the poor in eighteenth-century Bristol* (Cambridge, 1991).

10. For the above paragraphs see Barry, "The parish in civic life".

11. R. O'Day, *The English clergy: the emergence and consolidation of a profession 1558–1642* (Leicester, 1979); P. Collinson, *The birthpangs of Protestant England* (London, 1988); T. Watt, *Cheap print and popular piety 1550–1640* (Cambridge, 1991); I. Green, *The Christian's ABC: catechisms and catechizing in England c.1530–1740* (Oxford, 1996).

12. J. D. Walsh, "Origins of the evangelical revival", in *Essays in modern church history*, G. V. Bennett and J. D. Walsh (eds) (London, 1966), pp. 132–62; R. T. Vann, *Social development of English Quakerism* (Cambridge, Mass., 1969); D. M. Valenze, *Prophetic sons and daughters* (Princeton, 1975); T. W. Laqueur, "The cultural origins of popular literacy in England 1500–1850", *Oxford Review of Education*, **11**, 1976, pp. 255–75; D. M. Valenze, "Prophecy and popular literature in eighteenth-century England", *Journal of Ecclesiastical History* **29**, 1978, pp. 75–92; J. D. Walsh, "Religious societies: methodist and evangelical 1738–1800", in *Voluntary Religion*, W. J. Sheils & D. Woods (eds) (Studies in Church History **23**, 1986), pp. 279–302; S. Pedersen, "Hannah More meets Simple Simon", Journal of British Studies, **25**, 1986, pp. 84–113; D. Lovegrove, *Established church, sectarian people* (Cambridge, 1988); D. W. Bebbington, *Evangelicalism in modern Britain* (London, 1989); J. Garnett & C. Matthew (eds), *Revival and religion since 1700* (London, 1994); D. Hempton, *The religion of the people* (London, 1996).

13. J. Barry, "Popular culture in seventeenth-century Bristol", in *Popular culture in seventeenth-century England*, B. Reay (ed.) (London, 1985), pp. 59–90; J. Barry, "Piety and the patient", in *Patients and practitioners*, R. Porter (ed.) (Cambridge, 1985), pp. 145–76; J. Barry, "The press and the politics of culture in Bristol, 1660–1775", in *Culture, politics and society in Britain 1660–1800*, J. Black & J. Gregory (eds) (Manchester, 1991), pp. 49–81; J. Barry, *Methodism and the press in Bristol 1737–1775* (Bristol Branch of Wesley Historical Society, Bristol, bulletin no. 64, 1993).

14. Compare the findings in G. H. Jenkins, *Literature, religion and society in Wales 1660-1730* (Cardiff, 1978); Gregory, "Eighteenth-century reformation"; M. Spufford (ed.), *The world of rural dissenters 1520–1725* (Cambridge, 1995).

15. K. Wrightson, *English society 1580–1680* (London, 1982); D. Underdown, *Revel, riot and rebellion* (Oxford, 1985); M. Spufford, "Puritanism and social control?", in *Order and disorder in early modern England*, A. Fletcher & J. Stevenson (eds) (Cambridge, 1985), pp. 41–57; M. Spufford, "Can we count the 'godly' and the 'conformable'?", *Journal of Ecclesiastical History* **36**, 1985, pp. 428–38; Duffy, "The godly and the multitude"; M. Ingram, *Church courts, sex and marriage 1570–1640* (Cambridge, 1987); D. Cressy, *Bonfires and bells* (London, 1989); R. Hutton, *The rise and fall of merry England* (Oxford, 1994); A. Walsham, "'The fatall vesper': providentialism and anti-popery in late Jacobean London', *Past and Present* **144**, 1994, pp. 36–87; S. Amussen & M. Kishlansky (eds), *Political culture and cultural politics in early modern England* (Manchester, 1995); K. Wrightson & D. Levine, *Poverty and piety in an English village* (2nd edn, Oxford, 1995); M. Ingram, "Reformation of manners in early modern England" in *The experience of authority*, Griffiths, Fox & Hindle (eds), pp. 47–88.

16. D. W. R. Bahlman, *The moral revolution of 1688* (New Haven, 1968); Pocock, *The Machiavellian moment*; W. Speck & T. Curtis, "Societies for the reformation of manners", *Literature and History* **3**, 1976, pp. 46–51; A. G. Craig, *The movement for the reformation of manners 1688–1715* (PhD thesis, University of Edinburgh, 1980); T. Isaacs, "The Anglican hierarchy and the reformation of manners, 1688–1715", *Journal of Ecclesiastical History* **33**, 1982, pp. 391–411; G. Newman, *The rise of English nationalism* (London, 1987); D. Hayton, "Moral reform and country politics in the late seventeenth-century House of Commons", *Past and Present* **128**, 1990, pp. 48–91; J. Spurr, "'Virtue, religion and government'", in *The politics of religion in Restoration England*, T. Harris, P. Seaward & M. Goldie (eds) (Oxford, 1990), pp. 29–47; J. Innes, "Politics and morals", in *The transformation of political culture in Britain and Germany in the late eighteenth century*, E. Hellmuth (ed.) (Oxford, 1990), pp. 57–118; D. Hirst, "The failure of godly rule in the English Republic", *Past and Present* **132**, 1991, pp. 33–66; S. Burtt, *Virtue transformed* (Cambridge, 1992); L. Colley, *Britons* (New Haven, 1992); R. B. Shoemaker, "Reforming the city", in *Stilling the grumbling hive*, L. Davison, T. Hitchcock, T. Keirns & R. B. Shoemaker (eds) (Stroud, 1992), pp. 99–120; J. Spurr, "The church, the societies and the moral revolution of 1688", in Walsh, Haydon & Taylor, *The Church of England*, pp. 127–42; C. Rose, "The origins and ideals of the SPCK 1699–1716", in *ibid.*, pp. 172–90; C. Rose, "Providence, Protestant union and godly reformation in the 1690s", *Transactions of the Royal Historical Society*, 6th series, **3**, 1993, pp. 151–69; C. Durston, "Puritan rule and the failure of cultural revolution, 1645–1660", in *Culture of English Puritanism*, Durston & Eales (eds), pp. 210–33; A. Claydon, *William III and the godly revolution* (Cambridge, 1996).

17. J. Barry & K. Morgan (eds) *Reformation and revival in eighteenth-century Bristol* (Bristol Record Society **45**, 1994), pp. 1–62. I have explored this subject further in J. Barry, "Begging, swearing and cursing: the reformation of manners and the politics of religion in Bristol 1689–1715", in Barry, *Religion in Bristol*. See also M. Fissell, "Charity universal? Institutions and moral reform in eighteenth-century Bristol", in *Stilling the grumbling hive*, Davison, Hitchcock, Keirns & Shoemaker (eds), pp. 121–44.

18. W. Lamont, *Godly rule* (London, 1969); C. Russell, "Arguments for religious unity in England 1530–1650", in C. Russell, *Unrevolutionary England* (London, 1990), pp. 179–204; M. Finlayson, *Historians, Puritanism and English revolution* (Toronto, 1983) ; P. Lake & M.Dowling (eds) *Protestantism and the national church in sixteenth-century England* (London, 1987); P. Lake, "Anti-popery", in *Conflict in early Stuart England*, R. Cust & A. Hughes (eds) (Harlow, 1989), pp. 72–106; Morrill, *The nature of the English revolution*, Part I; A. Walsham, *Church papists* (Woodbridge, 1994); W. Lamont, *Puritanism and historical controversy* (London, 1996).

19. J. Miller, *Popery and politics 1660–88* (Cambridge, 1973); J. Scott, "England's troubles: exhuming the Popish Plot", in *The politics of religion*, Harris, Seaward & Goldie (eds), pp. 107–31 (although see S. Pincus, "The English debate over universal monarchy", in *A union for empire*, Robertson (ed.), pp. 37–62 for a critique of this); G. Schochet, "From 'persecution' to 'tolera-tion'", in *Liberty secured*, J. R. Jones (ed.) (Palo Alto, California, 1992), pp. 122–57; R. K. Webb, "From toleration to religious liberty" in *ibid.*, pp. 158–98; C. Haydon, *Anti-Catholicism in eighteenth-century England* (Manche-ster, 1993); D. Hempton, *Religion and political culture in Britain and Ireland* (Cambridge, 1996).

20. J. Barry, "The politics of religion in Restoration Bristol", in *The politics of religion*, Harris, Seaward & Goldie (eds), pp. 163–90; J. Barry, "Provincial town culture 1640–1780", in *Interpretation and cultural history*, J. H. Pittock & A. Wear (eds) (London, 1991), pp. 198–234. See also P. T. Underdown, *The parliamentary history of the city of Bristol, 1750–1790* (MA thesis, University of Bristol, 1948); P. Rogers, "Daniel Defoe, John Oldmixon and the Bristol riots of 1714", *Transactions of Bristol and Gloucestershire Archaeological Society* **92**, 1973, pp. 145–56; R. H. Quilici, *Turmoil in a city and an empire: Bristol factions 1700–75* (PhD thesis, New Hampshire University, 1976); N. Rogers, "Popular Jacobitism in a provincial context", in *The Jacobite challenge*, E. Cruickshanks & J. Black (eds) (Edinburgh, 1988), pp. 123–41; N. Rogers, *Whigs and cities* (Oxford, 1989); J. E. Bradley, *Religion, revolution and English radicalism* (Cambridge, 1990); M. Dresser, "Protestants, Catholics and Jews", in *The making of modern Bristol*, M. Dresser & P. Ollerenshaw (eds) (Tiverton, 1996), pp. 96–123.

21. A. Milton, *Catholic and reformed* (Cambridge, 1995).

22. W. R. Ward, *The Protestant evangelical awakening* (Cambridge, 1993).

23. C. Garrett, *Respectable folly* (Baltimore, 1975); H. Schwartz, *The French*

prophets (Berkeley, California, 1980); C. Garrett, "Swedenborg and mystical enlightenment in eighteenth-century England", *Journal of the History of Ideas* **45**, 1984, pp. 67–81; R. Gwynn, *Huguenot heritage* (London, 1988); O. P. Grell, J. Israel & N. Tyacke (eds), *From persecution to toleration* (Oxford, 1991); J. Champion, *Pillars of priestcraft shaken* (Cambridge, 1992). B. Cottret, *The Huguenots in England* (Cambridge, 1992).

24. J. W. Raimo, *Spiritual harvest: the Anglo-American revival in Boston, Massachusetts and Bristol, England 1739–42* (PhD thesis, University of Wisconsin, 1974); R. Mayo, *The Huguenots in Bristol* (Bristol Branch of the Historical Association, Bristol, 1985); A. B. Sackett, *James Rouquet and his part in early Methodism* (Wesley Historical Society, Chester, 1972); M. Dresser, "The Moravians in Bristol", in Barry & Morgan, *Reformation and revival*, pp. 107–48.

25. For which see Fissell, "Charity universal?"

26. A similar argument is made in Webb, "From toleration to religious liberty".

27. See *The report from the committee of the commons . . . to consider the petition of Richard Thompson* (London, 1680); *The vizar pluck't off from Richard Thompson of Bristol clerk in a plain and true character of him* (London, 1680); R. Thompson, *A sermon preached in the Cathedral Church of Bristol 21 June 1685 before his grace Henry Duke of Beaufort* (London, 1685)

28. J. Barry, "'The history and antiquities of the city of Bristol'", *Angelaki* **1**(2), Winter 1993/4, pp. 55–81, especially 72–4.

29. J. C. D. Clark, *English society 1688–1832* (Cambridge, 1985); J. C. D. Clark, *The language of liberty* (Cambridge, 1994).

30. Barry, "Piety and the patient"; J. Barry, "Public infidelity and private belief? The discourse of spirits in Enlightenment Bristol" (forthcoming).

31. T. Amory, *A sermon preached at the ordination of Edward Harwood* (Bristol, 1765); E. Harwood, *Proposals for publishing by subscription, a liberal translation of the New Testament* (London, 1765); E. Harwood, *A liberal translation of the New Testament*, (London, 1768); E. Harwood, *A letter to the Rev. Mr. Caleb Evans* (Bristol, 1767); E. Harwood, *A new introduction to the study and knowledge of the New Testament*, (London, 1767–71); J. Newton, *Reply to a letter to the Revd Mr Caleb Evans of Bristol* (Bristol, 1766); *Felix Farley's Bristol Journal* and *Bristol Journal*, passim late 1765 – early 1767; *Animadversions on the Rev. Mr. E. Harwood's affectionate and candid letter by a By-Stander* (Bristol, 1767); C. Evans, *The scripture doctrine of the deity of the Son and Holy Spirit, represented* (Bristol, 1766); C. Evans, *Brief remarks upon the Rev. Mr. Harwood's late extraordinary letter* (Bristol, 1767); C. Evans, *British constitutional liberty* (Bristol, 1775); C. Evans, *A letter to the Rev. Mr. John Wesley*, 3rd edn, (Bristol, 1775); C. Evans, *The remembrance of former days* (Bristol, 1778); C. Evans, *Postscript to the first edition of a sermon preached at Broad-Mead, Bristol, on the fifth of November last. Containing a letter to the author from a Romish priest, occasioned by that publication; together with some remarks upon it* (Bristol, 1779). On Evans, see Bradley, *Religion, revolution and English radicalism*, especially

pp. 127–92; R. Hayden, *Evangelical Calvinism among eighteenth-century British Baptists* (PhD thesis, University of Keele, 1991).

32. L. E. Elliott-Binns, *The early evangelicals* (London, 1953); H. Rack, "Religious societies and the origins of Methodism", *Journal of Ecclesiastical History* **37**, 1982, pp. 582–95; H. Rack, *Reasonable enthusiast; John Wesley and the rise of Methodism* (London, 1989); M. Noll, D. Bebbington & G. Rawlyk (eds), *Evangelicalism* (Oxford, 1994).

11

Was there a Methodist evangelistic strategy in the eighteenth century?

W. R. Ward

Recently Professor Hempton, under a title which suggested that he was going to plunge into this impenetrable thicket, actually plunged into another, that of what went on in the Methodist psyche in the eighteenth century, and made some progress, nobly resisting the temptation to refurbish E. P. Thompson's "psychic masturbation" (which always seemed to me a jolly good cheap vice, could one but think how to do it).[1] Progress with my question, which the simple-minded might suppose would be one of the first to be asked about the revival in the eighteenth century, seems, however, to be almost totally blocked by both the literature and the sources, and the best I can hope to achieve in this chapter is to indicate some levels at which the question may be asked. Two examples may illustrate the difficulties in the literature. Seventy years ago Fr Maximin Piette won all manner of prizes for a work of vast scope in which he attempted to set Methodism in the context of an eternal struggle to reform the Reformation.[2] This was in various respects an unsuccessful work, quite apart from the fact that Piette hardly had the mastery of the eighteenth-century church, let alone the rest of the background he needed; but above all he seems not to have grasped the conceptual difference between movements for reform and movements for revival. The word "revival" itself proved a red rag to a bull when Rupert Davies and Gordon Rupp came to launch the official history of Methodism in 1965. Their doctrine that "it would be dangerous and foolish to suppose that the norm of Christian renewal is a technique of mass evangelism", and that it should be replaced by the "normative" but unhistorical concept of "resurrection", was an attempt to evade an historical question and put down evangelical opposition to union with the Church of England by the kind of bluster very characteristic of those years.[3]

And yet are not the sources as bad? Take, for example, the proposition at the first Methodist Conference of 1744.[4]

Q. What may we reasonably believe to be God's design in raising up the preachers called Methodists?
A. To reform the nation, more particularly the church; to spread scriptural holiness over the land.

The straight answer to that straight question seems to put Piette absolutely in the right. Moreover, when Wesley attempted to explain what he meant by "reformation" in relation to the "infamous, scandalous rabble rout [of the mid-1740s] roaring and raging as if they were just broke loose with their Captain Apollyon from the bottomless pit", it was "the bringing them back (not to this or that set of opinions, or to this or that set of rites and ceremonies, how decent and significant soever) but to the calm love of God and one another; and to an uniform practice of justice, mercy and truth".[5] Reformation, in short, was a sort of eschatological category, almost equivalent to Davies and Rupp's incorporation in the resurrection. Late in life, however, a reflective Wesley, ascribed the taming of the mobs not to reformation or resurrection, but to the patriarchal wisdom of George III who at the time of preaching was just about to take leave of his sanity, pronouncing that "while I sit on the throne no man shall be persecuted for conscience sake"; and by this time the bold aims of the first conference had dissolved in Wesley's memory to a recollection of the early open-air preaching in London in which "these clergymen, all this time, had no plan at all. They only went hither and thither wherever they had a prospect of saving souls from death".[6] And, of course, the notion that the Methodist constitution could be providentially validated, as presented piece by piece unsought by those who were merely its instruments, was itself a godsend to later Wesleyan apologists striving to create acceptance for the system of authority they had inherited,[7] and to chairmen of districts seeking to marshal the troops.[8] It would seem that

Methodism, like the Second British Empire, occurred in a fit of absence of mind.

Clearly the evidence needs to have some pattern imposed upon it, and that process needs to begin with the recognition that the original Methodism of the late 1730s and 1740s had a history discontinuous with that of the Methodist churches. The clue to this is indeed given by the Conference assertion of 1744 that the mission of Methodism was "to reform the nation, more particularly the Church, [and] to spread scriptural holiness over the land". Early Methodism was a movement which never became a denomination, and it was composed of men and women in all parts of the United Kingdom, many of whom were interested in reform politics of the country party kind, some of whom, like Wesley himself, came from a Jacobite milieu, and nearly all of whom were involved in the various schemes to stiffen, rescue, or revive different groups of European Protestants associated with Halle or the inveterate rival of Halle, the Moravians. As a body they represented parties which had been outmanoeuvred by government patronage in the churches both of England and Scotland, and since public action was out of their reach, societary action was all that was available to them. What this group did was to supersede the old religious societies, to use them as a springboard for a variety of new activities, but to preserve much of the anti-corruption rhetoric of the old societies, and to turn it against Walpole and his successors.

The new societies, unlike the old, did not insist on church membership as a condition of society membership, but a network throughout the United Kingdom such as Wesley (and in a lesser degree, the Moravians) finally built up, and Whitefield, the great hero of the London religious societies, began to build up before he was diverted to other things, might well serve as a catalyst for reform in the Church, preserved as it was from the contamination of court patronage. The attractions of this milieu for Wesley, when in 1738 he returned from Georgia with his tail between his legs, are obvious. Even had he not been raised in a milieu tainted with Jacobitism, and returned from a nest of Jacobites in Georgia, he brought with him a sense of personal failure to find the public breach between Gibson and Walpole proclaiming the failure of the latest attempt to harmonize the roles of church and state. Whatever else Wesley's conversion at Aldersgate Street was or was not, it was a self-confessed incorporation into the new work of the religious societies, and it might easily have led to Wesley's becoming a Moravian.

To put the matter in this way is to draw attention to the fact that the conclusion of the observers in Halle that Whitefield was more important than Wesley at this stage of what may be called the Methodist movement was absolutely accurate. Much of the action in the 1740s turned round the efforts of the Countess of Huntingdon and her following of Tory politicians, a following enlarged by the recruitment of even the liberal Dissenter Philip Doddridge in the cause of pulling down Walpole, to create a situation in which White-field could be made a bishop. Dr Nuttall has shown in considerable detail how the evangelical leaders throughout the United Kingdom stood together behind this cause throughout the 1740s, with Howell Harris bringing in the Welsh interest.[9]

It is that other strange character, James Erskine, Lord Grange, who most clearly illustrates what was happening in this, the sole period of his prominence. It was Whitefield who put Howell Harris in touch with Erskine, and Erskine who used the success of Whitefield's evangelism in Scotland to suggest to all parties that the situation there had changed to the point where a revolution in party relations was conceivable. A vast report on the Scottish situation which he prepared for Zinzendorf was an effort to bring in the Moravian forces on a Catholic Christianity and anti-bigotry platform, and he repeated the tactic with Wesley and with Harris.[10] The ecclesiastical basis of Erkine's policy lay in the fact that he was a distant cousin of Ralph and Ebenezer Erskine who had gone into secession to form the Associate Presbytery, and who, having invited Whitefield to Scotland, attempted to tie him on his arrival to an impossibly narrow platform, turned against him, and left him free to evangelize with great success within the Scottish establishment. Whitefield indeed showed that the anxieties and stresses which had issued in secession could actually be used to promote revival, and if the opportunity were seized the whole complexion of the Kirk might be changed.

Erskine's intervention here had a two-fold significance. He was one of the most equivocal figures of the age. Rapidly advanced under Queen Anne, he had lost his preferment at the Hanoverian succession. Still worse, his elder brother, the Earl of Mar, having also failed to make his way with the new dynasty, became the leading organizer and general of the Pretender in the rebellion of 1715, and then his Secretary of State abroad. Erskine stood aside from this adventure, but much of the rest of his life was devoted to manoeuvres designed to save the Jacobites from the full penalty of their failures; in 1745 he encouraged the conspiracy of the Young Pretender, but condemned his arrival without an army.

The wives of both brothers gave them trouble, and may well have been in possession of evidence incriminating their husbands. At any rate in 1732 Grange celebrated his wife's death, having in fact had her abducted by men in Lovat (Jacobite) tartan to confinement for many years in St Kilda, and later in Assynt and Skye where she truly died in 1745. In the 1730s, however, Grange made the transition to legit-imate opposition, became secretary to the Prince of Wales, and helped to whip in the Scottish members for the final defeat of Walpole. The year before the '45 he wrote to Howell Harris that he had

> carry'd a message from my lady [Huntingdon] in your behalf to the Earl of Stair,[11] commander in chief of the Tories in England, and at the same time for some others in different countys, both of Whit[e]field's & Wesley's congregations, and had a very obliging and right answer from his lordship.[12]

Grange was invited to Wesley's Bristol Conference in 1745, and actually attended the London Conference in 1748. He and Charles Wesley seemed able to reduce each other to happy tears at will; he helped to get John Nelson out of pressed service in the army by providing a substitute; Charles Wesley redeemed a lost daughter of his from deism and reconciled her with her father. Moreover he longed for a "union of hearts between those of different sentiments [and especially between Harris and the Wesleys], without in the least meddling with these differences, or preaching or conversing of anything but true saving faith and repentance unto life",[13] and in this he represented a desire which was, despite periodical tetchiness, quite substantially achieved in the evangelical milieu in the 1740s, a period properly to be described as the "rise of Methodism", a Methodism which was not an extension of the personality and policies of John

Wesley. Above all, the active connection with the Leicester House interest shows very clearly what Wesley himself meant by "the reform of the nation, [and] more particularly the Church". Here in a special field was the politics of an alliance of Leicester House and country party groups, seeking to reduce the court interest and to strengthen what would now be called the private sector by evangelism in the field, the evangelism itself being the work of a multicoloured alliance of Calvinists, Arminians, Moravians, Welsh, Scots, and, before the 1740s were out, Irish. But the alliance knew that there was no hope of securing its wider interests, let alone of having Whitefield made a bishop, without court action through the reversionary interest.

There was perhaps nowhere where this programme had a more immediate relevance than in the lowlands of Scotland. For here the patronage question was a very live issue, Presbyterian scruples being exacerbated by the fact that crown and aristocratic patronage were amongst the resources exploited by Walpole to create a following for English purposes. Behind patronage lurked English assimilation, behind English assimilation lurked Moderatism and new theological fashions derived from Enlightenment, and behind high Reformed Orthodoxy there lurked, as perhaps nowhere else in Europe, bizarre memories of Reformed revival under persecution in seventeenth-century Ulster and the West of Scotland. It is this situation which accounts for the ambiguous relation of the Erskine brothers, Ralph and Ebenezer, to the English and Welsh revival circus, and to practitioners of the art as far away as America. Ebenezer Erskine was in many ways turned against the Kirk by the harsh treatment meted out by the General Assembly to the supporters of Edward Fisher's *Marrow of modern divinity*. This brought them the support of the Cameronian interest which was only too ready to regard rationalism as evidence of English assimilation. The result was that when Ebenezer Erskine, who had led the defence of the *Marrow* men, turned irreconcilably against the Assembly on a relatively small patronage question in 1732, he and his coadjutors were everywhere welcomed by the Praying Societies, and rapidly created a new denomination, the Associate Presbytery.

This was actually a secession movement, but in the seventeenth century such things had often been associated with revival, and might be again. The upshot was that the Erskines's works were translated into Welsh, while John Wesley's propensity to encounter the phenomena of abnormal psychology in his earlier meetings is supposed to have been encouraged by the advice of Ebenezer Erskine, and finally Ralph Erskine, after a long correspondence, invited Whitefield to Scotland to assist in the cause. As everyone knows, this invitation produced instant disaster, and Whitefield went on to commence his triumphs in a parish of the Kirk, Cambuslang, which had been made miserable by the sort of Cameronian contumacy which rallied to the Erskines.[14] Here clearly the prominence of the patronage question, and the English cultural baggage which seemed to go with it, made the causes of reform and revival hard to combine; reform seceded, revival went on in the Kirk most notably in its elemental struggle in the Highlands. Moreover the strategy of Lord Grange (a distant relative of the Erskines) becomes comprehensible. He might well want a "union of hearts", for what he wanted was a shift in the balance of forces in the Kirk, ahead of the time when that shift was completed by the accession to court of the reversionary interest, Leicester House.

This last matter, ostensibly the most rational aspect of the evangelical strategy, proved to be its biggest, but not its only, gamble, as the first stage of the revival fizzled out in extraordinary symmetry with the revival in America and in most parts of Europe. In 1751 Frederick, Prince of Wales, died as the result of a blow from a tennis ball, and the heart of the strategy was gone. In addition Lady Frances Hastings, the sister of Lady Huntingdon, died, Lady Huntingdon's daughter became dangerously ill and she herself was ill. Among the Leicester House connections, Bolingbroke died in the same year, and Philip Doddridge also died. The Moravians went bankrupt and never regained their expansiveness. Howell Harris gave up the fight for the time, and Whitefield went back to America. In 1753 Wesley was taken seriously ill and wrote his own epitaph, and, although he recovered, he seemed to despair of the prospects of a mission within the Establishment. Certainly the days when his movement might aspire to reform the nation or the church had gone for good, and, though he could not yet know it, a different kind of success which he was to achieve, recruiting a good number of society members, and a very much larger penumbra of non-members, ensured that whatever scriptural holiness he did spread through the nation did not result in the creation of a holiness sect. Still more the attempt to retain echoes of Wesley's phraseology in America simply showed how the substance had been forgotten. The Christmas Conference in America in 1784 adopted the formulation "to reform the continent, and to spread scriptural holiness over these lands".[15]

"Continent" and "lands" show how they conceived their mission as a vast struggle with the brute facts of American geography, how they began with no conception of an American nation, how they encountered no single established church, and how they could hardly begin work in the new republic by talking about reform. (Indeed the first item for which there was a vociferous American Methodist call for reform was the Methodist Episcopal Church itself). In short the disasters of the early 1750s suggested a providential reading of history exactly the opposite of that which the evangelicals required. Lady Huntingdon and Wesley proved, however, to be great survivors, and each continued to make something of what they had established in the 1740s. In the 1770s she and Howell Harris were still negotiating with the heads of the church for the ordination of her students. Wesley, by contrast, was creating an institution which was neither a church nor a society as traditionally understood, and whether what he did embodied anything which can be called a strategy calls for an inquiry at both the macro- and the micro-level.

As regards the macro-level I can for the most part refer to what I have already written in the introduction to the new edition of Wesley's *Journal*.[16] Wesley made much in England of his mission to the poor and was of course well primed with Scripture warnings against the dangers of wealth and those who enjoyed it. But he professed no objection that "a few of the rich and noble are called", and, perhaps in a broad hint to the Countess of Huntingdon, would "rejoice if it were done by the ministry of others".[17] But in England Wesley came from a political milieu which had been beaten both in politics and the church, and, until he himself had come back to court and became a national institution at the end of his life, there was not much he could expect to do within the circle of those attracted by the court. Like so many of his kind, he perceived new beginnings in the reign of George III. But many of the most interesting passages in the *Journal* show Wesley puzzling over the very uneven responses which he obtained from social groupings with whom he had a good deal of rapport, such as coal-miners. He came to despise the miners of Kingswood among whom he first began open-air evangelism in comparison with those of Gateshead or Plessey in Northumberland; nor did he think much of those of Sunderland.[18] In the *Journal* he is struggling to construct for himself a sort of sociology of religion, and, like an honest man, admitting the difficulty in fitting the facts to any pattern of interpretation.

From one point of view, the main interest of Wesley's claims of a self-conscious mission to the poor, is the contrast which they form to what he actually did in Scotland and Ireland. Wesley seems never to have been quite at home in Scotland, and contented himself with quite contradictory caricatures of the Scottish people. All the more remarkable then that he always had friends (as well as a few enemies) among the Scots clergy, men like John Gillies who would give him invitations and arrange his itineraries, that he could be passed from hand to hand by the evangelical aristocracy, especially on the distaff side, great ladies such as Lady Maxwell and Lady Glenorchy, Lady Henrietta Hope, the Countess of Leven, Lady Banff and the Countess of Buchan to whom he became chaplain. Still more remarkable, the Arminian Wesley made it his business to be in Edinburgh at the time of the General Assembly in each of the four years, 1763–66. No doubt this owed something to the same considerations that took him to Allendale in Northumberland at the precise moment when the lead-miners had their half-yearly payday and beano, namely that there was a throng to meet and influence; but he seems to have hoped for something from the Assembly itself. What this was he does not disclose, and seems certainly to have left empty-handed. In Scotland Wesley was clearly prepared to start at the top of the social pile much more than in England, but he never worked out a consistent mission strategy, the confusion he bequeathed was made worse in the age of Valentine Ward and Jabez Bunting,[19] and has not been resolved to this day.

Ireland was a still worse case, for Wesley's Irish journals although full, are constructed entirely on old-fashioned principles of adventurous *res gestae* and are almost without general reflection. In Ireland as in Scotland Wesley was hoping for familiar signs of well-ordered Englishness, and occasionally found them.[20] In the circumstances it is very extraordinary that it took him a decade to discover Ulster. His Irish missions began in Dublin, went due west across the centre of the country to Athlone and then in a great sweep southwards, in the course of which permanent strongholds were established in Cork and Bandon.

There was one respect in which Wesley's English experience stood him in good stead in Southern Ireland. Huguenot immigration had been in the end sealed off by the government of Louis XIV, and one of the conundrums of the second quarter of the eighteenth century was how the religious situation in England would be affected by their gradual assimilation. The London Huguenots were very heavily concentrated in the west in the Savoy and Soho, and in the east in Spitalfields, Whitechapel and Wapping. During the period immediately after his conversion, when Wesley's work was very closely based on the religious societies, great numbers of Huguenot names appear in his diary, a sizeable minority of the early membership at his society at the Foundery (conveniently located for Spitalfields) were Huguenots, and when he began to administer communion to society members in premises not episcopally consecrated he accepted the invitation of Dr Deleznot, the pastor of a Huguenot congregation in Wapping, to use his chapel. In the mid-1740s he put the work on a firm base by acquiring the Huguenot chapels at West Street, Seven Dials in the west, and in the east at Grey Eagle Street, Spitalfields, using them, among other purposes, to educate dissenting Huguenots in the ways of Anglican liturgical worship. It was the same story in Bristol; and even in the 1750s Wesley was grateful for the services of Fletcher and the Perronets in preaching to congregations in French.[21]

The willingness of the Huguenots to respond to a live religious appeal, however alien to their theological heritage was an encouragement to Wesley to try again in Ireland, which was full of unassimilated religious minorities. When Wesley encountered the Huguenots at Portarlington in 1750, revivalism seems already to have been the order of the day;[22] but he was most attracted by the Palatines who had been settled on a group of estates in Southern Ireland in the reign of Queen Anne. He liked them, which helped: "These have quite a different look from the natives of the country, as well as a different temper. They are a serious, thinking people. And their diligence turns all their land into a garden".[23] Here was an almost Silesian situation of a German-language population deprived of their church but clinging to their Luther Bible. They perceived echoes of Reformation preaching in Wesley, responded vividly, and rewarded him by taking Methodism to America. Two of the pioneers there, Philip Embury and Barbara Heck, were Palatines. A half-length American portrait of the latter shows her piously clasping her Bible, the *Luther* Bible. Picking up the Palatines gave Wesley's cause a boost of the same kind that picking up other evangelists' preaching rounds gave him in England; and Wesley was on the whole kindly received in the Church of Ireland, to whose clergy he brought a pleasing change of cultivated company from across the Irish Sea.

The initial hope seems clearly to have been the conversion of Catholics, and with the Catholic cause in Ireland at about its lowest ebb Wesley's hopes were not as unreasonable as those of the often ferocious evangelists who came after him. Quite apart from preparing himself for the outer darkness by strenuous application to the Protestant historians of Ireland, Wesley clearly did not like the Irish, whom he found "ignorant", "squalid" and "fickle", worse than the more barbaric Scots, and it is clear that his work among them was dependent not, of course, on the absentee aristocracy, but on resident gentry and men of property to a degree which would have been unthinkable in England.

There were two other peculiar factors in the Irish situation. The garrison was ubiquitous, and it is striking how much of Wesley's Irish ministry was devoted to the troops. In more than one case, conversions among the troops were the agency of conversions among the civilian population;[24] at least one distinguished Methodist preacher was recruited from the Irish garrison; and when Wesley preached at Waterford, "the major of the highland regiment standing behind me, with several of his officers, many of the soldiers before me, and the sentinel at the entrance of the court",[25] or inside the castle at Charlemont with all the soldiers drawn up,[26] or inside the barracks at Limerick, Athlone or Cappaquin,[27] he was making absolutely clear where he stood in relation to the Ascendancy. More generally the skyline in small Irish towns was distinguished from that of their English counterparts by four prominent features, the distillery, the barracks, the court house and the jail. Law enforcement being a far more tense affair even in Wesley's lifetime than in

England, his habitual preaching in the court house must have had a chilling effect upon the Roman Catholic population. Most spectacularly at Birr, he preached out of doors before the memorial to the Duke of Cumberland, the butcher of Culloden, on its 58-foot column, and, building a chapel by the court house, jail and excise office, he made absolutely clear what he was about; despite recruiting a handful of ex-Catholic preachers, he guaranteed that he could reap no great Catholic harvest.

So far as the Protestant population was concerned, the problem in Wesley's later years was to know *how* to be establishmentarian. Wesley could not wish away his anti-American stance which was so profitable in England when the Irish responded vividly to the destruction of the American part of the old colonial system. The result was that the Methodism which survived him in Ireland, survived mostly under the wing of the Irish Church and partook of its Orange sentiment, yet broke up rather than remain a religious society within the Church.

On the positive side, Ireland with its subordinate Conference formed the model for Wesley's constitutional disposition of his community after his death, a disposition it proved impossible to carry out in its entirety, and it produced a larger Methodist family than Scotland. On the negative side, Methodist connexionalism also took the steam out of the Irish revival. From an early date it proved impossible to get English Methodist preachers (Charles Wesley being the first among many) to accept Irish appointments; while the Irish had been lured in numbers, and some with distinction, to the lusher pastures of English circuits. Ireland, like Scotland, had hardly been the much-vaunted mission to the poor of Wesley's English work, and had accomplished somewhat less than it might have done, because of the confusion which surrounded it from the beginning.

There is no need to say a great deal about Wesley's work on the micro-level because once his tendency to insist on random nostrums and some very long-running myths among the Methodist people are stripped away, the essence of the matter is fairly clear. He did insist vehemently on the maintenance of itinerant preaching, that is a ministry not church-based, and in this respect he found a faithful disciple in Asbury in America, who got the American preachers off their bottoms in the eastern seaboard towns and propelled them into motion in the interior. It is clear that from an early stage Wesley's own itinerancy was a highly organized affair.[28] The impression given in the *Journal* that Wesley rode into the sunset solo to address throngs assembled by the unaided agency of the Holy Spirit is misleading on both scores;[29] and before long he had arranged a programme which enabled him to get round the entire connexion every two years. "My course [as he not unfairly described it to a correspondent in 1771] has been for several years as fixed as the sun".[30] Where, in the first instance, Wesley or his preachers might go was commonly determined by the accident that hospitality was available;[31] the self-conscious mission to the poor was from the beginning modified by the need for regular hospitality.

The next stage was earnestly to try to capitalize the early religious impressions made by the preaching by incorporating people into societies,[32] a process for which Wesley would often leave one of his accompanying preachers behind when on his rounds.[33] These societies, which were more open in membership than the old religious societies, were nevertheless closed for many purposes,[34] and were so much the ark of the Wesleyan covenant, that in places where it proved impossible to form a society he and his preachers were apt to assume that this was a sign from the Holy Spirit that they should move elsewhere.[35] There were places (such as London) where, from the beginning, the numbers in society were too large to manage and the process of breaking them down into classes (theoretically numbering about a dozen)[36] and bands, had to begin at once. Writers on Methodist history have been too prone to take the rules of bands and societies as a literal description of what they were. Wesley's insistence on society membership is plain enough, but societies were not quite universal.

In Pembrokeshire, where from an early date Wesley agreed not to compete with the Welsh movements, he went ahead (against his better judgement) without societies,[37] and also in Cornwall, which was always disorderly.[38] Again, classes varied in size with the skill and popularity of the leader; John Pritchard had to break his up into four, and varied the official diet with united prayer meetings.[39] It is quite clear that the mechanism of society, class and band provided a stable environment for many touched by the preaching, and a powerful institutional suggestion that conversion might be the beginning of the Christian life but was not to be looked upon as its end. At its best, the class meeting provided an effective education in the management of experimental religion,[40] could lead to a great outpouring of the spirit and ingathering of souls,[41] and became a "fruitful nursery" of preachers, local and itinerant.[42] The class meeting thus became a legend, and more than a little of a burden upon the Methodist community. That burden, as Whitehead remarked, fell in the first instance upon Wesley himself, who did not shrink from attempting to regulate the whole machine in detail as it grew, and it is clear that the class meeting itself was in some trouble from the start. There were classes which never held the new recruits who were put in them;[43] there were others like the one in Nottingham, begun by Wesley himself in 1743, which he purged from top to bottom in 1746.[44] In fact before the end of the eighteenth century the class meeting was being undermined by many changes in the pattern of recruitment. The longer the Methodist community lasted, the more it was recruited from the children of members, and the more it was likely to develop churchly instincts and feel that it ought to provide a home for all sorts, whether they took to the class meeting or not. Moreover the connexion developed powerful new means of evangelism. Of these the cottage prayer meeting was the most spectacular,[45] and the Sunday school at least potentially the most important; and at this point the Methodist empiricism which had made a legend of the class meeting turned to other things. What kept the class meeting going as long as it did was partly the fact that the Methodist legend was reinforced by the pietist movement throughout the Protestant world, and partly the capacity of small-group religion to answer the immediate needs of participants, and to change form and content without their realizing it.

Finally, Wesley deserves credit for perceiving the movement of people through his system and out of it with far more equanimity and sense than those disappointed Catholic triumphalists who write about it in terms of "leakage". "It is well [he wrote in 1777] if a third part of those that at first set their hands to the plough endure to the end".[46] A loss of two thirds, in other words, was a consequence of that increasing freedom of choice in matters religious which made both the Methodist and the contemporary Catholic revival possible, and which bequeathed to this country, even after the efforts of the doctrinaires of the nineteenth century, a society blessedly free from a religious caste system in which people are not free to change the religious viewpoint to which they were born. And as Wesley was wont to point out, not without rubbing of hands, this growing freedom of choice permitted the steady growth of a dynamic movement in a way that the convulsive establishment-revivalism of New England did not.[47]

I would like to end on a somewhat negative note by reference to a rather charming work of American Methodist scholarship.[48] Writing of American Methodism immediately before and after independence, that is in Wesley's lifetime, Professor Richey summarizes a complex and subtle argument in these propositions:

> that community, fraternity and order characterized early Methodist ecclesial experience; that Methodist religious experience demanded fresh terms, an idiom generated out of the religious life itself but evocative of Scripture as well; that this vernacular presupposed and actually flowed from the routines and rhythms of the Wesleyan movement, a movement which had already elaborated its own grammar of the Christian life; that the vernacular and Wesleyan languages existed in creative tension, giving a movement run on authoritarian and hierarchical (albeit rather unpretentiously hierarchical) bases a popular and egalitarian appeal; that on this creative tension, the church imposed in 1784, when it formally organized itself, an episcopal idiom, adopted to give legitimacy to and make ecclesial sense of the religious life that Methodism had sustained; and that this particular Pentecost – the juxtaposition of the three idioms and particularly the imposition of episcopal terminology on the dynamisms of early Methodism – yielded a linguistic cacophony that Methodists may never have adequately decoded.

American Methodism, in short, inherited the "language of Canaan", that common language of European pietism, which in America had been made a folk idiom by the first Great Awakening in the 1740s. It was natural to them to talk of the Spirit "falling" upon a meeting, for people to have "melting experiences", to "find great freedom", to be knit together in "love", to call each other "brother", and "rejoice in the prosperity of Zion". Yet this language never found its way into the official canon of Methodism, and my impression is that on this side of the Atlantic it became more characteristic of Primitive than of Wesleyan Methodism. Americans had of course to master the official language of English Methodism, of class, society, quarterly meeting, conference and so forth, and this they did by taking the formulations of the British *Large Minutes* into their own documents in due season. These two languages were of course different, but not as different as the episcopal language which Wesley borrowed from the Church of England and adapted for American purposes. And eventually the Americans had to cope with a republican language, as the British had to cope with a language of democracy. Whether these languages could in the long run be made to harmonize or coexist was a question.

Community and fraternity were ritualized and internalized in the love-feast where individuals gave their testimony and shared what was most personal to them; they bonded themselves to one another, to the Methodist society and to Christ. Inevitably the experiences at the love-feast as now recorded in cold print have a certain formulary quality, but there is no mistaking the genuineness of the emotion they released. William Watters reported of one:

> I . . . believe Heaven above will differ more in quantity than in quality. Never did I hear such experiences before. Our eyes overflowed with tears, and our hearts with love to God and each other. The holy fire, the heavenly flame, spread wider and wider, and rose higher and higher.[49]

What happened at the quarterly meetings was that the church offered itself as an alternative social body to the world. It began on the Saturday by withdrawing to order itself in circuit business and preaching. The next day was a public celebration beginning at 9 am with a love-feast to which non-members could only attend two or three times, followed by communion at 11 am, public preaching at 12 noon, memorial services, marriages and baptisms. Crowds running into four figures would assemble from far and wide for these events, and in an Old South which defined itself in terms of community events such as dances, horse races, cockfights, elections,[50] Methodism was offering itself as an alternative community of grace, and one which at first could even include black slaves. It was in the quarterly meetings, where the ideals of community, fraternity and order were best balanced, where Methodism most fully displayed its wares and in that sense was most fully the church, that revivals occurred; occasions to care for the circuit's business became festivals for religious renewal. I am normally profoundly sceptical of apologias for episcopacy or other forms of church government based on the assumption that the outward form of the church must display to the inquirer its inner essence. It really seems, however, that at least at quarterly meetings and to some extent at conference level American Methodism had found an outer form which displayed its inner essence, and because of that fact it had discovered an evangelistic strategy; the revivals actually followed.

Did such a thing exist in the United Kingdom? The various languages employed by the Americans were all imported from here as, with modifications, was the constitutional machinery they operated. Quarterly meetings were imported into Wesleyan Methodism in the late 1740s from the round established in the North Midlands by John Bennet.[51] Bennet had included devotions with his quarterly meeting which were sometimes of notable blessing,[52] and also included the disciplinary function of inquiry into the spiritual welfare of societies which were carried over into Wesleyan Methodism.[53] It is also true that at the beginning Cornish quarterly meetings were accompanied by watchnight meetings,[54] and that the annual conferences were sometimes accompanied by mass communion services, of a kind which seem to have ceased soon after Wesley's death.[55] But after re-reading thousands of eighteenth-century Methodist letters and the not inconsiderable quantities of quarterly meeting records which survive and suggest that the eighteenth-century quarterly meeting was already the business meeting it still is, I cannot find any trace that these gatherings were the liberating affairs that they were in contemporary America, and certainly they seem to have given rise to none of the jolly pilgrimages associated with Gwennap Pit or, later, Mow Cop. In other words the British Methodists failed to find a memorable evangelistic strategy which was within the grasp of their American brethren. Why was this so?

The hazards of attempting to prove negatives in history are notorious, but it is worth, in conclusion, making a few suggestions. The first is that in America the revivalistic aspects of quarterly meeting and conference were perpetuated in the camp meeting. The camp meeting was welcomed into the fold by Asbury, and enabled the American Methodists to believe that their primitive ethos was being maintained, when in fact their order was being transformed into organization, their language of Canaan was being supplanted by the Wesleyan and episcopal languages of their hierarchy.

The camp meeting in short enabled Methodism to change while appearing to stay the same. The way in which it in the first decade of the nineteenth century became the touchstone dividing the forces of order and those of life in English Methodism is familiar and does not need retelling. What is worth saying is that the minute regulation which Wesley thought proper to apply to his religious societies was probably always excessive, that the highly organized stage manage-ment of at least some of his love-feasts really put order above every other virtue[56] and that shortly after his death quarterly and district meetings were regarded in the Wesleyan inner sanctum as having been instituted for disciplinary and business purposes.[57] Add to this two other liabilities which the British suffered in comparison with the Americans. The "language of Canaan" (though officially favoured by the Moravians) had not enjoyed the popular diffusion given it in America by the first Great Awakening; the British had less idea how to "let their hair down" religiously than the Americans. And popular attitudes were more deeply influenced here by that most grossly overrated incubus of European Christianity, a Catholic church order, which affected even those who resolved to do without it.

Notes

1. D. N. Hempton, "Motives, methods and margins in Methodism's age of expansion", *Proceedings of the Wesley Historical Society* **49**, 1994, pp. 189–207 [Reprinted in D. N. Hempton. *The religion of the people. Methodism and popular religion, c.1750–1900* (London, 1996), pp. 3–28].
2. M. Piette, *John Wesley: sa réaction dans l'evolution du Protestantisme* (Louvain, 1925), Eng. tr. *John Wesley in the evolution of Protestantism* (London, 1938), p. 3.

3. R. Davies & G. Rupp (ed) *A history of the methodist church in Great Britain*, vol. I (London, 1965–88) pp. xvi–xvii.

4. *Minutes of the methodist conference*, vol. I (London, 1812–54), p. 9.

5. J. Wesley, *A farther appeal to men of reason and religion part III* (1745), *Works*, Bicentennial edn. vol. XI. p. 322.

6. J. Wesley, *Sermon no. cvii* (1788), *On God's vineyard* §4. 2, §2. 2, *Works*, Bicentennial edn. vol. IV.

7. J. Whitehead, *Life of the Rev. John Wesley*, vol. II (London, 1793–6), pp. 99–100. Whitehead saw no inconsistency with this view in also quoting (vol. II. p. 315) a minute of the first conference which suggested that the "hither and thither" understanding led to waste of time:

    > Q. Is it advisable for us to preach in as many places as we can, without forming any societies? A. By no means, we have made the trial in various places, and that for a considerable time. But all the seed has fallen as by the high-way side. There is scarce any fruit remaining.

8. John Rylands Library, Methodist Church Archives (hereafter JRL, MCA), MS Address by Joseph Entwisle, Hull, 21 June 1802.

9. G. F. Nuttall, "Howell Harris and 'The grand table': a note on religion and politics, 1744–50", *Journal of Ecclesiastical History* **39**, 1988, pp. 531–44.

10. For a fuller account and references to sources see my *Protestant evangelical awakening* (2nd printing, Cambridge, 1994), pp. 322, 333–5.

11. The second Earl of Stair (1673–1747), a former Whig, was disgraced under Walpole and became a leader of the opposition to Walpole in Scotland. In 1741 two-thirds of the Scottish MPs were returned in the anti-Walpole interest. The connection between Grange and Stair vividly illustrates the former's equivocal position, for Stair, reinstated in favour after the fall of Walpole, was made commander-in-chief of all the forces in South Britain in 1744 when a Jacobite rising was feared.

12. *Selected Trevecka letters (1742–1747)*, G. M. Roberts (ed.) (Caernarvon, 1956), p. 140.

13. *Ibid.*, pp. 191–2.

14. For references see W. R. Ward, *Protestant evangelical awakening*, pp. 329–335.

15. R. E. Richey, *Early American Methodism* (Bloomington/Indianapolis, 1991), p. 36.

16. Wesley, *Works*, Bicentennial edn. vol. XVIII *Journals and Diaries*, W. R. Ward & R. P. Heitzenrater (eds) (Nashville, 1988), vol. I, pp. 62–79.

17. Wesley, *Works*, Bicentennial edn. vol. XXI: *Journals*, vol. IV, p. 233.

18. Wesley, *Works*, Bicentennial edn. vols. XXI, XXII: *Journals*, vol. IV, pp. 464, 503; vol. V, p. 48.

19. W. R. Ward, "Scottish methodism in the age of Jabez Bunting", *Records of the Scottish Church History Society* **20**, 1978, pp. 47–63; A. J. Hayes & D. A. Gowland (eds), *Scottish Methodism in the Early Victorian Period*, (Edinburgh, 1981).

20. Wesley, *Journal*, N. Curnock (ed.) (2nd cdn, London, 1938), 3 June 1789; Wesley, *Works*, Bicentennial edn. vol. XXI: *Journals*, vol. IV, p. 69.
21. G. E. Milburn, "English methodism and the Huguenots", *Proceedings of the Wesley Historical Society* **45**, 1985, pp. 69–79; P. P. Streiff, *Jean Guillaume de la Flécherè. Ein Beitrag zur Geschichte des Methodismus* (Frankfurt, 1984). Even in 1765 Wesley preached a charity sermon for the Spitalfields weavers. T. Jackson (ed.), *Lives of the Early Methodist Preachers*, vol. VI (London, 1872), p. 33.
22. Wesley, *Works*, Bicentennial edn. vol. XX: *Journals*, vol III, p. 346.
23. Wesley, *Works*, Bicentennial edn. vol. XXI: *Journals*, vol. IV, p. 368.
24. Wesley, *Works*, Bicentennial edn. vol. XX: *Journals*, vol. III, p. 349; *Journal*, Curnock (ed.), April 29, 1787.
25. Wesley, *Works*, Bicentennial edn. vol. XXII: *Journals*, vol. V, p. 448.
26. *Journal*, Curnock (ed.), June 20, 1778; 15 June, 1787.
27. Wesley, *Works*, Bicentennial edn. vol. XXII: *Journals*, vol. V, p. 366; *Journal* Curnock (ed.), 17 April, 1 May, 1789.
28. Wesley, *Works*, Bicentennial edn. vol. XXVI: *Letters*, F. Baker (ed.), vol. II. pp. 131, n.19, 208–9.
29. How it was done is described in my paper on "John Wesley, traveller", in my *Faith and faction* (London, 1993), pp. 249–263.
30. J. Telford (ed.), *The letters of John Wesley* (London, 1931), vol. V, p. 278.
31. Dr J. A. Vickers has shown that the whole of Hampshire and Dorset was (not very well) missioned from Salisbury and Shaftesbury because Wesley had a roguish brother-in-law in the one, and a friend, John Haime, in the other. *Methodism and society in central Southern England, 1740–1851* (PhD thesis, Southampton University, 1986), pp. 67, 70.
32. L. Tyerman, *Life and times of John Wesley* (6th edn London, 1890), vol. ii, p. 5.
33. Jackson (ed.), *Lives of the early Methodist preachers*, vol. V, p. 181.
34. Rumours of the dreadful abuses which followed opening society meetings were current. *Ibid.*, vol. V, p. 191 (cf. vol. IV, p. 6); JRL, MCA, Tyerman MSS, vol. III, fo 442.
35. Wesley, *Works*, Bicentennial edn. vol. XX: *Journals*, vol. III, p. 423; JRL, MCA, vol. II, fos. 280–81.
36. Wesley, *Works*, Bicentennial edn. vol. IX: *The Methodist societies, History, nature and design*, R. E. Davies (ed.), p. 70.
37. Wesley, *Works*, Bicentennial edn. vol. XXI: *Journals* vol. iv, p. 424.
38. For an impression of the general atmosphere in Cornwall, see J. Rule, "Methodism, popular beliefs and village culture in Cornwall, 1800–1850", in *Popular culture and custom in nineteenth-century England*, R. D. Storch (ed.) (London, 1982), pp. 48–70.
39. Jackson (ed.), *Lives of the early Methodist preachers*, vol. VI, p. 258.
40. *Ibid.*, vol. VI, p. 28. An impression of how another class worked is given in Wesley, *Works*, Bicentennial edn. vol. XXVI: *Letters*, vol. II, pp. 94–5.

41. Jackson (ed.), *Lives of the early Methodist preachers*, vol. V, p. 297.
42. Whitehead, *Life of Wesley*, vol. II, p. 290.
43. Jackson, *Lives of the early Methodist preachers* vol. I, p. 242.
44. R. C. Swift, *Lively people. Methodism in Nottingham, 1740–1979* (Nottingham, 1982), pp. 3, 8.
45. JRL, MCA, Tyerman MSS 2, fo. 258.
46. Telford, *Letters of John Wesley*, vol. VI, p. 255.
47. Wesley, *Works*, Bicentennial edn. vols. XX, XXI: *Journals*, vol. III, p. 447; vol. IV, pp. 18–19.
48. Richey, *Early American Methodism*, pp. 1–2.
49. *Ibid.*, p. 4.
50. See R. Isaac, *The transformation of Virginia, 1740–1790* (Chapel Hill, North Carolina, 1982).
51. H. Rack, *Reasonable enthusiast: John Wesley and the rise of Methodism* (London, 1989), p. 246.
52. J. S. Simon, *John Wesley and the advance of Methodism* (London, 1925), p. 128.
53. *Ibid.*, pp. 147–8, 154–8.
54. *Ibid.*, p. 185.
55. Tyerman, *Life of Wesley*, vol. III, pp. 271, 497, 584.
56. For examples of Wesley's application of disciplines of procedure and time, see his *Journal*, Curnock (ed.), vol. VII, pp. 255, 259.
57. MCA, JRL, William Smith to Joseph Benson n.d. [*c*.1795].

12

The making of a Protestant nation: "success" and "failure" in England's Long Reformation[1]

Jeremy Gregory

This chapter has arisen from teaching a number of courses in religious history, from the late medieval to the late modern periods, during which I have become increasingly struck by what appear to me to be underlying common methodological and conceptual concerns faced by historians working on religious themes from the sixteenth to the nineteenth centuries, but who, nevertheless, are not always aware of work in periods deemed to be different from their own. The matter was crystallized when, in two review articles published recently, I learned on the one hand from Diarmaid MacCulloch that the Reformation had been a "howling success" by the early seventeenth century in its aim of making England into a Protestant nation (noting that when Civil War broke out in 1642, it was fought overwhelmingly between Protestants), and on the other hand I was informed by Simon Green that the Victorians saw their own time as the beginning of the Christianization of the British people (of which Protestantization was a part).[2] What is going on here? Do these two historians mean different things by terms such as "Christian" and "Protestant", do they (and/or their sources) differ in their ways of measuring religious commitment, or are we talking about change over time (in this case a real decline in religious sensibility)?

One possible solution, which might appeal to both historians of the seventeenth and nineteenth centuries, although it would probably find less favour with historians of the eighteenth century,[3] is that during the sixteenth and early seventeenth centuries England had indeed been Protestantized, but, because of the secularizing tendencies of the century and a half after 1660, there was a need to start the whole process off again, allowing historians to talk of a "religious revival" in the Victorian period.[4] Another possible answer is that the remarkable upsurge in the number of Catholics after 1800, for whom a re-converted nation appeared a real possibility, made the need to Protestantize seem more urgent.[5] A third, and perhaps rather more plausible explanation, is that many of those who might well have called themselves Protestant were not, or at least not in the eyes of the clergy and those members of the laity who considered themselves part of the religious elite. The problem which I had in reconciling these two review articles opens up the interrelated conceptual and methodological concerns of this chapter: when was England made into a Protestant nation, and how historians have attempted to measure the success of that endeavour?

The question of timescale is clearly important. Alongside the perennially fascinating, and certainly unresolved question of why the English Reformation happened, historians have become increasingly preoccupied with the question of how it happened. Over a decade ago Christopher Haigh formulated a useful (and influential) schema whereby he suggested that the answers given to this second question could be broadly classified under four heads: it was either a "rapid" Reformation imposed from "above", or a "rapid" Reformation from "below", a "slow" Reformation from "above", or a "slow" Reformation from "below".[6] Whilst some historians have expressed doubts about the applicability of the Haighian model, and in particular have worried about the binary opposites implicit in the formula (and added other variables in accounting for the uneven social and geographical spread of the Protestant message, such as north/south; centre/peripheries, town/country, youth/old age, and gender), it has certainly been a stimulating framework for discussion.[7]

But in some ways, the resonances of Haigh's schema have not been fully explored. Historians have paid more attention to the implications of the "above" and "below" aspects of the question, than to the chronological problem within Haigh's model: the question of when the Reformation happened. The confident assertions of A. G. Dickens, that England was by 1553 so firmly Protestant that Mary's attempt at Counter-Reformation was necessarily bound to fail,[8] and of G. R. Elton, that England in 1558 was more Protestant than anything else,[9] have been challenged by revisionists who, increasingly it seems, incline to the slow Reformation model.[10] Yet even for those historians who favour the slowest of slow Reformations, England was effectively and to all intents and purposes a Protestant nation by the end of Elizabeth's reign. Not only is this the view of historians sympathetic to the cause of the Reformation, it is an opinion shared by Catholic historians such as Eamon Duffy, who has been the most recent and the most vigorous defender of the strengths of late medieval Catholicism: "by the end of the 1570s", he has remarked, "whatever the instincts and nostalgia of their seniors, a generation was growing up which had known nothing else, which believed the Pope to be AntiChrist, the Mass a mummery, which did not look back to the Catholic past as their own, but another country, another world".[11]

At one level, of course, it must be true that England was Protestant by the late sixteenth century. If we define a Protestant nation as one that was not Catholic, or one that was indeed anti-Catholic, then there seems no doubt of this. Evidence of all kinds, from historians of national identity, to social and cultural historians, and to estimates of Catholic strength, indicates that the majority of Englishmen and women (save perhaps in Lancashire, some areas in the north east and the west Midlands, and in the few pockets of parishes in the south which conformed to John Bossy's model of seigneurial Catholicism) clearly identified themselves as anti-Catholic (or perhaps, rather, anti-papist), to such an extent that popular celebrations, the lighting of bonfires and the ringing of bells marked Protestant highdays and holidays within the calendar.[12] Indeed Jeremy Black has argued that "anti-Catholicism" was the major ideological determinant for most seventeenth- and eighteenth-century English people, marking them off from a foreign "other",[13] and Linda Colley's exploration of national identity in the eighteenth century has amply demonstrated the role of anti-popery in forging a concept of Britishness.[14] Such statements seem to confirm Jan Albers' point that we need to think of religious identity in broadly-based social and cultural terms, which could encompass enormous variations in theological understanding, and which removes us from the snare of rating or grading religious commitment on some sort of piety scale.[15]

Yet the methodological problem of Albers' position, it seems to me, is that she comes close to saying that if people in the past saw themselves as Protestant, then historians ought to view them as such. But we need to recognize that, even in the period, there were doubts about the real meaning and significance of such anti-popery. As late as 1724, Daniel Defoe, after nearly two centuries of anti-Catholic propaganda, could despair of those "who would spend the last drop of their blood against popery . . . [and] do not know whether it be a man or a horse".[16] We clearly shouldn't conflate a virulent anti-Catholicism (which as Colin Haydon has demonstrated penetrated far down the social scale) with a rigorous or even perhaps with a sufficient understanding of Protestantism.[17] How far does evidence of deep-rooted anti-Catholicism mean that the English were a Protestant nation in any meaningful sense? Christopher Haigh (again) has usefully observed that churchgoers in the late sixteenth century were "de-Catholicised but unProtestantised. What they were not is a good deal clearer than what they were".[18] He himself has interpreted the complaints of Puritan writers to suggest that what was more apparent by the early seventeenth century was the failure rather than the success of the Protestantization process (which, for him, helps account for the acceptance of Laudianism in the parishes).[19] Indeed some historians, echoing the laments of early seventeenth century Puritans, have argued that far from creating a truly Protestant nation, the upheavals associated with the first century of the Reformation had created a godless nation, one where large numbers stayed away from church, neglected the sacrament, and indulged in shopping on Sundays. For Robert Whiting, the century witnessed "less a transition from Catholicism to Protestantism than a decline from religious commitment into conformism or indifference".[20]

This raises the methodological problem of how one should gauge the extent and the degree to which Protestantism succeeded. In answering this, a number of definitional and conceptual problems spring to mind. What, for example, did a Protestant nation look like? How far need it have been a "confessional" state comparable to those emerging in early modern Germany?[21] In any case, how should an individual's commitment to Protestantism be measured? Attendance at church can be counted, but it is impossible to penetrate the personal commitment of believers, or their sincerity. Furthermore, what demands did Protestants make of individuals before they could be regarded as Protestants? To what extent did parishioners have to be able to read and understand Protestant doctrine before they could accept its arguments? To put it bluntly, do things need to be coherently understood to influence thought and behaviour? Moreover, how far is instruction a way to measure the effectiveness of the Protestant message? (These are of course concerns not only facing modern historians: the problem of establishing the degree of commitment required before being counted a Protestant, and indeed defining what was meant by Protestant, provided the very stuff of the religious debates in the three centuries after 1530).[22]

One of the problems in assessing the extent to which the English had been Protestantized at any given moment is that the sources are ambiguous. My title is in part a reference to a debate amongst historians of the European Reformation, inaugurated in 1975 by Gerald Strauss, who controversially argued that, largely because of the methods employed in educating people into the fundamentals of the Protestant faith, the German Reformation was, at least until the late sixteenth century, more a tale of "failure" than a "success" story, creating indifference rather than religious commitment.[23] The most obvious pieces of documentary evidence, such as visitation returns (the sources which Strauss himself exploited to indicate the failure of the German Reformation to disseminate the essentials of Protestant doctrine) are fraught with interpretative problems, dealing as they do with the outward behaviour of parishioners, and being essentially the view of the religious professionals.

Some instances at any point in the period from the 1530s to the early nineteenth century (and beyond), it is true, can be used to subvert Strauss's picture of failure, suggesting that his gloomy analysis needs to be more nuanced: evidence can certainly be found of a religiously well-educated laity who regularly attended divine service and received the sacrament, who sent their children and servants to be catechized, and who, in the view of one early seventeenth-century minister, made England "the only nation, almost, that doth openly and solely profess the true religion of God".[24] But, it cannot be denied that a recurring theme of such replies is a sense of failure and frustration. Clergy frequently complained of the theological ignorance of their parishioners, and often behind their complaints is a sense of nostalgia for a religious world which had been lost, with regular comments on the decay of religious practice, and at times a suggestion that secularization was occurring.[25] In 1602, even after the efforts of the godly pastors so admired by Professor Collinson, Josias Nichols lamented that only one in ten of the inhabitants of the parish of Eastwell in Kent, which had 400 inhabitants of communicable age, understood the fundamental elements of Protestant doctrine.[26] A similar point was made in 1676, by incumbents responding to the Compton census,[27] although there is perhaps some excuse here because of the ways in which the Civil War had interrupted the Protestantizing process (or at least that part of the process approved of by the Church of England).[28]

But as late as 1758, the rector of Bapchild informed the archbishop of

> the great ignorance of the lower sort of people, and servants, in religious matters, not only indeed in this, but in all other parishes in this country, in which I have ever been concerned. There is hardly one in three, that I have ever met with, that knows who Jesus Christ is, and the need and design of his coming into the world.[29]

Similarly, a Norfolk cleric in 1843 remarked that after thirteen years of preaching the gospel he was firmly convinced that his efforts had been an entire failure.[30] The point of these instances is to demonstrate that, according to some definitions, the Reformation was not even assured by the early nineteenth century.[31]

Such complaints by the religiously zealous of the religious habits of the rest of the population are, however, probably a misleading guide to the religious commitment of parishioners, provoking historians to question how far can one take the assumptions of the religious diehards as evidence of the success or of the failure of the Protestant enterprise. Just because there was concern about the lack of progress does not mean that there was no progress at all. Nevertheless, the recurring clerical dismay about the religious commitment of large sections of the parish has encouraged historians to wonder about the true nature of those deemed "ungodly" and of what has been termed "popular religion".

One of the most influential ways of talking about "popular religion" has been to oppose it to the "religion of the elite"; a whole tradition in historiography, from Keith Thomas, writing on the sixteenth and early seventeenth centuries, through to Jim Obelkevich, writing on the mid-nineteenth century, has highlighted the "magical" and "superstitious" elements within a popular religious culture, stressing the antagonism between this and the official Protestant religion.[32] Yet, as so often with models which implicitly oppose "elite" and "popular" habits of mind, we might have underestimated the ways in which the official Protestant message could percolate through society, and we may have exaggerated the gulf between "elite" and "popular" religiosity. Whatever the situation in the sixteenth and seventeenth centuries, Mark Smith, in a provocative study, has demonstrated the far-reaching social purchase of the Anglican Church in the most surprising of periods and in the most surprising of places: Lancashire in the late eighteenth century, which may represent an improvement on the earlier situation. He argues that popular culture, at least in Oldham and Saddleworth, was saturated with a "diffused Christianity", shown for example in the custom of marking dough and butter with the sign of the cross so as to preserve them from the influence of evil.[33] It could be that Eamon Duffy's suggestion that for the pre-Reformation Church the term "traditional" religion (so long as we remember that this was not as static as the phrase might imply) should replace the term "popular" religion in discussing a shared, rather than a bifurcated, religious culture,[34] has some applicability for the way in which the Protestant faith was able to relate to popular culture in the centuries after 1530.

What we might also be able to learn from the visitation returns is not necessarily that the Reformation in England was a failure (although some historians might suggest that it was), but to indicate that it should be seen as a continuing and complex process and not as an event with a straightforward beginning and end. Indeed, I would want to offer a rival interpretation to the usually limited chronological focus (often amounting to less than a century) which has ended consideration of the Reformation in 1559, 1603 or 1640, by emphasizing the long and drawn-out nature of the English Reformation. Even if the political Reformation had been won by the seventeenth century, there was still much to do in bringing the Protestant faith to the hearts and minds of the English people, and this was a process which took centuries rather than years or decades. Furthermore, we will have an improved understanding of what the Reformation implied, and its broad social consequences, if we track its influence and its ideology well into the eighteenth and early nineteenth centuries, for arguably only then were the effects of the Reformation seen in the parishes (such as a professionalized clergy and a religiously-educated laity).

In the process of making England Protestant, it might be suggested that historians are currently talking about three interrelated, but in some ways distinct, aspects of the process which we now label under the umbrella term of the "English Reformation", and while there was clearly an overlap in aims, they need to be unpicked in order to evaluate "success" and "failure". First, there was the process of de-Catholicization, the weaning away from the old faith. This entailed the dismantling of some of the traditional forms of worship, and was often accompanied by an intense iconoclasm which aimed to destroy an entire religious system.[35] Secondly, and this might have gone hand in hand with the first type of Reformation, there was a process of Protestantization (a process, which in its initial stages entailed making committed Catholics into committed Protestants). It was these first two types of Reformation which represented the areas of greatest success in the sixteenth and early seventeenth centuries, although historians have frequently pointed to the dangers of reading changes of heart into the evidence of changes of behaviour, and even the process of iconoclasm could be a protracted business. For example, Margaret Aston has shown that "as late as the 1770s die-hards in Gloucestershire were moved to erase a tombstone inscription which seemed to proclaim a belief in prayers for the dead".[36] And the processes of de-Catholicization and Protestantization could be unrelated. Robert Whiting, for example, has argued that "the destruction of Catholicism . . . owed . . . less to the rise of Protestant convictions than to the motive power of essentially secular compulsions."[37] Thirdly, there was the far harder task of Christianization, the attempt to make those who appeared irreligious into committed Christians, let alone into committed Protestants. This third aspect of the Reformation was not, of course, limited to Protestants, and a number of historians have demonstrated the similarity (and indeed the continuity) of the Catholic and the Protestant attempts to transform the religious behaviour and attitudes of those considered to be irreligious and ungodly.[38]

In some ways, of course, the aims of "de-Catholicization", "Protestantization" and "Christianization" were bound up with one another, but noting their different aims and objectives, does help us to observe shifts in priorities at specific periods, in different regions, and even among individual clergy, and to recognize that success or failure in one of these objectives was not necessarily matched by success or failure in other areas. For example, despite the current stress on the slow speed of the Reformation, a number of scholars have reminded us that as far as de-Catholicization is concerned, Henry VIII was in fact extremely successful in eradicating the major elements of Catholic worship. We ought to acknowledge the remarkable speed in which those essential elements of late medieval Catholicism (such as monasteries and pilgrimages) disappeared. On this definition of Reformation, Henry comes very close to complete success.[39] The difference in these three objectives has been most fully articulated by historians of the Reformation in Ireland: most notably Aidan Clarke who has argued that the Church of Ireland "confined itself to the manageable task of providing properly for the spiritual needs of those who were already Protestant", and by David Hayton who has recently shown how late seventeenth- and early eighteenth-century Protestant clergy saw their main task, not of proselytizing Catholics (de-Catholicization), but of strengthening the nominally Protestant base.[40] We might usefully apply this to the English context, where even when the Catholic threat at home was negligible, in the face of what appeared to be the forward march of Catholicism in Europe in the late seventeenth and early eighteenth centuries, the priority was to repel that advance. Because of the fear that through indifference, ignorance, and moral decline the Protestant interest was losing ground, the major imperative was seen as strengthening the Protestant majority, rather than converting the Catholics.

Seeing the Reformation as three separate strands begs the question not only of when the Reformation ended, but also when it began. Patrick Collinson has suggested that as far as the process of de-Catholicization is concerned we need to start from the time when Catholicism in England was first challenged and end with the final extinguishing of its political hopes: the three centuries from Wycliffe's first intellectual repudiation of the Church in 1378 to the overthrow of the Catholic James II in 1688–9[41] (although Jacobite historians would no doubt want to extend this latter date to as late as 1745–6 when the danger of a Franco–Spanish alliance seeking to return a Catholic monarchy to Britain seemed real).[42] Some historians would argue that aspects of the Protestantization process (such as the interest in individual and private religious practice, and the concern with literacy), can be found in a "premature" reformation with its origins in the fifteenth century.[43] And as far as the conversion of the lives of the ungodly is concerned, it has been argued by Martin Ingram that this needs to be fitted into a process going back perhaps a thousand years or more.[44]

Stressing the continuing Reformation (the Reformation as *longue durée*), might encourage us to avoid getting bogged down in discussions over terminology, such as the disputes amongst European historians over the beginnings and endings of the "first", "second" and "third" Reformations,[45] and the confusion amongst historians of England over the precise demarcation between the "early" and the "late" Reformation.[46] Continuity may, of course, refer to the absence of change, but, as Peter Burke has pointed out, the term can also be used to describe a particular kind of change, a change which was more or less even in rate and constant in direction.[47] More fundamentally, stressing the long and drawn-out nature of the Reformation, might help us concentrate on the making, and the constant remaking of the Reformation. Whilst some historians have characterized the Anglican regime in particular as suffering from inertia and hidebound by tradition, that is not the way it seemed to those involved in the process of handing down the Protestant message. The ways in which Protestant (and perhaps above all Anglican) attitudes were diffused is often described in terms of metaphors such as "survival", "inheritance" or "legacy". One needs to make an effort to remember that this inheritance was not automatic, and indeed that it had to be worked for; it did not just happen by some kind of osmosis, but was rather a constant process of taming, breaking in and educating each new generation, rather like a gardener's battle against weeds or a housewife's against dirt – unending, but not necessarily to be seen as pointless or without effect.[48] Above all, we should remember that well into the early nineteenth century contemporaries were not sure that the Reformation would survive at all (hence the difficulties over Catholic Emancipation in 1829; and the *frisson* caused by what appeared to some to be the Tractarian "Counter-Reformation").

In discussing the fashioning of a Protestant nation, historians have spent a great deal of time in looking at those who can be called the makers of the Reformation. The key group, of course, in England as elsewhere, were the clergy. A major theme in the historiography has been to study the creation of a cadre of officials charged with implementing Protestantism in the parishes, usually under the concept of the professionalization of the clergy, an umbrella term covering the various attempts to re-fashion the clergy along Protestant lines, replacing the intercessor of the Catholic Church with the educative and pastoral roles of the Protestant minister. This development encompassed clerical recruitment, education and training, and ought to be seen as a process lasting several centuries, rather than, as some historians have suggested, being limited to a couple of periods of intense activity, such as the late sixteenth century and the mid-nineteenth century.[49] And if we are talking about the making of a Protestant nation, then the clergy of the Church of England represented the group most likely to think (and possibly to act) in national terms. Their recruitment, education and contacts made them the national profession *par excellence*, and it was they, possibly more than any other section of society, which furthered the creation of a Protestant national identity.

But we also need to look at the mechanisms by which the Protestant message was disseminated and transmitted throughout society. Here, what needs to be highlighted is the massive educational endeavour which underpinned the spread of the Reformation in England. Many of the religious movements and revivals from the sixteenth to the nineteenth centuries, such as Puritanism, Methodism and Evangelicalism, can be explained as renewed efforts in this direction. For all clergy in the post-Reformation world, the sermon was the principal mode of communication (although there were debates about how and where sermons should be delivered), and some groups emphasized the importance of preaching over other

317

pastoral attributes. We ought to pay particular attention to the role of print culture in establishing religious norms, such as through reading the Bible, the writing and the learning of catechisms, the printing of sermons and devotional literature.[50] We should, of course, recognize that this educational mission was not just an English, or even merely a Protestant phenomenon. John Bossy, amongst others, has forcefully argued for the common shift towards a print religion in both Catholic and Protestant countries.[51] And, it has been suggested that if England stands out as a regime with a high degree of interest in the printed Bible, it was because of the well-established pre-Reformation tradition of having a Bible in the vernacular.[52] Yet it might be worth observing that Protestantism did put special emphasis on literacy and understanding. We might note, for example, the extraordinarily high literacy rates in Scandinavia (in some areas a staggering 90 per cent of the population could read by 1700) which go a long way to explain how it was that the Reformation was so assured there by the mid-seventeenth century.[53]

But if the spread of literacy and the related educational endeavour have been seen as vital factors in accounting for the success of the Reformation in England, it has also been suggested that the same process also accounts for the failure of the Reformation amongst some social groups. It can, for instance, be maintained that the Protestant stress on literacy made the message inaccessible to the illiterate poor, and some studies have argued that this led to a further alienation of the poor from the "official" religious culture, perhaps creating disaffection towards the religious establishment, rather than Christianizing those deemed to be ungodly.[54] And there is some evidence which indicates that the desire to give information through the diffusion of literature which told the reader not only of the right way to live their lives, but did so by outlining the heresies which had to be avoided, could have unimagined consequences. Robert Payne told the Society for the Propagation of Christian Knowledge in 1729 that, although he held Bishop Gibson's pastoral letter against infidelity, which had mentioned the writings of the free-thinkers Toland, Tindal, Collins and Wollaston, in high esteem, "as the poison to which it is an antidote has not spread amongst the poor, he does not think it advisable to put into their hands",[55] and Charles Bean similarly remarked that the clergy in these parts [Kent] have generally thought it not prudent to put the refutations of infidelity into the hands of their country parishioners, lest it should excite them to the curiosity of trying the strength of a poison to which they are hither absolute strangers and think it more beneficial to give them catechetical, devotional and other practical tracts against the common vices.[56]

Yet we also need to stress, as some recent research has done, the attempts to bridge the gap between the literate and non-literate worlds, either through the commitment to spreading literacy through various educational initiatives, such as grammar schools, charity schools, Sunday schools, and the tracts distributed by the SPCK, which arguably helped to create a ladder joining the two worlds,[57] or through exploiting forms of communication such as visual images and music which might transcend the written word.[58] In any case, the binary polarity implicit in the distinction between literate/illiterate and between print/oral culture may be too schematic. We ought to remember that Protestantism was a religion of the word, not just of the book, and that there were ways in which the word could reach even the illiterate. A number of scholars have remarked on the ways in which print culture could in fact permeate oral culture: it was, for example, a well-attested tradition to have books and sermons read aloud. And as late as the 1840s, members of the congregation at Waterhead in Lancashire, responded to the problems caused by illiteracy by learning much of the service by heart.[59]

In disseminating the Protestant message, we need also to point to the effect of regular attendance at church services, above all through the auspices of the Church of England, where the constant hearing of the Anglican liturgy, most notably via the Book of Common Prayer, inculcated religious knowledge in the hearers. Evidence from the parish of Hernehill in the 1830s has shown how the majority of the poor in the parish – many of whom became followers of the Courtenay rising of 1838 – were regular attenders at the parish church, possessed Bibles and other religious books, and that a significant number were dedicated members of the church choir.[60]

Acknowledging the long-term nature of the Reformation might also help us to think again about the development of Nonconformity and Dissent, and the position of groups who to some extent rivalled what might be termed "mainstream Anglicanism". On the one hand, it was precisely the debates about what constituted a real Protestant which fuelled the development of Protestant rivals to the Church of England. The appearance of religious groups in the sixteenth, seventeenth, eighteenth and nineteenth centuries, which, to varying degrees, seem to have stood outside mainstream Anglicanism, and which have had their own lively historiography, such as the emergence of Puritanism, the rise of Laudianism, the origins of Methodism, the impact of Evangelicalism, and the nature of the Oxford Movement, as well as the existence of more obviously dissenting groups, might usefully be seen as a logical consequence of the English Reformation, not only working out tensions which were inaugurated in the early sixteenth century (especially concerning Church authority and organization), but perhaps more significantly for our purposes, finding different ways of furthering the Reformation in the parishes.

It can also be suggested that these surges of religious activity represented some kind of generational revolt, and it might also be possible to attempt a sociology of revival where, most commonly, young men, dissatisfied with contemporary religious practice (perhaps we should also call them "alienated intellectuals")[61] joined together to form alternative religious cultures. On the other hand, stressing the common aims behind these seemingly diverse groups helps to suggest that the historiographical tendency to emphasize differences between religious movements and to compartmentalize them into separate historical agendas (partly because of religious propaganda, partly for historiographical convenience, partly because of an excessively "denominational" approach to religious movements) has been misleading. Rather, we need to emphasize the similarities and connections, both in ideas and personnel, between religious groups, so that seemingly opposed movements can be shown to have shared not only a common inheritance, but could also indulge in shared alliances, which makes it difficult to talk of definite and distinct groupings. Here I would point to the parallel debates in historiography over the distinctions between "Puritans" and "Anglicans" in the late sixteenth century,[62] between "Calvinists" and "Arminians" in the early seventeenth century,[63] between Anglicans and "Dissenters" in the late seventeenth century,[64] between Methodists and Anglicans in the eighteenth century,[65] and between Evangelicals and High Churchmen in the early nineteenth century,[66] all of which increasingly are seen by historians to have had common pastoral aims, and where the polarities were less sharp than used to be believed. Moreover, from the vital perspective of the parish, these distinctions look more and more blurred. Puritanism, Laudianism, Methodism, Evangelicalism and Tractarianism, as well as "mainstream Anglicanism" represented an attempt to mould religious sensibilities. Instead of concentrating on the differences between the Church of England and its rivals, it might be worthwhile to think of different religious movements in terms of cycles of Reformation endeavour. For whatever their differences, the professed aims (and often the methods) of these various groups were often strikingly similar.

In understanding the relationship between these groups and the Church of England, we need to see them not only in terms of reacting against the established church, but more positively in terms of emerging from and drawing on the church, often building on Anglican pastoral initiatives. Patrick Collinson has shown that some of the supposed hallmarks of Puritanism, such as lectures and prophesy-ings, were entrenched within contemporary Anglicanism.[67] Similarly, John Walsh has demonstrated how far the Methodist interest in the group meeting drew on Anglican models of religious societies.[68] We might also point to the ways in which certain supposedly "evangeli-cal" initiatives, such as the development of Sunday schools in the late eighteenth century, not only had support from all sections of the church, but were often in fact instigated by High Churchmen.[69] In any case, the fluidity of relations between the Church and Dissent allowed "nonconformist" styles and techniques to be re-absorbed (and de-radicalized) within the Church, demonstrating how religious litera-ture such as that by John Bunyan could transcend its denominational roots.[70] These shared aims and the common inheritance of these religious groups and movements supplied the basis for the large amount of interdenominational co-operation, which, as a number of studies have shown, was a constant feature of the English religious landscape.[71] Denominational histories have frequently used sources which suggest conflict, and have tended to play down the common inheritance of these groups, but we need to go beyond such sources to admit the considerable evidence of tolerance and co-operation which might exist in practice. For instance, Timothy Davies has found evidence of co-operation in the 1660s even between Anglicans and Quakers, usually seen as the group who displayed the greatest antagonism towards the Church of England establishment.[72]

The fact that Protestant groups in England in the centuries after 1530 had much in common, especially in their pastoral aims, should not be surprising since recent historians have suggested that there were also similarities between Catholic and Protestant ways of spreading the Christian message.[73] Mark Byford, for example, in a pioneering study of the impact of Protestantism in Essex, has forcefully argued that a great deal of what clergy before and after the Reformation preached and taught was fundamentally the same, allowing him to call the Protestant Reformation a "religious revival", rather than being a new departure.[74] He points to the wide range of pastoral manuals published during the sixteenth century concerning moral advice which stood outside conventional Reformation controversy. In a similar vein, Brad Gregory has demonstrated the ways in which the Puritan Edmund Bunny literally plagiarized the pastoral writings of the Jesuit Robert Parsons, since their essential concern, to instill what Gregory has called "rigorous religion" into their parishioners was practically identical.[75] And in the seventeenth and eighteenth centuries there was a well-established genre of editing Catholic manuals of devotion for Protestant use.[76] The existence of similarities between seemingly opposite religious standpoints makes the use of religious labels a difficult task. For instance, the terms "Puritan" and "godly" could be applied to devout Catholics as well as to devout Protestants.[77] And the Protestant William Sheppard was vilified for calling himself a "Jesyutt", meaning, as he tried to explain, that he was a follower of Jesus, and not a Jesuit priest.[78] But the fact of continuity between the Catholic and the Protestant pastoral messages may have helped the early success of the Reformation, easing England's transformation into a recognizably Protestant nation. As Byford argues, the more the values emphasized by Protestantism can be seen to have been already present in English religious culture, the less daunting seems its prospect of successfully spreading.[79]

One reason why historians have ignored the problem of the long Reformation is because several aspects of that endeavour, such as the regulation of people's behaviour, have been side-tracked into the rather different categories of "moral reform" and the reformation of manners, which are often viewed as secular rather than as religious concerns. Although historians have analyzed the various "movements" to reform manners, such as those in the late sixteenth and early seventeenth centuries, in the mid-seventeenth century, in the late seventeenth and early eighteenth centuries, and in the late eighteenth century, they have usually been discussed in terms of social control, and as separate from the religious reformation.[80] It is true that, until the historiographical divide of 1660, the reformation of religion and the reformation of manners are seen as being inter-related, but, even those such as David Underdown who recognize a congruence between religious and moral reform (often under the category of "godly" reform), argue for the end of godly reformation by the late seventeenth century.[81]

In particular, Shelley Burtt, in her recent study of the early-eighteenth-century movement for moral reform has seen this as the period which witnessed the switch from a religious to a temporal justification for action, leading her to make a distinction between churchmen and moral reformers.[82] And Joanna Innes, in her elegant dissection of the campaign for the reformation of manners in the 1780s, distinguishes between religious traditions (which emphasized sin), and secular concerns (which emphasised the social consequences of immorality, idleness, and improvidence).[83] But it is possible to suggest that "religious" and "moral" reform were twin aspects of the concern to create a Christian commonwealth, and that this priority continued to influence attempts at moral reform well into the nineteenth century. Indeed historians appear to want to have it both ways. A long-observed criticism of late seventeenth and eighteenth century Anglican sermonizing was precisely that it was too concerned with morality and behaviour. Idleness and drink continued to be condemned for religious reasons.[84]

Furthermore, campaigns for moral reform were one of the most obvious ways in which co-operation between different religious groups could be manifested, providing a common ground for a large number of shared educational and social initiatives. This is not to suggest that these same campaigns did not cause tensions also: in the early eighteenth century, for example, there were debates about how far the Church of England should be the dominant partner in any such alliances; and what relations should be with Protestant Dissenters. But, in the context of the Long Reformation, it is worth noting that some of the "new" religious movements justified themselves in part as being a renewal of efforts at the reformation of manners.[85]

In conclusion, we may recognize that taking a long-term view of the Reformation raises several points which need to be stressed. First, we might challenge the traditional periodization and the historiographical convention which has made a distinction between the vigour of religious activity before 1660 and the stasis after that date. (We might note, incidentally, a parallel in the historiography of the Catholic Church, which has led Hanns Gross to talk of the "post-Tridentine syndrome", an entropy and lack of spirit displayed in the Catholic Church after the late seventeenth century).[86] But seeing the limitations of the earlier period, the period conventionally labelled as the era of Reformation, might help us to see better the achievements of the second period. Indeed, it might be that the success of the Reformation comes later than we once thought. Secondly, we need to appreciate how far the need to spread the Reformation was a common concern for all Protestant groups within English society, and that this common aim should be stressed against the traditional picture of inter-denominational rivalry. Moreover, it was the Church of England (through its national clergy and its pastoral initiatives) which played a continuing (and a leading) role in furthering the Reformation. Thirdly, in evaluating the question of "success" and "failure", we might recognize that to a large extent a Protestant nation was always something to aim for, a process of becoming, rather than of being. Patrick Collinson has indeed suggested that the attempt to create a truly godly society was bound to fail: for Protestants, whose self-perception was defined by opposing the papist "other", always needed to be fighting against something, so that complete success could never have been achieved.[87]

Notes

1. I am grateful to George Bernard, Tony Claydon, David Hempton, Hugh Mcleod, Mike Snape and Lucy Wooding for discussing an earlier version of this chapter. A slightly condensed variant has appeared in *Church and People in Britain and Scandinavia* I. Brohed (ed) (Lund, 1996), pp. 159–80.

2. D. MacCulloch, "The impact of the English Reformation", *Historical Journal* **38**, 1995, p. 152; S. J. D. Green, "Unestablished versions: voluntary religion in the Victorian north", *Northern History* **XXX**, 1994, p. 193.

3. See, for example, J. C. D. Clark, *English society, 1688–1832. Ideology, social structure and political practice during the ancien régime* (Cambridge, 1985), and the contributions to *The church of England, c.1688–c.1833. From toleration to Tractarianism*, J. Walsh, C. Haydon & S. Taylor (eds) (Cambridge, 1993).

4. For aspects of that "revival" see O. Chadwick, *The Victorian church* (London, 1970), and *Religion in Victorian Britain* G. Parsons and J. R. Moore (eds) (Manchester, 1988).

5. In Kent, for example, the growth in Catholic numbers – in part as a result of the influx of Catholic *emigrés* – was dramatic. In 1803 it was estimated that there were only 600 Catholics in the whole of the county; by 1814 this had risen to 3,317; C. Buckingham, *Catholic Dover* (Canterbury, 1968), p. 32. See also J. F. Supple-Green, *The Catholic revival in Yorkshire, 1850–1900* (Leeds Philosophical and Literary Society, **XXI**, 1990. It was perhaps such a rapid increase in numbers which led to a renewed anti-Catholicism: see, E. R. Norman, *Anti-Catholicism in Victorian England* (London, 1968), and J. Wolffe, *The Protestant crusade in Great Britain, 1829–1860* (Oxford, 1991).

6. C. Haigh, "The recent historiography of the English Reformation", *Historical Journal* **XXV**, 1982, pp. 995–1007.

7. See the comments in D. MacCulloch, *The later Reformation in England, 1547–1603* (London, 1990), pp. 125–143; MacCulloch, "England", in *The early Reformation in Europe*, A. Pettegree (ed.) (Cambridge, 1992), pp. 166–87; S. Brigden, "Youth and the Reformation", *Past and Present* **95**, 1992, pp. 37–67; P. Crawford, *Women and Religion in England, 1600–1720* (London, 1993). The ways in which regionalism affected the spread of the Reformation can be seen in the contrast between P. Clark, *English provincial society from the Reformation to the revolution: religion, society and politics in Kent, 1500–1640* (Hassocks, 1977) and C. Haigh, *Reformation and resistance in Tudor Lancashire* (Cambridge, 1976). It may be worth noting that the effects of geography have also been seen as "the most potent and most mysterious" factor accounting for religious differentiation in France: R. Gibson, *A social history of French Catholicism, 1789–1914* (London, 1989), p. 170.

8. A. G. Dickens, "The early expansion of Protestantism in England, 1520–1558", *Archiv für Reformationsgeschichte* **78**, 1987, p. 220.

9. G. R. Elton, *Reform and Reformation: England, 1509–1558* (London, 1977), esp. pp. 382–9.

10. Especially the contributions to C. Haigh, *The English Reformation revised* (Cambridge, 1987). Note Haigh's own comments in the Conclusion, p. 214: "By the 1580s, however, the Protestants had effectively won the struggle". This is somewhat at odds with his later comment that "[t]here might have been no Reformation: indeed, there hardly was one": "The English Refor-

mation: a premature birth, a difficult labour and a sickly child", *Historical Journal* **33**, 1990, p. 459.

11. E. Duffy, *The stripping of the altars. Traditional religion in England, c.1400–1580* (New Haven & London, 1992) p. 593.

12. J. Bossy, *The English Catholic community, 1570–1850* (London, 1975), pp. 149–81; D. Cressy, *Bonfires and bells. National memory and the Protestant calendar in Elizabethan and Stuart England* (London, 1989).

13. J. Black, *The British and the grand tour* (London, 1985), p. 189. For the role of anti-Catholicism as the dominant ideology of the seventeenth century, see also M. Finlayson, *Historians, Puritanism and the English revolution: the religious factor in English politics before and after the interregnum* (Toronto, 1983).

14. L. Colley, *Britons!: forging the nation, 1707–1837* (New Haven, 1992).

15. J. Albers, "'Papist traitors' and 'Presbyterian rogues': religious identities in eighteenth-century Lancashire", in *Church of England*, Walsh, Haydon & Taylor (eds), esp. pp. 319–20.

16. D. Defoe, *The great law of subordination consider'd* (London, 1724), p. 20.

17. C. Haydon, *Anti-Catholicism in eighteenth-century England. A political and social study* (London, 1993).

18. C. Haigh, *English Reformations. Religion, politics and society under the Tudors* (Oxford, 1993), p. 290.

19. C. Haigh "The church of England, the Catholics and the people", in *The reign of Elizabeth I*, Haigh (ed.) (Basingstoke, 1985), pp. 169–220.

20. R. Whiting, *The blind devotion of the people. Popular religion and the English Reformation* (Cambridge, 1989), p. 268.

21. See, for example, E. W. Zeeden, *Die Entstehung der Konfessionem: Gründlagen und Formen der Konfessionsbildung in Zeitalter der Gläubenskampfe* (Munich, 1965) and his *Konfessionsbildung: Studien zu Reformation, Gegenreformation, und Catholischen Reformation* (Stuttgart, 1985). For some suggestions as to the necessary criteria for defining a Reformation city, which might usefully be extended to the definition of a Protestant nation, see J. Barry, "Bristol as a 'Reformation city'", above, pp. 261–84. Barry argues, however, that "the Reformation moment" came to an end c.1770, as after that date what appear to him to be new concerns began to dominate the social and political agenda. I am unconvinced by this. In thinking about what might be meant by a Protestant nation, Patrick Collinson has recently claimed that by the early seventeenth century England was a "Protestant nation, if not a nation of Protestants", in *The culture of Puritanism, 1560–1700*, C. Durston & J. Eales (eds) (Basingstoke, 1996), p. 46.

22. Historians of Catholic Europe have been engaged in a similar debate about how best to measure religious commitment. Some of the indices they have used (many of which will be familiar to historians of England) include: church attendance; numbers taking communion; recruitment to the priesthood, wills, reading matter, sexual morality: Gibson, *Social history of French Catholicism*, pp. 1–8.

23. G. Strauss, "Success and failure in the German reformation", *Past and Present* **67**, 1976, pp. 30–63. See also Strauss, *Luther's house of learning: indoctrination of the young in the German Reformation* (Baltimore, 1978), and Strauss, "The Reformation and its public in an age of orthodoxy", in *The German people and the Reformation* R. P. Hsia (ed.) (Ithaca, NY, 1988), pp. 194–214. For the debate see, J. M. Kittelson, "Successes and failures in the German Reformation: the report from Strasbourg", *Archiv für Reformationsgeschichte* **73**, 1982, pp. 153–75, and G. Parker, "Success and failure during the first century of the Reformation", *Past and Present* **136**, 1992, pp. 43–82.

24. William Whately, in 1623: quoted in P. Collinson, *The birthpangs of Protestant England: religious and cultural change in the sixteenth and seventeenth centuries (Basingstoke, 1988)*.

25. For example, the lament of William Backhouse, archdeacon of Canterbury in 1784 that the influence of religion "has diminished, is diminishing and ought to be increased": quoted in W. J. Gregory, "Archbishop, cathedral and parish: the diocese of Canterbury, 1660–1805" (D.Phil thesis, Oxford University, 1993), p. 250.

26. Quoted in S. Doran & C. Durston, *Princes, pastors and people: the church and religion in England, 1529–1689* (London, 1991), p. 82.

27. See *The Compton census of 1676. A critical edition*, A. Whiteman (ed.) (London, 1986).

28. But see J. Morrill, "The church in England, 1642–9", in *Reactions to the English Civil War*, Morrill (ed.) (London, 1982), pp. 105–24, for evidence of the strong survival of the Church of England even during the Interregnum.

29. Lambeth Palace Library, MS 1134/1, fo. 33.

30. Quoted in the manuscript diaries of Arthur Upcher (in private hands), vol. 2, p. 30.

31. cf. D. Bebbington, "Religion and society in the nineteenth century", *Historical Journal* **32**, 1989, pp. 997–1004.

32. K. Thomas, *Religion and the decline of magic* (London, 1971) and J. Obelkevich, *Religion and rural society: South Lindsey, 1825–1875* (London, 1976).

33. M. Smith, *Religion in industrial society. Oldham and Saddleworth, 1740–1865* (Oxford, 1994), p. 268.

34. Duffy, *Stripping*, introduction.

35. M. Aston, *England's iconoclasts*, vol. I. *Laws against images* (Oxford, 1988).

36. *Ibid.*, p. 3.

37. Whiting, *Blind devotion*, p. 266.

38. For example, J. Bossy, *Christianity in the west, 1400–1700* (Oxford, 1985).

39. R. Whiting, "Local responses to the Henrician Reformation", in *The reign of Henry VIII. Politics, policy and piety*, D. MacCulloch (ed.) (Basingstoke, 1995), pp. 203–226, and S. B. House, "Literature, drama and politics", *ibid.*, pp. 180–201.

40. A. Clarke, "Varieties of uniformity: the first century of the church of Ireland", in *The churches, Ireland and the Irish*, W. J. Sheils & D. Wood (eds)

(Oxford, 1989), p. 118; D. Hayton, "Did Protestantism fail in early eighteenth-century Ireland?: charity schools and the enterprise of religious and social reformation *c*.1690–1730", in *As by law established. The church of Ireland since the Reformation*, A. Ford, J. McGuire & K. Milne (eds) (Dublin, 1995), esp. p. 175.

41. P. Collinson, "England", in *The Reformation in national context*, B. Scribner, R. Porter & M. Teich (eds) (Cambridge, 1994), p. 81.

42. See for example, E. Cruickshanks, *Political untouchables* (London, 1979).

43. A. Hudson, *The premature Reformation. Wycliffite texts and Lollard history* (Oxford, 1988), but note Christine Carpenter's reservations about how far such developments anticipated a Reformation: "The religion of the gentry of fifteenth-century England" in *England in the fifteenth century*, D. Williams (ed.) (Woodbridge, Suffolk, 1987), pp. 53–74.

44. M. Ingram, "The reform of popular culture? Sex and marriage in early modern England", in *Popular culture in seventeenth-century England*, B. Reay (ed.) (London, 1988), p. 131.

45. For example H. J. Cohn, "The territorial princes in Germany's second Reformation, 1559–1622", in *International Calvinism, 1541–1715*, M. Prestwich (ed.) (Oxford, 1985), pp. 135–63; K. von Greyerz, *The late city reformation in Germany* (Wiesbaden, 1980), pp. 196–203; B. Nischan, "The second reformation in Brandenburg", *Sixteenth-Century Journal* **14**, 1983, pp. 173–87.

46. See for example, the dating of MacCulloch's, *Later Reformation* [1547–1603], which includes the Edwardian period as part of the second Reformation in England, whilst other scholars reserve the label "second Reformation" for the Elizabethan period. Also confusing in terms of chronology is Christopher Haigh's suggestion that there were four distinct Reformations in sixteenth-century England: *English Reformations*, p. 14.

47. P. Burke, "Concepts of continuity and change in history", *New Cambridge Modern History* **XIII** Companion volume (1979), p. 3. For fears over Catholic emancipation, see W. Hinde, *Catholic emancipation. A shake to men's minds* (Oxford, 1992).

48. I owe these analogies to George Bernard.

49. For example, R. O'Day, *The English clergy: the emergence and consolidation of a profession, 1558–1642* (Leicester, 1979); B. Heeney, *A different kind of gentleman. Parish clergy as professional men in early and mid-Victorian England* (Connecticut, 1976); A. Haig, *The Victorian clergy* (London, 1984).

50. On the significance of print generally, see E. Eisenstein, *The printing press as an agent of change: communication and cultural transformations in early modern Europe* (Cambridge, 1979).

51. Bossy, *Christianity in the west*.

52. Scribner, Porter, & Teich (eds) *Reformation in national context*, p. 219.

53. Parker, "Success and failure", pp. 78–9.

54. *Inter alia*, Thomas, *Decline of magic*.

55. SPCK, LB 234/7, p. 5.

56. *Ibid.*, p. 14.

57. See, for example, the remarks in I. Green, "'For children in yeeres and children in understanding': the emergence of the English catechism under Elizabeth and the early Stuarts", *Journal of Ecclesiastical History* **37**, 1986, pp. 397–425, and his *The Christian's ABC: catechisms and catechising in England, c.* 1530–1740 (Oxford, 1996).

58. On the role of printed images, see T. Watt, *Cheap print and popular piety, 1550–1640* (Cambridge, 1991). The role and power of music in conveying religious sentiments has been almost totally neglected. But some inklings of the possibilities of the subject can be found in W. Webber, *The rise of musical classics in eighteenth-century England. A study in canon, ritual and ideology* (Oxford, 1992); J. Gregory, "Anglicanism and the arts: religion, culture and politics in the eighteenth century", in *Culture, politics and society in Britain, 1660–1800*, J. Black & J. Gregory (eds) (Manchester, 1991), esp. pp. 96–100; and V. Gammon, "Babylonian performances: the rise and suppression of popular church music, 1660–1870", in *Popular culture and class conflict, 1590–1914*, E. & S. Yeo (eds) (Brighton, 1991), pp. 62–84.

59. D. Cressy, *Literacy and the social order. Reading and writing in Tudor and Stuart England* (Cambridge, 1980), pp. 14–16; Smith, *Religion and industrial society*.

60. B. Reay, "The last rising of the agricultural labourers: the battle in Bossenden wood, 1838", *History Workshop Journal*, **XXVI**, 1988, pp. 79–101.

61. The phrase, first used by M. Curtis, to describe Puritan lecturers in the early seventeenth century: "The alienated intellectuals of early Stuart England", *Past and Present* **XXIII**, 1962, reprinted in *Crisis in Europe, 1560–1600*, T. Aston (ed.) (London, 1961), pp. 295–316.

62. The debates over the relationship between "Puritans" and "Anglicans" are most obviously followed in the works of Patrick Collinson, especially in his *Godly people. Essays on English Protestantism and Puritanism* (London, 1993) and in Collinson, *The religion of Protestants. The church in English society, 1559–1625* (Oxford, 1982). Also, P. Lake, *Moderate Puritans and the Elizabethan Church* (Cambridge, 1982) and Lake, *Anglicans and Puritans? Presbyterianism and English conformist thought from Whitgift to Hooker* (London, 1988). See also M. Todd, *Christian humanism and the Puritan social order* (New York, 1987). Recent re-appraisals of some of the issues can be found in *The culture of Puritanism, 1560–1700*, Durston & Eales (eds) and W. Lamont, *Puritanism and historical controversy* (London, 1996). My argument here, and in what follows, is that we should – as many historians have been doing recently – recognize those elements and issues which united as well as those which divided groups and institutions. But, I am aware of the methodological problems this involves. It is worth recalling Peter Lake's statement that

"all religious historians, whether of Puritanism, Arminianism, or whatever, are faced with essentially the same definitional choice: do they go for tight and coherent definitions of their object of study and run the risks of tunnel vision, or do they opt for a more generous definition of their field and risk a consequent loss of precision and focus".

"The impact of early modern Protestantism", *Journal of British Studies* **28**, 1989, p. 303. My contention, however, is that historians of religion have in fact created false boundaries and distinctions in attempting to define discrete groups.

63. See N. Tyacke, *Anti-Calvinists. The rise of English Arminianism, c. 1590–1640* (Oxford, 1987); K. Fincham, *Prelate as pastor. The episcopate of James I* (Oxford, 1990); P. White. "The rise of Arminianism reconsidered", *Past and Present* **101**, 1983, 34–54; J. Davies, *The Caroline captivity of the church. Charles I and the remoulding of Anglicanism, 1625–1641* (Oxford, 1992). A. Milton, *Catholic and reformed: the Roman and Protestant churches in English Protestant thought, 1604–40* (Cambridge, 1994), p. 536, shows Calvinists who accepted some of the Laudian reforms.

64. J. Spurr, *The restoration church of England, 1646–1689* (New Haven & London, 1991); J. Ramsbottom, "Presbyterians and partial conformity in the restoration church of England", *Journal of Ecclesiastical History* **XLIII**, 1992, pp. 249–70.

65. On Methodism, and its links to the Church of England, see J. Walsh, "The origins of the evangelical revival", in *Essays in modern English church history*, G. V. Bennett & J. D. Walsh (eds) (London, 1966), pp. 136–62 and F. Baker, *John Wesley and the Church of England* (London, 1970).

66. See G. Rowell, *The vision glorious. Themes and personalities of the Catholic revival in Anglicanism* (Oxford, 1983), pp. 5–7, and E. Jay (ed.) *The Evangelical and Oxford Movements* (Cambridge, 1983). Peter Nockles argues that there was a High Church/Evangelical consensus which was only really broken by the Tractarians. In particular, he suggests that the Tractarian "counter-Reformation" was displayed by an antagonistic attitude to the sixteenth century Reformers which went against the grain of Anglican thought (including even Laudian) since the Reformation: *The Oxford Movement in context. Anglican high churchmanship, 1760–1857* (Cambridge, 1994), esp. pp. 122–27.

67. P. Collinson, "Lectures by combination: structures and characteristics of church life in seventeenth century England", *Bulletin of the Institute of Historical Research* **48**, 1975, pp. 182–213.

68. J. Walsh, "Religious societies: Methodist and Evangelical, 1738–1800", in *Voluntary Religion*, W. J. Sheils & D. Woods (eds) (Studies in Church History **23**, 1986), pp. 279–302.

69. See, for example the role of George Horne, who, as a firm High Churchman, supported the Sunday schools in Kent. See T. Laqueur, *Religion and respectability: Sunday schools and working class culture, 1780–1850* (New

Haven, 1976), pp. 21–36, who mistakenly assumes that Horne was an Evangelical. Horne also defended the Calvinist Methodists expelled from Oxford in 1768, suggesting an interesting connection between the "Hutchinsonians" and the Methodists. Similarly the interests of the firm High Churchman, Samuel Horsley, indicate that issues such as the anti-slavery campaign and philanthropic schemes which are often associated with Evangelicalism were in fact shared by a range of churchmanship: F. C. Mather, *High church prophet. Bishop Samuel Horsley (1733–1806) and the Caroline tradition in the later Georgian church* (Oxford, 1992), pp. 235–43.

70. On Bunyan's popularity within the Church of England, see Gregory "Anglicanism and the arts", pp. 90–1. A similar remark could be made of the music of Handel, which by the late eighteenth century was an opportunity for co-operation between the Church of England and Dissent: Webber, *Musical classics*, pp. 140, 245.

71. See, for example, Gregory, "Archbishop, cathedral and parish", pp. 181–241; Smith, *Religion and industrial society*. Co-operation can be seen not only in shared activities, but also in the ways in which people moved freely between different churches. This was still happening as late as the mid-nineteenth century; see, R. W. Ambler, *Lincolnshire returns of the census of religious worship 1851* (Lincolnshire Record Society **72**, 1979) esp. pp. 172, 189, 236.

72. T. A. Davies, "*The Quakers in Essex, 1655–1725*" (DPhil thesis, Oxford University, 1986), esp. pp. 261–312. My interpretation of the relationship between the Church and nonconformity receives support from the collection of essays in *The world of rural Dissenters, 1520–1725*, M. Spufford (ed.) (Cambridge, 1995), and from A. Urdank, *Religion and society in a Cotswold vale. Nailsworth, Gloucestershire, 1780–1865* (Los Angeles, 1990).

73. Bossy, *Christianity*. See also P. Marshall, *The Catholic priesthood and the English Reformation* (Oxford, 1994) and Marshall, *The face of the pastoral ministry in the East Riding, 1525–95* (University of York, Borthwick Paper 88, 1995).

74. M. S. Byford, *The price of Protestantism. Assessing the impact of religious change on Elizabethan Essex: the cases of Heydon and Colchester, 1558–94*, (DPhil thesis, Oxford University, 1988), abstract.

75. B. S. Gregory, "The 'true and zealouse service of God': Robert Parsons, Edmund Bunny, and the first booke of the Christian exercise", *Journal of Ecclesiastical History* **45**, 1994, pp. 238–268.

76. For examples, see Gregory, "Canterbury", p. 249.

77. Byford, "Protestantism", p. 5.

78. *Ibid.*, pp. 58–60.

79. *Ibid.*, p. 395.

80. K. Wrightson, "Alehouses, order and reformation in rural England, 1590–1660", in *Popular culture*, E. & S. Yeo (eds), pp. 1–27; K. Wrightson & D. Levine, *Poverty and piety in an English village: Terling, 1525–1700* (New York,

1979); M. Ingram, "Communities and courts: law and disorder in early seventeenth-century Wiltshire", in *Crime in England, 1550–1800*, J. S. Cockburn (ed.) (London, 1977), pp. 110–34; M. Ingram, "Religion, communities and moral discipline in late sixteenth and early seventeenth-century England: case studies", in *Religion and society in early modern Europe, 1500–1800*, K. von Greyerz (ed.) (London, 1984), pp. 177–93; D. Hirst, "The failure of godly rule in the English republic", *Past and Present* **132**, 1991, pp. 33–66; D. Hayton, "Moral reform and country politics in the late seventeenth century House of Commons", *Past and Present* **128**, 1990, pp. 48–91; D. W. R. Bahlmann, *The moral revolution of 1688/9* (New Haven, Connecticut, 1957); T. Claydon, *William III and the godly revolution* (Cambridge, 1996), esp. pp. 110–122; E. Duffy, "Primitive Christianity revived: religious revival in Augustan England", in *Renaissance and revival in Christian history*, D. Baker (ed.) (Oxford, 1977), pp. 287–300; S. Burtt, *Virtue transformed. Political argument in England, 1688–1740* (Cambridge, 1992); A. G. Craig, *The movement for the reformation of manners, 1690–1715*, (unpublished PhD thesis, University of Edinburgh, 1980); T. Isaacs, *Moral crime and the reform of the state: a study in piety and politics in early eighteenth-century England* (PhD thesis, University of Rochester, New York, 1979); Isaacs, "The Anglican hierarchy and the reformation of manners, 1688–1738", *Journal of Ecclesiastical History* **XXXIII**, 1982, pp. 391–411; M. Fissell, "Charity universal? Institutions and moral reform in eighteenth-century Bristol", in *Stilling the grumbling hive: the response to social and economic problems in England, 1689–1750*, L. Davison et al. (eds) (Stroud, 1992), pp. 121–44; R. B. Shoemaker, "Reforming the city: the reformation of manners campaign in London, 1690–1738", *ibid.*, pp. 99–126; Shoemaker, *Prosecution and punishment: petty crime in London and rural Middlesex, c.1660–1725* (Cambridge, 1991); J. Innes, "Politics and morals. The reformation of manners movement in later eighteenth-century England", in *The transformation of political culture. England and Germany in the late eighteenth century*, E. Hellmuth (ed.) (Oxford, 1990), pp. 57–118.

81. D. Underdown, *Fire from heaven: the life of an English town in the Seventeenth century* (London, 1992), esp. pp. 231–260.

82. Burtt, *Virtue, passim*, and see Burtt, "The societies for the reformation of manners; between John Locke and the devil in Augustan England", in *The margins of orthodoxy, Heterodox writing and cultural response, 1660–1750*, R. Lund (ed.) (Cambridge, 1995), pp. 149–69.

83. Innes, "Politics and morals".

84. Gregory, "Canterbury", pp. 272–75.

85. For evidence of the continuing interaction between religious and moral reformation in the eighteenth century, see *Reformation and revival in eighteenth-century Bristol*, J. Barry & K. Morgan (eds) **45** (Bristol Record Society 1994).

86. H. Gross, *Rome in the age of Enlightenment: the post-Tridentine syndrome and the*

ancien régime (Cambridge, 1990). But see L. Chatellier, *The Europe of the devout. The Catholic Reformation and the formation of new society* (Cambridge, 1989, originally published in French in 1987), which not only argues for the vitality of religious life in the eighteenth and nineteenth centuries, but also indicates the ways in which religious priorities helped pave the way for modernity and democracy. Something similar could be said of the English and Protestant context if we recognize that many of the elements which Raymond Williams in *The long revolution* (London, 1961) saw as the hallmarks of a modern, liberal society, such as the spread of education and literacy, and the extension of communications, were in fact the products of the long Reformation. For an American parallel, which emphasizes the dynamic (and modernizing tendencies) of religion in American life after 1700, see J. Butler, *Awash in a sea of faith: Christianity and the American people* (Cambridge Mass, 1990).

87. Collinson, *Birthpangs*, p. 154.

Index

Collinson, Patrick   25, 36, 39, 40, 152,
   263, 312, 315, 321, 324
Commons, House of   21, 239
Compton census (1676)   312
Conyers, Thomas   15, 96
Cooper, Elizabeth   103, 104
Copdock, Suffolk   174
Coppinger
   Henry   172
   Margaret   172
Corbet, Master   103
Cork, County Cork   294
Cornwall   22, 297
Cornwallis family   188
   Sir Thomas   170, 171, 177, 181, 191
Cox, Richard, Bishop of Ely   5, 8, 146,
   151, 154–6, 217
Crab, a weaver   250
Craig, John   171
Cranmer, Thomas, Archbishop of
   Canterbury   5, 6, 8, 9
   *Defence of the true and catholike doctrine
   of the sacrament*   20
Crashaw, William   44
Cromwell, Thomas   7, 8, 92, 93
Crook, Henry   100
Crowley, Richard   18, 19, 128, 205
   *An informacion and peticion agaynst the
   oppressours of the pore commons of this
   realme*   15, 16

Dane, William   117, 129, 134
Daniell family   183
Darrell, John   82
Davies, Julian   79
Davies, Rupert   285
Davies, Timothy   322
Davies, William   200
Dawson, William   206
Deane, James   131
Debney, Richard   96
Defoe, Daniel   310
Deleznot, Dr   294
Delumeau, Jean   1, 33, 36
   Catholicism between Luther and Voltaire
   33
Dent, Arthur   41
De Renty
   life of   56
Dering, Edward   121

Dettingen
   battle of   276
Devon   11, 22
Dickens, A. G.   4, 71, 117, 308
Dillon, Mr   185
Dilworth, John   209
Dixie, Wolstan   130
Dodd, George   123
Doddridge, Philip   288, 291
Dodgson, C. L.   73
Doncaster, Yorkshire   6
Dorothy, Sister   180
Dorrington, Robert   147
Doubleday, a servant   97
Downham, Cambridgeshire   151
Drewry, Mistress   210, 211
Drury, Henry   174
Drury, Robert   218
Dublin, County Dublin   294
Duffy, Eamon   2, 13, 21, 23–25, 71–84,
   118, 220, 236, 261, 309, 313
   The stripping of the altars   72–74
Dugdale, Gilbert   2
Dursley, Gloucestershire   51, 65
Dyer, William   276
Dyxe, John   99

Eachard, John   54
East Harling, Norfolk   182
Eaton, Samuel   244
Eccleshall, Staffordshire   46
Ecclesiastical Canons (1604)   183
Ecclesiastical Census (1603)   183, 191 n12
Edinburgh   293
Edward VI   37
Edwards, Thomas   24, 235–55
   Antapolgia   238, 240, 241, 247
   Gangraena   24, 236, 238, 239, 242–50,
   253
Edmunds, John   5
Elizabeth I   22, 76, 78, 87, 106, 144, 149,
   155, 170, 218
Elkpin, Sir William   131
Elmswell, Suffolk   189
Elsing, Henry   132
Elton, G. R.   309
Elveden (Elden), Suffolk   169
Ely, Cambridgeshire
   diocese of, courts of   156
   prison   199

INDEX

Offley, *contd.*
Robert 131
Thomas 131
Oldham, Lancashire 313
Old Pretender 297
Old Romney, Kent
minister of 57
Oliver, Dr 172
Order of Communion (1548) 13
Ore, Salop 131
Ormes, Cicely 103, 104
Osbern, Robert 97
Osiander, Andreas 5
Overton, Richard 239, 243, 245
Oxburgh, Norfolk 185
Oxford, Oxfordshire
gaol 214
Movement 278
University 4, 5, 8, 13, 21, 132
divinity scholars of 131
Oxfordshire 17

Page, Robert 201
Paget, Mr 210
Pagitt, Ephraim 243, 245
Palmer, Richard 125
Parker, Cuthbert 180
Parker, Matthew, Archbishop of
Canterbury 5, 8, 9, 15, 19, 96, 154
Parker, Thomas 172
Parker, T. M.
The English Reformation to 1558 71
Parkhurst, John, Bishop of Norwich
105, 170, 171
Parsons, Robert 42, 75, 177, 202, 217,
322
*Brief discourse containing reasons why
Catholics refuse to go to church* 178
Patrick, Simon, Bishop of Ely 54, 60
Paul, Vincent de, St 35
Payne, Robert 318
Payton, Alice 173
Pembrokeshire 297
Pentbridge, Staffordshire 46
Percy, John 205
Perkins, William 43, 83, 209
Perne, Andrew 23, 76, 152–7, 159, 162
Perronets, preachers 294
Peter, Hugh 81, 242
Master Peters last report of the English

wars 247
Peter, Richard 123
Pettons, John 92
Philpot, John 127
Piette, Maximin 285
Pighius, Albertus 9
Pike, John 188
Pine, William 272
Plessey, Northumberland 293
Pocock, John 261
Poley, Richard 178
Pollard, A. F. 14
Polle, Thomas 123
Portarlington, Leix and Offaly 294
Prayer Book 56, 78
(1549) 13, 43, 59
(1552) 20
(1662) in Welsh 55
Praying Societies 290
Preston, Thomas 199, 206
Primer (1553) 19, 20
Pritchard, John 297
Privy Council 13, 21, 96, 100, 101, 106,
150, 160, 170, 203, 211
Puckering, Sir John, Lord Keeper 201
Purchas, Joshua 211–13, 217

Quakers *see* Society of Friends
Questier, Michael 24, 77, 80, 82

Reay, Barry 235
Redemptorists 35, 64, 82
Redgrave, Suffolk 176
Redhead, Robert 203
Redlingfield, Suffolk 181, 187, 188
Reformation Society 59
Registry of Papists' Estates (1717) 184
Return of Papists (1767) 187–8
Reve, Robert 175
gentleman 175
Rich, William 172
Richardson, Charles 216, 217
Richey, R. E. 299
Rickinghall Superior, Suffolk 177
Ridley, Nicholas 5
Rigby, John 210
Robinson, Francis 219
Rockett
Susanna 172
Thomas 172

344